THE
ALTARS
OF AHAZ

HOW A THERAPEUTIC CULTURE
BLINDS US TO THE CLAIMS
OF THE GOSPEL

EVANGELINE A. THIESSEN

Published by
VMI Publishers
Sisters, Oregon
www.vmipublishers.com

ISBN: 9781933204369
Library of Congress Control Number: 2007928298
Author Contact: thiesseneva@yahoo.ca
Printed in the United States of America
Cover design by Joe Bailen

FOR PAUL:

When you promised,
"For better or worse, for richer or poorer…"
you had no idea how much that promise would cost—
but you kept your commitment anyway.

TABLE OF CONTENTS

PREFACE AND ACKNOWLEDGEMENTS

I NEVER STARTED out planning to write a book. I started out looking for God. In that search, I began to buy more and more books, then more bookshelves in which to shelve them, then more books, until my husband began complaining about the piles of books that could no longer be contained in our shelves. I wish I could thank all those people who have been pilgrims before me and who wrote their wisdom in books that allowed the path to be made a little clearer for those, like myself, who trail behind. The spiritual life is not fed on novelty; it is nourished by putting down roots in the soil nourished by those who have gone before. I was not looking for new ideas, but a way to ground my life in the ageless and the eternal. Although those authors may not have agreed with the ways those ideas blossomed in me, it was their shared wisdom that provided the rich soil that allowed new life to grow for me. I know it would be impossible to adequately acknowledge all the roots of the ideas expressed in this book, but I hope the references given cause others to go back into our rich shared Christian heritage where a mother lode of treasures is stored just waiting to be unearthed.

Medieval Christians followed a practice called *florilegia* (it was actually something they picked up from the ancient Greek and Latin people). In the same way that bees look to withdraw the sweetest nectar from flowers, so the medieval saints would find sayings that contained the essence of truth. They would take those choicest and distilled morsels, collect them in books, and then pass them around so they could be cherished and savored by the many. Long before I had heard of the practice I, too, had started writing out favorite sayings in books so that I could go back and reread and meditate on them at my leisure. Again, I originally had no intention of writing a book, so the idea that I might at some time need to find the source of those sayings did not occur to me. When using those (now source-less) sayings, I attribute them to the original authors, and I hope they are the impetus to cause others to follow that scent, but I am sorry I cannot direct readers to exact book, page, and title.

When life took a dark turn, I attempted to withdraw from life and polite society. There were some, however, who ignored my "No Trespassing" signs and came offering friendship, challenge, and the realization that it wasn't people that I was tired of, but rather, the old ways of relating. Laura, Evelyn, Kyle, Jane, Wilda—you gave me a foretaste of Christian community and the knowledge that relationships are only safe and healthy when grounded in something higher than ourselves.

I am blessed by my family, a family who offered unwavering love, support, encouragement, criticism, and a place to test my ideas. Thanks Wyndham and Amy, Matt and Petra, and Zoe. Special thanks to Paul.

I now need to admit to a personal bias—I do not like inclusive language. I, too, have been deeply wounded by the male power-mongers in the church who thought it their God-given duty to put me in my place. I, too, have been at a place where I found it almost impossible to read parts of the Bible because male language and pictures of oppressive power seemed to equate God with what was worst in human relations. I, however, kept on reading until I could see that just because God is referred to by means of masculine pronouns does not mean that God is male. I noticed that, "God created man in his own image... male and female he created them" (Genesis 1:27). Both the male and the female are needed to reveal the nature of God. The word *man* in the Bible, therefore, meant me, a female. I could finally see that in God there was no "male nor female, for you are all one in Christ Jesus" (Galatians 3:28). With that realization I could finally turn to all those who had so badly mutilated the image of God and of our divided humanity and could both forgive and be reconciled to them. The feminization of the image of God will never bring that healing; it will only fracture the Light of God according to a different bias. Inclusive language always seemed to me, therefore, to be a sign of personal failure, a failure to be brought to that place beyond language where our words and broken images no longer hurt and offend but where they are healed so that we can discover the unity and wholeness that God desires to draw us into. However, acknowledging that we still live in a fallen world where our images of God are broken and flawed, I have chosen to capitalize all pronouns referring to God to acknowledge that just because we apply masculine language to God does not mean that God is male; God exists on a different plane than our broken associations.

CHAPTER ONE

THE ALTERS
OF AHAZ

H ell, I have been told, is not a place, but a condition. In that case, it was also my home address. I now know that our understanding of hell comes largely from metaphorical constructs. God uses parables, allegories, metaphors, and dream-like visions in order to reveal what we are not yet capable of rationally grasping and understanding. My hell, however, was not a metaphorical or allegorical construct, but an existential reality. It was an entrapment—a life constricted and bound by dead ends, destroyed dreams, fractured relationships, and mired in deep depression.

I could empathize with the images of constriction that St. Theresa of Avila, a Catholic saint from the sixteenth century, used to describe her experience of hell. St. Theresa had asked God to show her what hell was like so she would know what God's mercies had rescued her from. She described hell in terms of constriction, writing, "I found I was placed in a cramped condition… a constriction, a suffocation, an affliction… Those walls, which were terrifying to see, closed in on themselves and suffocated everything."[1] It was in her description of hell that I realized I could recognize my former residence.

I now live in an increasingly spacious place—metaphorically speaking, that is. I love how the Bible describes salvation by using metaphors of spaciousness:

"Enlarge the place of your tent, stretch your tent curtains wide, do not hold back; lengthen your cords, strengthen your stakes. For you will spread out to the right and to the left " (Isaiah 54:2, 3).

"The boundary lines have fallen for me in pleasant places; surely I have a delightful inheritance" (Psalm 16:6).

"He brought me out into a spacious place; he rescued me because he delighted in me" (Psalm 18:19).

"You have not handed me over to the enemy but have set my feet in a spacious place" (Psalm 31:8).

I have since learned that the Psalms' "spacious place" comes from a context of Hebrew words we now translate as "being saved."[2] Having come from a religious background where "being saved" was central to one's religious identity, I was surprised to discover that the word "salvation" occurs more frequently in the Old Testament than in the New, and it was not seen as a ticket to bliss in the afterlife, but was rather deeply rooted in this present and earthly life. I, too, now see my salvation in terms of the long process that drew me out of my preceding hell to be given life among the widening horizons depicted in those gospel passages.

This book, however, is not a story of that process. It is, rather, a book written in response to the questions that arose out of that dark, broken, constricted place in which I found myself. After a life of attending church, serving the church, baking for church functions, teaching Sunday school, sitting on church committees, and financially supporting the church, I finally found myself to be broken, empty, and needing the life I believed the church existed to provide. That is when I began to notice what the church had actually become. When life was going well, then religion as tradition, as form, and as intellectual adherence to a system of beliefs was sufficient. When life broke, however, I realized that in order for religion to save, it would need to take hold of life at a much deeper level. That is when I began to notice what difficulty the church was having in mediating God's life to our broken lives. In fact, to a large extent, it seemed to have given up trying; it had just called in the assistance of the therapeutic to cover for God. I told myself that I just happened to be in one church that had gotten lost; changing churches would provide answers to what was troubling me. That began a long quest, during which I eventually gave up, becoming just one of a growing number of modern seekers who cannot give up the search for the answers to the hunger, the loneliness that drives us heavenward, but who have become wary of the institutional church as a present mediator of ultimate realities.

Our world now offers us a smorgasbord of answers to the spiritual quest—old religions, Eastern religions, new religions, and ways to discover and create one's own religion. I sampled and got lost, but in the midst of all that confusion, a curiosity awoke in me as to what really lay at the heart of the religion I had been born into. One day I picked up my Bible, opened it to the front page, and began to read.

Now, in a sense, the Bible was very familiar to me. All those years of church services, retreats, camps, study groups, and lectionary readings had in fact created an over-familiarity that blinded me to what was actually revealed in those Scriptures. As I began to read my Bible from cover to cover, and then over and over again, I became engaged in its life in a way I had never experienced before.

Coming from an evangelical tradition, I had been taught to stand firmly on the Scriptures. Unfortunately, I must have been standing on them so firmly, or had been so complicit in spreading them and defending them, that my energies had become deflected from the need to learn how to read them, how to meditate on them, how to get angry over them, doubt them and struggle with them. Now, however, I began to engage them in a wholly new way, a way that began to open up my life to their scrutiny. I had begun to examine the Bible for answers to my questions, but the roles were soon reversed—the Bible began to examine me and challenge me to respond to its questions. "Little Gidding" by T.S. Eliot best articulates where I eventually found myself:

"We shall not cease from exploration
And the end of all our exploring
Will be to arrive where we started
And know the place for the first time."

My question is—why did my journey seem inimical to attending church? Why did my freshly sprouting faith seem most threatened by religious institutions? To answer, it is perhaps first necessary to ask what the purpose of religion is. The philosopher William James, a pragmatist who turned the study of religion into a dry, dispassionate, analytic affair, gave the answer to that question. In his book entitled *Varieties of Religious Experience,* James concludes his classic by stating that all religions ultimately arrive at the same place, at a meeting point that has two parts:

1. An uneasiness; and
2. Its solution.

1. The uneasiness, reduced to its simplest terms, is a sense that there is something wrong about us as we naturally stand.
2. The solution is a sense that we are saved from the wrongness by making proper connection with the higher powers.[3]

I now know why I loved church when all was going well, but could no longer go when life broke apart. I was finally in a position to notice that the church's answers to those fundamental questions were no longer religious answers. It had erected a new altar that blocked the view of God's altar—a new altar that used therapeutic systems for its structural stones, replacing the need for the religious insights that once gave answer to our human unease.

The story of Ahaz and his two altars has become, for me, a metaphor for much of our present day religious life. The story of the altars of Ahaz, and how the second altar came to be erected, is told in 2 Kings 16:10–16:

"Then King Ahaz went to Damascus to meet Tiglath-Pileser king of Assyria. He saw an altar in Damascus and sent to Uriah the priest a sketch of the altar, with detailed plans for its construction. So Uriah the priest built an altar in accordance with all the plans that King Ahaz had sent from Damascus and finished it before King Ahaz returned. When the king came back from Damascus and saw the altar, he approached it and presented offerings on it. He offered up his burnt offering and grain offering, poured out his drink offering, and sprinkled the blood of his fellowship offerings on the altar. The bronze altar that stood before the Lord he brought from the front of the temple—from between the new altar and the temple of the Lord—and put it on the north side of the new altar."

"King Ahaz then gave these orders to Uriah the priest: On the large new altar, offer the morning burnt offering and the evening grain offering, the king's burnt offering and his grain offering, and the burnt offering of all the people of the land, and their grain offering and their drink offering. Sprinkle on the altar all the blood of the burnt offerings and sacrifices. But I will use the bronze altar for seeking guidance. And Uriah the priest did just as King Ahaz had ordered (2 Kings 16:10–16)."

The altar had always been a place for the meeting and exchange of life's forces. The people brought their first fruits, their grain, their animals—their life's work, life itself—to be offered up to God, and the priests, representing God, sprinkled the blood that provided the atonement for them. By that means life, and the tangible signs of that life, were brought under and reconciled to the life of God.

What Ahaz did was separate the spiritual from the tangible. He kept the original, God-ordained altar available for the spiritual side of their being, but erected a new altar for the visible, pragmatic, and concrete aspects of their humanity. Ahaz was astute. There will always be times of emergency when we feel we need a direct line up to God. It is expedient keeping the old altar with its options open. For the most part, however, Ahaz seemed to understand that to keep religion functioning expeditiously, human planning and design are needed. The altar on which the people placed the fruit of their work and life was therefore no longer an altar erected according to the revelation and guidance of God, but was rather a construction of human design. Ahaz was a pragmatist. The altar in Damascus was probably the altar of Tiglath-Pileser, the conquering Assyrian king. Tiglath-Pilaser was powerful, and when Ahaz saw his own failures set against Assyria's successes, his temptation to link up with what was currently successful would have been overpowering. Ahaz wanted to be effective, and he therefore needed to cover all his bases. So he also offered sacrifices to the gods of Damascus, even though they had been defeated, just in case there was some lingering power there (2 Chronicles 28:23). Soon the dominant power structures of the age were setting the terms of religion:

"King Ahaz took away the side panels and removed the basins from the movable stands. He removed the Sea from the bronze bulls that supported it and set it on a stone base. He took away the Sabbath canopy that had been built at the temple and removed the royal entryway outside the temple of the Lord, in deference to the king of Assyria" (2 Kings 16:17, 18).

The God of their covenant had not made an appearance in quite a while, so why not chase proven results? An obsequiousness to the power structures of the time quickly followed. However, Ahaz discovered that once pragmatism and effectiveness were allowed to set the terms of religion, then dispersion resulted. Soon, shrines were set up throughout the land with everyone worshipping what worked for them. One of our final views of Ahaz comes when he "shut the doors of the Lord's temple and set up altars at every street corner in Jerusalem" (2 Chronicles 28:24).

What is significant about Ahaz is that he did not destroy the original altar. He could have truthfully claimed evangelical adherence to God's revealed purposes. After all, he still had the altar to be used for more spiritual matters. But Ahaz did something much, much worse—he managed to relegate that God-ordained altar to a place of insignificance for the actual people, and for the reality of their actual lives.

In the Old Testament, the fire on the altar that consumed the visible signs of the people's life and work represented the Presence of God meeting man at the place of God's choosing. At Pentecost, the fire representing God's Presence became dispersed and settled on individuals. The individual now became the new altar on fire, revealing and containing the Presence of God. Now each struggling, creating, working, communicating, loving life was to be an altar that revealed the Presence of God. We, however, have destroyed the wonder of that revelation by again consigning God to a spiritual side of our being.

Once again we, like Ahaz, have found it easier worshipping at two altars. True religion is about faithfulness, not effectiveness, but that is a truth hard to hold onto when the visible world is so present with us. It is hard to orient our lives around the invisible; in the rush and commotion of life, we tend to forget that just because something is not visible does not mean it is not real. So, instead of the uncertainty, struggle, and (at times) terror involved in forming a life around God, we have created a new dualism. We have kept the original gospel for the spiritual side of our being, but then have erected another altar on which we can place our physical, practical, everyday lives.

It is our tangible, everyday lives, however, that we are asked to place on the altar before God. Instead of the surrender and commitment inherent in that act, we have instead allowed the dissolution of the gospel's greatest truth: the truth of the Incarnation. The Incarnation reveals that human flesh and human life are God's chosen medium by which He reveals Himself. The God of Abraham, Isaac, Jacob, and the Father of Jesus has chosen life—human life—as the book into which He writes a story about Himself. Our salvation consists in opening up our lives to God so that He, with divine penmanship, can inscribe another unique, never-to-be-repeated story revealing another facet of His reality and nature. We, however, have allowed the tension of body/soul, lived existence/spiritual existence, visible/invisible, to disintegrate. We have chosen to live worshipping at two altars rather than engage in the messy tension of the Incarnation, of the meeting between seemingly disparate elements.

To a large extent, the church now lives with two contradictory answers to the question of our unease, and the degree to which the church has become dependant on the therapeutic for answers is the degree to which it has allowed secular humanism to erect its altar inside the church. Those fundamental religious questions—Who are we? What has gone wrong with us? What shall we do about it?—are now being answered within the church from two contradictory sources. We have reduced the Gospel to theories of some nebulous realm of soul, spirit, and afterlife, and then have erected an altar for our concrete, tangible lives out of the hard stones of the science of the therapeutic. If many of us spiritually hungry seekers do not go to church, it may be because the view of God's altar has been obliterated and the altar that has taken its place is the same one we have seen in the world. Therapeutic answers have been allowed to replace religious answers to our unease.

This book is my attempt to dismantle Ahaz's altar. We were created to worship. We were created for community. The spiritual journey should not be a solitary journey, but an ever-increasing number of us spiritual seekers are finding it difficult to find what we are looking for in the church. This book was written out of a desire to again see the church become what it was meant to be—a place of one altar.

Over the last century, many of our greatest and most creative minds have been turned towards man as a subject of inquiry. Psychiatry, psychology, and the social sciences have come up with a lot of profound insights and clues as to who we are and how we function. I enjoy and learn a lot from reading their works. I agree with Augustine that, "All truths are God's truths"— and the therapeutic offers truths. However, there is an anxiety or unease that is fundamental to our humanity and it will never be eradicated. The question of that unease and how we can surmount it is fundamentally a religious question; it lies at the heart of all religions. When the church invites the therapeutic in to erect its competing systems and structures, offering answers in competition to the Gospel, then it is a destructive force in the church.

One cannot lump all the knowledge from psychology, psychiatry, and the social sciences into a unifying system. I need, however, some term to identify the knowledge systems from science and secular humanism that have been invited into the church to compete with and displace religious answers to those basic existential questions and understandings. For lack of a better phrase, I shall use the term *the therapeutic*.

CHAPTER TWO

LIFE
IN THE
BORDERLAND[4]

O ne cannot, I know from experience, criticize the role of the therapeutic in the church without also having to face the inadequacies and abuses that have made turning to the therapeutic for help seem a necessary corrective. We seem to be caught in a Catch-22 situation. The more pronounced God's absence and silence becomes, the more the church seems justified in enlisting the aid of the therapeutic. The more dependent the church becomes on the therapeutic to provide answers to our unease and feelings of being lost, the more pronounced the absence and silence of God becomes. The problem is thus exacerbated as the church is then increasingly stripped of all its stories and testimonies that give witness to the Presence of God with us. That, in turn, further justifies the ever-growing need for an ever-expanding role and dependency on the therapeutic to cover for the ever-growing silence and distance of God.

I tend not to waste my energies trying to defend the church. I, too, have shared the modern disillusionment with the church. I believe that the modern church's growing dependence on the therapeutic has at least one of its sources in the tradition in which I was raised. Religion was an all-pervasive influence. Gospel words surrounded all the parameters of life. Even as a child, however, I began to realize that quietly desperate lives were being lived behind those religious pieties. Bright gospel assurances were being laid like an oil slick over very troubled waters. The mouths of those whose eyes bespoke fear made claims of victorious Christian life. Those who lived lonely lives surrounded by fractured relationships were testifying to the love of God. There seemed to be a major disconnect between what people desperately needed to believe and the lonely, unhappy lives they actually lived. There is nothing more disillusioning and destructive of faith, I have discovered, than getting a good glimpse of the gap that exists between the beliefs people claim with their mouths and the reality of lives that contradict those words.

I needed a life that was more authentic, more real. I wanted an examined life, and psychology and the therapeutic offered systems, words, and tools that made me feel I was living a more authentic, real, truthful existence. We have now had a long time to observe what happens when the therapeutic is allowed free reign in the church. It did fill a vacuum that had been allowed to grow, but at what cost?

The ground of our lives needs to be ploughed open before that seed of faith can germinate and take root. Applying gospel words to lives that don't open themselves up to their scrutiny is like planting seeds on top of hardened soil. Religion without the interiorizing of its beliefs can provide a hard, glittering surface behind which we can hide wounds, passions, fears, and insecurities. When religion doesn't transform us, it becomes a hardened, whitewashed, deceptive surface behind which our real selves can cower and hide.

However, fully acknowledging the shortcomings of religion and the way we use it as an accomplice in our attempts to hide from God and from the truth of ourselves, I think it is time to recognize that our attempts to "save" religion and cover for its failures by marrying it to the therapeutic have only created new problems. All the therapeutic plowing of the soil of our lives seemed to be every bit as destructive as the hardened, impenetrable soil I had observed as a child. It was as though a host of would-be farmers showed up with all their tractors, harrows, ploughs and shovels only to discover that nobody had brought the seed. As Isaiah wrote:

"Listen and hear my voice; pay attention and hear what I say. When a farmer plows for planting, does he plow continually? Does he keep on breaking up and harrowing the soil? When he has leveled the surface…. Does he not plant wheat in its place, barley in its plot, and spelt in its field? His God instructs him and teaches him the right way" (Isaiah 28:23–26).

In attempting to "cover" for God by bringing the therapeutic into the church, we have eliminated a Living God from people's lives. The gospel offers us life—real, meaningful, purpose-driven life—but it is that life that seems to keep slipping away from us.

When my husband and I were in London, we rode the underground trains. Every time the train stopped, a voice would come over the speaker, saying, "Mind the gap." The gap between the train and the platform was obviously treacherous enough to bear repeated warning. The warning was such vintage London that t-shirts were sold with the inscription: "Mind the Gap." I have wondered if the t-shirts should not be bought in bulk and dispersed to all who enter the church. The gap between gospel promise, gospel life, and the place where we find ourselves living out our everyday lives is a place of special importance, but also of special danger to the life of faith.

The therapeutic is a dangerous addition to the church precisely because it meets us at the gap between gospel promise and actual life, and then seductively offers its own methods of response. There will always come a time when we, like the boy in the story of "The Emperor's New Clothes," look around and need to admit that we don't see evidence of what everyone is talking about. Those who stand at that point telling us we don't need to see evidence of the new—new clothes, they say, are "imputed"—they have just not read their Bibles very carefully. Jesus' parable of the wedding banquet in Matthew 22 clearly teaches that it is not enough to accept an invitation to the banquet; one must be clothed in new attire befitting that banquet. However, those who would import the therapeutic to sew us clothes of health to cover our nakedness and deformities will not sew us clothes that survive our mortality. Their patterns of health come from the secular realm.

There will always be a gap that exists between gospel words, religious rites, and the reality of our everyday mundane lives. Those who tell us that faith means believing in spite of that gap will turn us into spiritual schizophrenics. Real faith is about connecting the words to life, about interiorizing the gospel story. Those who attach therapeutic knowledge to gospel words to give them more weight and tangibility will not serve the gospel, but will actually rid those gospel words of their ability to lead us someplace completely new.

There are probably few moments in faith more pregnant with possibility than when our eyes are opened to what the Gospel actually says, and in that seeing, we find ourselves saying with the disciples: "Who could ever accept that?" It is at that point that we stand on the borderline of grace. Acknowledge someone else's right to lead, our own inability to know the steps, and the dance between heaven and earth can begin. True religion is not about moralism, social activism, religious work, or even about an eternal insurance policy against fire; it is about the dance. The dance is everything. There will always be those who cannot hear the music so, thinking to aid religion, gather the hard edges of the Gospel into a moral pattern they attempt to forcibly apply to man. What they create is a moral hair shirt that kills all life and allows for no movement. However, there are also those who wait for those who come against the impossible demands of the gospel in order to offer the therapeutic wares that they sell. With their supposedly more scientific understanding of human nature, they can whittle away all the hard edges of the gospel. Unfortunately, the dancing ground that grace needs in order to teach its steps is also thereby destroyed.

Faith is about the journey we are led on when we notice the silence and distance of God. It can be the seeming absence and silence of God itself that may be the most profound message we ever receive from Him. Those who help us avoid the silence by means of human words formed into theological formulas, dogmas, and creeds will not serve a Living God as much as create spiritual wastelands, but those who help us deal with the absence of God by means of importing therapeutic systems will do

God no favors. They will only consign all their people to perpetual spiritual infancy, and since there is no permanent stasis in the life of faith, then spiritual atrophy and death.

The fact is that we, as Christians, often seem to be living in a place that is neither here nor there. We have escaped from Egypt, but are not living in any Promised Land. Our existence seems to be suspended in some borderland defined neither by what we left behind nor by the glorious gospel promises.

The life of faith is actually lived in that creative space between Gospel promise and actual life. Faith calls us to live in three dimensions—time, space, and eternity—in a world trapped in two-dimensional living. We live caught between eternal yearnings and the competing desire to secure the life we have now on our own terms. It creates an unbearable tension. The therapeutic has amassed an impressive amount of knowledge to assist us in integrating our lives into that borderland. Most of us, however, can't live there indefinitely. The call of eternity is too strong within our hearts. But neither can we fully trust the unknown and move on. So, instead of movement, we devise ways of living in that borderland indefinitely, turning its tension into a permanent state. I have discovered that there are two primary ways of avoiding spiritual growth in order to create settlements of pseudo-security: by means of religion and by means of Gnosticism.

Religion is necessary. At the same time that I have grown disillusioned with the church I have also come to see the need for religious form and tradition. Religion provides the foundation and framework that allows faith to grow in a healthy environment. We are surrounded by too many living examples of spiritualities that have shed the forms of religion thinking that subjective experience is sufficient for the life of spirit. God may be spirit, but so is Satan; magic, superstition, and the occult are all part of spiritual life. Spiritualities that place their faith in the subjective rather than the trusted forms of religion are just asking to be led astray.

I was born in Saskatchewan, a province known for its wheat farming. I come from a large family of grain farmers. When the Bible uses the image of wheat as a symbol for the spiritual life it strikes a deep resonance with what I can understand. Religion is like the wheat plant that produces the grains of wheat. There is a lot of visible stem and leaves that grow before the head ripens and matures. When Jesus spoke of the final separation of wheat from chaff he was not speaking of the separation of good from evil. Chaff is not evil; it is necessary. No one has ever devised a way of growing wheat without chaff. Chaff is the husk, the stem, the plant, and the protective coating that encases the kernel of wheat allowing for its maturation. I know of few uses for chaff other than to produce and house the kernels of wheat until they mature, but as such, it is absolutely necessary.

The Bible repeatedly likens the spiritual life to the growth of that kernel of wheat. It is a sad fact of wheat farming, however, that one can grow fields of stalks that never mature into heads of wheat. The prophet Hosea made that same observation:

"The stalk has no head; it will produce no flour" (Hosea 8:7).

The wheat plant can still grow to a glorious height with stem, leaves, and husk intact, but produce nothing more than visible form. Religion that forgets its purpose is like that empty stalk. Satisfied with the visible, it can produce form and structure with no inner life.

There is another danger encountered by those who grow wheat; it is a disease called smut. Smut is a disease that gets into the head of wheat and infects and changes the very nature of the kernel. When those smut balls open, they let off a foul odor and infect all healthy growth around. Gnosticism functions in the same way as that smut. *Gnosticism* means "knowledge" and it is the attaching of a system of knowledge to a religious system. It can be the human attempt to cover for the gap and seeming failures of religion without having to leave the framework of religious system. Gnosticism basically functions as a disease or parasite, attaching itself to an established religious system and slowly living off of its life. Early Christian Gnosticism (second century) was largely influenced by Greek wisdom. In our world, it is the therapeutic that has taught us ways of approaching reality which has allowed Gnosticism to again flourish.

Greek Gnosticism is significant for us in that I believe it created the environment that allowed for the reaction of modern, therapeutic

Gnosticism. Christianity was born in a world that was Hellenized in thought. Our world has never surpassed or completely freed itself from the wisdom of early Greek thinkers such as Aristotle and Plato. Early Christian history shows that the first church fathers were conflicted over what to do with the Greeks. Some thought Christianity meant making a break with Greek wisdom (Jerusalem and Athens, they said, were not compatible). Others, the winning camp, thought Plato and Aristotle could be baptized, Christianized, and thus brought into the church. Since the Greeks thought that the soul needed to break with the body in order to be free to grow, and since this created an enmity between the soul and human nature, the decision to integrate Greek wisdom into the Christian church proved to be a fatal error. It allowed the work of the Incarnation to be undone. The insidiousness of that error became evident as Christian man struggled with what to do with his human nature. A lot of the excesses of the medieval church and their ascetic extremes can be attributed to that fateful attempt at integration. The church has never fully recovered from that Gnostic blend.

It was Plato, not Jesus, who split the body and soul apart. The Incarnation was meant to bring those two natures back together. It was Plato, not Jesus, who denigrated human nature. Jesus took on human flesh to show us that we need not be ashamed of our bodies. Plato claimed the body was a prison. Jesus taught that it was a temple. For Plato, the body got in the way of the freedom of the soul. Jesus made His body the central symbol of the new religion, body and blood becoming the sacramental means by which God's life was imparted to us. In Christianity, flesh and blood have a sacred purpose; they are the medium by which the life of soul is nurtured.

Greek philosophers such as Alcinous and Celsus condemned the early Christians for getting so caught up in the world of sensible things that "they are unable to breathe the pure intellectual air where true knowledge of God is found."[5] The early Christians, in contrast, believed God's greatest and final revelation of himself came not in ideas but in a human life. Early monasticism was devised not as an imitation of the life of Christ, but rather an imitation of the Platonists (and the Greek Pythagoreans who came before them), "who sometimes lived in communities under vow, renounced a normal life in the world, and waited in some lonely place for a final revelation."[6]

The Greeks saw salvation in terms of immortality for their souls. Under their influence, the early Christians began to dismiss the revelation of a God who came to be with us on earth, who loved the world, and who was "an ever-present help in trouble" (Psalm 46:1). They, too, began to see salvation in terms of the soul, and their salvation became ever more ethereal, otherworldly, and futuristic.

As the Greek disdain for the body increasingly infected the Christian church, soon they were refusing to glorify their creator for being "fearfully and wonderfully made" (Psalm 139:14), rather seeing a disdain for their nature as a form of spiritual superiority. Bonhoeffer aptly noted, "The man who renounces his body renounces his existence before God the Creator,"[7] but the early Gnostics saw the body mainly as a vehicle of temptation. Paul may have said, "Everything God created is good" (1 Timothy 4:4) and that God "richly provides us with everything for our enjoyment" (1 Timothy 6:17), but soon, denying the goodness of the world and ascetic extremes became seen as the means of spiritual progression.

Jesus said he came not to condemn but to save the world; His followers devised ways to avoid the world and leave it behind. Jesus said, "God so loved the world," but His followers developed a suspicion and horror of the world. The great gospel story of spirit being made flesh so that flesh could be reborn as spirit got turned into a story of rejection of the flesh. Rather than spirit redeeming nature, they turned religion into a corrosive, destroying the very nature it was meant to redeem. With all their ladders of perfection supposedly leading to a higher life, the Medieval Christians seemed to forget that we were not designed or invited to be celestial beings; we were created to be human beings.

I realized what a Gnostic being I had become when I found myself reacting in horror the first time I really saw Jesus, as a resurrected being, being touched, eating, and wearing a body. I realized my hope had been for a time when I would be pure spirit. Jesus dashed that hope. Christianity is as much about becoming human as it is about becoming spiritual.

Modern Gnosticism may be a late and final reaction to Greek Gnosticism. For centuries, man had denied his human nature, attempting to become a pure spiritual being. It didn't work. Then the Enlightenment taught us to become thinking animals, the life of soul and spirit being denigrated, eliminated, or ignored. The only reality deemed trustworthy became that which could be apprehended according to the supremacy of the mind or by our physical senses. Without an acknowledgement of the human being as a living soul, the Enlightenment also proved disastrous for our human natures. Man the "Rational Being" increasingly became man the irrational and unreasonable animal. Somewhere along the line, the human entity—with its soulful longings, its emotions, desires, passions, and human depths—demanded to be heard. The result has been a world madly attempting to fill our inner void with bogus therapies and spiritualities. The therapeutic, offering us its aid, is again teaching us ways to approach reality that is nourishing and spreading a new Gnosticism. I believe part of the current debate over Jesus—was He God? Was He only human?—is a projection of the confusion we feel about ourselves. Who are we? Spirit, soul, flesh, mind; how are we to think of ourselves?

Both forms of Gnosticism—Greek and the therapeutic—create the same problem. They keep our natures split. They offer no unity to the tension in our being. The Incarnation—the uniting of the human and divine, of spirit with flesh, which lies at the heart of the Gospel—is in both cases destroyed. The church now lives in an unnatural tension—having never completely purged itself of the former Gnosticism, it has become vulnerable and fallen victim to the latter Gnosticism. I suppose this book is one long argument that culminates in the final chapter with the conclusion that we have journeyed long and hard to rid ourselves of Greek Gnosticism, only to find that we have become enamored by a new Gnosticism, and that our integration of the gospel with therapeutic sensibilities has allowed for an even more dangerous and virulent form of

Gnosticism. What I would like to argue in this book is that much of what comes in the name of Christianity is only tangentially related to either orthodox Christianity or else the teachings of Jesus. Much of what currently is done in the name of Christianity is actually the blossoming of a new Gnosticism. But that is to get ahead of myself. Let us first look at the arguments.

The failings of religion are not reason enough to justify bringing the therapeutic into the church, with its competing answers to questions of our nature and our existential unease. Ecclesiastes 3:11 says that God has "set eternity in the hearts of men; yet they cannot fathom what God has done from beginning to end." Any attempt to understand the human animal that refuses to take into account that divine spark will miss what is most important and unique in our being. When the therapeutic, which was originally anti-religion, finally came to that realization, it transferred its ways of seeing onto the spiritual realm and taught us ways of seeing that are Gnostic, not Christian. The therapeutic cannot produce real wheat; it infects wheat's attempts to grow.

The problem with growing older is that we finally have to face the consequences of the paths we have chosen. I'm old enough to have grown disillusioned twice: once by religion and secondly by the therapeutic systems we have used to support it. The first disillusionment came from observing religion that had gotten detached from life; the second disillusionment came from observing life and the attempts to live it freed from the framework of gospel truths.

The great danger now in the church lies in creating a false dichotomy, contrasting religious life that has grown stale with the allure of the therapeutic with its seeming pragmatism. The real danger is not that of becoming disillusioned with the church; the real danger lies in allowing something like the therapeutic to cover for God so effectively that, in avoiding disillusionment, we become accustomed to life without God.

CHAPTER THREE

THE
HUMILIATION
OF THE WORD

I t seems almost heretical criticizing the presence of the therapeutic in the church. After all, organizations like Focus on the Family and Christian counselors have become completely embedded in the church structure and they claim to be working towards the same ends as the church; inner healing is offered and family values and moral ends are being loudly trumpeted. Criticizing the therapeutic in our day can feel as though one were attacking something as sacred as God, Himself. Few seem willing to question whether religion and the therapeutic should have become such close bedfellows.

What few seem ready to acknowledge is that one of the casualties of that Gnostic pairing has been the Word, its slow devaluation occurring so insidiously that even evangelicals seem unaware of how its message has been sidelined. Therapeutic effectiveness has rendered as obsolete the necessity to discover the way the Word works in drawing us into its life. Wonder, reverence, mystery, worship, and obedience have fallen to the wayside, but rather than lamenting their demise, we celebrate the healing, the guidance, and the self-awareness that human knowledge systems can provide. Why learn the slow, circuitous and mysterious ways of God if the therapeutic can affect our healing, reveal our identities, and give us a sense of our worth without so much struggle and effort? Are those not gospel ends just rendered easier?

If one believes, as I do, in the need to return to the Word as the means by which we are formed and guided through life; if one believes in the Word as the means by which we are healed and transformed, then trying to defend its worth in a world caught up in a fascination with therapeutic effectiveness is frustrating. Trying to defend the Word from its critics and detractors eventually brings one up against, to use the phrase coined by Jacques Ellul, "The humiliation of the Word." In a world addicted to pragmatism, simple answers, and therapeutic lingo, we have lost our ability to believe in and see how the Word can sufficiently answer the questions of our humanity.

We may give lip service to the words in 2 Timothy 3:16, 17, "Every part of Scripture is God-breathed and useful one way or another—showing us truth, exposing our rebellion, correcting our mistakes, training us to live God's way. Through the Word we are put together and shaped up for the tasks God has for us" (The Message), but in actual life, we have lost our faith in the Word to speak to the reality of our tangible existences. It is in the very evangelical churches that pride themselves on their adherence to the Word that one can find some of the greatest dependence on the therapeutic for answers to the "real" issues of life. How did that come about?

I grew up in evangelical churches where the supremacy of the Word was verbally assented to. The shrillness and stridency with which the Word's supremacy was acclaimed never diminished, but the actual relevance of the Word to the everyday particulars of life was slowly eroded. Which came first? Did the seeming inefficacy of the Word create the vacuum which allowed the therapeutic to fill the void, or did the influence of the therapeutic slowly infiltrate the church, rendering as obsolete the necessity to learn to use the Word as a sufficient guide to life? Whatever the order, not allowing the Word to speak in its own way on its own terms has given rise to the fallacy of its ineffectiveness. I have learned that before one criticizes the role of the therapeutic in the church, one should be ready to defend the Word against accusations of its irrelevance.

Before I seem too judgmental, I must start by admitting that I, personally, have been part of the problem. I remember getting up at a meeting in a church where the minister had been urging us to read our Bibles and arguing that the Bible had so little to say to my tangible, actual existence. I didn't realize at the time that I was saying little about the efficacy of the Word and everything about the place where I, myself, was spiritually.

There is a woman who has become an icon for me, a visible representation of a truth that I found hard to discover. She was someone I had known superficially for years. Our paths crossed repeatedly but we never became close because we had so little in common. I prided myself on my competence; everything in life, for me, needed to be under firm control, whereas she was constantly overwhelmed by life. For her, the smallest details of life seemed to become mountainous obstacles for her to cross. We attended the same church for a while, but we were too different in personality to have ever become soulmates or, for that matter, to have even enjoyed much of each other's company. Our paths diverged, I didn't see her for years, and then I heard through the grapevine about how terrible tragedy had struck her family. I told myself that she was the last person in the world to be able to handle the tragedy, and that she would certainly disintegrate, incapable of handling the depth of what had happened.

I was therefore surprised when, several months later, ready to pay for my groceries in a Safeway store, I spotted her in one of the checkout lines ahead of me. I didn't know what I would be expected to say, so I thought the best way to handle the situation would be to choose the longest line— she was near the front of a line—pick up a magazine to read, and pretend I hadn't seen her. I read until I reached the counter, paid for my groceries, and then just as I was about to walk out I looked up and, to my horror, saw the woman I was avoiding standing right in front of me. By the look on her face I could tell she was feeling just as reluctant to see me. There was no polite alternative but to walk out together. I did a quick mental check and decided that the best way to proceed would be to pretend I hadn't heard of the family disaster. I would mutter some irrelevant pleasantries and then we would part as quickly as possible.

I need not have worried. As we walked out of the store together she began to talk, and as she spoke, I realized I no longer had any idea as to whom this woman was. The woman who stood beside me radiated strength, she radiated courage, and strangest of all, she radiated gratitude: gratitude as she told of a God who, honoring her middle-class respectabilities, had touched her, been with her, and whose mercies she claimed to see running throughout the perimeters of the tragedy. In a strange twist of irony I, who had prided myself on my competence and ability to control every aspect of my life, was increasingly becoming incapacitated and mired in body-numbing depression while she, who had never seemed to be able to manage the pressures of life, was confident and calm and assured. What was even more surprising was that the language she used to describe her peace and assurance was gospel language. The language I had publicly dismissed as having so little relevance to my tangible, concrete existence was the language she used to describe her state of peace. As I left the Safeway parking lot, I realized that she had just brought me what I had long been looking for—the "scent of water."[8]

That Safeway woman became an icon for me because she taught me that for gospel words to have power they need to first make their way through the medium of a human life. To one who had dismissed gospel words as being irrelevant to everyday life, she was a sign, a visible manifestation, of the power of the Word when it has been made real in one human life. Her image and the message it revealed would repeatedly return to my mind.

It was at the darkest period of my life that I, who was trying to retreat from all contact with people, began meeting up with broken people who were looking for help. At a time when I had withdrawn from life, turning my home into a fortress that was supposed to keep all of life out, coincidences allowed cracks to appear that would allow these people in. I had turned to the Bible looking for clues as to the reality of God, and had an ever-increasing sense of my journey being guided and accompanied, but for a rationalist, I had certainly not come upon certainties that would allow me to speak of what I felt I was discovering. And yet, the coincidences whereby these people had come into my life were too pronounced to be called just coincidences. I would tell myself that if I couldn't help myself, I certainly couldn't help anyone else, but then the Safeway woman would appear in my memory. I would remember how she spoke of God in a way that brought a glimmer of hope into my life and then I would repeat to myself what I had learned from her, saying, "Never, never speak any more than has been realized, actualized in one's own life; but as much as one has discovered, speak that!"

I drove down to the Fraser River one afternoon, promising myself that I would not leave until I had answered a letter, a chore that I had been putting off for far too long. It was to be a letter to a woman who was so mired in deep depression she was finding it difficult keeping on with life. I didn't know what to write. When I tried to articulate my hope, it all seemed to distill itself into question and subjective experience. What I really wanted to say was that after an entire life of struggling with deep depression I had finally found peace—not peace arising out of life, but peace given as a gift to meet ever-darkening days. What I wanted to say was that for the first time in my life, I had discovered one morning what real joy felt like—joy that had broken through in order to counter the darkest period of my entire life. What I wanted to say was that I had discovered that I had a soul; there was something in me that could become aware of and then cling to that which lay beyond a disintegrating life. But a soul is not cognitive and I couldn't yet clearly understand it, much less articulate it. I felt uncomfortable with religious language. I had developed an allergy to the religious language I had grown up with and yet, as I struggled to write, it was gospel language that gave form to what I had been going through. Struggling to remain honest—what did I still believe, what was wishful thinking, where was the boundary line between faith and self-deception?— I got rid of all the words that still lived in the realm of blind hope, blind faith, and wishful thinking. With great inner struggle I finally got to the point at which I could honestly say, "There, as much as one can ever say they know anything, I know that." I mailed the letter, drove home, and as I walked into the front door, I suddenly realized what I had done. I, for whom all God-language had once become stale and dead, that I had filled an entire letter with gospel clichés. I, who had always cringed at overly pious verbiage, that I had filled an entire letter with the very words I would have once called the religious trite. As I felt the shame washing over me, I told myself that she was certainly going to think that I had lost my mind.

To my great surprise, I actually received a letter in reply. It said she had read my letter so many times that she almost had it memorized. The correspondence continued. She said my letters were a sign of God's care for her; they were a salve to wounds; I had what many wanted.

Since then I have frequently thought back to Kierkegaard and how he separated gospel words into those that come from deep filing cabinets and those that come from living springs. Gospel words, I realized, that come from deep filing cabinets can come with all the added erudition of higher learning and can be vested with all the power that officialdom can bestow upon them, but if the speaker has not personally drunk the water from a Living Source, then those words will ultimately only add to the air the scent of dust and mothballs. E. M. Bounds aptly wrote, "The spoken word cannot rise in its life-giving forces above the individual. Dead people give out dead words, and dead words kill. Everything depends upon the spiritual character of the speaker."[9]

What the woman in the Safeway parking lot taught me was that gospel words that have been allowed to break us, reform us, lead us through valleys of overwhelming darkness till finally the words themselves break open and reveal the life-giving Spirit that lies within and beyond them—those words, I discovered, can be spoken in the middle of a Safeway parking lot with no pulpit, no vestments, no music to create a holy mood, and they can still come with all the power of some mighty river washing over one. I, who had stood in that church hall saying that gospel words did not speak to my concrete existence, had discovered, finally, that they are the most relevant words of all.

Before I could discover how the gospel is "sufficient," however, I had to learn how to separate the Word from the literalist readings of Scripture that I had linked it with. Part of my problem came from how I had understood the words from John 1: "In the beginning was the Word." I believe that the impression I, from my background, was given was that the Word was synonymous with the Scriptures, and in particular, a certain understanding of the Scriptures as pertaining to a specific denominational interpretation. With that interpretation, it is small wonder that there was not more visible evidence of the Word taking root in human life. The Bible had been turned into a dead, literalist object, an idol, a "letter that kills."

Since Christianity is known as one of the religions that rely on a Holy Book, it is interesting comparing the Christian Scriptures with other religions that use a sacred book. The Jews, of course, believe that the Ten Commandments were written directly by the finger of God and that God gave the other laws directly through Moses. The name *Koran* means "something to be recited," and Muslims believe the Koran to be the words of God, Himself, revealed to Muhammad by the angel Gabriel. The Mormons believe that the angel Moroni gave golden plates to Joseph Smith, which he then translated into the *Book of Mormon*. In contrast, neither Jesus nor His disciples passed along recorded scriptures that they then claimed were sacred. The first gospel of our Bible was not even written until about thirty years after Jesus' death. Our Scriptures did not reach their current form until a few hundred years after the life of Jesus. Clearly in Christianity the Word does not mean the same thing—direct, literal inspiration—that it does in other religions. In a sense, Christianity is closer to Buddhism in that it is a life, not a book, which is at the center of its beliefs. So when we, in Christianity, believe in the supremacy of the Word, what exactly does that mean?

For the Greeks, later for the Scholastics, and much later for the Enlightenment thinkers, the concept of Word, or logos, was that of the rational principle that governs all creation. There were principles and laws under-girding all of the cosmos and we lived best when we oriented our lives according to their rhythms. There is truth in that interpretation. The cosmos is intrinsically rational. If the Word was that rational principle, then obviously the mind was the means whereby we approached it. That, however, would give reason a preeminence that allowed it to master and control the mystery. A concrete example of that approach could be seen in a book a religious organization sent me that promised to answer, categorize, and summarize all the arguments for the Christian religion. It also offered to refute all the main objections to Christianity, as well as offering answers to the hundreds of questions that querying minds might ask about the life of faith. It was an impressive attempt at comprehensive apologetics but it, too, turned the Word into a reductionist, dead object. It eliminated the Living Word in order to make faith comprehensible to the human mind. Something still seemed to be missing.

I later came to discover that among the earliest theologians, the concept of logos was identified more with the Holy Spirit than with the idea of wisdom or rational principle.[10] With that interpretation, the first chapter of John would then read, "In the beginning was the Spirit, and the Spirit was with God, and the Spirit was God."[11] That interpretation seems to lie much closer to the Hebrew idea of logos as being "that which comes from God to fulfill his purpose in and for the world."[12]

During the Enlightenment years, with their overemphasis on reason, the reality of the Word was largely interpreted as rational principle. Now, with a burgeoning interest in spiritualities making intuition and spirit the focus of interest, it is the Word as the external, intelligible, and revealed order ordained by God, which is being neglected or destroyed. Unlike modern spiritualities where subjectivity reigns, however, in Christianity, the work of the Holy Spirit is never separated from the Word as revealed order or truth. In Christianity, objectivity and subjectivity are combined; it is always Spirit and Word together that are linked to become the means of our transformation.

"The Word became flesh and made his dwelling among us" (John 1:14)—this forever rescues the Word from stagnating into something dead or inanimate; it is a Living Word. Linking Jesus with the Word means that what will forever remain incomprehensible, obscure, remote, and outside of human understanding has chosen to enter human time to become visible, particularized, and revelatory. The knowledge we thereby gain is not general, abstract, or conceptual, but is instead particular and relational. The Word speaks through the Bible, but is not the Bible. The early Christians did not have our Bible as we know it—what they had was the verbal witness of those who had known Jesus and the reality of the Holy Spirit. As long as the Word is interpreted to mean the Bible, a book that we read like any other book, then its life will remain cut off from us. However, by entering into the life of the Living Word, the Bible becomes the guide, the map, and the inerrant clues to life and to what lies beyond itself without becoming a dead object.

John 1:1 also states, "The Word was God." Deuteronomy 30:14 says, "The word is very near you; it is in your mouth and in your heart so you may obey it." Word as God, as the Holy Spirit, as Jesus, and as the inner witness to the Trinity—what I finally came to realize was that the Word is an all-encompassing reality that both lies beyond and yet runs through our time-bound lives, a reality towards which all our truest words point.

The Word thus understood draws me out of my tangible, pragmatic, everyday life to alert me to the reality of another whole plane of existence. It releases me from time-bound, visible reality and invites me to enter and live in the dimensions of eternity. It tells me that I am not living in a closed, determined system, but that there is both a pre-ordained order and a spiritual presence that permeates creation, something that I, as a creature with a soul, can be awakened into awareness of and live in harmony with. The Bible is the book that reveals and offers the language and narrative of the soul.

Living by the Word, therefore, does not mean adapting a literalist, legalistic application of the Scriptures to our lives; it means living in awareness of the spiritual realm where order and Spirit reign. The God who heals, restores, redeems, and reconciles is forever waiting to break into history. For that to happen, however, we need to live before timeless Word, not human words. Therein lies the problem. We cannot see how the Word relates to life itself unless we let go of our obsession with the visible, concrete, and pragmatic. We may believe in a supernatural world in the sense that we hope to reside there in some afterlife, but fail to comprehend the significance of the supernatural for our everyday, mundane existences. We don't have the time or the patience or the faith for the mysterious and circuitous ways in which the Word becomes visible and en-fleshed in human history. The demands of the Way—"Seek ye first the Kingdom of God, and his righteousness; and all these things will be added unto you" (Matthew 6:33 KJV)—are being supplanted by the relevant, the pragmatic, the concrete, and the effective.

Before the end of the nineteenth century, it was assumed that learning how to read the Bible was almost as important as what was in the Bible. The Bible was not seen as revealing literal truth as much as it was the lens through which one caught a glimpse of mystery and the infinite glory of God. It was the scientific revolution that gave us the strange idea that we could read the Bible for facts and literal truth in the same way that we read scientific journals. The Word, however, has more in common with deep symbols and myths than the information bites and reducible systems that surround us. Properly used, the Bible meets us at a place deeper than the cognitive structures we attempt to live by, and in our co-operative response, it gets turned into a Living Word. The Living Word must be freshly discovered and struggled with ever anew if it is going to reveal its life. The temptation will always exist to seek refuge in information, facts, concrete images, reducible structures, labels, categories, systems, diagrams, slogans, and psychobabble.

Our desire to reduce reality to the visible and concrete is an old failing and obsession. It was the call of the pragmatic and concrete that had the Israelites consistently falling for foreign gods: gods who offered fertility for their fields, flocks, and wombs, or gods who offered healing for illnesses and help conquering enemies. Their seduction, in other words, lay in their relevancy; not only were they symbolized by concrete images that could be seen, touched and approached by the human senses, but they were associated with blessings and rewards that secured their relevancy. The Israelite God, in contrast, offered a covenant that would teach them how to live. As long as they lived according to that covenant, God promised to provide for their needs. The promised benefits were secondary; the obedience and relationship would have to come first.

Mark 4:24, 5 admonishes us to "consider carefully what you hear…
with the measure you use, it will be measured to you—and even more.
Whoever has will be given more; whoever does not have, even what he
has will be taken from him." Our ability to hear and appropriate the Living
Word will always depend on what we have done with what we have
already received. With every choice and act, we are either increasing our
capacity to hear the Living Word or are deadening our receptors so that it
cannot penetrate.

It is we who decide whether the Word remains a Living Word or
whether it dies. The God of the Scriptures is a God who goes into hiding.
His eyes are said to roam the earth looking for those who seek Him. God,
in other words, has put a high premium on allowing us our freedom of
will. God also places a high premium on relationships. Healthy relationships are dependent on ever-increasing levels of mutual commitment, self-
disclosure, vulnerability, and growth; they begin to atrophy as soon as one
party is no longer interested in the needed effort required for growth. In
viewing the mess within our world, we can either say there can be no God,
that God doesn't care, that He is helpless, or that He has chosen to hide
His hand in order not to override our free will. The Word must be actively
pursued if it is to be prevented from "falling to the ground" or sinking into
oblivion and irrelevancy.

The Bible is a book that has something to appeal to almost everyone.
Try living into its reality, however, and it can be the most frustrating book.
Try to speak God's words against the background of His absence, distance,
silence, and into the needs of ordinary people struggling with concrete,
tangible life and one will know the temptation to either lose one's faith in
the Word or else devise means whereby one can be kept from becoming
disillusioned. We can inadvertently turn the Living Word into a dead
object in order to protect it. We can turn the Word into spiritual gloss that
we apply to something more concrete, like a therapeutic framework. Or we
can turn the Word into a theology that can exist separate from the messiness of life. We can also become isolationists, creating communities of religious retreat and ironclad certainty wherein everybody lives according to

some unspoken agreement to ignore doubts, questions, inconsistencies, and realities. Perhaps the reaction of choice to the Word nowadays is to become introspective, using oneself as a baseline against which to measure truth, and then becoming the judge of the Word according to one's own understanding. Since the Word is no longer "Other" but rather a projection of our personal understanding, then we avoid disillusionment, for the interpretation will just change according to our varied situations. Unfortunately all of those responses create the kind of hypocrisy that has the world denying the reality of faith, for no concrete sign of the Word is made evident.

Rarely do we see the Word "become flesh" in a way that convinces us of its power and validity. It seems to be the mark of the spiritually mature, however, to be able to know how to respond to and speak the Word "in season." The Word used in a way that can free and enlighten seems to be spoken by those who come out of long dialectic struggles of the Word being allowed to reveal life, life lived according to Word, until Biblical time finally becomes our time and we know our lives to be lived in eternal time.

It should not surprise us that the Word has so much trouble taking root in our lives and culture. After all, it was Jesus who gave us the parable likening the sowing of the Word to a farmer planting seed—that seed was trampled on, snatched away, and choked by weeds. Even that which managed to take root was soon scorched by the sun and insufficient soil. I cannot help but react to the parable by thinking that the sower should have been more careful of his seed: what wastage, what desecration, how inefficient. Living in a secular world, however, where religious language is still loosely and carelessly broadcast, makes me realize that the parable describes reality as we see it in our world. There is still so much God-talk and religious verbiage, with so little sign of the Kingdom among us.

We live in a time of the devaluation of the Word. However, rather than sharing in its humiliation and working for its re-valuation, much of the church has chosen, instead, to itself become an accomplice to the great compromise of the Word.

CHAPTER FOUR

THE GREAT COMPROMISE

Gospel words are not always Living Words. The words of Scripture are just human words until the Spirit that first breathed them into life breathes them afresh into our lives. Gospel words taken on their own can save no one. They are, however, the assigned meeting place for our encounter with the One who can save us. It is not words but the Holy Spirit that brings the experiential knowledge of God and His redeeming truths to us and personalizes the gospel words in a way that makes salvation personal and real. It is gospel words, however, that are the medium the Spirit uses to reveal that life. Christianity is ultimately about a person, not a theology that systematizes and defines words—but we need words to illuminate and reveal that person. In Christianity, words are important.

It is interesting, therefore, living in a world increasingly filled with spiritualities that approach Divinity directly through intuition, bypassing the need to struggle with words. It is alarming to see how Christianity, a religion that supposedly centers itself around the Word, is succumbing to pressure to get caught up in cults of silence. Prayer retreats, books on prayer, and spiritual directors are increasingly becoming focused on modes of silence. We are taught about meditation, relaxation, centering, emptying our minds, breathing and concentration techniques, yogic positions, and mantras, all of which take us to where our words disappear into silence. It seems that when we lost our sense of the Word as being crucial to the forming of our lives, then all our human words became devalued in the process.

In Christianity, as opposed to Eastern religions, words have great value. They are instrumental in our search for and approach to God: "Take words with you and return to the Lord" (Hosea 14:2).

For centuries, people have learned how to pray using the Psalms as a guide. The Psalms do not offer us techniques, ways into silence, or exercises that empty our minds—they offer us words that run the full gamut of human emotion. The Psalms are a school of prayer; they give us the courage to articulate and then bring the full range of our emotions and our humanity before God. In the New Testament, when the disciples asked Jesus how to pray, He did not offer techniques or ways into silence; He gave them words. Again, in Christianity, words are important.

In the Scriptures, words are depicted as the measure or the container that receives and mediates Mystery (Mark 4:24), and in the way and to the degree that we provide the measure, its bounty is said to be multiplied. Gospel words are depicted as the sword that cuts through our illusions and delusions to bring us back to that pre-linguistic Word so that all our human words, like filings before a magnet, can get their true bearings. Gospel words are depicted as a light to our path, so that in a dialectic of word revealing life, life revealing word, they can lead us to where we know the reality towards which they point as our surest reality. Gospel words, I have found, are like guardrails—the only safe, sure ones I have found—that help us safely navigate and enter Mystery. But as with light, measure, sword, and guardrails, words have to keep their shape in order to do their work.

The problem is, words don't stay still. Words are constantly slipping in their meanings, sliding into new meanings, being emptied of meaning, being misunderstood, compromised, abused by those who wish to use them for personal reasons, or being manipulated by those who have personal motives for doing so. We are deluded if we think words are only used to communicate. In our world, they seem to be largely used for opposite purposes: to obfuscate, to rationalize, and to create illusive fronts behind which we can hide. It is Christianity that offers a Word pre-existent, pre-eminent, and external to human language so that our human words can get their bearings. It is therefore that pre-linguistic Word that gives meaning and authority to all our human words.

For both Christianity and the therapeutic, words are the tools of the trade. More than that, since both deal with our problems in living and with problems inherent in being human, they end up sharing many of the same words, or else offer competing words for similar states of being. They both offer us understanding of our lives, our relationships, and ourselves. It was perhaps inevitable that when we failed to perceive how the Word worked in forming our lives, we next attempted to rescue it from irrelevancy by integrating it into therapeutic frameworks of understanding. At first glance, it seems a natural marriage, since their concerns are so similar— the human creature with all of its anxiety, stress, and emotional cravings. One writer succinctly observed that, "There is a sense in which modern psychiatry should be included with the world religions, for although no pretense of religion is made, yet the same raw material is taken—man with his storm and stress, his tension and anxiety—and the same result sought, namely, release, not by supernatural means, but by natural ones."[13]

Perhaps it time that we engaged in some self-examination, looked at the two gospels we have tried to blend, and then had the courage to ask: do they exist in harmony with one another, do they compete, or does one actually subvert the other?

Let us look at the shift that has occurred. The Episcopal priest Alan Jones noted that "Idolatry is now called addiction. Sin is called neurosis or pathology. Salvation is called liberation or individuation."[14] With that shift in language, are we providing a truer, more scientific understanding of a person's nature, are we merely finding new, more updated words for the same reality, or are we actually shifting or destroying certain realities? According to our perceptions and answer, we will either be searching for a missing redeemer or a good therapist.

The church has been drawn into a huge paradigm shift. Karl Menninger, M.D., in his book, *Whatever Became of Sin?*, wrote that the "clergyman's morally burdened parishioners became the psychiatrist's complex-laden patients; sin became symptom, and confession became psychotherapy."[15] What is that shift in understanding doing to the realities that words are meant to reveal?

The integration of the therapeutic into the church has completely altered the conceptions of self that we, as Christians, once held. When we took the "self" words from our Christian heritage—self-control, self-denial, self-surrender—and then allowed them to be coupled with the "self" words from the therapeutic—self-actualization, self-realization, self-fulfillment, self-awareness—did we actually think we could integrate the two fields or did we just feign ignorance as we obliterated an entire field of awareness?

Both religion and the therapeutic exist to help us understand ourselves. However, do they give us compatible answers? In the nineteenth century, "character" was a word that gave form to how we defined ourselves. Character was a concept of self that was formed according to convictions and was also the language used to describe the measure of our success in living up to those convictions. It was always linked to moral expectations and was oriented towards "work, building, expanding, achieving, and sacrifice on behalf of a larger good."[16] Character was a meaningful way of defining one's self in that it was always linked to duty, honor, integrity, and right action, and therefore it offered a point of view that was helpful in setting goals and making choices. Implied in "character development" was the idea of life as a progression whereby we were challenged to work towards specific goals.

Character eventually became seen as being too closely tied to ethics, and so, as a concept, it had to be replaced. The therapeutic offered us the concept of "personality" instead. The newer concept of personality was not based on convictions or moral expectations, but rather, according to "emancipation for the purposes of expression, fulfillment, and gratification."[17] Personality still contained connotations of characteristics that were stable, set, and fixed. Now, however, thanks to the progressive thinking in the therapeutic field, we are being helped to define ourselves according to "identity." Identity is something that we establish outside of external reference points and according to personal preference. Having lost all our traditional road maps and external reference points, our main mission in life has become that of creating and defining our own personal identity. Character, personality, identity—when we change the words we use, we also change the lens through which we see, form, and interpret reality.

"Conversion" and "salvation" are also words that once had meaning and existed at the heart of living religion. They signified the re-ordering of all our realities around God and were based on faith and trust. As the therapeutic language of integration, "inner reorganization," and "conflict resolution" filled our lexicon, the need to re-orient our lives around a Transcendent source was eliminated. Instead, integration was achieved through self-understanding and by ordering all our realities around the personal ego. It was ourselves we needed to focus on, not some external reference point.

We have taken the words that come naturally when man measures himself by the Transcendent—words like humility, meekness, gentleness, poverty—and have exchanged them for those "self" words that come natural when we take our measure by the measure of man: self-authenticated, self-assured, self-affirmed, self-aware, self-confident, self-conscious, self-interested. Whereas self-control was once a Christian virtue, now it is seen as a form of bondage to the super-ego and must be worked through in a way that brings release. We pretend not to notice when self-discipline becomes replaced by self-expression, when the need for self-transcendence is turned into the sacred need to express oneself, and we feign ignorance when the self thus formed is not Christ-like, but rather, an egotistical monster.

Many of the words from our Christian heritage still fill the air, but with greatly altered meanings. Words like "soul," "spirit," and "spirituality" may have become popularized, but they have been emptied of their Christian meanings in order to form the containers that have been filled with the liquid of Jungian thought.

The therapeutic prides itself on being morally neutral, so the language of right and wrong is being been replaced by the language of sickness and health. What is "good" or "right" has been replaced by what is "normal" or "healthy"; anyone attempting to make a value judgment is apt to be viewed as uptight, intolerant, or badly inhibited. The pursuit of righteousness has been replaced with the pursuit of happiness. Moral law has become reduced to just a value perspective, and old authoritative codes are being replaced by self-referencing language. The kingdom of God is only acceptable as long as it is a social order designed according to secular ideals rather than a place where God's authority reigns.

"Truth" is a word that has been greatly re-ordered. Whereas truth, in the past, was assumed to be an external reality that one ordered one's life around, now the individual subject is left to define truth and reality. The only truth we live by is expressed in the motto, "To thine own self be true." We have psychologized life, looking inwardly for truths that would have once been external to the self.

Jesus may have modeled the servant's heart, but now, being servant to our neighbor can be diagnosed as "compulsive helping," and loving our neighbor as ourselves has become "relationship addiction." Love is no longer selfless but is an instinct that arises out of the libido.

Whereas suffering is seen to be of great value in Christianity, it has no purpose in psychology. It is, therefore, the purpose of the therapeutic to reduce pain, but it does that without regards for the rights of others, or without regard for ethical considerations. We may give lip service to a gospel that offers us the language of dying, offering up one's life, being poured out for others, but the weight of our lives is increasingly being carried and formed within a linguistic framework created by the language of personal rights and self-fulfillment.

Journaling is an activity that is held in high regard both by saints and by those who have entered therapy. I am surprised, however, by the fact that so few seem to notice the difference between the two. Spiritual autobiography was essentially a story about God and how He was working out a unique story in one human life. It was God-focused. Modern journaling is self-focused and introspective; it is essentially another of our narcissistic activities. It is no longer an attempt to remember and record the trail of Transcendence as it weaves a pattern in a human life, but rather, it augments the self as an entity worthy of great examination and attention. Both use the language of journey, but then blur the distinction of destination, as though a journey towards God and a journey into oneself are both of equal import.

My journey into Christ and towards God soon became a journey into rediscovering the original reality and meaning of gospel words. The biblical assertion of, "Deep calling to deep" (Psalm 42:7), drawing us to where we could begin to leave behind some of the sediment of our lives, was not, I discovered, compatible with a life of scouring through the muddied waters of repression, projection, and the unconscious.

If Jesus now stood in our midst telling the story of the Pharisee and the tax collector (Luke 18:10, 13), would the tax collector's cry—"God, have mercy on me, a sinner"—be recognized as man's first glimpse of himself standing naked before the Holy, or would he be diagnosed as suffering from low self-esteem and referred to therapy? Achieving "insight" may be the goal of therapy, but when it managed to replace "repentance" as that experience of catching a true glimpse of ourselves before God, something of great depth was lost.

If self-knowledge, as Freud taught, can really bring our freedom, then there is no room for the call of faith, which can draw us beyond what we can initially understand. If self-knowledge can affect our transformation, then grace can be little more than a bar code that will have us eventually scanned into heaven—regardless of how self-obsessed and how stinking and rotten our nature has become.[18] Grace then confirms and validates our ego rather than being the power of God helping us to overcome it.

Sin can no longer be seen as it was once defined, as the choosing of our own way, if we've filled our churches with those who help us choose our own way. Sin cannot be, as Martin Luther defined it, as "humans turned in on themselves," if we've filled the church with those who help us turn in upon ourselves, so sin has to become morality, usually sexual morality. Our baptism can no longer signify a dying to self if the self is precisely what we have become pre-occupied with, so baptism becomes an initiation rite into the company of the elect.

Our gospel words will be emptied of all their meaning if we speak of "the peace that passeth understanding" on Sunday and then receive it in the form of Prozac or Zoloft in the week, or if our "joy unspeakable" comes in tablet form, created by a pharmaceutical company. Or if we hear of our glorious freedom in Christ from the pulpit and then spend our weekdays being told that we are products, beings determined by our past or by the collective unconscious.

Forgiveness was the gospel reality that I stumbled over. It seemed humanly impossible and unnatural. It was also, I saw, the only condition placed on our receiving of divine forgiveness. The therapeutic, I discovered, offered a much easier approach. As the psychologist Paul Vitz wrote in *Psychology as Religion,* the story of the prodigal son is currently being re-enacted over and over in our world as the wayward son returns from his life among the pigs and refuses to confront his parents with the words, "Father, you have sinned and are no more worthy to be called my father."[19]

Reading the lives of past saints made me aware of how different their view of the Trinity was from our culturally conditioned view. Once our universe became filled with our bloated selves, there was certainly no room to bow down before anything higher than the Almighty Self, so God had to become that which we find within ourselves—our Higher Self, or the power inherent within. If Jesus came to bring new life within, then why not just call the creative life within us the Christ and give it free reign? And the Holy Spirit—well, one cannot know that reality without knowing the fear of the Other, so why not just call whatever moves pleasantly within us the spirit and follow that?

As I went back through history looking for those who had known God, for those who had an experiential relationship with a Living God, I became aware that one thing they all had in common was a different gospel than I had been living with. At first I was confused, because all the words I had grown up with were there. Those words, however, seemed to add up to a different story than the one I had been raised with. I eventually came to understand that we have allowed our gospel words to be shaped by the power of our culture's understanding. We all hear the gospel through our own cultural lens and, as William A. Dyrness pointed out in *How Does America Hear the Gospel?*—in our case, the gospel is forced through the lens of individualism, self-sufficiency, and self-esteem. By the time the gospel makes it through the filter of the "imperialistic sense of self,"[20] there may be very little gospel left.

In studying the lives of the saints, a very different gospel was revealed to me. The past saints inhabited the gospel words they spoke, and in so doing, they used and revealed those words in a way that purified them and allowed me to see them as though for the first time. It made me aware of how quickly we can lose hold of eternal truths when the words that are to reveal them have been allowed to slip, shift, or be emptied of their meanings. I came to firmly believe that the Gospel can be destroyed most effectively not by any frontal attack—that has traditionally only sharpened and strengthened the gospel and faith—but by slowly shifting or emptying gospel words of their meanings.

The historian Adam Nicolson, in his book on the history of the writing of the King James Bible, noted that, "The flattening of language is a flattening of meaning. Language which is not taut with a sense of its own significance, which is apologetic in its desire to be acceptable to a modern consciousness, language in other words which submits to its audience, rather than instructing, informing, moving, challenging and even entertaining them, is no longer a language which can carry the freight the Bible requires. It has, in short, lost all authority."[21]

We need to enter the world of the Bible and tune our hearing to its cadences if we are going to know the life of which it speaks. Gospel words that have been allowed to shift their meanings out of a desire to please or to be relevant will be dead, lifeless words. Nicolson further noted that in linguistic history, "Languages lose aspects of themselves, whole wings of their existence withering, falling off, disappearing into the past."[22] He then asked the sobering question: "Does English no longer have a faculty of religious language?"[23]

Psychoanalyst Leslie H. Farber noted that, "The mode of speech appropriate to being human is not the mode appropriate to human objects. Having used only the single mode of scientific knowledge for the past hundred years or so, we are uneasily aware that this was the wrong mode—the wrong viewpoint, the wrong terminology, and the wrong kind of knowledge—ever to explain the human being."[24]

Scientific language—the language of biology, chemistry, physical processes, and the language of the therapeutic, which still claims to be a science—is insufficient to explain the human being with his misery, desires, dreams, despair, and anxiety. By allowing the language of science to infiltrate the church, and by allowing its vocabulary to articulate and form our humanity, religious language has increasingly become stale or set aside. When religious language becomes stale or irrelevant, we lose the only language structure that is sufficient to articulate the richness and fullness of what it means to be fully human.

It has never been enough to just preach the gospel; sheer gravity seems to constantly pull gospel words down into the morass of each culture's meanings. It is the challenge of each succeeding generation to reclaim those words, to rid them of cultural accretions, to free them from the entanglement of Gnostic blends, to bring them back to their original meanings, so that they become resonant with higher truth, so that they become windows into the reality of another Kingdom, so that they can mediate God's life-giving Presence to our everyday lives. Gospel words need to be constantly rescued or they degenerate into empty cliché and reverberate with the hollowness of the religious trite.

Both psychology and religion give us competing answers to the questions of our existence, the questions of: Who are we? What has gone wrong with us? What we should do about it? In offering us answers, they have to share much of the same vocabulary, or else offer us competing vocabularies. A tension is created, which causes traditional religious definitions and understandings to shift, crack, be undercut, and dissolved.

The words that were to be our markers pointing to another higher life are quickly disappearing to be replaced by a whole new therapeutic vocabulary. The words that remain in our vocabulary are being redefined. Even when we recognize the words from our Christian heritage, their meanings too often have been either altered or destroyed. The Word may have been sharper than any two-edged sword, but it is becoming blunted almost beyond usage by common, shared usage.

Perhaps A. J. Conyers, in his book *The Eclipse of Heaven,* was right when he ended his book with the terse comment, "Only heaven can prevent theology from becoming psychology."[25] It is the Transcendent that is being eliminated from the gospel in our attempt to integrate it with the therapeutic. Perhaps it is time to look at the two gospels we have tried to integrate and see if there has been an integration, or if there has been a complete subversion of one gospel.

Life:
A Secular or Sacred Endeavor?

FAITH IS ULTIMATELY about life and how we see and live it. Yes, it is about learning a circuitous approach to life—"Seek ye first the kingdom of God and all these things will be added unto you"—but it is about life nonetheless. That may seem a simple and obvious observation, but it is often the simplest truths that are the hardest to grasp.

If I had to name one significant moment that was decisive for my ultimate spiritual formation, it would be the moment I entered the "Religion" section in the main branch of the Vancouver Public Library and found books that treated life and faith as two facets of one and the same reality. Religion, for me, had been about correct belief, not experiential reality. In the library, I was confronted with the possibility of another approach to God.

I had always lived in a religious environment. My evangelical heritage had left knowledge of the Bible and Christian truths deeply ingrained in my being. I knew the correct theology about God, atonement, Christ, and everything else that would apparently secure my salvation, but when my life shattered, what I knew, at an existential level that was much deeper than all that theology, was God's absence and silence. The breaking of life revealed the large gap that existed between the biblical knowledge that I held in my head and the seeming absence of God that left a haunting loneliness at the center of my being. Eventually, all the theological structures I had erected in my head and thought I believed in came crashing down.

I found, however, that I was not capable of living without a framework into which to place my life. I needed some reason to get out of bed in the morning that was greater than chores and chitchat. Now suspicious of the church, I went to the city library and chose four sections— philosophy, the classics, psychology, and religion—and decided that somewhere in those stacks of books I would find a new framework for life.

If one is formed by the North American culture and finds oneself in emotional turmoil, psychology is the obvious first place one turns for answers. I found a lot of useful words, ideas, and insights in the psychology section that I could apply to my life. However, it was there in a large book on depression in women, written by a female psychiatrist, that I found the one word that re-routed me to that other aisle: *loneliness*. This psychiatrist named it as the most painful human emotion and said that we will go to any lengths to avoid it. Then she changed the subject and avoided it herself. However, in the naming of the pain that sat like a permanent ache in the center of my being, I realized that I had finally received a diagnosis. The shattering of life would not have been so bad if only there were not that debilitating loneliness, hunger, emptiness that filled the core of one's being, leaving one feeling quite desperate at times. I went to the computers (this was so long ago computers in the library were something new) and entered the word "loneliness." Two items came up—one was an essay by Cicero and the other was a book by a Catholic priest named Rollheiser called *The Loneliness Factor.* In the book on loneliness, Rollheiser told me, by means of a long and convincing argument, that I was looking for God and that loneliness is the means God uses to draw one to Him. The loneliness at the center of my being, according to Rollheiser, was a God-shaped, God-sized, and God-created hole that only a real God would be able to fill. The moment I read those words, I knew in my depths that I had always known it to be so. I had just been waiting for someone with the courage to say it.

The advantage of looking for God in a library as opposed to a church is that the search isn't narrowed by one denomination's theology and interpretations. After the Catholic priest, I discovered a charismatic writer who also spoke of God as an experiential reality that one could encounter in this life, a reality that could meet and then fill that well of loneliness. From that point on, my thirst for this God became unquenchable. Philosophy, I discovered, was a help-meet in the search; answers are of dubitable value unless they come with questions, and philosophy, at its best, does help us face and frame the questions. History became a new interest; it was a treasure trove of clues. My search for God became the new framework that gave meaning to life; it gave me sufficient reason to get out of bed each morning.

Where my search eventually brought me was to a completely new way of viewing life itself. I began to find writer after writer who taught me to see my life, itself, as the place of divine meeting. As Teilhard de Chardin wrote, "By means of all created things, without exception, the divine assails us, penetrates us, and molds us. We imagine it as distant and inaccessible, whereas in fact we live steeped in its burning layers." Evelyn Underhill wrote, "The God of nature and of our natural life makes that natural life the material of revelation,"[26] and Simone Weil also observed, "The essence of created things is to be intermediaries.... They are intermediaries leading to God. We have to experience them as such."[27] If all created things are intermediaries revealing God, then we must acknowledge, with Kathleen Norris, that, "It is in the realm of the daily and the mundane that we must find our way to God." Our daily lives are imbued with the Holy; in fact, as Karl Rahner noted, "The highest sacrament is meant to be the sacrament of our every day."[28] That is why Thomas Merton could say, "It is in the ordinary duties and labors of life that the Christian can and should develop his spiritual union with God," and Jean-Pierre De Caussade could observe, "You seek the secret of union with God. There is no other secret but to make use of the material God gives us." It is in life itself, these writers were saying, that God questions and challenges us, and it is in life itself that we begin to make out the outline of the God who became Immanuel, a God with us. Oswald Chambers wisely offered, "If I obey Jesus Christ in the seemingly random circumstances of life, they become pinholes through which I see the face of God."[29] All the writers agreed that our salvation is a process that comes through our response to life: "The conditions with which God has surrounded us are the only possible way of salvation for us; these conditions will change as soon as we have made full use of them, having transformed the bitterness of offences, illnesses, labors, into the gold of patience, absence of anger, meekness" (Alexander Elchaninov).[30] The anthropologist Mircea Eliade, noting how Christianity is unique among world religions in the meaning that it gives to history, wrote, "This, for the true Christian, creates an exceedingly difficult situation....

He has continually to choose, to try to distinguish, in the tangle of historical events, the event which, for him, may be charged with a saving significance."[31]

I needed to hear the same message spoken over and over again before, slowly but surely, its truth began to sink in. What I was finally forced to acknowledge was that if God seemed silent and absent then it was because I was looking for Him in the wrong places. As an evangelical, I was used to looking for God in the realm of ideas or theology; after reading and spending time with those within the charismatic movement, it was tempting to look for God in the supernatural. What I needed to do was to refocus my attention onto life itself. If I was sincere in my search for God, then what I needed to do was open up my life itself to make it the means of communication. As was translated in *The Message,* "Take your everyday, ordinary life—your sleeping, eating, going-to-work, and walking-around life—and place it before God as an offering" (Romans 12:1).

Life, I finally came to realize, was the medium of our meeting with God. Christ plays in our lives in all the people and all the details, and choice-by-choice we answer. The Living God was the God of all the processes of life, life itself being the means whereby we were questioned, tested, challenged, and revealed. Life was the means whereby we communicated to God our interest in relationship, and life was the means by which God responded. It was also in our life's choices that we reflected back to God who we think He is, what we think of Him, and how seriously we regard His relevance in our world. It is not, I came to see, what we say with our lips that is the real confession faith— it is what we say with our lives.

Perhaps a simple example can be used to illustrate how life itself can become a medium of communication. There was a time when my family went through a period of deep darkness. My family home was then in Surrey, one of the municipalities that border Vancouver. Once a week, I would drive out to Surrey, where I would be confronted with intractable problems that would send me emotionally spiraling down into some deep pit of darkness. No matter how well I prepared myself emotionally, the trip home would invariably be one of deepest gloom. It was on one of my return trips when, again mired in a depressive hangover, I came to the crest of a hill and was suddenly caught up in a moment of epiphany. It was triggered by the sight of a bridge—a bridge that stretched across the Fraser River, forming a base from which it produced web-like spires extending up into the heavens. And there it was that the glory was to be seen. The reach of the bridge penetrated endless sky, clouds, mountains, flowing rivers, and deep rolling valleys. As tears came to my eyes, the bridge became, for me, an instant symbol of hope. That which man had created—a bridge—had been allowed to penetrate the heavens, and rather than marring their beauty, the glory of the earth and heavens enveloped it and gathered it into their endless horizons. The moment brought a return of hope—hope that my seemingly futile efforts would eventually be accompanied and gathered up into a larger story that would ultimately be one of glory. Noah had his rainbow to remind him of God; I had my bridge.

From that time on, I would leave Surrey and drive expectantly, wait-ing for the moment at the crest of the hill when I would once more be confronted by that vision of hope. I suppose I had hoped the emotional intensity would return. It never did. But it didn't need to. I was created, I realized, with a mind that could hold that moment in its memory, and rather than bring back the emotion, it could add reflection and insights so that the moment deepened into a permanent symbol of God's promise and faithfulness.

The degree to which we have stripped the world of the numinous can be seen by the way in which modern minds might approach and interpret the incident of the bridge. Enlightenment thinkers, following Kantian logic, would have said that nature was not a place of communion but rather a place where, by an extension of the will, I could manipulate and master the entire situation. The bridge and family dynamics could all be forced into structures of understanding that reason could formulate and control. Once the entire situation was under the control of reason, there would be no room for intimations of glory. The logical positivists would have assured me that every time I approached that hill, the same combinations of bridge, sky, and mountains would have appeared; values and feelings, however, were of another realm with no connection to the bridge. I could have, therefore, gone to see a psychiatrist for help in understanding the powerful emotion that had overwhelmed me. He could have helped me delve into my past to find root causes or, if I found the emotion unsettling, he could have offered chemical relief to escape its recurrence. Sartre and the existentialists could have convinced me of my right to re-create myself, to exist as an unencumbered self. As a being with freedom from commitments and ties, I had no need to go to Surrey. The deconstructionists would have said I was in error looking for or wanting meaning. A bridge, a sky, some water, and mountains are never any more than just that. To desire some further meaning is to desire an illusion. Hegel and countless moderns who now use the language of spirit could have allowed me my emotions as part of a vaporous, universal spirit, but my sense of being confronted by the Holy meeting me in my particular moment of time with my personal history and personal problems would have been an anathema to them.

If we are to ever again see life as a sacred endeavor, then we will need to learn how and what to focus on. Einstein said, "It is the theory which decides what can be observed." It was Einstein's theories, which could not initially be proven, that taught the scientists what to look for so that his theories could eventually be validated. Paul Tillich defined *faith* as "the state of being ultimately concerned."[32] By remaining focused on ultimate realities, those realities then become the revealing lens through which we view our daily, mundane lives. We ultimately see according to the lens we use in our approach to the world.

In John 12:28, we are told that a voice spoke out of heaven. Some said an angel spoke, while others said it thundered. The same phenomenon was interpreted two ways—as either a natural or a supernatural phenomenon—according to the ability of the hearer to perceive the reality. At the coming of Pentecost (Acts 2), many were amazed at the ability of ordinary men to speak in all the languages of the world. Others, however, merely laughed and accused them of being drunk with wine. Those who cannot bear transcendence will always find a way to rationalize away the divine. Elizabeth Barrett Browning put the same idea in a poem:

> Earth's crammed with heaven,
> And every common bush afire with God;
> But only he who sees takes off his shoes;
> The rest sit around it and pluck blackberries.

The greatest significance of our practical ways of seeing may be in what we are thus prevented from seeing. We by nature tend to focus on the visible and concrete. That is why the therapeutic is so tempting. It helps us see life in terms of understandable categories and empirical data, offering knowledge that is helpful and insightful. That is not the problem. The problem is that it teaches us ways of seeing that destroy our ability to see God at work in the world.

We have fundamentally changed the way we orientate ourselves in the universe. At one time, God was seen as the reality in which we live, move, and have our being. When God gave Adam responsibility for the tending of creation, He strategically placed mankind between Himself and the created order. Our primary relationship was with God; the created order reflected that relationship. The Old Testament reveals the intricate relationship between mankind and creation—when man lives in harmony with God, then all of creation is blessed and radiates that harmony; when man strays, then the earth feels the brunt of that betrayal and drought, pestilence, and the ravaging of the earth follow.

Modern man has destroyed that divinely appointed order, placing nature between himself and God. Nature is now the reality in which we live, move, and have our being. God has been shoved out of His own creation, consigned to living in a deistic sphere away from the world that man has now claimed dominance of. God has been reduced to a God of the gaps; at those places where disease, death, and natural calamities occur, we call on God to fill those crevasses of need. However, as we become ever more adept at conquering all of nature, including now the reality of our own inner natures, the gaps through which we might get a glimpse of God become ever more narrow and sparse.

The writer/medical doctor Christine Sine reported a conversation she had with a missionary from West Africa who was shocked to discover that there in Ghana, the missionaries were not invited to the prayer meetings of the local people. Since the foreigners taught them how to make some income, how to plant crops, and gave out medical advice and pills, it was assumed that they did not believe in prayer except for specific religious purposes. The missionaries had been so focused on helping they were not even cognizant of how they were modeling an attitude of self-sufficiency rather than a reliance on any reality higher than their own effectiveness.[33]

It was not only the Enlightenment that shoved God out of His world; religion also played a role. Before the Reformation, the sacraments were at the heart of the community of faith experience. In the sharing of the sacraments, the Christian community was giving witness to the fact that it is through bread and wine—through the most basic and common elements of life—that God's life is mediated to us. With the Reformation, the focus of the service shifted, and the message, not the sacraments, became central. The comprehensibility of the Word, rather than participation in Mystery, was emphasized.

When the focal point of the religious service was allowed to shift from the sacraments to the message, then another great shift began to happen; evangelism was allowed to replace the Incarnation as the heart of the Christian gospel. Spreading the gospel began to supplant becoming the gospel. *Israel,* the name for the chosen people of God, means "one who struggles with God". After the Reformation, the struggle increasingly became an intellectual struggle rather than a life struggle. The emphasis on grace over works and the horror instilled with regard to any human effort that could be interpreted as works also added to the separation of religion from life.

The more faith became associated with assent to certain doctrines and beliefs, rather than a way of life lived in faithfulness and trust, the more religion became an ever-expanding clash of ideas. However, eventually it became evident that even the most orthodox beliefs cannot heal, comfort, or transform individuals. The therapeutic became a seeming godsend as it entered the church at the very time of growing disillusionment with religion.

By bringing the therapeutic into the church, we are claiming control of yet another area in which we once would have looked to God for help. The needs that once had us seeking the face of God, or at least acknowledging our estrangement from Him, are now being served (often with religious language attached) by those whose credentials are not their ability to walk close to God and discern His movements, but rather by those with training in systems of knowledge derived from secular schools of thought.

Few of us will ever seek God because of a sudden desire for piety. We seek God for exactly the same reasons we go to a therapist. We recognize that there is something wrong with us—we have unmet emotional needs, or life has fractured, leaving us in despair. My knowledge of God cannot be separated from a marriage that had reached its end, a rebellious teenager, deep depression, incurable illnesses that had no more medical hope, and broken relationships. Life provided the fracture lines through which the light of another reality could finally shine.

Simone Weil wrote, "The danger is not lest the soul should doubt whether there is any bread, but lest, by a lie, it should persuade itself that it is not hungry." It is imperative to resist the temptation to fix life's problems. Few of us will learn trust or dependence on God unless we are brought to the place where we have run out of other options. We need our problems much more than we need their resolution or some pragmatic solutions. For the sake of our souls, we need to feel our insufficiency much more than we need to be taught self-reliance. A church that is anxious to help us solve our problems rather than helping us to find and see God in our problems is going to be a church that lacks spiritual depth. A church that helps us see our problems through a therapeutic lens rather than with God as the reference point is going to be a church that slowly loses its Christian message.

Both Christianity and the therapeutic are about life. They both offer us frameworks through which to see and interpret life, they both offer us help in getting through life, and they both help us develop the mindset that helps us conceptualize our purpose in life. By trying to relegate religion to the world of spiritual realities, and by giving the therapeutic the right to direct and interpret our physical lives, we have created a dichotomy that removes God from the processes of life.

When we refuse to see life as a sacred mystery, life inevitably becomes a problem to be solved by professionals. Under the care of professionals we, ourselves, become reduced to chemistry and biology instead of being seen as spiritual beings. Each day, however, I have multitudinous opportunities to reveal whether I see myself as an eternal being or whether I live as a product of all the forces around me that have formed and are forming me still. Each day I awake to be faced with the choice of whether I will live with the grain of worldly life, or whether I will struggle to live against its grain. Each day, in other words, I choose whether I will live in ways that allow the soul to grow and increase its capacity to apprehend God or deaden its capacity so I can adjust better to life in the world

We, ourselves, were meant to be part of the mystery allowing God to be made visible in the world. When the men of the Old Testament asked God to reveal His name, God's reply was that he would be known as the God of Abraham, Isaac, and Jacob. By taking on the names and choosing to identify with Abraham, Isaac, and Jacob, God chose to reveal Himself through men who were too insignificant to warrant mention in any secular historical records. They were men who were revealed to be lying, deceitful, double-minded trouble-rousers, men whose faith wavered according to circumstances, and who were manipulative and greedy. They would alternately live lives of dependence and obedience to God, and then would wrest life back to be lived under their own control as they became impatient with the slow and uncertain ways of God. They were men with menial jobs, men who had trouble with their wives, and whose kids gave them trouble. But their God was something else. At the places where their mundane lives were made open to the reality of God, they themselves became bearers of a story about God.

The New Testament asks us to view our lives in the same way. When God became revealed in Jesus, He was again using human flesh as the means of revealing Himself. Jesus was known as the son of David, God placing himself in the lineage of man and again becoming fully identified with human life. At the center of the gospel is that recurrent theme: life itself is revealed as the medium whereby God makes Himself visible: "You show that you are a letter from Christ, the result of our ministry, written not with ink but with the Spirit of the living God, not on tablets of stone but on tablets of human hearts" (2 Corinthians 3:3). Catholic priest Marko Rupnik was basically saying the same thing when he wrote: "A person filled with the light and the fruits of the Holy Spirit becomes a living compass pointing towards God. That person becomes an image, a likeness of God. That person becomes a word of God that others can see and touch."[34]

Similarly, John Shea, in his book *Stories of God,* recounts the legend about the time that God, "angered by inaccurate reporting and editorial guesses about who he is and what he is about, hired the human person as a scribe and began to dictate his story.... Finally the last word having been spoken, the exhausted God sat down.... The scribe finished the last word and stood up with the outrage of someone who has been plagiarized, "But this is my story"."[35]

The legend is a retelling of the same profound truth—God remains invisible until He can be revealed through the medium of a particular human life.

I once read—and I can't corroborate it—that the Christian culture is the only culture that has a literary genre called "Spiritual Autobiography." Ever since Augustine discovered that his search for God ended up being a search whereby he discovered himself and wrote his *Confessions,* we have had a tradition of telling stories of God by telling our stories. A faith that has no stories of God to tell is a faith that never learned how to walk.

I remember with what a strain I used to try to get through certain passages of the Bible. The details with regard to the Temple were boring and endless, with their exhaustive details about cubits and linen and such. Then one day, as I was forcing myself to get through those passages because they were my reading for that day and I always read a book from cover to cover, my attention was jolted by the sudden interjection of a verse from the New Testament: "Don't you know that you yourselves are God's temple and that God's Spirit lives in you?" (1 Corinthians 3:16). If I were to see myself as a temple, I realized that in comparison to all that attention to detail, my life was a testimony to sloppy living. I was a master of wasted time, gloom masked the glory of life around me, relationships were an effort, and depression blinded me so that I could not see the giftedness of life. I didn't notice the details or the glory of life: I was just focused on getting through the day. I suddenly became aware that the Living God is a God for whom all details matter. Whether God ever chooses to inhabit the temple we prepare is up to Him; our responsibility is to pay attention to all the details.

In the Old Testament, the ark, the temple, the clothing, and all the particular instructions were given as a way of teaching the people the difference between the sacred and the profane. In the New Testament, the sacred entered the profane; it is for us to develop the eyes to see the sacred in all the details of life. Christ assails us through all the particulars of life, and then in life, itself, waits for us to notice and respond.

There is a reason why I think it is especially important at this time to rediscover the connection between faith and life. We live in a pluralistic world where a lot of blending of belief systems is taking place. Crucial to understanding Christianity's uniqueness is an awareness of the significance of the Incarnation and the sacramental life.

I have already told how my search for God began after my religious system had crumbled. I didn't know, therefore, what or whose God I was actually looking for. As I searched, becoming aware of how people in other denominations and other religions expressed the Transcendent, I felt increasingly disoriented and lost. Slowly, however, I began to see the threads that were universal and common to all that searched with their whole heart, mind and soul. I became convinced that the Bible was correct when it said that there is a light that shines on all men that come into the world. I became convinced that, as the Gospel of John put it, there is a Word, a unifying principle or force that has always penetrated and informed all reality. God has set the terms for all life on earth: "God did this so that men would seek him and perhaps reach out for him and find him, though he is not far from each one of us" (Acts 17:27). God reveals Himself to all: "For since the creation of the world God's invisible qualities—his eternal power and divine nature—have been clearly seen, being understood from what has been made, so that men are without excuse" (Romans 1:20). In my reading of the Bible, I noticed how the examples of evangelism were always in the form of "to what you have already received I can now add." There was always an assumption of previous knowledge of God. For a while, I lost my ability to believe in the necessity for the unique revelation of Jesus. For a former evangelical, that was a frightening place. However, where my search for truth and understanding eventually brought me was back to my Christian roots with the ability to see, for the first time, the uniqueness of Christianity. The clue to its uniqueness lies in life; Christianity's uniqueness lies in the Incarnation and in sacramental living.

The Incarnation showed us that human life is the vehicle God has chosen to make Himself visible. As Evelyn Underhill wrote, "The deep mysteries of the Being of God... cannot be seen by us, until they have passed through a human medium, a human life." The sacraments reveal that it is in the most common elements of life itself—bread and wine—that God has chosen to reveal Himself. It is the very stuff of everyday life that is the bearer, harbinger, and container of mystery.

Our life's story is the message, the medium, and the end of it all. The Judeo-Christian religion is unique in the importance it places on history as the place where God reveals and works out His purposes. Eastern religions teach meditation and offer practices that can bring one to places of heightened awareness, but of what? Life is seen as an illusion. Christianity, in contrast, teaches us that it is the stuff of life itself in which meaning is to be found.

In Christianity, we are taught that prayer is how and where we bring life before God, prayer being a place of struggle before it is a place of peace. Other religions, in contrast, offer techniques and exercises that bring one to a place of peace separate from life.

In Christianity, we do not break through or destroy consciousness or leave the world behind in order to get in touch with Pure Being. On the contrary, we use our conscious awareness in order to learn to see God acting in the world. Eastern religions, in contrast, offer ways whereby life and the conscious ego are transcended.

New Age and Eastern religions emphasize the unity of all life; human individuality is lost. Christianity, in contrast, emphasizes the supreme importance God places on every individual life. Other religions tell of reincarnation, of the recurrent return of life, or else of some final absorption where our identity is dissolved. Individual life obviously loses its importance when it is destined to be absorbed into the All or consigned to return in a new form. In Christianity, however, the end of life is pictured differently: "And the books were opened; and another book was opened, which is the book of the life of each man."[36] At the end of life, our story will be read—it is the permanent record that we carry into heaven.

If we stopped to analyze our heart's deepest longings, I think most of us would admit that the need to find meaning in this life is as important as the need to exist after death. We do not only need salvation in the afterlife, but also to be saved from futility and meaninglessness in this life. Christian salvation cannot be understood fully without recognizing that all we do—even the cup of cold water we give—will ultimately be acknowledged and rewarded. That is why Paul could advise people to be rich in good deeds, for thereby, "In this way they will lay up treasure for themselves as a firm foundation for the coming age" (1 Timothy 6:19). The details of our lives are saved to be brought into the next life (or else burned up if not worthy). My days are not draining away like sand in an hourglass; I can live my days in a way that allows them to become permanent, to be taken up to become the fabric of a new life. Life—all the mundane, particular details of life—are therefore not meaningless, but have eternal significance. In the words of N.T. Wright, "Acts of justice and mercy, the creation of beauty and the celebration of truth, deeds of love and the creation of communities of kindness and forgiveness—these all matter, and they matter forever."[37] It is the Christian religion that gives the greatest value to personal life, personal choice, and to all the details of life. Eugene Peterson encapsulates well the uniqueness of Christianity when he writes:

> Salvation does, of course, deal with the condition of the soul, but "soul," remember, is a totalizing term; there is no soul apart from history, with all of its economics and politics, science and geography, literature and arts, no soul apart from work and family, body and the neighborhood…without a firmly historical grasp of salvation, many end up living timidly, scurrying like scared rabbits into religious holes where they maintain their faith in reduced dimensions; others over-compensate by living obnoxiously, like barking dogs voicing spiritual contempt for and superiority over history.[38]

A salvation relegated to some nebulous realm of soul and spirit that bypasses life is not Christian salvation. That, precisely, is why it is so important that life not be allowed to come under the umbrella of secular humanism and its therapeutic systems. Life is a sacred, not a secular, endeavor.

The second way in which Christianity is unique is in the belief that at the heart of the universe is not a void, nor an impersonal unity, nor even a dominating Allah, but rather, a personal, loving Presence. A Christian is someone who knows God in His final, most complete revelation—as a Father. When Jesus said, "There is no way unto the Father but by me," He did not say there was no other way to God, but rather there was no other way to God as Father. Jesus used the term "Father" over 170 times in the New Testament. Fatherhood implies a personal, caring, communicating being who is defined in terms of relationship. That is the uniqueness of Christianity. As James Mulholland wrote, "For Jesus, God was the father we cry out for when we awake in the darkness, in the grip of a nightmare. God was the mother who dries our tears and kisses away our pain when we fall and skin our knee. God was a parent—intimate, loving and committed."[39]

The fatherhood of God was a concept that had been introduced in the Old Testament, but it had been a failure. In Jeremiah 3:19, we hear God's disappointed lament, "I thought you would call me "Father"." The Israelites did not want the intimacy with God that fatherhood implied; they wanted a deistic God who was a source of power but stayed at a great distance. In the New Testament the humility of God became evident. God came in a form that allowed us to torture Him, to spit on Him, and, ultimately, to kill Him, but no longer could we banish Him from the earth and consign Him to some deistic sphere outside of His own world.

When we are taught to see life in secular terms, our relationship to God automatically changes. God is no longer Father to us in our broken humanity, but He is again relegated to a distant sphere, while knowledge, not faith and relationship, determines the shape of our lives. The Bible says that eternal life is to know God. We are defined eternally by our relationship to God here on earthly soil. God known as Loving Father is a relationship that was mediated and made possible by the work of Jesus Christ. It is a relationship that is not there to the same degree in any other religion. I am not a Christian because of certain dogmas or correct theology—though without correct theology I will be tripped up in life. No one is going to be sitting at St. Peter's gate when I leave this world demanding that I pass a theological exam in order to enter the pearly gates. I am defined eternally by my relationship to God here in this world while still walking on earthly soil. Here, in this life, I found myself in some great freefall of my being. I cried out for help, and to my surprise, I discovered I was not alone. From that point on, it was God's Presence that made all the difference. That is how I survived; I discovered God as a Loving Father.

In our post-Freudian world, viewing God as personal and in terms of fatherhood is seen as infantile projection, a regressive device preventing us from gaining maturity and assuming control of our lives. Or so the therapeutic informs us. Religion, in our world, has again become acceptable as long as we view spirit as universal, impersonal, and of unity of substance.

The view of God as Father is an anathema to modern sensibilities. God as Father implies attitudes and realities that the therapeutic rejects and works against.

Just because we have a vague sense of God in our lives and hold ideas of Jesus in our heads does not mean we know God in His final revelation in Jesus, as loving Father to our broken, fallen humanity. Whenever we are ready to turn God into an abstraction, to remove Him from the processes of life itself, we will move outside the realm of orthodox Christianity.

Faith is a gentle flower. In order to keep its life, it needs to be ever-expanding its root systems into all the minute particulars of life itself. The soil of life is the soil of faith. In bringing the therapeutic into the church, the inextricable link between life and faith has been destroyed. Trying to separate faith from life, however, is like cutting a flower from its roots; that cut flower will either die, will wither, or, more likely, will ossify into life-less religion. Religion, if detached from life, becomes that ossified or pressed flower; it will be able to beguile and deceive by still having the form and contours of what once had life but it, itself, will have no more present life than the cold stone or the lifeless medium that surrounds it. Real faith needs the soil of our mundane existence to keep its life. In Christianity, religion and life became inextricably linked.

Reductionism versus Mystery

WE LIVE IN A WORLD that is ever-increasingly being reduced to psychological self-understanding. One historian noted that, "Today Americans turn to psychological cures as reflexively as they once turned to God."[40] Schools, churches, workplaces, hospitals, all offer therapeutic help in places where they perceive our need. The social-welfare systems and the justice systems have become increasingly dependent on psychology in order to understand and further their own processes. Disasters are met with therapeutic intervention. Talk shows have turned therapeutic wisdom into a form of entertainment. Self-help books fill bookstores. Normal conversations with friends tend to get peppered with therapeutic jargon and insights. Whereas religion once provided the overriding framework that enveloped our society, now religious assumptions are slowly being eroded to make way for therapeutic effectiveness. We have slowly been socialized into seeing life, our selves, and our society through the new, more modern lens of psychological understanding.

The change in vision has come about so slowly and seductively that I think we are often unaware of what a major shift in understanding has occurred and how much we have lost in the exchange. Aside from all the obvious purposes and benefits of religion, one of our great losses has been our ability to conceive of life as a mystery. Whereas faith had once given us a vision that allowed us to live expansively, now a reductionist mindset has set in. Reductionism, in philosophy, is the belief that it is the nature of complex things that they can always be explained by reference to simpler things. According to my Oxford Dictionary, *reductionism* is "the practice of analyzing and describing a complex phenomenon in terms of its simple or fundamental constituents, especially when this is said to provide a sufficient explanation." We were created with souls capable of growing into awareness of things unfathomable, eternal, and infinite, and then to be drawn into their life. We have preferred to focus on the empirical self, that self that is visible, concrete, and that can be slotted into predicable categories.

Our lives, however, are a question addressed to us from God, and when God is the reference point around which we orient our lives, then room is left for constant growth, never-ending journey, and endless challenge. Although we never arrive, we are, in the process, being continuously stretched. When we eliminated God as the center around which we oriented life, then meaningful, purposive life became a pursuit of happiness, or self-fulfillment, and consequently, a problem to be solved, for happiness and fulfillment can only be discovered as byproducts and will elude us when they are our desired ends in life. Once life became a problem rather than a question, the lens that once allowed us to see life as mystery became replaced by mindsets that taught us to see life in terms of systems, categories, and diagnoses, and just when we thought we could be reduced no further, we next became a protoplasm of biological and chemical definition that the pharmaceutical companies could come to the aid of psychiatry to help manage.

It would not be so alarming if there were any sign of it improving our society, but the opposite seems to be the case. As the aforementioned historian concluded: "The persistence of Americans' faith in psychological happiness is troubling. No matter what the age or particular circumstances, Americans seem reflexively to turn to psychological cures. And rather than offering real psychological insight, these cures are vapid therapies. There is little rigorous psychological thinking in our culture. Rather, we embrace fast, simple, and often mindless solutions."[41]

I spent my time in a therapist's office. I left when I began to feel like the door-mouse in the Mad Hatter's tea party. I felt as though someone were trying to stuff me into a container that was just not going to fit. It seemed to me precisely what didn't fit, what wasn't touched by psychology's knowledge and categories and techniques that was giving me trouble. But how was I going to articulate that "something more" when everywhere, even in the church, the assumption was that psychology had the answers?

Greek mythology has given us a story that gives form to our reductionist tendencies; it is the story of Theseus and his need to outwit a marauder name Procrustes. Procrustes was a skulking evil-doer who waited along the road for any travelers coming along that he might be able to ambush; any he managed to lay his hands on would be summarily tied to his iron bedstead. The travelers, of course, would not initially fit in his bed. Some needed to have heads and limbs chopped off. Others needed to be stretched. However, by the time Procrustes was finished with them, they all fit perfectly in his bed.[42]

I've often wondered if our fascination with the therapeutic is not just the refusal to carry the weight of our glory. Being created to be sons of the Living God, we only want to live by the measure of common man. We want to look like the Joneses, not like Jesus Christ. Refusing to accept the Biblical claims as to our real status, we have preferred, instead, the comfort and the commonality of that Procrustian bed. Perhaps our spiritual journey can only begin when we have tired of the many ways we are diminished and formulated and are ready for "something more."

Of course, religion does not always broaden our horizons. Often it is used for the opposite purpose—to create small enclaves of pseudo-certainty so that one can ignore how many and how large the questions of life really are. However, it is precisely because so many of us have fled religious roots that have been attempts to oversimplify, reduce, and create airtight systems that I find our fascination and faith in the therapeutic to be puzzling. In our growing dependence on the therapeutic, we have just exchanged one fundamentalist system for another. Our dependence on the therapeutic has not allowed us to embrace mystery in our lives, but has rather introduced us to systems that are even more reductionistic and dogmatic. We have exchanged religious fundamentalism for secular fundamentalism—the boxes may be different, but they provide us with the same approach to reality. It would seem that we are not only willing to allow, but also actually want ourselves, boxed, labeled, systematized, and reduced. We now accept theories and techniques and biological answers to the question of our existence that are even more reductionistic and destructive of mystery than the oppressive religious roots we left behind, and we have done it with a naivety that has made the religious fundamentalism we condemned seem like intellectual heaven. And all the while, the real mystery of God and of ourselves has eluded us.

Being boxed and placed six feet under is the final destination of the human animal, but many of us want to hurry the process and be boxed while still alive. Real life, however, is itself question, quest, struggle, and challenge, both bitter and sweet, part inspiration and part despair, at times a burden and then a joy, vacillating between being meaningful and then empty, both painfully and darkly uncertain and yet beguiling us with its mystery, alternately a problem and yet intriguing us with hope. We, since Eden, have been saddled with a curse, and yet our deepest longings strain towards redemption. The depths of life are as important to our final destination as are the highs, our failures are as important as our successes, and our handicaps as important to our final outcome as our gifts. From the viewpoint of faith, all those conditions are necessary for the cultivation of a soul that is strong and mature.

Living within a therapeutic framework can give one the sense, for a while, that life is understandable and controllable. Real life, however, in order to be lived to the fullest, exposes us to the full gamut of experience, and attaching labels to our reactions and thus internalizing the challenge only removes us from the field of life. To avoid the richness and yet the challenge of life, we turn to the therapeutic for aid in reducing life to a definable problem, a problem that we approach in terms of categories, systems, labels, and diagnoses—a problem that we approach in terms of utility, not meaning. And yet, as one psychiatrist who left her orthodox training wrote, "Human diagnosing is a contradiction in terms. To be human is to be boundless, multitudinous."[43]

Trying to live life by means of therapeutic categories and understanding is like asking Vincent Van Gogh to create a masterpiece by means of a paint-by-number set. It was precisely his novel use of paint to eliminate literal contours and lines and his use of unrepresentative color that allowed Van Gogh to create canvasses that came alive and shimmered with light. Our lives are like that canvas; they are a gift given by God that we return to Him after life painted over with our attempts at discovering the meaning, the richness, the purpose, and the giftedness of life. To turn them into a paint-by-number creation predetermined by therapeutic categories and labels is to deface the very gift of life.

The psychiatrist Robert Coles has written: "We hunger after certainty. We want 'orientations' and 'conceptual frameworks' and carefully spelled out 'methodological approaches'. We want things 'clarified'; we want a 'theoretical structure', so that life's inconsistencies and paradoxes will somehow yield to man's need for a scrupulous kind of 'order'. For some it is a matter of so-called 'objectivity': man's behavior at some 'level' can be made utterly straightforward, can be submitted to the linear workings of a particular psychological or sociological theory."[44]

Trying to fit man into a scientific framework, however, is bound to distort as much as it clarifies. The more we search for the secret of what it means to be human and how we become human in the annals of science, the farther we may be traveling from the answer.

What we so often fail to realize is that in our desire to have life clarified, ordered, and objectified, we are eliminating from life all capacity for mystery, awe, and wonder. We can, as a result, manage life, but in so doing we also become incapacitated for relationship, for meaning, and for worship. All wonder over the giftedness of life disappears as soon as we begin to see life in terms of pathology, categories, and symptoms.

By attempting to reduce life to the predictable and understandable, we destroy the very genius of man—our ability to escape determinism. Life was meant to be an exciting adventure. So why do we look for people who can convince us that we are products of our past, controlled by the collective unconscious, or determined by chemistry and biology? Psychology works from a base that derives its shape from common humanity. It takes the mystery out of human life and turns it into a problem; it subverts wisdom by glorifying subjective experience; it redirects our vision from the external and from the world in order to internalize all reality. It categorizes and generalizes in order to avoid the unique, the particular, and the unpredictable.

Otto Rank was one of the favored "sons" of Sigmund Freud. Gradually

Rank, however, found himself out of favor with Freud as his own views increasingly diverged from those of his former mentor. In *Psychology and the Soul*, Otto Rank wrote that, "Realistic psychology is the death knell of the soul, whose source, nature, and value lie precisely in the abstract, the unfathomable, and the esoteric." Like a butterfly pinned to a board, a living soul will slowly die when forced to live with fixity, definition, and with our reductionist tendencies. We were created to live expansively in mystery; before a living God, we are always stepping out before the new, the yet unexplored, the yet to be discovered. We cannot be reduced to a case study filed away by those who create general categories discovered by studying mass or average man. Life lived by faith will create as many stories as there are individuals who attempt to walk its path.

Robert Coles, the aforementioned psychiatrist, chose to teach literature rather than psychiatry to medical students, perhaps because, as he said, "We have systems here to explain everything—except how to live. And we have categories for every person on earth, but who can explain just one person?"[45]

Nietzsche once wrote that the human psychologist studied men either to gain advantage over them or else to allow himself to feel superior to them, "To have the right to look down on them, no longer to confuse himself with them."[46] Nietzsche was cynical, but he was also right in his observation of how psychology, with its grab bag of labels, diagnoses, categories, types, etc., does give us the feeling that we can stand apart from and distance ourselves from our neighbor. I bristle whenever I am in a conversation where we are discussing a puzzling individual and then someone comes out with some therapeutic label that they think explains the individual and all conversation stops. One can almost hear the collective sigh as a puzzling individual has thus been reduced and encapsulated by a therapeutic category. Naming gives us the feeling of being in control, in the know, when in fact it can limit our vision rather than expand it.

We all need to orient ourselves in the world; ascribing words to objects helps us get our bearings. There are words, however, that help us define our context, bring us into relationship, and point towards meaning;

there are also words that attempt to classify and organize all reality so that it can be managed and reduced to utilitarian function. Reality thus remains anonymous and objectified. Knowledge comes when we, like Adam, can attach labels to all reality around us. Wisdom comes from realizing what we destroy or diminish by attaching labels.

Alexis de Toqueville, in his observations about why the Americans showed such a propensity towards generalizations, observed that:

> The Deity does not view the human race collectively. With one glance He sees every human being separately and sees in each the resemblances that makes him like his fellows and the differences which isolate him from them. It follows that God has no need of general ideas, that is to say, He never feels the necessity of giving the same label to a considerable number of analogous objects in order to think about them more conveniently . . . . General ideas do not bear witness to the power of human intelligence but rather to its inadequacy, for there are no beings exactly alike in nature, no identical facts, no laws which can be applied indiscriminately in the same way to several objects at once.[47]

God, the incomprehensive One, chose to reveal Himself by means of taking on a particular form and a particular name, entering a particular time in history, and identifying Himself with a particular cultural identity. God revealed His greatness by means of uniqueness and particularity. There is significance and importance in the one-of-a-kind.

Psychology, in its study of man, does come up with a lot of useful truths. "Empirical Man" is a reality that lends itself to observation. Problems arise, however, when we regard its truths as prescriptive rather than descriptive. There is truth in a lot of psychology's observations. That is not enough reason, however, to try to crawl into its boxes or to see our neighbor in terms of its categories. Although psychology can tell us about the average, it is precisely the average that is our enemy. As E. Herman wrote, "No genuine spiritual height can ever be attained along the path of the average. It is in our steady and unremitting struggle with the average that our salvation lies: to conform to the average is to lose one's soul."[48]

In living before God, we learn to accept mystery and uncertainty rather than certainty and precise definition. After all, as the Russian priest Alexander Elchaninow noted: "Only dead bodies and outworn ideas have precise outlines; those that are alive, are encircled by a variable and ever changing aura, filled with radiance and the breath of life. All definition and fixation in our human plans restrict and frieze up this breath of life."[49]

In *The Secular Mind*, the psychiatrist Robert Coles observed that, "With God gone for so many intellectual pioneers of the last two centuries, the rest of us, as students and readers, as seekers mightily under their influence, have only ourselves left as 'objects' of attention."[50] When our attention was on God, we lived expansively. When our attention turned onto ourselves, the quest for clues to the subject matter meant an ever-increasing reduction of our humanity, as we became the matter under study. Coles points out how humanity at large has slowly allowed its attention to shift from theology to philosophy to psychotherapy to biology to chemistry. Now we look to neuroanatomy, neurochemistry, and neurophysiology for clues as to who we are. That progression in the therapeutic field has been a progression away from what it means to be uniquely and fully human. At every step of that journey, we have allowed ourselves to be reduced a little more. We have become matter to be analyzed and studied.

There was a time when we viewed ourselves differently. We were living souls. We believed that our bodies housed souls that permeated and defined who we are. It was therefore in our search for God, the God who had breathed His own breath into us, that we discovered the reality of ourselves. That journey was one of expansion, not reduction. It was not about definition or prescription, but rather about discovering the meaning and worth of life. What was revealed by that journey was that we are not just matter—we matter.

The Scriptures teach us that each one of us is a unique thought in the mind of God. Living, growing faith will draw us out of our Myers-Briggs and other categories to teach us how to live before ever-expanding horizons of awe and wonder. Those who allow themselves to be defined or fitted into a therapeutic system, category, or label are allowing themselves to be seen as less than they are in the eyes of God.

Who Are We? Two Answers

BOTH CHRISTIANITY and the therapeutic claim they can help us understand who we really are. Then they give us different answers. Christianity claims that we are made "in the image of God": it teaches us to view ourselves through the lens of the eternal. The therapeutic, in contrast, is about man using his rational faculties and turning them onto himself in order to create rational systems to explain all that he observes. As the sociologist Ernest Becker noted, "All that psychology has really accomplished is to make the inner life the subject matter of science, and in doing this it dissipated the idea of the soul."[51]

Scientific precision, however, has not solved the enigma of the human animal. We humans are the only animal that attempts self-analysis and who struggles through such long periods of introspection and self-reflection. We are the only species of animal that talks to itself, who is aware of inner division, who is aware of its mortality and fragile state, and who roars with laughter at jokes revealing its own absurdity. And yet for all that, we are also the only animal who seems to be confused as to who we actually are.

A good example of that confusion can be seen in the self-reflection carried on by Charles Lindbergh as he made his historic solo flight across the Atlantic. Exhausted after hours of flying, but at the same time reflective as to who it was doing the flying, he gives us his reflections as to the tripartite division he discovers within himself:

> For immeasurable periods, I seemed divorced from my body, as though I were an awareness spreading through space, over the earth and into the heavens, unhampered by time and substance, free from the gravitation that binds men to heavy human problems of the world. My body requires no attention. It's not hungry. It's neither warm nor cold. It's resigned to being left undisturbed. Why have I troubled to bring it here? I might better have left it back at Long Island or St. Louis, while this weightless element that has lived within it flashes through the skies

and views the planets. This essential consciousness needs no body for its travels. It needs no plane, no engine, no instruments, only the release from flesh, which the circumstances I've gone through make possible. Then what am I—the body substance which I can see with my eyes and feel with my hands? Or am I this realization, this greater understanding which dwells within it, yet expands through the universe outside; a part of all existence, powerless but without need for power; immersed in solitude, yet in contact with all creation? There are moments when the two appear inseparable, and others when they could be cut apart by the merest flash of light. While my hand is on the stick, my feet on the rudder, and my eyes on the compass, this consciousness, like a winged messenger, goes out to visit the waves below, testing the warmth of the water, the speed of wind, the thickness of intervening clouds. It goes north to the glacial coasts of Greenland, over the horizon to the edge of dawn, ahead to Ireland, England, and continent of Europe, away through space to the moon and stars, always returning, unwillingly, to the mortal duty of seeing that the limbs and muscles have attended their routine while it was gone.[52]

As fatigue begins to take over, Lindbergh goes on to speak of the terrible struggle he encounters within:

I'm beginning to understand vaguely a new factor which has come to my assistance. It seems I'm made of three personalities, three elements, each partly dependent and partly independent of the others. There's body, which knows definitely that what it wants most in the world is sleep. There's my mind, constantly making decisions that my body refuses to comply with, but which itself is weakening in resolution. And there's something else, which seems to become stronger instead of weaker with fatigue, and [sic]element of spirit, a directive force that has stepped out from the background and taken control over both mind and body. It seems to guard them as a wise father guards his children.[53]

Who was the essential Charles Lindbergh flying that aircraft across the Atlantic? Was it the body, the mind, or the essential spirit that seemed to be watching over both?

The soul or spirit of man can never be discovered; its reality is infused. It is like the blood flowing through our veins—we are unaware of its presence until something goes wrong. Our modern attempts to objectify the human being are like a doctor treating a sick patient without taking a blood test. Soulful longings, deep inner torment, existential anxiety, all imply an elusive "something more" in the heart of man, but the more we try to capture that "something more" by our rational powers, the more it will elude us. The enigma of our existence lies in the fact that we cannot discover who we are on our own or by means of human reason. Although our physical natures can be studied, analyzed, labeled, and categorized, for the discovery of the nature and reality of soul, we need revelation.

It is the need to know who we actually are and the question of why we exist that lies at the heart of living religion. Whereas it was to religion that we once turned looking for answers to the enigma of human identity it is now the therapeutic that has become our primary source for self-understanding, the therapeutic now offering competing secular answers to the same questions that religion once existed to answer. Freud described the analyst as a "secular pastoral worker."[54] The whole therapeutic field following in his footsteps has been attempting to impose secular, rational answers where religion once held sway. In so doing, they are destroying precisely what it is that makes us unique: the soul.

The Christian Scriptures reveal us to be divided creatures. The Bible refers to us in terms of flesh/spirit, old man/new man, and old creation/new creation. One side of our nature is visible, tangible, and definable; the other side needs revelation in order to be understood. We were fashioned out of the earth, but then God breathed His own life into us. He placed eternity in our hearts (Ecclesiastes 3:11), but then left us confused and unsettled as we tried to live as earthly beings. We were created to be immortal and yet are mortal; we are an inconsistent blend of both eternal longings and animal instincts. We were created to be amphibious beings, beings capable of living in two realities—temporal and eternal—simultaneously, and yet we so often prefer and even struggle to close the doors of perception so that we can adjust better to life in this world. In the words of Wayne E. Oates: "Faith is like adding a third dimension to one's perspective of his destiny when only two have been used thus far. This calls for a whole change of identity from a two-plane existence of time and space to a three-plane existence of time, space, and eternity. The eternal dimension provides both height and depth, deals with both life and death, both things present and things to come, powers and principalities."[55]

Any attempt to understand man without taking that third dimension into account will obliterate rather that illuminate what it means to be human.

The enigma of our selves is further complicated by the fact that the Bible claims we have to lose and leave our selves in order to save and find ourselves. It is not enough to assign our physical natures to the realm of science and then turn to religion for some spiritual knowledge, as to some nebulous realm of soul. We need to choose one locus around which to orient our entire being. As beings containing both the divine impulse and animal instincts and nature, we are left with the freedom to choose around which locus to orient our being. The paradoxical nature of our being becomes evident in that if we live according to our visible human nature, allowing free reign to our natural instincts and passions and ordering life according to our own human understanding, we become inhuman—less than human. However, if we deny our nature, lose our selves in order to live out of a Transcendent source, then it is precisely our human nature that is redeemed and perfected. We become fully human, fully alive.

All of created nature lives bound by laws except for man. We alone were created with the ability and freedom to choose which nature we will acknowledge and live out of. Thomas Traherne was a seventeenth century

Christian mystic who reveals God as saying to man: "All other things have a nature bounded within certain laws; thou only art loose from all, and according to thy own council in the hand of which I have put thee, may'st choose and prescribe what nature thou wilt to thyself . . . . We have made thee neither heavenly nor earthly, neither mortal nor immortal, that being the honored former and framer of thyself, thou mayest shape thyself into what nature thyself pleasest!"[56]

Traherne was elucidating the paradox that the Psalms place before us. They tell us, ""You are "gods"; you are all sons of the Most High'" (Psalm 82) but then they add, "You will die like mere men." They also say, "I am fearfully and wonderfully made" (Psalm 139:14), but then go on to add, "I am a worm and not a man" (Psalm 22). Inflation and deflation are built into our very being, the two poles we oscillate between as we struggle with the paradoxical reality of our nature.

We, according to Dietrich Bonhoeffer, were unitary beings before the fall: "Man has only been divided in himself since his division from the Creator."[57] At one time, God's warning to Adam that he would die if he ate of the forbidden tree seemed like an idle threat. After all, Adam was said to have lived over 900 years. I later realized that the death that became mankind's curse was a spiritual death. Adam's body lived on, but no longer could Adam live in relationship with and in a continuous awareness of the Presence of God. He was reduced, instead, to a two-plane existence where the world and an intractable nature, not God, were the primary realities with which he must negotiate. It was the cross—that second tree—which allowed the curse of the first tree to be overcome. The cursed banishment from God's Presence was superseded by reinstated relationship. Once again, we could be made spiritually alive; once again we could become awakened into awareness of that parallel Kingdom that provides the third dimension to life.

Being creatures of two natures, it is inevitable that we will find ourselves at war within. That contrary and often warring division is well articulated in a Jewish story about a master and how he taught his students to approach life. As he explained,

Every person must have two pockets. In one pocket should be a piece of paper saying, 'I am but dust and ashes'. When a person is feeling too proud, he should reach into the pocket and withdraw the paper to read it. In the other pocket should be a piece of paper saying, 'For my sake, the world was created'. When a person is feeling disheartened and lowly, he should reach into this pocket, withdraw the paper and read it. For each of us is the joining together of two worlds. Of clay we are fashioned, but our spirit is the breath of God. We must seek to balance in our lives what is ordinary and what is holy, what is creaturely and what is sacred.[58]

Gregory Nazianzen, a church father writing back in the fourth century, also gave words to our paradoxical state as he contemplated the strange nature of the human animal: "God set this 'hybrid' worshipper on earth to contemplate the visible world, and to be initiated into the invisible; to reign over earth's creatures, and to obey orders from on high. He created a being at once earthly and heavenly, insecure and immortal, visible and invisible, halfway between greatness and nothingness, flesh and spirit at the same time... an animal en route to another native land, and, most mysterious of all, made to resemble God by simple submission to the divine will."[59]

Unfortunately, faced with the enormity of what the Bible reveals about who we truly are, we have devised ways to avoid facing the implications of our revealed state. Both the therapeutic and, unfortunately, sometimes religion can be the means we use to avoid facing reality in order to live a "lie that covers over the painful ambiguities of man's worm-godlikeness— the despair of the human condition, the miraculousness of it tightly interwoven with the stink and decay of it. Religion as unrepression would reveal both truths about man, his wormlikeness as well as his godlikeness. Men deny both in order to live tranquilly in the world."[60]

Too often, we seek help that will aid us in our attempts to avoid the frightening implications of our revealed state, preferring instead to live in a reduced state in order to escape the mystery, the enigma, the ambiguity, and the paradox of our very being.

Since religion was first and foremost to be directed towards the revealing of the invisible, the immortal, and the spiritual side of our being, why did it become so enmeshed with the therapeutic and its rational ways, which reduce man to the visible, to flesh, and to the earthy? Madeleine L'Engle expressed well the awe and wonder we should feel when contemplating our assigned place in the universe: "As I read the Old and New Testament I am struck by the awareness therein of our lives being connected with cosmic powers, angels and archangels, heavenly principalities and powers, and the groaning of creation. It's too radical, too uncontrolled for many of us, so we build churches which are the safest possible places in which to escape God. We pin him down, far more painfully than he was nailed to the cross, so that he is rational and comprehensible and like us, and even more unreal."[61]

Religion was meant to reveal how we become reborn as spirit, how we can again become reconnected to the "heavenly principalities and powers." It was to offer us a vision, a narrative that would allow us to rise from our worm-like bellies and stand straight as eternal sons of God. When religion became wedded to psychology, it lost its vision; we were helped, instead, to adjust to being just flesh, biology, and chemistry.

Although psychology claims to be able to help us with self-understanding, what is the basis of that understanding? The psychologist Allen Bergin did a search through what were considered important psychology reference books and textbooks to see what they had to say about religion and belief. What he found was that, "An examination of 30 introductory psychological texts turned up no references to the possible reality of spiritual factors. Most did not have the words God or religion in their indexes."[62] Whereas surveys in America show that over 90% of the general population believes in God, when the American Psychiatric Association and the American Psychological Association were polled, they found that only 43% of its members believed in God.[63] In fact, one study showed that 40% of psychotherapists believed that, "Organized religion is always, or

usually, psychologically harmful."[64] In 1975, the president of the American
Psychological Association noted that, "Present day psychology and psychiatry in all their major forms are more hostile to the inhibitory messages of
traditional religions' moralizing than is scientifically justified… our fields
are apt to invoke tradition and religious heritage only to explain malfunc-
tions, be it neurotic individual guilt or collective social prejudice."[65]

Since much of the therapeutic is based on a hostility to traditional religion, it is strange that the church was so eager to welcome it into its midst.

It is the concept of soul that we will have to rediscover if we are going
to be able to accept our nature as revealed in the Scriptures. We will need
to again concede that there is something in us that will never be reduced
to biology, chemistry, or observable human nature. As Coventry Patmore
wrote, "Those who know God know that it is quite a mistake to suppose
that there are only five senses."[66] The soul has intuitive capabilities that can
readily be dismissed by the scientific mind, but for the saint who has
allowed the capacity of soul to be nurtured and to grow, the soul is the
birthplace and the home of the divine.

It was the Apostle Paul who gave us words to express the inner duality and conflict that we discover within ourselves. Paul realized that with
his encounter with the risen Christ, something from a future age and reality—something that he referred to as a "deposit" or as the "first fruits"—
had entered his own sense of reality and had drastically altered it. Paul's
cry— "Wretched man that I am! Who will rescue me from this body of
death?" (Romans 7:24)—is the cry of someone who has tasted the Spirit
of a new age, but realizes that he must express it through a body of death.
As James Dunn noted, "The warfare does not end when the Spirit comes;
on the contrary, that is when it really begins."[67] Inner struggle is one of the
surest signs of being "born again."

Not only did Paul live in awareness of the division within his nature,
he also became aware of living within two time zones— present and the
eschatological end. Paul could claim that we have been justified (Romans
5:1), but then in the next breath say that, "We eagerly await through the
Spirit the righteousness for which we hope" (Galatians 5:5). Paul speaks

of redemption received (Ephesians 1:7), but then also eagerly awaited (Romans 8:23). Paul can say, "Now is the day of salvation!" (2 Corinthians 6:2), but then speak of the process of being saved (1 Corinthians 1:18). Paul tells believers that they have, "Clothed yourselves with Christ" (Galatians 3:27), but then asks believers to, "Clothe yourselves with the Lord Jesus Christ" (Romans 13:14), as though it is something that they yet needed to accomplish. Paul claims we have been adopted as sons (Romans 8:15), but then claims that we groan inwardly awaiting our adoption as sons (Romans 8:23). Paul speaks of resurrection as both a past and a completed fact (Colossians 3:1), but also a future promise (Romans 6:5). Those contradictions can only be resolved by the recognition of man as a being living in divided realities—the reality of the future as well as that of the present—the reality of being born as Spirit while still living in a body of flesh. That tension, as Dunn noted, "Is set up precisely by the fact that the Spirit by his coming begins to reclaim man for God, to contest the sway of man's selfish passions, his self-sufficiency and self-indulgence, and, if man wills, to defeat them."[68]

In a sense, then, the Christian can be defined as one who recognizes himself to be a divided being, a person at war within himself. The temptation has always existed to eliminate the tension by means of a Gnostic solution, by positing a salvation that can bypass the flesh. For the Gnostic, his body was irrelevant to his spiritual self. It is thought that the Corinthians addressed in 1 Corinthians 12:3—the ones who could say, "Jesus be cursed" —were Gnostics.[69] They felt they could denigrate the humanity of Jesus because they had discerned His essential, spiritual core. No one, on the other hand, can say, "Jesus is Lord" unless they have, by the Spirit, truly been awakened into the reality of the spiritual realm and can therefore know that Jesus, the now invisible one, is Lord and has relevance to our raging lusts, our broken relationships, our possessions, dreams, and the rest of our tangible, everyday lives.

Paul actually found himself caught between two opposing worldviews. It was the "not-yet" of his eschatological belief that separated him from the Gnostics who believed that, since the body did not matter, they had already arrived. They, like much of modern-day religion, believed themselves saved irrespective of the state of their human natures. Paul, on the other hand, believed that the Spirit was given precisely to redeem the flesh; therefore, the "not-yet" part of his message. They were not yet saved. Jesus, too, had spoken of the Kingdom that had arrived, but was not here yet. Paul was acutely aware of that tension.

Unlike the Gnostics, in Judaism—where Paul's roots lay—messianic hopes lay entirely in the future. Paul found himself in conflict with them, too, because of the "already here" aspect to his message. Paul's emphasis on the Spirit already given as a sign of the effectively completed work of Christ bringing hope, salvation, and resurrection separated him from his former compatriots. Paul is such a reputable guide precisely because he makes visible the struggle that the Spirit would draw all of us into, the invitation to live by the Spirit while living in a body of flesh—to live fully into the reality of a Kingdom that has already developed a beachhead in our world, but has to be expressed in a world that has not yet welcomed it, but rather lives in hostility to it.

Who are we? The revealed answer is that we are a complex blend of the human/divine, mortal/immortal, and flesh/spirit. Those who study the empirical self are not usually wrong in their observations; they are just severely limited by their observations of the visible. As long as we continue to allow the therapeutic to tell us who we are according to human under-standing, help us define and understand ourselves according to biology, chemistry, and the physical side of our being, as long as we allow the "empirical self" to replace the soul and revelation as our primary means of self-definition, then the completed, full, revealed reality of ourselves as sons of the Most High will not be fulfilled in us.

Knowledge Systems versus Narrative

WHETHER WE ARE CONSCIOUS of it or not, we all place our lives into some narrative structure. Our lives are held together and given form by some story that we tell ourselves, a story we tell in order to give meaning and purpose to our daily actions. We used to have communal stories. Unfortunately, that is now changing. Mircea Eliade, the historian of religion, claims that before the Enlightenment, no people had ever tried to live without a large cosmic, supernatural story that provided the referential background that man could place his life into. Myths, archetypes, and mysteries had provided the setting into which man placed his life and that gave him answers to the reasons for his life in temporal time. We are now becoming impoverished by our lack of stories.

What surprised me in reading about archaic religions and myths was how many themes seemed to be universal. Even Israel's cultus and beliefs resonated with the other narratives. When our Bible refers to God as that in which we all live, move, and have our being, of a primordial, pre-existent Word running through all reality, of witness being made to God in all creation, of a God who is not far from each one of us, the history of religions bears that out. We all are connected to the same reality and we all struggle to give words and form to what we experience. The uniqueness of the Judeo-Christian religion does not lie in the fact that it tells a completely unique and different story, but that it claims to be historical.[70] The Judeo-Christian religion claims that at certain particular moments in time, God enters history in a revealing way that corrects, enlightens, or confirms that which man has already intuitively grasped. For example, the following is a story that was historically re-enacted throughout civilization. I've included it in the imaginative form rendered by Stephen R. Lawhead:

> A young man is sleeping in a hut by a lake. It is near dawn. As the sky brightens in the east, a group of armed men appear. They enter the hut, seize the young man and bind his wrists with leather cords. The men carry their prisoner to a waiting boat, and the boat is pushed out into the lake. They then row the boat to an island in

the center of the lake where other men are waiting. The prisoner is brought before these men and made to kneel before them. No one speaks. They watch and wait, their faces impassive. The sky grows gradually lighter. As the sun breaks above the horizon, the foremost man steps over the prisoner and withdraws his hand from beneath his cloak. He is holding a knife, and as the first rays of the new sun strike the youth huddled at his feet, the man raises the knife and swiftly plunges the blade into the young man's neck. The youth makes no attempt to escape; he does not struggle or resist. He slumps silently to the ground as his lifeblood gushes forth into a bowl that is quickly set aside. Satisfied, the murderers smile as the young man dies. And when he has breathed his last, they set upon the corpse with sharp knives, hacking strips of flesh from the body. The flesh is eaten and the bowl of blood passed hand to hand. Each man drinks, spilling a few drops upon the ground before raising the bowl to his lips. Lastly, the still-warm heart is carved from the victim's chest. This grisly treasure is presented to one of their number—another young man who has been standing by, witnessing this gruesome ritual. The youth receives the heart, slices a small piece, and eats it.[71]

In early civilization, every culture had a similar story that was told and then ritually acted out. The young man was the king who gave his life so that the tribe could survive another year, the shed blood was given to replenish the life of the gods so that they could bring another year's harvest, and it had to be re-enacted every year. Into a world where in all its reaches a similar story had been told, Christianity claims a Living God entered to correct what had been wrongly grasped by intuition; blood was shed not for the needs of a dying god, but by a dying god for the needs of a needy world. It did not need to be repeated endlessly, but was offered once for all, and the king didn't need to be sacrificed, but the one who was sacrificed became king.

A second example is in the story of Abraham and Isaac. Throughout the Old Testament we hear of a god named Molech. The neighbors of the

Israelites told stories of how this deity, a vengeful deity, needed to be appeased by the sacrifice of first-born sons. Now, the Israelites had a similar story in that the covenant between the Israelites and their God also required that first-born sons were to be devoted to God. That devotion, however, never required extinction. Throughout the Old Testament, God repeatedly expressed his anger at the Hebrews who sacrificed their children in the fires of Molech, a thing He said He never asked them to do, a thing He hadn't even thought of, and a practice He found especially repellent. Something in the cosmic story had become perverted.

The Hebrews, in contrast to the pagans, had been given a story about how at a certain point in historical time God, wanting to create a people who would reveal who He really was, called a man named Abraham, and when Abraham had passed the childbearing years, He gave him a son named Isaac. When Isaac had reached some maturity of years, God then asked of Abraham precisely what the competing god Molech asked of his followers: God asked Abraham to bring Isaac, build an altar, and sacrifice Isaac to Him. Abraham, in his obedience, gave to all mankind a story of how the children given to a Living God are not destroyed in the fires of some god's anger or need, but are rather returned to become the very vehicles of God's promise and blessing. No longer need man project his own inexorable fear and guilt out onto the visage of God; through Abraham and Isaac, God gave His people a story of how He, Himself, would provide the sacrificial lamb that would take away that fear and guilt.

It is also of interest comparing the Biblical account of the creation of the female with the myths of the pagan cultures. One story claimed that Athena, the favorite daughter of Zeus, sprang fully formed from the head of Zeus. Woman as an idealized and romanticized image projected from the head of man is a universal phenomenon. Another story told was that woman was created by Jupiter and sent to Prometheus as punishment for stealing the fire of the gods. That first woman was Pandora who, in her box, brought to earth all of its ills. Woman as the source of all earthly evil is another universal prejudice. Other pagan stories emphasized woman as a sexual object; the pagan gods were a fornicating lot that always seemed to be betraying, chasing, and harassing the female and then producing human offspring. Compared to the pagan stories, the Hebrew myth is truly profound. Eve came out of Adam's side—male and female were meant to stand side by side as helpmates. Eve was not created out of functional necessity, but because Adam was lonely; the relationship was foremost. Eve was created out of Adam's rib—Adam had to give up something of himself in order to be in relationship. With that as a foundational story, could the role of women in the church have become such a divisive issue if the Bible was read as a story rather than a source of proof texts?

In another chapter (Chapter 4:G) I also tell the pagan story given as an explanation for our essential loneliness. Rarely has the particular message of the gospel been impressed upon me more than when I have seen it highlighted against the backdrop of the stories that other peoples were telling. Much has been made in the last century of our need for de-mythologizing the Scriptures. What we really need is to re-mythologize them. The Bible is a story, not a textbook of propositional and doctrinal truths.

The universality of religious themes is explained in Christianity by the imminence and transcendence of God. God's Holy Spirit moves through all of creation, seeking to draw all life back to its source. That is what Aldous Huxley called the Perennial Philosophy—the idea that the "divine Ground of all existence is a spiritual Absolute, ineffable in terms of discursive thought, but (in certain circumstances) susceptible of being directly experienced and realized by the human being."[72] Without revelation or Word, however, our intuitive instincts are inadequate. It is in the acknowledgement and recognition of revelation and of Transcendence that we are given form for what we have already been intuitively prepared for.

Until the Enlightenment, religion had always given form and story to what we had intuitively grasped and had already sensed the Spirit to be doing. We were acknowledged to have souls that could apprehend more than our minds could ever grasp, and narrative was the way we could articulate what could not be reduced to definitions and simple understanding. With the Enlightenment, that changed. Religion was turned into another cognitive system, another thing we could figure out with our minds.

It is now known that our cognition functions along two tracks: propositional and narrative. The first operates according to universals that can be de-contextualized. The narrative mode, on the other hand, is impossible without imagination and empathy and it requires a grounding in concrete, tangible life. The two approaches are exemplified by comparing the differing ways the Greeks and the Jews spoke about God. The Greeks spoke about the essence of God; they would have used phrases like the "ground of all being" or as the "unmoved mover." The Jews, in contrast, knew that God was beyond definition; they instead talked about what God did. They knew that it was in telling stories about God that He was revealed. The Christian religion only operates effectively when it is seen as narrative. With the Enlightenment, however, we again attempted to approach religion as propositional truth. The evidence of its failure now surrounds us.

The same systems of knowledge that propel big business now inform the church on how to run successful programs. The same therapeutic systems that help people find inner healing without God are now functioning effectively in the church. Forms of worship have more to do with current entertainment tastes than being in tune with the Spirit or with the long histories of man worshipping God. One writer referred to that triad—business acumen, therapeutic understanding, and the entertainment industry—which has now infected the church as the new Unholy Trinity. The necessity of placing our lives into a narrative structure that's too ambiguous and outdated to fit our natures with ease or without struggle has been simplified by having it reduced to propositional, theological systems that fit nicely into three-point sermons.

However, when the gospel is turned into a theology rather than a narrative, it loses its ability to speak to our human condition. Much of our problem with the Bible arises out of the fact that we try to read the Bible as a legal document rather than as a story. The Bible, however, is essentially a love story between God and man. It starts out with the story of how God created a world that He declared to be good and then placed man at the apex of creation—man as a being with whom He could be in relationship. The rest of the Bible is a story of man's refusal to be in relationship, of his many attempts to distance himself from God, and of God's contin-uing attempts to reach out to him. We will always run into trouble when we try to turn what is essentially a love story into a legal or a philosophi-cal or a moral document.

Current liberal thinking would have us believe that much of the Bible can now be relegated to the time and ways of mythic thinking. Modern man, so they claim, has become rational, rendering as obsolete the story-telling ways of the Bible. It is precisely in looking at our rational world, with its fascination with the occult, horoscopes, and New Age religion, its susceptibility to image versus content, its gullibility before advertising, and its vulnerability to propaganda, that convinces me that modern man is no more rational than ancient man. No, we humans will always be a combination of the rational and the irrational, creatures linked by both story and fact, living between revelation, inspiration, and logic. It is story that leaves room for new intuitive insights, new applications, and constant imaginative expansion. It is story that keeps truth from being reduced to theological systems and moralistic reduction.

The Bible is fairly unique among sacred books in its emphasis on nar-rative. The very framework of the Bible is a narrative structure. The Bible's individual books reveal the ongoing story of God's revelation in history. The Biblical story has a beginning, an end, and in between, we have the gradual unfolding of the story of God's purposes and the meaning of his-tory. Many of the individual books of the Bible are also stories, stories that further elucidate the great story. God's most complete revelation of Himself in Jesus is based as much on the story of His life as in any individual words He spoke. Even the words Jesus spoke were often in the form of story. Contrast that to the Buddhist sutras, which have little narrative, or to the Koran, which consists of gathered revelations that do not rely on narrative for their sequence, and one has to acknowledge that it is not only what the Bible says that is unique, but also the manner in which it says it.[73] Any attempt to reduce Christianity to doctrine and theology will miss some-thing vital; in order to know what it is all about, we will first have to learn how to get ourselves into the story. The more we discover and know its reality, the more we will realize that what we know can be stated by means of story, but not reduced to facts.

What the Bible seems to understand is that we are hardwired for narrative. When we try to reduce it to fit into a theological structure, or else attempt to distill its secrets by means of proof texts, we simultaneously destroy the very mode by which it works. The narrative form is an intrinsic part of its reality. As one writer expressed it, "Without a grasp of the plot that holds everything together, the Bible is as vacuous as a mosaic in which the tiles have been arbitrarily rearranged without reference to the original design or as a poem constructed by stringing together random verses from the Iliad and Odyssey and imagining it was Homer."[74] So it is the entire Bible, with its narrative structure, that resonates within us, because we, too, are only able to see life as a meaningful venture to the degree that we see ourselves placed within a larger story. We see, understand, and define ourselves according to the narrative we have running inside our heads. Barbara Hardy has noted, "We dream in narrative, daydream in narrative, remember, anticipate, hope, despair, believe, doubt, plan, revise, criticize, construct, gossip, learn, hate and love by narrative".[75] It is, therefore, novels, and not case studies, that can most fully reveal who we are. As the philosopher Alisdair MacIntyre observed, "Man is in his actions and practice, as well as in his fictions, essentially a story-telling animal. He is not essentially, but becomes through his history, a teller of stories that aspire to truth."[76] It is by means of telling ourselves stories that we can believe in ultimate order, plan, meaning, and purpose even though we live in disordered worlds.

We moderns are adept at amassing amazing amounts of facts, details, and trivia. At the same time, we are destroying the structures that can place all that knowledge into a coherent, meaningful whole. What I ultimately found that changed my life was a narrative that was ultimately mystery, not reductionist system, where I was a participant and co-creator but not in control, where I could learn dependence at the expense of self-sufficiency, where I gave up autonomy in order to be in relationship. In looking for some framework in which to ground my life, I eventually found myself back in the very religious framework I thought I had left behind, but now with a difference; it was no longer a religious system or a theology I believed in, but it had become, rather, a story I found myself placed inside. Unless the imagination is kindled, we don't act or connect our lives to what we claim we believe. We need a powerful story to motivate us, to draw us into its life.

The historian of religions, Mircea Eliade, identified faith as the one way in which the Judeo-Christian religion was unique. Mircea Eliade claimed, "The discovery of faith as a religious category was the one novelty introduced into the history of religion since Neolithic times."[77] Faith meant the interiorizing of the stories. Each person was to be an epiphany, a story of God. Faith is the discovery that a story told thousands of years ago about wilderness, rebellion, darkness, and resurrection is actually our story, and slowly we discover all the reference points for our lives in its many-layered richness.

We, unfortunately, are usually content to leave the Gospel relegated to the realm of theology and propositional truth until some tragedy or adversity allows us a new vantage point in which to view the Bible. That is why the book of Job is a book of such comfort for those who know suffering. It shows the ineffectiveness of theological argument in the face of real tragedy. Nowhere in the book of Job does God answer the questions of Job or the great questions of life. What the book says, in effect, is, "Forget the logical arguments spun out by those who sit together at their ease and discuss the ways of God...Let me tell you a story."[78] There comes a time in perhaps all lives when all the theology, concepts, and ideas we have held about God seemingly turn to dust and we feel like choking in their stifling air. The only things that can possibly keep faith alive at that point are real-life stories of God.

If I look back on my churchgoing days, it seems an inordinate amount of pulpit and study time was devoted to the epistles and the letters of Paul. In retrospect, I think it appealed to our intellectualism. The writings of Paul could keep one arguing and discussing forever, allowing one to feel one was really engaging with the gospel. I eventually found that the best way to be purged of our over-intellectualizing tendencies was to read the Old Testament. The Old Testament is a great antidote for religion that has gotten too otherworldly, too cerebral, or too idealistic. It has immediate shock value. Dietrich Bonhoeffer, from his prison cell, asked, "Why is it that in the Old Testament men tell lies vigorously and often to the glory of God (I've now collected the passages), kill, deceive, rob, divorce, and even fornicate (see the genealogy of Jesus), doubt, blaspheme, and curse, whereas in the New Testament there is nothing of all this?"[79] Alone in his prison cell, it was the Old Testament that was increasingly capturing the mind and imagination of Bonhoeffer. As he came to say, "In my opinion it is not Christian to want to take our thoughts and feelings too quickly and too directly from the New Testament."[80]

It is in the Old Testament that we get the large story which has Jesus as its climax. In reading the story of God's attempts to create a people who would reveal Himself, we become aware of the problem to which Jesus provided the answer. It is in the Old Testament, if we have the courage to keep reading, where we discover that it is a story told about ourselves. It is then, and not much sooner, that we are ready for the New Testament. Otherwise, we become confident of finding answers when we haven't yet even asked the proper questions. The New Testament may offer us effective teaching and answers; the Old Testament, however, offers us the story behind it.

The fallacy in the thinking within the therapeutic movement lies in their belief that knowledge can change us. It doesn't. We need to catch a vision of something so large and so gripping that it compels us to devote our lives to it. When religious narrative was allowed to provide our inner resources, then love, faith, and purposive existence kept our personalities from getting sucked up into the black hole of our inner vacuity. The way we have been turned into ourselves, analyzing, defining, and labeling, one would think we were afraid of becoming an amorphous vapor that didn't exist without definition. What narrative does is turn us outside ourselves. Our lives are given meaning by connecting with a story that has already been going on before our earthly entrance and continues on after we make our exit. We are never more alive than when we feel our lives to be part of a larger story.

Through narrative, we learn to see with other eyes, enter the world from another viewpoint, empathize with the lives of others, and imaginatively expand our horizons. Narrative rescues us from thinking that is egocentric, self-absorbed, and petty.

The therapeutic would help us see ourselves in terms of systems and categories. Narrative, in contrast, deals with particulars. It is through particulars, and not categories, that we are given a glimpse into the universal. That is why reading a good storybook, which may seem like a solitary activity, can be our link with and preparation for life in the greater community. It helps us to see the universal through the particular.

When I first started reading the Bible, passionately looking for a God I could believe in, I thought I was looking for facts. I was also reading a lot of other books by people who seemed to know God intimately. After a while, something strange started to happen. It was as though I could see three streams—the Bible, the writings of the saints, and my life—all merge to become one stream. Time would seem to stop as I meditated on the intricacy and the wonder of it all. I would always catch myself, castigate myself for lack of discipline—after all, there was still so much to read— and promise myself that I would stop such foolishness. But the more I read, the more those moments happened. Much later, I would come upon books on meditation and contemplation and realize that the purpose and end of all Biblical reading was precisely to find oneself at those moments, moments in which one knows one's life to be placed in and defined and revealed by that Biblical story. I, however, was an Enlightenment product; I was reading to gather information. The early church, I later discovered, actually had a name—*lectio divina*—for the kind of reading I had discovered. This was reading turned into a divine conversation, reading that allowed one to enter a reality that was timeless and that could sweep one up into its eternal currents.

True religion is about the deep down, truest things. At that level, the mind cannot explain or sum up exactly what is happening; for understanding, we need narrative to provide a glimpse into the mystery. With the Enlightenment, we stopped defining ourselves by means of story. We ignored the soul and its intuitive, imaginative, emotional capabilities. We failed to realize that the soul may not be cognitive, but it has the capacity to apprehend greater truths than can be captured and reduced by the mind. Stories, music, nature, and art can touch us in ways that our minds cannot put words to. Knowledge is not sufficient to explain our lives or determine their meaning. Science, for example, may explain exactly and in great detail the biological reasons for why my father died, but it can offer no reason or solace for my grief. Biology may explain the sex drive, but not be able to explain my love for one human being. Psychology can attach a label to my unhappiness and prescribe a drug to deaden the pain, but it cannot give me a sufficient or meaningful reason for continuing on with my existence. Therapeutic systems may be able to categorize and provide labels for every individual, but they will never be able to predict or cause the formation of a single saint.

Psychology leaves us with the impression that we humans were incapable of understanding ourselves before it came on the scene. As Aldous Huxley aptly observed, "One of the most extraordinary, because most gratuitous, pieces of twentieth-century vanity is the assumption that nobody knew anything about psychology before the days of Freud. But the real truth is that most modern psychologists understand human beings less well than did the ablest of their predecessors."[81]

Psychology did not give us more self-understanding or self-awareness; it just changed the way we defined and came to an understanding of ourselves. In the past, we saw ourselves reflected through myths and stories; we defined ourselves according to the narrative structure we placed our lives into and according to the role we saw ourselves playing. Even Freud needed to return to the world of myth and the story of Oedipus to give us his Oedipal Complex.

We err when we think the therapeutic can turn life into a fixity that can be captured by labels, systems, paradigms, or constructs. One psychoanalyst wryly noted, "It is a matter of some irony, if one turns from psychology to one of Dostoyevsky's novels, to find that, no matter how wretched, how puerile, or how dilapidated his characters may be, they all possess more humanity than the ideal man who lives in the pages of psychiatry."[82]

Life is not a fixity, but more like an intricate spider's web vibrating and shimmering in the dew, wind, and sun of the universe while held ever so precariously and ever so lightly to the corners or the branches that keep it grounded.[83] It is more like an ocean voyage, all shifting and movement, which tries to keep its bearings by some distant shoreline, its only fixity lying outside of itself. It is narrative that best provides the attachments or reference points that still allow for that movement and freedom. Story allows for those moments of inspiration when we suddenly realize we've caught sight of a truth about ourselves or the universe that we can use as one of the reference points around which to orient our life. We give credence to the role of inspiration when we say things like, "It suddenly came to me," "It struck me," "For the first time I saw," or, "I was hit by sudden inspiration." We need to catch sight of something outside of ourselves that remains elusive in order to discover how to live. We don't need more knowledge, but more inspiration.

The last meta-narrative we told ourselves and trusted in was the one the Enlightenment taught us— the story of continual progress. It was a story that was proven to be false by ensuing history, and in disillusionment, we have since refused to believe anything larger than the personal stories that we, ourselves, create. The large meta-narratives that once united us into communities of common purpose have now been deconstructed, and in their shattering, we have been left as isolated individuals, all trying to script isolated, personal stories.

Perhaps the most devastating result of losing a large narrative into which to place our lives is the fragmentation of our being. We now think atomistically. By turning into ourselves, and by self-examination, we become a sum of many parts; we become our roles, our interests, our pathology, and our habits. Without a large narrative into which to place our lives, we lose our ability to see ourselves as a unity. Only a large, mythic story and the concept of soul can again restore that unity to our being.

The sociologist Robert Bellah, in his book *Habits of the Heart,* looked at the question of why the American Dream seems to be approaching a state of crisis. He observed, "We certainly did find that the language of individualism, the primary American language of self-understanding, limits the ways in which people think."[84] As Walter Brueggemann noted, "Reduced speech leads to reduced lives."[85] At one time, the primary story or language of the American people had been that of God and country. The language of individualism had been secondary. Now it has been reversed. God and country are certainly referred to repeatedly, but as secondary languages subservient to the supremacy of the self and rampant individualism.

Taking the Christian story with its spiritualized account of history, its eternal horizons, its cosmic explanation for the purpose of man, and trying to run it as a subplot to a primary language or paradigm formed by man's theories of self, is like taking an advanced computer program and trying to run it through a computer with insufficient memory. Those eternal horizons are not going to compute. Our realities will have become limited, instead, to the narrow parameters of our ever-diminishing selves.

The Unconscious versus Transcendence

BOTH CHRISTIANITY AND PSYCHOLOGY invite us to break through the crust of surface consciousness to become aware of that which is not yet either cognitive or visible. Both Christianity and the analytic tradition claim that to know ourselves, we need to understand depths and forces that lie below or beyond our surface consciousness. The analytic tradition claims that much of our behavior is determined by the unconscious; that which remains unknown and unrecognized by the individual can be precisely what is active in determining one's actions and responses. It is, therefore, into the personal history of the individual that the analytic tradition would turn one in an attempt to make conscious all that yet remains hidden. In contrast, Christianity locates the individual within a large cosmic story wherein good and evil battle, but of which the individual remains largely unconscious. Unconsciousness is therefore a problem, for the individual who remains unaware of those larger forces is going to become an unwitting vehicle for the transmission of evil in the world. Greater consciousness, therefore, is a goal for both those in Christianity and the therapeutic movement. They disagree, however, over what it is we are to become conscious of.

The idea of the unconscious is a way for scientific, rational man to admit that there is more to our existence than what our reason and senses can understand without having to use the outmoded language of God, devil, or good and evil. We can admit to powers and forces beyond our rational control without having to acknowledge traditional understandings. The therapeutic offers us countless systems to explain all of visible human life. Their theory of the unconscious allows them to also claim authority over the invisible realm.

It came as a surprise to me to read history and realize that it was not Freud who "discovered" the life of the unconscious. It was actually a philosopher named Friedrich Schelling who, in philosophy, first used the term the "unconscious." Freud happened upon the writings of Schelling in a circuitous way, and then claimed and applied the concept of the unconscious to medical psychology. It was originally in the writings of Schelling that the traditional battle between good and evil got turned into a developmental struggle whereby unconscious matter slowly became conscious until it could reach its fulfillment in man who became self-conscious. All nature, according to Schelling, was of one unified substance moving towards man's realization as a self-conscious being. Schelling and his theory became very popular in his time. Then Schelling's wife died. His idealistic beliefs in unity, in all-spirit, were shattered when he needed to make sense of diversity and evil. Schelling did an about-face and returned to orthodox Christian roots. No longer did he believe in a unitary psychic force out of which we humans derive our consciousness, but rather in the powers of being that religion gives words to and that we humans encounter; it was the struggle between the nature of good and evil that the individual was immersed in and not just a developmental struggle. Schelling no longer thought in terms of Ultimate Reality being a psychological projection or wishful thinking, but acknowledged that we have roots that go down into Ultimate Reality itself, a reality that is other than and greater than our personal being.[86] He acknowledged that there are powers of being that are separate from, and yet act on, the human psyche, and on one's soul, which influence both one's conscious thinking and the unconscious mind, but yet they do not derive from it.[87] The powers of being, he acknowledged, had a reality in themselves separate from man.

In spite of Schelling recanting all of his early work, it was picked up and made full use of by others. It was Freud, especially, who took the idea of the unconscious and brought it to where it could become a part of modern thinking. We all, according to Freud, have mental processes that are made up of thoughts, feelings, and ideas that are largely left in the realm of the subconscious. It was what remained unconscious that largely influenced our actions and that could then become responsible for mental illness and problems in behavior and relationships. It was by becoming conscious of all that lay in those subconscious depths that human beings could again regain control of their lives and actions.

Freud was a rationalist and materialist. His discovery of the uncon-scious, however, was taken up by many of a very different ilk. Carl A. Raschke claims that it was World War I and its destruction of the old world order and old certainties that had many searching for new faiths and new gods. They found what they were looking for in the discovery of the unconscious. Suddenly, dreams, intuition, fantasy, and imagination had validity—they were products of the world within. In a world where rea-son and established order had collapsed, people could retreat into the comfort of knowing, as Raschke wrote,

> "Within" was more genuine than the "without." The visible world may have perished in flames, but the world which manifested itself in the unmediated flow of intimation and fantasy had a greater weight and significance. Unconscious reverie harbored more insights as to the nature of things than conscious delibera-tion and logical analysis…. Whereas the time scheme of ordinary experience seemed broken and meaningless in the disarray of betrayed hopes and promises, the buried freshet of personal imag-ination might possibly contain hints as to the actual meaning of life. Deep behind the mask of the average person's consciousness might be concealed a timeless absolute. Self-knowledge might be the portal leading to an existence of an entirely different order.[88]

What the new theories offered was a retreat from the world that had become unsafe, untrustworthy, and frightening—a retreat into an internal, personal world.

The idea of the unconscious strategically shifted the human being's place in the world. No longer was man significantly placed inside a story of good versus evil and given the opportunity to become a co-creator in the world, bringing good out of evil, but he was placed, instead, at the pin-nacle of an unconscious chain of being. By becoming self-conscious and integrating all one's awareness into a personal story, he would be respon-sible for creating a self-realized, authentic self.

With reality becoming internalized, it was necessary to make some pact or accommodation with evil. It was Carl Jung, a disciple of Freud's, who removed the language of good versus evil from our lexicon and replaced it with the concept of the "shadow"—the dark side of our being—which needed to be accepted, made conscious, and then integrated into our self-understanding. We were not to think in terms of evil, but rather in terms of the shadow manifesting itself. Perhaps the naivety of that attitude can be best seen in an interview that Jung did with an American correspondent named H. R. Knickerbocker in 1938. After calling Mussolini warm, human, and a man of good taste and style, he then went on to give his impression of Hitler: "There is no question but that Hitler belongs in the category of the truly mystic medicine man…since the time of Mohammed nothing like it has been seen in this world. This markedly mystic characteristic of Hitler's is what makes him do things which seem to us illogical, inexplicable, curious and unreasonable…. So you see, Hitler is a medicine man, a form of a spiritual vessel, a demi-deity or, even better, a myth."[89]

As Jung unwittingly revealed, without an understanding of the nature of evil, one can too easily be seduced by it.

The idea of the unconscious has had a powerful effect on modern thinking. Life was no longer to be understood and interpreted according to transcendent values, but rather according to the unconscious life that we find within. God, Freud claimed, was a projection of man's unconscious. Religious beliefs and rites could therefore be interpreted in terms of unconscious mechanisms. In fact, religion was seen a sign of man's immaturity on the road to self-actualization. The idea of the unconscious removed an exterior plumb line or reference point around which we sought the measure for self-understanding and made introspection, instead, the means whereby we came to insight and enlightenment. Transcendence was eliminated in order to make the knowing ego the center of one's own personal universe.

The Bible also reveals lack of consciousness to be a problem. The Bible claims that our battles are not against "flesh and blood," but against spiritual forces. We tend to live much of our lives unconscious of the greater significance of our lives and actions. From the cross, Jesus cried: "Father, forgive them, for they do not know what they are doing" (Luke 23:34). Peter, in addressing a Jewish crowd, spoke similarly when he claimed, "Now, brothers, I know that you acted in ignorance, as did your leaders" (Acts 3:17). Evil gains its power precisely because we remain unconscious of its nature and the part we play in its dispersion. We are bit players in a large cosmic drama. It is not inner unconscious mechanisms or what is suppressed and repressed within that we need to focus on, but rather the nature and reality of good and evil—forces that are external to ourselves.

The unconscious is formless and chaotic. We were not meant to be authors of our own story, attempting to tame and order those chaotic regions. We are, rather, invited to turn, to allow all the emerging awareness, memories, hurts, and brokenness to be held before a Transcendent Light so they can be reordered into a new story. The narrative thus formed will not only be a human story, but also an eternal story. It is when we allow God to take all the emerging chaos of the unconscious and form it into something new that we, ourselves, become a story of God.

Perhaps the difference between forming life around ideas of the unconscious and that of Transcendence can be seen by means of an incident. Someone close to me who works in the medical field was at a group meeting where case studies were being discussed. The person who related the story to me spoke at the meeting of how impressed he was by the attitude of the parent of a handicapped child. When the parent was asked about how he and his wife were coping, the father said, "Life doesn't get better than this." The response of the psychiatrist at the group meeting was, "What denial." Greater consciousness is not sufficient for transcending either ourselves or what life throws in our way. It does not allow us to rise above what we can't understand, nor does it allow us to live a supernatural life.

The difference that catching a vision of transcendence makes can also be illustrated by another personal story. There was a time, several years ago, when someone near me became ill. They seemed to enter a dark world of compulsions, terror, and madness. My heart broke as I heard

Tony (not his real name) say, through tears, "I had so many dreams, and now I'll never live a normal life." I knew fear as I heard Tony say, "I'm psychic. I should kill myself." When Tony would say, "The devil told me" or "God says," I felt a chill enter my heart. Of course, a history of drugs and psychiatry followed.

I have come to believe that for some things in life to be borne, there must be meaning, a higher purpose. Perhaps everything can be borne if surrounded by meaning. It is meaninglessness that destroys us. I began to spend a lot of time with Tony, helping him to see and interpret all that was happening to him in terms of God, of Transcendent Reality. I discovered how deeply mental illness is connected to religious questions—questions of life, identity, meaning, guilt, helplessness, and ultimate purpose. I discovered that one of the main characteristics of mental illness is that all concepts of God and religion get very badly distorted. I had always liked my religion in Laodicean style (Revelation 3)—not too hot, not too cold, but just nice and respectable—but as I watched Tony struggle, I became firmly convinced that there is a malevolence that exists in our world. What Tony struggled with was not just biology and chemistry; what he needed to be free of was greater than a faulty consciousness. I consistently urged Tony to accept the God of revelation—a God of love, acceptance, forgiveness, and a God that gives life, not a god of distorting compulsions. Slowly, Tony became aware of the Presence of a God that began to counter the god of his illness. Tony eventually stopped his psychiatric sessions; he found it was the Biblical narrative that gave meaning to what was happening.

There came a time when I heard Tony say, "If I never get any better than this, I can handle it now." And then finally, the surest sign of a true faith journey—gratitude. I heard Tony say, "I needed that (the illness)" as he realized that so much good had come out of being ill that he had become grateful for the illness.

It was one day in prayer that what I suppose is best described as a "communicating presence"—though more traditionally referred to as God—assured me that the person I just described was now going to be healed. That week Tony went off all his remaining medication and has been perfectly healthy ever since. His life became another story about God.

Sometime later, I heard someone discussing Tony's radical change in personality and attributing it to some theory they had read of systems of change. I finally lost my composure and blurted out, "What is it about you and your religion that can't say the word "God"?" Human understanding was insufficient to explain a truly radical transformation of personality.

A third incident arises from having lunch with a minister and a psychologist associated with the church. The minister told of baptizing a woman that week who had lived a hard life and who found that when she came to church, all she could do was cry. The psychologist immediately related that to a sign of pathology and then related the experience of counseling another woman who kept crying in church. He determined it was out of grief for a dead husband and unresolved issues, so he brought a coffin into the counseling sessions so she could get mad and vent her last words to her husband. That reminded the minister of another woman who would cry whenever she entered church so, thanks to our ability now to rummage through the unconscious for hidden material, it was discovered that in the previous generation, her father had had a traumatic experience in church. Supposedly, the grief the father felt in church had just been visited on the daughter, where the implication was given that in becoming "conscious," it had also been resolved. Both men seemed satisfied with how the women had been "cured"—their tears had stopped. However, if tears, as I believe, are a sign of God's nearing Presence, then could it have been God that the women were cured of?

My lunch made me aware of how deeply I wanted to be part of a community where I could say the word "God"—where "God" wasn't a word left in the church sanctuary, but was recognized as the reality in which we all live, move, and have our being—where God, not the unconscious, is articulated as the reality we have to deal with in all the lived moments of our mundane, or exciting, or terrifying lives—where, once again, we acknowledged our lives to be connected to higher realities.

God is the reality in which we all live, move, and have our being. One can, as Freud, Jung, and the others following them did, just eliminate Divinity, turning the powers that be into an impersonal, unconscious, random, and chaotic sea striving towards consciousness. The benefit of that approach is that it casts us in the role of God, bringing order out of chaos by making it conscious. We can become the author of our own story, choosing how we will bring order out of randomness. However, by becoming free of God, we will discover that we are not free at all; we have just become atoms in a sea of random, chaotic, meaningless, dark, unconscious humanity.

The same Spirit that hovered over pre-creation chaos still hovers, offering to breathe life into all that tries to rise and live by that which lies beyond man's dark, collective, unconscious humanity. But for that, we need to acknowledge and live by Transcendence.

Integration versus Overcoming

I WONDER IF IT IS POSSIBLE to become allergic to certain words. I certainly developed a hypersensitivity to the word "integration." It is one of those buzzwords from the therapeutic that seems to have snuck into our conversations with little accompanying thought as to what it really signifies. At first I, myself, couldn't understand my oversensitivity. It was only when I began to study the lives of the saints and mystics that I began to understand my aversion to that word.

If one wants to cultivate an interest in the mystics—those passionate followers of the Light—then a good guide is Evelyn Underhill. Evelyn Underhill was an academic (the first woman to become a Fellow of King's College, London, and the first woman lecturer to have her name on the Oxford University List) whose special area of interest was mysticism. Mysticism, for Underhill, was not an esoteric interest, but was rather, as she defined it, "The expression of the innate tendency of the human spirit towards complete harmony with the transcendental order."[90] Mysticism, in other words, was a universal calling—we just needed to learn to recognize its call and then learn how to respond.

Evelyn Underhill's seminal work was a large, almost unreadable, tome called *Mysticism*. Near the end of this large work—in which she studies the mystics of all religious traditions, but especially those in Christianity—Evelyn Underhill asks, "What do these things mean for us; for ordinary unmystical men?"[91] Her answer: "The germ of that same transcendent life…is latent in all of us; an integral part of our humanity."[92] We do not need to recognize that latent germ of life before being drawn by its power; without recognition, we just explain it in human or in lesser terms. However, as Underhill points out in her book, if one were to recognize, nourish, and then allow that latent seed to grow, then one would find oneself placed on a path that always forms itself into a similar pattern. It is that path or pattern that is important to recognize, for when we see it made visible in the lives of the saints and the mystics, we will recognize that they are responding to the same call that has invited us to follow. It is when we study what the mystics—with their lives lived in full surrender to some cosmic rhythm—wrote large with their lives that we begin to recognize the cadences that are also resonating in our own lives. Without that recognition, we live lives that are reduced and fall far short of our God-given potential.

According to Underhill, that mystic path begins with a point of "awakening," "turning," or being "born again"—different traditions use different words. We need to acknowledge that divine spark of life and welcome it within. There then comes a time of "purgation," "sanctification," "holiness," or "discipline'—again, people apply different words—as one realizes that to follow the Light means being changed by that Light. Underhill then describes periods of darkness, of psychic upheaval, and of emotions increasingly becoming split between inflation and deflation. Life centered on ourselves and our old habitual ways of response are being challenged. In terror, we may give up the journey in order to re-assert our need for control and easy peace. Unfortunately, our world, and often even religion, are too ready to come to our aid, offering us ways to "integrate" the chaos according to human understanding, replacing the faith journey with modes of self-understanding, and helping us to re-assert control over the chaos by fortifying our ego rather than by learning the new lessons of faith.

According to Underhill, there is another option; it is the option chosen by the mystics. That option consists of using the inner upheaval as an opportunity to re-order one's life and ways of seeing around a reality that lies outside of and beyond our disintegrating, chaotic selves. Those that choose that option will slowly find themselves drawn along a path of enlightenment or illumination, a path along which one increasingly becomes aware of who it is one is reaching for, and the attendant knowledge that always comes with it—the knowledge of who we are as we increasingly stand revealed by that Light. For the mystics, adversity and suffering are seen as gifts; they are what caused them to flee to the sheltering Presence of God.

What the lives of the saints and mystics next reveal is that once life has become centered around God or a transcendent source, then where they are finally brought is to a new place of unity, a unity no longer formed with the self at center, but rather formed around a transcendent Other. For many of the saints and mystics, it was a unity so complete that they could say, as that mystic St. Augustine once said, "Love and then do what you will." Most of us mere mortals will not get to that point in this life but, as another mystic, Dante, portrayed so graphically in his *Divine Comedy,* it is the growing peace, the growing joy, the growing certainty, fulfillment, and freedom of the journey, that makes the journey almost a sufficient end unto itself.

If Evelyn Underhill is right, if living faith always forms itself into a journey of similar pattern, then when an awakened interest in the transcendent is coupled with inner psychic upheaval, in emotions diverging with ever-increasing gaps between highs and lows, in an increasing awareness of one's inner lack of health, then if at that point the church calls in the therapeutic to "integrate" that turmoil around the personal ego and its need for control, then it may be a Living God and the Holy Spirit that they are working against. What is more, if the therapeutic is successful in re-integrating that psychic upheaval and inner chaos around the core of the self and its ability to live by self-understanding, then the greatest significance of what they will have just accomplished is that they will have just aborted that spiritual journey. The church that aids in that re-integration may be lauded for the pragmatic and concrete evidence of its usefulness, but in actual fact, it will have been false to its purpose—the creation of living souls who can live in response and co-creation with a transcendent reality.

The word "integration" is a word that I have never discovered in my Bible. I suppose that if it were used in the sense of our integrating our lives around the reality of God, then it would be compatible with Biblical beliefs. But I have never heard it used that way. When I hear the word used, it is always used to describe our ability to gather all the pieces of our life around a core of our own understanding.

If the church is successful in helping us get our lives back together into an integrated whole centered on the ego and our own understanding, then what has it gained other than a reputation for effectiveness? Adversity and need can be seen as the God-given impediments that stop us on our journey towards self-reliance and self-realization in order to initiate us into a new way of life. After all, the ultimate questions of our selves, of death, of purpose and meaning, have not been removed by therapeutic intervention, only bypassed or postponed.

We humans are hybrid creatures. When our lower nature is given free reign, then the soul has no option but to atrophy and die. However, when the eternal side is allowed to take charge, our natural life is redeemed and restored to its created splendor. We can never be unitary or fully integrated beings until either the animal or the eternal side of our being has been allowed to predominate, causing the other part of our being to be subsumed, re-ordered, overcome, or to atrophy. I suppose that is why I have always reacted so strongly against the word "integration." Every time I heard that word in the church setting, I knew that the ego had been allowed to assert itself at the expense of something else—a step of faith—being taken. According to therapeutic theories of integration, well-adjusted people have adjusted their lives to the situations they found themselves in rather than the reality of God—lives where personal ego, not God, reigns supreme.

The concept and language of integration actually descends from Carl Jung, who thought that the shadow and dark side of our being should be accepted and brought into the life of the whole man. Nothing in man should be denied, repressed, or cut off. Jung considered Christ to be an archetype of the self. The problem was, in Jung's view, that Jesus was an insufficient archetype for modern man in that He failed to reveal the shadow side of our being. Jung wrote in *Christ, A Symbol of Self:* "The Christ symbol lacks wholeness in the modern psychological sense, since it does not include the dark side of things but specifically excludes it in the form of a Luciferian opponent."[93] Jung thought that the Christian symbol of the Trinity should be changed into a quaternity so that Satan could be included. It was that foursome aspect—with evil included—that

Jung thought to be a better archetype for what actually lay within the unconscious of man. Jung would have had no patience for the Bible's assertion that, "God is light; in him there is no darkness at all" (1 John 1:5). As the philosopher Iris Murdoch noted, "The perfectly integrated personality, as presented by Jung as an ideal, must include some notion of a pact with, or somehow reassessment of, what is evil in the soul."[94] Therein lies the source of our modern therapeutic language of integration. Man's end was to be seen as the final acceptance of all that he discovers within himself, including the dark side. As a concept there can be few ideas that fly farther from the reality of Gospel teaching.

The Bible, in contrast to all that talk about integration, instead uses the language of overcoming. As it states in 1 John 5:4, "Everyone born of God overcomes the world." Jesus' assertion that He had overcome the world used to perplex me, as it was evident that He had not overcome the world in any sense that we usually conceive of that term. Jesus created no political movements, did not destroy His enemies (they destroyed Him), He did not overcome poverty to rise in society, He won no visible wars, He did little to change the corrupt nature of the Pharisees and Sadducees who had gained control of organized religion, and He seemingly did nothing to eliminate Roman oppression. In the ways that we in the world normally think of "overcoming," Jesus was a failure. In fact, by the time of Jesus' death, His claims to have overcome the world could, in practical terms, be said to be false: Jesus had made no visible difference to the world in which He lived. Clearly the overcoming of which Jesus spoke was of a different order than the terms in which we normally conceive of it.

"Overcoming" is a word that becomes a repeated refrain in the book of Revelation. Our Scriptures end with Revelation, wherein we are offered the image of a triumphant Christ holding out the crown of life to those who have overcome. The historian N.T. Wright has pointed out that Jesus, in His coming to earth, deliberately changed the symbols by which the Israelites understood their religion and history.[95] In the Old Testament, God revealed His power over evil by helping the Israelites overcome the Assyrians, the Canaanites, the Philistines, and the Moabites. Evil was external, interpreted according to nationality. In the New Testament, Jesus changed the symbols. God's power over evil was revealed in the healing of the sick and in casting out demons. The miracles symbolized and illustrated the new message that Jesus came to preach, the message that what was wrong with the world was that which could be found in each and every individual. A major thrust of Jesus' message was to turn man's attention away from viewing evil as something extraneous to himself and to view it, instead, as that which is internal: "Nothing that enters a man from the outside can make him 'unclean'.… What comes out of a man is what makes him 'unclean'. For from within, out of men's hearts, come evil thoughts, sexual immorality, theft, murder, adultery, greed, malice, deceit, lewdness, envy, slander, arrogance and folly. All these evils come from inside and make a man "unclean'" (Mark:7:14, 20).

According to the Bible, we are capable of recognizing evil in the world because it has dropped its seeds in every one of our human hearts. It is within our own hearts that the battle over evil is begun. The greatest enemy we will ever fight is the one we discover within ourselves. As Solzhenitsyn discovered in prison, "Gradually it was disclosed to me that the line separating good and evil passes not through states, nor between classes, nor between political parties either—but right through every human heart—and through all human hearts."

George Macdonald wisely recognized our need to overcome the enemy within when he wrote, "To be made greater than one's fellows is the offered reward of hell, and involves no greatness; to be made greater than one's self is the divine reward, and involves a real greatness."[96] The kingdom of God is born within wherever something of the kingdom of this world is overcome.

The difference between the Old and New Testament concepts of overcoming can by seen in the two visions of St. Francis of Assisi. St. Francis, in a dream, had a vision of swords, helmets, shields, and spears formed in the shape of and carrying the sacred insignia of the cross. St. Francis saw it as a call to arms, and as he rode off to war, it was with a boast on his lips—"I shall come back a great prince." However, he did not become triumphant, but rather, ill. Sick, disillusioned, and humiliated, St. Francis received another vision in which he was told, "You have mistaken the meaning of the vision. Return to your own town." St. Francis was even more confused. Spending day after day in listless confusion, he rode out into the country one day, only to be confronted by a leper. At the sight of the leper, "He knew instantly that his courage was challenged, not as the world challenges, but as one would challenge who knew the secrets of the heart of a man. What he saw advancing was...his fear coming up the road towards him; the fear that comes from within and not without."[97] Courage, he realized, came not from overcoming the armies of Perugia or Sicily, but rather from overcoming the fear that lurks within. St. Francis jumped from his horse and ran to embrace the leper. In that embrace, he knew that he had decisively overcome and conquered something important within himself. Later, as he rode on, he turned to see that the leper had disappeared.[98]

Jesus' turning the language of warfare, which is so prevalent in the Old Testament, into an interior battle was new and unique, but not unprecedented in His world. There was one group that seems to have predated the Pauline and early Christian recognition of our battles being inner struggles; it was the Qumran sect, as we now know from the Dead Sea Scrolls: "Until now the spirits of truth and perversity have contended within the human heart. All people walk in both wisdom and foolishness. As is a person's endowment of truth and righteousness, so shall he hate perversity; conversely, in proportion to bequest in the lot of evil, one will act wickedly and abominate truth. God has appointed these spirits as equals until the time of decree and renewal...deciding the fate of every living being by the measure of which spirit predominates in him."[99]

Already in the Qumran sect, the idea of life's great battles being inner battles had predated the teachings of Jesus. With Jesus, the inner world of man moved to the forefront of attention.

The overcoming, which is repeated as a refrain in Revelation, is therefore an inner victory. In order to re-make the world, we must first be inwardly re-made. The world will do its best to impose its fallen order, views, and way of life on us. If we are to be victors, then we, like Jesus, will have to overcome like Jesus did: in an interior struggle wherein the kingdom of God overcomes the kingdom of the world.

That overcoming, however, is easier said than done. As long as we are content to integrate all of life around the ego and its propensity to live according to self-understanding, then we need never become aware of what the early desert monks referred to as the demons that battle it out within the individual soul. As long as we swim with the stream of our own instincts and desires, we will know little inner conflict for, as Fenelon observed, "While we go with the stream, we are unconscious of its rapid course; but when we begin to stem it ever so little, it makes itself felt." Everyone who tries to follow the way of Jesus will discover a deep inner division within themselves; they will discover that we exist as creatures of two natures and one will have to overcome the other in order to thrive. In fact, it seems to be the very act of turning and of trying to live out of a reality higher and other than our ego that can unleash and fan into flame all the hell-fires burning within us, the fires of anger, bitterness, greed, lust, and envy. I have come to appreciate and see the truth of Dante's vision of hell as the place where we burn forever with the fires we did not put out in this life.

I now know that it wasn't just coincidence that a growing interest in the Transcendent came with a growing awareness of what an angry person I was. The Light of God's approach will always begin to illuminate our inner life to us. I tried to fight the fire of anger through more self-aware-ness, through analyzing the root causes, but that was like pouring oil on the flames. It just convinced me that my anger was justified. It didn't help that wherever I looked, I seemed condemned for the very anger I could-n't control. I read, "Do not fret—it leads only to evil" (Psalm 37:8), and, "Man's anger does not bring about the righteous life that God desires" (James 1:20). Finally, one night, I admitted my inadequacy. I told God that I couldn't get rid of the anger, but I relinquished it and asked Him to take it away. That night I had a dream. Through my dream came the people I had been so angry with, and into the dream came the knowing that Christ was in all those people; those were the very people whose sins and insensitivities Christ died to take away. What He died to take away I had no right holding onto. A peace came over me that lasted a few days. Then I decided to go back and pick at a few of the old sores to see if they were really healed. The fires of anger came back with a vengeance. I was no longer angry; I was anger personified. Finally, the anger frightened even me. I decided that I was tired of my anger. I would fight it until it was finally overcome. It was an uphill battle. I discovered that prayer was the only safe place for certain memories to be allowed to resurface: "Prayer is the womb we curl into, the dark, closed, often silent place where we are formed in Christ-likeness, where strand by tangled strand our willfulness and selfishness is unraveled and stitch by painstaking stitch the Spirit's work is knit together in us."[100]

I learned mental discipline—"Whatever is true, whatever is noble, whatever is right, whatever is pure, whatever is lovely, whatever is admirable—if anything is excellent or praiseworthy—think about such things" (Philippians 4:8)—for we eventually become what we keep our minds on. I learned that if one persistently cries out for help, then grace leaves its ethereal realm of theological abstraction to become the presence of someone entering those depths to live them with us, a God who will not rescue us from the consequences of our lives, but rather enters their depths to live them with us. I learned that if one prays for one's enemies as we are told to, then God helps one to see them as He sees them, and hate dissipates. I learned how to bring spiritual disciplines into my life, for I discovered that one's soul needs nurturing to keep its life just as much as a body needs food to stay alive.

It was easy to believe in God in the midst of a dream that removed anger. The instant peace, however, did not transform all of life and its processes that had turned me into such an angry person. I hadn't struggled through all the ramifications of what relinquishing that anger would mean. There were so many people to forgive. I had to learn new attitudes. I had to stop expecting too much of people. I had to learn to accept those in whom I could see many flaws. I had to learn that mercy trumps justice. It was in suffering that wisdom came. By bringing the Light of God into my anger and allowing layer after layer of life to be revealed in that Light, I slowly learned that forgiveness, understanding, wisdom, and knowledge of Kingdom realities eventually become the precipitate of that inner struggle.

I grew up with stories like Paul's Damascus Road experience. I couldn't help but pick up the idea of that being what salvation was about: an instant experience. Then I started to read history and realized that we have avoided preaching the gaps. History reveals that Paul, upon his conversion, was a disruptive influence in the church. He therefore needed to leave to live separate for a while. There were approximately ten years (different scholars give different time estimates) between Paul's Damascus Road experience and his call to begin his missionary career. Much of that time seemed to be spent making tents in Tarsus. What there seems to be more consensus on is the fact that three of those years were spent alone in the desert. Slowly but eventually, Paul's disruptive zealotry got turned into a charitable zeal that God could finally use. His preaching mission began.

The crucial question is—what was the cause of Paul's transformation? Was it the overwhelming Damascus Road experience or was it the ten years (many alone in the desert) that changed him? If one believes it was the experience, then one may be more Gnostic than Christian. We need to catch a vision; we need to experience God's overwhelming grace in our lives if we are going to be able to change. But God does not destroy our human natures. It is in the struggle that we are slowly transformed. It is at all those places of overcoming that the new Christ-life is born within us. The more our fallen nature is overcome, the more we will increase our capacity for God.

Both Christianity and psychology are aware that we humans are inwardly conflicted beings, beings who struggle within ourselves. Both offer advice as to how to approach that inner struggle. One offers us help in integrating the inner chaos around the ego and its ability to live according to its own understanding. The other is an invitation to orient our being around a transcendent source, a choice which will inevitably pitch us into a battle against all within that lives in conflict with that other world.

Integration versus overcoming; the two different words offer competing linguistic and perceptual frameworks around which very different lives will be formed. One linguistic framework derives from Jesus Christ, the other from Carl Jung. The difference between those words is not only a matter of semantics, but rather, of totally different world or Kingdom views.

Relationships: Knowledge versus Love

BOTH CHRISTIANITY and the therapeutic are ultimately about relationships. The Gospel tells us that love is the summation, the perfection, the completion, and the totality of the gospel. It tells us that the end of faith is to love, and that love covers over a multitude of sins. It tells us that those who love know God, and that our love of God can be tested for genuineness by watching our relationship with our neighbor. It goes on, in I Corinthians 13, to give us a running list of all that man does and would like to do in the name of religion, and then tells us that it all means nothing if it is done without love. In Galatians 5:6, we are told that, "The only thing that counts is faith expressing itself through love."

The gospel then goes further. Not only does it say, "God is love," but also it shows us in the life of Jesus what that love looks like when it has become incarnate in a human form. There is something almost scandalous about the way Jesus could love. In a Jewish culture where women were never allowed to let their hair down in public, where a woman with her hair down had just given her husband sufficient grounds for divorce, one can almost feel the shocked silence as Jesus watched a prostitute loosen her hair to wipe His feet. Jesus' response was surprising; He accepted her gesture and then turned to the men for whom judgment would have come easy and, reading that easy judgment written out on their faces, He rebuked them.

Jesus touched all those in need, allowing himself to become ritually unclean. Jesus was born in a culture where holiness meant the avoidance of contamination from innumerable sources. Jesus allowed himself to become contaminated in order to get close to the outcasts of society. He left the circles of the pious in order to associate with those with whom the religious of the day would not be seen.

In a world that had become Hellenized in thought—in Greek culture the love of boys was a man's great delight—it would have been prudent to keep all suggestion of Greek influence and improprieties at bay. Jesus was part of a Hebrew subculture that condemned sodomy, and yet we are given the picture of the Last Supper with the "disciple Jesus loved" laying his head on Jesus' breast. I used to wonder why the Holy Spirit needed that detail added; certainly it would have been prudent to keep far from all suggestion of indiscretion. Jesus, however, could love in ways that could destabilize those of lesser purity.

Jesus also allowed His associations with women to contravene all that was considered acceptable or appropriate for His time. In His relationships with women, Jesus was a subversive force that would ultimately threaten the very structures that defined male-female roles and relationships. Jesus, by ignoring the prohibitions and traditions that circumscribed relationships, revealed depths of intimacy and love that surpassed, and therefore could ignore, human traditions.

When Jesus was invited to dine at a Pharisee's home, a Pharisee who should have been the natural ally to the furtherance of His goals, Jesus destroyed all the facades of social etiquette in order to pronounce the six woes—forever de-linking Godly love with political correctness or social niceness.

I used to hoard and nurse every insult, hurt, or insensitivity—real or imagined—and then used that wall of offense as a means of keeping all people at a good, safe distance. I suppose that is why I was so shocked when I realized that in the Garden of Gethsemane, Jesus, knowing that Judas had just betrayed him, nevertheless approached him and addressed him as "friend." Loving those who had hurt you was so far beyond the pale of my understanding that I knew there had to be something more than human involved. And then, of course, there was that even greater feat of love; when crucified, Jesus prayed for those who were responsible for His death and asked God for their forgiveness.

What these stories all reveal is that Jesus was capable of loving beyond all the boundaries that we consider to be appropriate and normal. What Jesus made evident was that love—spiritual, gospel love—was not to be equated with either sentimentality or with our instinctual drives. It could not be made synonymous with our feelings, desires, emotions, or passions. God-revealed love lay on another plane entirely.

If to love like Jesus is our goal, then we must acknowledge that we are in trouble. Love is the one thing we are not capable of. We've been too badly broken, our foundations were too badly laid; our psyches are riddled with fracture lines. There seems to be an empty hole at the core of our being that wants to suck up all life into its vortex of need; if that doesn't work, we project that same neediness out in an inhuman attempt to control all life around us. Our neighbors unearth within us the entire spectrum of negative emotions, from envy to lust to hate, but love is conspicuously absent. We find it hard to even peer over the huge walls of defense created by our egos in order to see our neighbor adequately. We instead use our neighbor to feed our egos, calculating the personal advantages to association. We see our neighbor in utilitarian terms, in terms of our needs. We use our neighbor as the measuring stick against which we compete, or as a mirror whereby we can see ourselves reflected and thereby know that we exist. If love should happen to be awakened in spite of it all, it quickly gets derailed into lust. The only love we seem to be capable of is self-love, and that, precisely, is what is going to destroy us.

Love desiring to be awakened is a powerful force. Its roots are primitive and universal. At first it may present itself as something negative: a hunger, a loneliness, a psychic ache, a deep sorrow, an unfulfilled desire, a numbing sense of alienation. Without a revealed and articulated goal towards which to channel its force, it can become an energy driving us towards some indeterminate and often destructive end. In a short period of time, I knew two women who broke up families in order to pursue sexual affairs because, in their words, they felt the need for "something more." True religion is about the longing for "something more" that can drive us to erratic and destructive behavior if we do not know how to articulate, understand, and channel its energy.

We have been deeply imprinted at a level where human reason struggles for understanding. If we use the Biblical image of God breathing His own breath into us, then the imprint from the God of love will leave us with yearnings that draw us back to their source. If, on the other hand, we choose to define and express those longings in terms of the animal or instinctual side of our being, then the longings themselves, unable to be contained by our nature, can instead become our torment and downfall. Those longings are, in themselves, neither holy nor carnal; they find their definition according to the ends toward which they are directed.

It was Freud who initially taught us to articulate that imprint in terms of sexuality, turning sex into one of our dominant pre-occupations. Thanks to Freud, the God who draws us with His love was turned into an infantile projection, and our attempts at loving God were labeled as sublimated sexual urges. Although much of Freud's teachings have been dismissed, we have never managed to regain a balanced view of our sexuality.

What we have lost sight of is the difference between interpreting the latent force within as sexuality or as love. The former view interprets that innate drive as existing as part of our unconscious, and therefore, as being primitive and with roots that lie deep within our own being. The other view interprets our deepest longings as due to an imprint that has its source in the Transcendent; as such it is the means by which we are drawn outside and beyond ourselves. Real love does not deny any part of our nature, including the physical, but it is grounded in and points towards the eternal. By pointing to and intimating that which lies forever beyond our reach, it leaves us with desires and longings that, in this world, remain unfulfilled; the longings themselves seem imbued with the holy in a way that makes their temporal satisfaction a disappointment.

Ever since Freud placed sexuality at the center of how we understand ourselves, we have been trying to reduce love to an instinctual drive. We have taken the energy that is love and removed it from the realm of religion and have instead relegated it to the libido, a component of an impersonal life instinct. We have depersonalized the universe, and without the ability to believe in a personal God who by love draws us to Himself, we can only see that innate force within as leading us to better, more passionate, and more driven sex.

The problem is, love awakened can seem like a messy fusion of all loves and impulses. Our challenge in life is to rightly order that energy so that we achieve and reveal the fullness of our potential glory. The latent energy is universal. It is for us to choose how we will interpret and channel it. Awakened desires do not come with attached labels differentiating them according to their objective ends. We need to choose the ends towards which to direct their energy. As Wayne E. Oates noted, our loves "are distinguishable from each other by their object, not by their origin and nature."[101]

Too often we fail to adequately understand or direct our desires; we just leave them as a messy fusion. The erotic pop queen Madonna exemplified that when she said, "Passion and sexuality and religion all bleed into each other for me."[102] That assimilation is evident in her songs and videos, where she incorporates religious imagery into highly eroticized performances. Scott Peck, the psychiatrist who wrote the immensely popular *The Road Less Traveled,* also revealed that confusion when he explained his adulterous affairs by writing, "I was questing, through sexual romance, at least a brief visit to God's castle." Of course, that fusion of drives is not new. The pagan cultures in the Old Testament incorporated sexual orgies and shrine prostitution into their religion, revealing the same messy fusion of the divine and the erotic. And it was not only the pagans who got confused by their inner drives: the priest Eli's sons also slept with "the women who served at the entrance to the Tent of Meeting" (1 Samuel 2:22). Spirituality and sensuality are so intimately linked that confusion easily results.

When God is the final reference point around which all our other loves find their harmony, then our loves are enriched, channeled, and find their culmination in the love of God. When we find some lesser reference point to be the focus of our desires, then our loves will become strained. As C.S. Lewis noted, "We are half-hearted creatures, fooling about with drink and sex and ambition, when infinite joy is offered us, like an ignorant child who wants to go on making mud pies in a slum because he cannot imagine what is meant by the offer of a holiday at the sea. We are far too easily pleased."

John Eldredge observed that we have basically three choices in life:

"(1) to be alive and thirsty, (2) to be dead, or (3) to be addicted."[103] When we choose God as the end of our desiring, then we will never be sated here in this life, but the desire itself can keep us alive to the journey and our lesser desires will be kept in their proper ordering. However, allow our longings to be displaced from the infinite onto the finite and they will become our addictions; they will become the fire that consumes us. Eldridge offered his observation as to what the majority of people do with their desires: "Most of the world lives in addiction; most of the church has chosen deadness."[104]

Love may be what lies at the heart of the universe, but for us mortals, it presents itself as a problem. Perhaps the nature of the problem can be seen through the story of Ulysses and the Sirens. Ulysses, as the story goes, had fought the Trojan War and was making his way back home to his wife Penelope. He had been warned about Sirens ahead who sang a song so powerful and seductive that all who came within their range and heard their song would jump overboard and be drowned in the sea. Undaunted, and wishing to hear their song, Ulysses had his sailors tie him to the mast with ropes, and then had the sailors stop up their ears with wax. As their ship passed the Sirens Ulysses struggled, begged to be free, but unable to hear him, the sailors just tied his ropes even tighter.

The song of the Sirens is one that we will all hear at some point on our way home. The song of love is the most powerful force in our universe, and when we hear its haunting refrain, it will evoke one of three responses within. It can evoke a moral response, a response of fear that is too often, unfortunately, taken up by the church. Religion that has allowed morality to become its focus and end is depicted in the Bible as religion that is hopelessly immature or else lost: "Do and do, do and do, Rule on rule, rule on rule" (Isaiah 28:10).

Too often, in religion, making sure that everyone is bound fast by the prescribed ropes is presented as though that were the goal and end of religion. We, however, cannot learn to love by being frightened of love. As Simon Tugwell observed, "We cannot learn to love God by learning not to love. If we kill off in ourselves the faculty we have for desire, then we shall paralyze our faculty for loving God."[105] If we are to learn to love like Jesus, then we are going to have to pass through the inferno of our passions.

The second response is to put our intellectual faculty in charge; reason and self-understanding are deemed to be sufficient to keep us safe. That is akin to throwing away the ropes entirely. Hear those Sirens and one will know immediately our capacity to rationalize anything. Not only will the therapeutic, with all its theories, be of no value before the Siren's song, but it will just be pressed into the service of justifying one's leap into the sea.

The third response is the most torturous one—allowing the Sirens their song, but believing in the necessity of the ropes. At some point, we all think that it is the ropes that are the cause of our torment; rid ourselves of them and we shall be free. Although the ropes in themselves don't heal us, they do keep us safe while we are being healed.

I felt uneasy when I first started reading many of the church fathers and found they not only used the language of love, but also even used erotic imagery when speaking of and addressing God. I later realized it was because they had allowed their sexual energy to become subsumed and to become the driving force that drove them to God. Origen considered *eros* to have been implanted in us by God, and it was *eros* itself, he claimed, that would return us to God. *Eros* may have gone awry with the Fall, but by turning it from the objects onto which it had become displaced—the material world and human objects—and by redirecting it back to its original source, it could be transformed, again becoming the powering force allowing for the soul's ascent to God.[106] St. Augustine called the Christian life one of "holy desire".[107] Catherine of Sienna wrote that, "Sensuality is a servant, and it has been appointed to serve the soul."

In Christianity, sex is therefore seen as having purpose and substance. It has sacramental value, pointing beyond itself, becoming the model, and providing the vocabulary for the divine/human relationship. No longer is it to be seen as pure instinctual drive feeding itself, but rather as the energy that can be subsumed for higher purpose. To see what happens when sex loses its ability to point beyond itself, one has to again remember what happened in the pagan religions; they divinized the sexual drive, inter-preting their longings in terms of sexuality. When our drives lose their ability to point beyond, they become defined by our primitive instincts, our unconscious urges, our animal desires, and not by the call of the transcendent and holy.

In a society that is allowing love to be increasingly reduced and defined as an instinct arising from the libido, the church needs to reclaim its message. Bonhoeffer wrote from prison, "God wants us to love him eternally with our whole hearts—not in such a way as to injure or weaken our earthly love, but to provide a kind of *cantus firmus* to which the other melodies of life provide the counterpoint."[108] Our love of God does not destroy our human loves, but rather blends them into a healthy harmony. Allow sexual love to assert its independence from any higher authority and our loves will instead become a polyphony, each singing its own tune and creating noise, not music. If sex is the pinnacle of how we achieve ecstasy and a sense of transcendence and fulfillment, then our entire nature will be drawn down towards the instinctual level of the animals. As it says in Ecclesiastes 3:18, "As for men, God tests them so that they may see that they are like the animals." Our latent drives may be instinctual, as in the animals, but the ability to harness their energy and use it towards a higher purpose is unique to man.

Christian love can be identified with instinctual passions only in the way that a tree can be identified with the seed from which it sprang; the latent power and design are there in its inception, but it has to be put in the ground and die to its initial form before it can grow into its new life. That is why Otto Rank, the disciple of Freud who later distanced himself from his teacher, wrote that only in love expressing itself beyond sexuality does man discover and realize his truest self.

In a world obsessed with sex, a re-examination of chastity may be in order. Chastity is not the absence of sex as much as keeping it in harmony with the right ordering of reality. There is a striking difference between Jesus' attitude towards women and many of His followers who believed in celibacy. Many monks who preached celibacy were misogynists; they had a real fear and disgust for both women and sex. Jesus, on the other hand, demonstrated a love and intimacy with women that could only be seen as revolutionary, subversive, and scandalous in His time. Jesus' singleness was not a condemnation of sex as much as a sign of hope. We will all come to a place of disillusionment and disappointment with our human loves. Love makes us vulnerable, and it is hard to risk ourselves unless there is something larger than human love to ground us. Jesus, fulfilled and complete in His singleness, offers an example that holds hope to all who are rejected, disillusioned, betrayed, disappointed in love, or who have loved deeply only to have that love destroyed by death. It was in relationship with His Father that He found wholeness, perfection, and completion. Jesus did not live in a spiritual realm that denied human loves. On the contrary, as already mentioned, there was something supernatural about the way Jesus demonstrated human love. As long as our love of God is kept pre-eminent, then our other loves are safe to grow; the love of God will be the ground that nurtures and allows all our other loves to blossom.

The inability of human love to fully satisfy is a universal phenomenon and is reflected in our myths. Our deep longing and need to be in relationship was told long ago in Plato's Symposium in the form of a story. At the beginning of our race, the story goes, there was a male-female creature with two faces, four arms, four legs, four ears, and the rest as one can imagine. Man thus united proved to be a threat and a nuisance to the gods, so Zeus devised a means whereby man would be weakened—cutting him in half. Man ever after has lived as a divided being, each half living incomplete and longing for the other half from which it has been severed.[109]

It is interesting comparing the Greek myth with the Hebrew myth, which also gives form to our deepest longings. We once lived, we are told, in a garden of innocence where our primary relationship was a divine-human one. Having succumbed to the temptation to eat of a forbidden fruit, denying the imposed limitations of divine command, we found ourselves severed from our primary relationship, banished from the garden where we lived with God. About to part ways, God turned to our first mother, who had first eaten that forbidden fruit, and said, "Your desire will be for your husband" (Genesis 3:16). From that point on, transference was built into our very being. Ever since Eden, we have been searching in the faces of our neighbors for that which we have lost, craving an end to our loneliness, forever aware of our loss and of being incomplete alone.

The two myths elucidate the difference between pagan and Christian culture. Both myths recognize our incompleteness; the pagan myth places our completion in another human being, while the Hebrew story places it in the restoration of relationship with God.

Love can be such a problem for us precisely because it was never meant to be fully satisfied in this life. In Ivan Klima's novel *Love and Garbage,* the narrator comes to the profound realization that, "There is little that comes so close to death as fulfilled love."[110] What the narrator realized within himself was a need "from time to time, to reach out to emptiness, to let longing intensify within me to the point of agony, to alternate the pain of separation with the relief of renewed coming together, the chance of escape and return, of glimpsing before me a will-o'-the-wisp, the hope that the real encounter was still awaiting me."[111] Love is always truest and safest when we recognize and accept the gap between our longings and their inability to be fully met in this world here below.

Our human loves are a foretaste and a way of approach to the divine/human encounter. To fail to realize that is to place a strain on human love that it cannot bear. We will demand others to fill the well of loneliness and need which is of God-sized, not human-sized, dimensions. Christopher Lasch has noted that in our day, "People demand from personal relations the richness and intensity of a religious experience."[112] When we take our God-sized longings and try to fulfill them by means of human relationships, they become both our torment and a source of deep disillusionment. Only in seeking God as the final fulfillment of our longings will we be able to turn towards our neighbor and be kept from the ultimate boredom and disillusionment that are inevitable in human relationships. Only in turning to God will we be kept from expecting others to carry burdens that only God is large enough to carry. Only in relationships held together by divine laws of forgiveness and self-giving will we be safe to live together. As P. T. Forsyth aptly wrote, "We can trust love only as it is holy."[113]

There was a time when I thought we were handicapped by having only one word—"love"—to cover the whole field of relationships. After all, the Greeks had numerous words to differentiate between love of family, the Divine, friendship, and sexual love. It seemed inappropriate to use the same word for our feelings for God and also for our sexual relations, which are driven by passion and desire and can be little more than animal instinct; for our family relationships, which are tainted by bitterness; or for our friendships, which are motivated by competition and envy as much as by good friendly feeling. Eventually, however, I saw the wisdom of allowing one word to encompass all our loves. Our loves are like an interlocking web. Destroy one part and all the others are threatened. In their proper place, all our loves become a seamless whole that have their source in God and find their culmination in the spiritual.

Not only has the therapeutic handicapped us by defining our deepest imprint in terms of sexuality rather than love, but also with its emphasis on the ego and self-understanding, it creates an individualistic, autonomous, self-authenticated self than can exist outside of community. In Christianity, in contrast, community is integral to the message. Christianity is about learning to see the Presence of God in our actual lives and then allowing each and every encounter to both reveal and challenge us. So many spiritualities, both ancient and modern, emphasize isolation and solitude. Although solitude is a necessary spiritual discipline, its purpose is to prepare us for community, not to remove us from it. Monasticism, which started in the end of the third century, was formed by St. Basil and Pachomius in reaction to the early hermetic movement which, (how very like our day), was a movement of individual spiritual seekers all finding their individual paths to God. St. Basil and Pachomius, in contrast, saw in the extreme mortification and asceticism of the hermits a lot of what could be regarded as spiritual arrogance, individualism, self-centeredness and willfulness. Basil realized that the solitary life gave little opportunity to practice the love of one's neighbor. Without community there was little chance to develop charity, humility, and all the other virtues that form the heart of the transformed life. It is in community, after all, that we are revealed, defined, and transformed. Basil, realizing the necessity of community for the formation of the soul, was one of the first to set up rules for life in monastic community.

In contrast to our modern penchant for self-love, individualism, and autonomy, the Gospel offers us two images that show us how love goes to work forming Christian community. The first is of Jesus approaching the end of His life as a seeming failure. He had tried to train a group of disciples to carry on His message of the kingdom of God, but with little visible success. One disciple, He knew, was about to betray Him, another was about to deny Him, two had just demonstrated their ignorance of the Kingdom by fighting over who got to be first in that Kingdom, and they were all about to be scattered, leaving Him. Having one last chance to pass along the keys to the Kingdom, He gathered the disciples around him and offered to wash their feet. In case they missed the point, He asked, "Do you understand what I have done for you? ...I have set you an example that you should do as I have done for you" (John 13:12). That incident is iconic for what forms the heart of Christian community. We cannot save or claim ultimate responsibility for our neighbor—to try would be hubris, taking on the role of God. But if we stand before our neighbor in the position that Jesus showed us—that of non-judgmental attachment, of loving association, of willing servant-hood—we might become the channel God uses for bringing His life to them.[114]

We have, I believe, allowed the Reformation concept of the "priesthood of all believers" to become perverted. We now use the concept to affirm our individualism and our freedom from higher authority rather than to make us aware of our responsibility; we are the means by which God's life is mediated to our neighbor. Having noted abuses in the church, the Reformation meant to free us to stand alone before our God, not needing another mediator. Judging by our growing dependence on therapists, however, it would seem it was a responsibility too great to bear. Whereas priests once heard our confessions, we now go to paid professionals. Therapeutic counselors have taken over where priests and spiritual directors once held court. Self, not God, has become the focus of attention. Carl Jung saw early on the inverse relationship between interest in psychology and religion, and said, "The wave of interest in psychology which at present is sweeping over the Protestant countries of Europe is far from receding. It is coincident with the mass exodus from the Church."[115]

What Carl Jung did not foresee was that at some point, in order to stave off the exodus, the church would begin to bring the therapeutic couches into the church.

My daughter-in-law is a priest. The diocese taught her that any member of the congregation who came to see her more than three times should be referred on to a psychologist. In our modern world, it would take me more than three visits to convince most people they had a soul, much less to teach them how to nurture its life, how to discern its movements, and warn it of dangers. That is the best recipe I have ever heard for creating congregations of soul-dead, ego-driven people. Perhaps that is why the church has been declining in numbers and in influence while Alcoholics Anonymous (A.A) and all of its spin-offs have become so popular and successful. The Twelve Steps of A.A. demand that the individual acknowledge powerlessness, surrender one's life to God, and accept personal responsibility; it then sets out the terms for the restoring of relationships. It is small wonder that A.A has so many success stories, while the church is becoming increasingly ineffectual. The A.A. emphasis on God, personal responsibility, and community is at the heart of the gospel, a threesome focus that is destroyed by the therapeutic. A.A. showed more wisdom than the church when its founder explained, "Alcoholics Anonymous will never have a professional therapeutic Class.... For our purpose, we have discovered that at the point of professionalism money and spirituality do not mix . . . . Every time we have tried to professionalize our Twelfth Step, the result has been exactly the same; our single purpose has been defeated."[116]

I remember having lunch with someone who told me that it was hard going through as much pain as he was going through and not have anybody know. We may be able to survive alone behind a glittering facade when life is going in our favor, but when life breaks, we will be confronted with the true existential depth of our loneliness. Rather than offering Christian community where we would learn to become priests to each other and help each other place our lives in the great context of God's unfolding story, we have allowed professionalism into the church. Tetzel selling his indulgences in pre-Reformation Germany did not desecrate or trample on holy things more completely than we have by allowing the therapeutic into the church to place itself where communities were meant to be formed. We have prostituted the holy by allowing relationships to be reduced to appointment, professionalism, and payment at the end. A minister who stands at the place of our brokenness and despair and uses his position to set up a referral base for the therapeutic is functioning as a pimp rather than as priest of a Living God.

The second image offering us a clue to how love works towards the formation of community was offered shortly after the foot washing: in the sharing of the communal meal. Jesus offered his disciples one cup and one loaf of bread to be broken and shared. Then He said something that could have only confused them at the time—that it was His own life that was thereby being shared. By means of His own life being broken and shared, He was initiating a new era, an era wherein the Spirit was about to come and unite them in a way that the world and society could never know. When Jesus said, "Where two or three come together in my name, there am I with them" (Matthew 18:20), he was offering them a mode of relationship that was unique to Christian community, that of soul touching soul and being united in the burning fire of the Eternal Spirit. An example of that reality was given in the story of the disciples on the road to Emmaus, who found that a journey spent sharing their grief with the unexpected Christ in their midst ended up with their saying, "Were not our hearts burning within us?" (Luke 25:32). We long for intimacy, but sex cannot penetrate our being to where the deepest well of loneliness lies. When Jesus is the center around which our relationships revolve, then He can bring unity, a sense of community, and an intimacy that the world can never know.

Christianity offers us the vision that can unite souls around a single purpose. Dietrich Bonhoeffer wrote, "Christianity means community through Jesus Christ and in Jesus Christ. No Christian community is more or less than this. Whether it be a brief, single encounter or the daily fellowship of years, Christian community is only this. We belong to one another only through and in Jesus Christ."[117]

Christian community is formed wherever Jesus Christ has been allowed to be the vision and center of relationship. Jesus came not only to become mediator of a new relationship with God, but also with our brother. Romans 12:5 says, "In Christ we who are many form one body." Outside of that unifying reality, only our differences and brokenness become evident.

My husband has repeatedly accused me of being a hypocrite, speaking of the necessity of community while I, myself, don't attend church. I tell him that I discovered Christian community after I stopped going to church. Churches that call themselves Christian can become so focused on things carnal—such as numbers, building programs, competition, aesthetics, and therapeutic efficiency—that the living Christ is no longer the central reality of their meeting. Christian community, in contrast, happens whenever we allow the living Christ to be the mediating influence in our approach and encounters with others. When we look for the Christ-life in our brother, it helps us to see past the deformities in character to see the eternal core that God loves in spite of it all. It keeps us from attempts to control our neighbor and helps us focus on coming alongside what we can see God doing. It means that where once our ego reigned supreme, creating distance, a way has been opened to transcend the ego that blocks human love. It frees us from seeing our neighbors in the ways our culture would have us see them—according to social or economic class or pathology or race or religion—and helps us to view them as God views them. It keeps us from reacting to others out of the wellspring of hurt in our own lives and teaches us to react, instead, according to the perfected image of humanity that God revealed in Jesus. Seeing Jesus as the mediating reality keeps us from attempts to "help" our neighbor outside of reference to Christ, for anyone who tries to help another without first discerning the will of Jesus will be destroying Christian community. It creates an air of expectancy, for when Jesus is truly mediator, then we know that we have no right to "save" or interfere in another's life without first developing the awareness and humility that comes with realizing that Jesus was there first. If many a religious leader would only have kept their focus on the God-in-between, they would not have fallen into sexual misconduct, for one cannot lust after what Jesus has asked us to serve, and when we have learned to see Jesus in the one we serve. When we keep Jesus at the center, we learn that love is not actually an emotion. It is, rather, "The right way to respond to reality. It is the right relationship to being, including our own being."[118]

Our fierce individualism is now destroying community and the important friendships that find their home within it. Friendship is the highest and most difficult of our human loves. Aelred of Rievaulx, the twelfth century Cistercian monk, translated the verse, "God is Love" as, "God is friendship." Even Divine love in its highest form manifests itself as friendship: "I will not now call you servants, but my friends" (John 15:15). Unlike our other loves, which are based on instinct and desires or heredity or necessity, friendship is optional to us human beings. It is also the most difficult to maintain, perhaps because it requires our learning to see outside ourselves. It is predicated on finding a common goal that captivates our imagination and energies. Saint Exupery wrote, "Love does not consist in gazing at each other (one perfect sunrise gazing at another!) but in looking outward together in the same direction."[119] Yeats also acknowledged the need for a common external vision when he said that the greatest experience life offered was "to share profound thought and then to touch."[120]

At a time when I had given up on church, I began to meet people who also had broken lives and admitted to spiritual longings. We began to meet on a one-to-one basis to share insights we had gotten out of our Bible readings, other readings, our prayer lives, and the places where we felt

God near, and to share how we thought all that related to our lives. One day when I had talked to two different people, I sat down to supper to have my husband ask how my day went. I began to speak of the terrible things that were happening to the two people I had just talked to. My husband, obviously having had a bad day himself, interrupted me to say he was tired of depressing lives. I stopped, surprised. I had never thought of the two people as having depressing lives. I thought of them as people through whom the Light of God was shining. As I listened to them, I felt I could almost see the silhouette of God shadowing all that happened to them; they allowed me to keep my faith at a time when I could see no sign of God in my own life. It was the following week when I was again having coffee with one of those "depressing lives" that I was surprised to hear her say she could see no sign of God in her own life, but then in a change of voice that gave great emphasis to her words, she told me how she could really see God at work in my life. I got my first big insight into how Christian community was to work—a community that met to help each other see God at work in each other's lives.

John Shea, in his book *Stories of God: An Unauthorized Biography*, articulated how the formation of Christian community takes place:

> When we reach our limits, when our ordered worlds collapse, when we cannot enact our moral ideals, when we are disenchanted, we often enter into the awareness of Mystery. We are inescapably related to this Mystery which is immanent and transcendent, which issues invitations we must respond to, which is ambiguous about its intentions, and which is real and important beyond all else. Our dwelling within Mystery is both menacing and promising, a relationship of exceeding darkness and undeserved light. In this situation with this awareness we do a distinctively human thing. We gather together and tell stories of God to calm our terror and hold our hope on high.[121]

The life of faith will draw us all through dark valleys and terrifying terrain. When God withdraws, we need a community that keeps talking

about God until once again our vision clears and we can again see for ourselves.

In the therapeutic encounter, one does not meet in order to share stories of God or learn to recognize Jesus as the mediating reality in our relationships. One meets, rather, to gain the knowledge and insights as to
learn how to live independently. The therapeutic places the self, not God,
as the lens through which we view all relationships. Its focus is on individualism, not community. It is knowledge, not love, which becomes our
anchor. I know that there are counselors who refer to God, and even
include prayer in their sessions. Their epistemology, however, comes from
the secular realm and is based on systems of knowledge, not faith. The
truth is that psychology does not have the tools, language, or perceptual
framework to understand either a godly person or the spiritual life. As the
Catholic priest, Marko Rupnik, observed:

> A Gnosticism with psychological tendencies is easily recognized
> because people "affected" by it, finding themselves faced with an
> authentically lived spiritual life, lack the precise epistemological
> tools to know and judge such a life. It is because of a psycholog-
> ical gnosticism that the deeds of some holy lives are judged as
> having nothing to say to the world and at best, should only be
> shown as "episodes" in the showcase of history. Those who judge
> lack the relational dimension of love as a sphere in which to
> understand gestures, mentality, and spiritual practices. It hap-
> pens, therefore, that even the most loving gesture, driven by an
> intimate knowledge of the word of God and truly undertaken as
> a free act, comes to be judged by psychological gnosticism as a
> violence to oneself, as a religious fanaticism, etc.[122]

From within a therapeutic mindset, the saint will be seen as a fool,
signs of grace will be interpreted as pathology, and a transcendent life will
be construed as the inability to perceive the needs of the self. Because of
its different approach in understanding, psychology will never be able to
either form a saint or understand one.

At one time, relationships and community had provided the lens through which we came to an understanding of ourselves and through which we were formed and transformed: "As iron sharpens iron, so one man sharpens another (Proverbs 27:17).   C. S. Lewis observed, "As soon as we are fully conscious we discover loneliness. We need others physically, emotionally, intellectually; we need them if we are to know anything, even ourselves."[123] As the sociologists in the bestseller *Habits of the Heart* noted, "We find ourselves not independently of other people and institutions but through them. We never get to the bottom of our selves on our own. We discover who we are face to face and side by side with others in work, love, and learning.[124]

All human encounters are capable of questioning, testing, challenging, and revealing us to ourselves, and all human encounters have the potential for being moments of epiphany where we recognize the Christ-life that plays in life around us. No system of knowledge can replace our need for relationships, which can aid us in our struggle into health. We need fewer professionals and more spiritual friends.

Unfortunately, as Daniel Yankelovich noted, in a society seeking self-fulfillment, the individuals in that society "do not see themselves as part and parcel of an ongoing social world, progressively discovering themselves in relation to their work, their friends, families and the larger society. Rather, they are isolated—some might say existential—units, related intimately only to their own psyches."[125] We have created the idea of a psychological self that can be analyzed and understood in a vacuum separated from society, from history, and from family, religious, and friendship groups. The "true self" that we try to discover in isolation, however, can be as false as the "false selves" we jettisoned in order to live what we thought would be an examined life. The self that can find and understand itself in isolation is an illusion.

Rather than allowing community (or lack thereof) as the means whereby we are revealed, the therapeutic encounter is like a retreat from life where we can take time out to conceptualize, analyze, and create paradigms and constructs that explain our lives to us. When I first went to a therapist, I thought I had finally found the perfect relationship. I was delighted to be able to talk about myself uninterrupted with nobody from my life there to challenge my stories. Never before in my life had I been in a space where it was all right to talk about me and me alone. Never before had I been in a relationship where the other person existed to listen to me and me alone. I didn't have to feel embarrassed over what I revealed because I knew I would never meet the therapist in my real life. I liked paying at the end because that made it a relationship with very clear boundaries; he was paid to listen to me, so I was in control. What the therapy session was not about, then, was how I lived my real life. It set up an unreal clinical environment. In that sterile environment, I quickly realized how easy and tempting it would be to create a version of my life that was rationalized and a deceptive illusion. There were no reality checks in place. That therapeutic encounter was seductive and tempting precisely because it had no relationship to real life.

The therapeutic and its insistent orientation towards the personal self have destroyed the webs of relationships and networks of communities that once mediated our sense of self to us. We, however, were not thus freed from dependence on others; we just became dependent on therapists. The sociologist Frank Furedi has observed that "Therapeutics creates a demand for itself by continually compromising the informal networks of support that people rely on to negotiate the challenges of daily life."[126] He further noted, "As our dependence on informal relations diminishes so our subservience to the professional grows. The weakening of informal relations is proportional to the growing power of therapeutic ones."[127]

Not only does the therapeutic emphasize the needs of the individual over the life of the community, but it actually causes us to become suspicious of all our private relationships. Christopher Lasch has observed that the therapeutic, arising out of "dissatisfaction with the quality of personal relations" has in turn advised people "not to make too large an investment in love and friendship, to avoid excessive dependence on others, and to live for the moment—the very conditions that created the crisis of personal relations in the first place."[128] Families have become the place where we are taught to look for the toxic roots of all our unhappiness. Mutual interdependence has been replaced by self-reliance. Labels like "relationship addiction," "co-dependency," and "relational dependence" have instilled a fear in us of getting too close to each other. We are being driven from all potential intimacy.

The therapeutic makes much of the unencumbered self, the fully individuated self, and the autonomous self. It posits a self freed from the institutions, society, and the cultures that have traditionally been seen to form the individual. Relationships, commitments, and obligations, are all being made to sub-serve the self. The sociologist Frank Furedi further noted, "One of the direct consequences of the professionalisation of relationships is to diminish our sense of dependency on one another. Professional intervention not only complicates relationships, but also undermines the ability of people to communicate and interact with one another. This is not an accidental outcome of the therapeutic imperative. Contemporary therapeutic culture is distinctly hostile to the informal networks that bind people together."[129]

I find it ironic that in a religion where love is given as its end, fulfillment, and the sign of its genuineness, those who are supposed to lead us into its reality now go off to pastoral counseling seminars where they learn about appropriate boundaries, safe distance, professionalism, and dispassionate involvement. I remember the shock I felt when I talked to a minister who had just attended one of those seminars and been persuaded by its seeming wisdom. Apparently, according to what he had just been taught, distance helps to keep the lines of authority secure. The necessary transference supposedly requires an "ideal" or authority figure, not someone who comes alongside and is vulnerable and open; closeness or attachment would cause "interference." The art of spiritual direction had given way to active listening. Apparently, it was thought, in the right environment of being listened to, insights could arise from our own depths. I could not help but feel that, in contrast to spiritual direction, it could also just be a case of inner emptiness meeting more emptiness.

The apostle Paul is the New Testament character who gives us the model for pastoral ministry. He does not seem to have heard of dispassionate involvement. About his Jewish brothers, he wrote, "I have great sorrow and unceasing anguish in my heart. For I could wish that I myself were cursed and cut off from Christ for the sake of my brothers" (Romans 9:2). He allowed all his personal boundaries to be destroyed: "I face daily the pressure of my concern for all the churches. Who is weak, and I do not feel weak? Who is led into sin, and I do not inwardly burn?" (2 Corinthians 11:28). Paul didn't seem to believe in the need for safe distance—"We were gentle among you, like a mother caring for her children. We loved you so much that we were delighted to share with you not only the gospel of God but our lives as well, because you had become so dear to us" (1 Thessalonians 2:7, 8). He saw no need to restrain his emotions: "For I wrote you out of great distress and anguish of heart and with many tears, not to grieve you but to let you know the depth of my love for you" (2 Corinthians 2:4). He had no seeming fear of "over-involvement." From his letters to Timothy and in his attempts to have Onesimus re-instated, we know his willingness to get deeply and intimately involved in people's lives. Paul also seemed unafraid of vulnerability; he exposed his weaknesses and freely admitted to having not yet "made it." Paul, in other words, lived in direct contradiction to much of what our ministers are now learning in their pastoral counseling seminars.

In contrast to the stance of authority, professionalism, and safe boundaries, the Gospel, I believe, calls us to vulnerability and transparency. We are told that a lamp is not hid under a bowl, so "in the same way, let your light shine before men" (Matthew 5:16). Paul Tillich wrote, "The saint is a saint not because he is good, but because he is transparent for something that is larger than he is." In the same vein, Frank Laubach asked, "God, what is man's best gift to mankind? To be beautiful of soul and then let people see into your soul." God's Light is revealed through vulnerability and openness.

If the Christian church would live out the implications of its message, then it would exist as a condemnation and an alternative to our modern

society which focuses on individualism, and which has developed a narcissistic preoccupation with the needs of the individual self. The only form
of love the therapeutic can help us with is self-love. And yet self-love is
what Maximus the Confessor called the "mother of the passions" because
of the way it "distorts our desires and turns them into vices."[130] Once self-
love has infected our vision then a world that should induce worship, ado-
ration, and bring us into relationship only serves as a backdrop against
which we see only ourselves reflected. Our health is not evidenced by our
ability to love ourselves but rather with our ability to love our neighbor.

The therapeutic can offer us a lot of information about our neighbor,
but in the end it cannot teach us how to love our neighbor. Love is another
realm for which psychology has no keys. I found it significant that in
Dante's *Divine Comedy*, Virgil (as representing Reason), could guide Dante
through hell, but to move on towards heaven, Beatrice (representing
Love), had to take over as guide. At some point, knowledge and love have
to take separate paths.

Early Christianity became a powerful force because of the capacity for
love that it demonstrated. Jesus initiated a way of community that was to
bring a foretaste of eternity here in our midst. The book of Acts claimed,
"The multitude of those who believed were of one heart and one soul"
(Acts 4:32, NKJV). The world observed—"My, how they loved each
other"—and then responded to the appeal of that love.

Christianity offers us a vision, a way of being in community that
allows love to be brought into a dark world. It has given us a story that
can unite us and turn us into pilgrims who are becoming the people of
God. We have preferred sex and professionalism. We live in a world where
we tell our deepest secrets and reveal our souls to paid professionals, and
then think we need to sleep with everyone else we are attracted to. Under
those conditions, our souls have no hope but to shrivel and die.

Self-Love versus Accepting Love

WE LIVE IN A CULTURE where everyone is working hard at learning to love themselves. It reminds me of the efforts of Sisyphus. Sisyphus was the mythological figure who was condemned to endlessly rolling a stone up a hill; every time he neared the top, that stone would again roll back down, requiring him to commence his efforts yet again. I, like Sisyphus, would often have days when I felt pretty good about myself; in fact, on those days, my self-image would begin to inflate like a balloon that was being dangerously filled with too much air. Then life itself would prick that balloon. That new self-love could never withstand the onslaught of reality as each day would bring new failures, new opportunities to acknowledge inadequacies, new recognition of guilt, and new embarrassment, with life itself causing that supposedly necessary self-love to elude one as certainly as Sisyphus's stone would once again roll away. Self-esteem is obviously not a rock to stand on—it is, rather, an elusive stone that constantly slips away.

We live in an age when low self-esteem has been cited as the cause of almost every societal problem. In his book The *Psychology of Self-Esteem,* the author Nathaniel Branden wrote, "I cannot think of a single psychological problem—from anxiety and depression, to fear of intimacy or of success, to spouse battery or child molestation that is not traceable to the problem of poor self-esteem".[131] The need for self-esteem, self-acceptance, and self-love has become a modern cultural myth that is rarely challenged. It has caused one psychologist to write, "Recently a powerful movement has emerged in the field of mental health and education. The core, nucleus, and compelling force in this movement is the construct of self-esteem."[132] Each age has its dominant myths that are formative to the construction of personal identity; the construct of self-esteem has become crucial to the way we in the modern world think about ourselves.

Our supposed need for self-esteem has even made it into the political arena, which has only furthered awareness of its message. California assemblyman John Vasconcellos was instrumental, in 1986, in getting

Resolution 65 passed in the California Legislature, which mandated that a task force be established to find effective means to enhance the self-esteem of all Californians. Resolution 65 stated: "The epidemics of violence, drug abuse, teen pregnancy, child abuse, chronic welfare dependency, and educational failure threaten to engulf our society, and it appears that self-esteem may be our best hope for a preventive vaccine to develop an immunity to these and other self-destructive behaviors."[133]

Vasconcellos also stated, "It is becoming more evident that the development of healthy self-esteem may, as well, be the missing piece of the puzzle of our otherwise seemingly intractable social problems such as violence, alcohol and drug abuse, teenage pregnancy, a child's learning, a disabled person's capacity to become self-sufficient, and others."[134]

The psychologist Branden had established self-esteem as one of our basic needs; he regarded it as "the single most powerful force in our existence… the way we feel about ourselves affects virtually every aspect of our existence: work, love, sex, interpersonal relationships of every kind."[135] If self-esteem is truly a basic need, then perhaps that is why J.M. Brooks, the Executive Secretary of the California School Boards Association, felt justified in saying, "Sure, it's vital to teach Johnny and Mary Lou to read and write and think and compute, but if they don't learn to love themselves and each other, the rest isn't worth anything."[136]

Since psychology is supposed to be a science, it is of interest noting the studies undertaken in an attempt to validate the already previously held beliefs in self-esteem. In an attempt to justify the push for self-esteem that it had already mandated into legislation, California, in 1987, put in place a means of testing. What one of the key authors of the resulting report had to admit was that the expected association between low self-esteem and social problems could not be found. What had to be admitted, instead, was that "the association between self-esteem and its expected consequences are mixed, insignificant, or absent."

That failure to find a link between self-esteem and behavior did not, however, diminish the momentum of the self-esteem movement; after all, the idea had always been based less on fact than on blind faith. Other tests around the country were also administered in an attempt to prove what psychologists had already decided to believe in. They, too, were disappointing. Research among US college students, for example, showed that during the period when self-esteem rose, their SAT scores actually declined.[138] A social scientist, Dr Roy Baumeiser, did research that found that not only were people with low self-esteem not prone to aggressiveness, as had the prophets of the self-esteem movement claimed, but acts of violence were most likely to be committed by those who had a high opinion of themselves: "Conceited, self-important individuals turn nasty towards those who puncture their bubbles of self-love."[139] In addition, a major study done in Britain amongst 15,000 school children found, "Youngsters with high self-esteem were more likely to take illicit drugs than those whose confidence was low,"[140] and that "it is confident children who are more likely to be racists, to bully others and to engage in drunk driving and speeding."[141] The author of the British report actually likened the enormous therapeutic industry spawned by the self-esteem movement to the marketing of snake oil.

What the self-esteem movement has managed to do is blind us to what the Bible actually says about how we should view ourselves. The Bible teaches us how to die to self, not how to love ourselves, but that has not stopped those who ravage the Bible looking for proof texts to re-enforce already held views from finding one lonely verse to aid in the self-esteem movement—the command of Jesus to "love your neighbor as yourself" (Matthew 22:39). There are those who take that verse as a Biblical injunction commanding us to love ourselves. That always seemed to me like a twisted way to pervert what the gospel says in order to get back to what I and the rest of humanity are most engrossed in: self-love. We all naturally spend most of our time, energy, money, and attention on ourselves, so when the gospel tells me to accord the same for my neighbor, it seems strange to see the verse turned into a justification for more self-love.

It was Erich Fromm who presented us with the thesis that we needed to seek our own happiness first, after which love of neighbor would flow out as a "phenomenon of abundance." What Fromm did not want to recognize is that self-love is boundless—it has no determined boundaries or limits. It seems to only grow the more it is nurtured.

Living in a culture that emphasizes the need for me to accept myself, love myself, and forgive myself, it was with great delight indeed that I read my Bible and discovered that there, finally, was one book that never told me I had to love, accept, or forgive myself. What it told me, instead, was that to the degree I lived in openness before God I would be forgiven and loved and accepted in spite of it all. What a relief that was. Spiritual health, I discovered, unlike psychological health, is not a place where I think well of myself, but rather a place the gospel leads me into where I don't have to spend much time thinking of myself at all. In the words of Simone Weil, "It is not up to me to think of myself. It is up to me to think of God. And it is up to God to think of me." True religion turns me out of myself.

True Christianity is not a vehicle designed to help us feel better about ourselves; it teaches us what to do when we realize that we don't feel very good about ourselves. In Chapter 1, I mentioned the observation by William James that all religions meet at that point where we recognize that there is something wrong within us; there is an unease that lies in the heart of our being. Karen Armstrong has rightly observed that "a deep-rooted anxiety is part of the human condition: this is not neurotic, because it is ineradicable and no therapy can take it away."[142] True religion meets us at that place of our anxiety or unease.

At one time, we might have called that unease "guilt." That is a terminology, however, that is no longer considered acceptable, for the therapeutic has given us a horror of the concept of guilt. Guilt implies some external measurement that we have not lived up to. That is why, in the past, it was a mechanism that was seen as necessary, it being the means whereby we were socialized into the demands of a society. Now, however, guilt is seen as a sign of personal pathology, something that should be gotten rid of or else avoided at all costs. When the subjective, autonomous self has ceased to define itself by anything outside of itself, then guilt is irrelevant; it only gets in the way of feelings of self-esteem.

The therapeutic exists as a contradiction; it offers us a supposed non-judgmental space where we will know complete acceptance, but in order for us to acknowledge our need for its services, it has to convince us that we have problems and are unacceptable in our current state. The therapeutic is big business, constantly needing to expand its client base to find a market for its product. It does that by filling us with unrealistic goals, by creating diseases, and by pathologizing the details of normal life. By presenting us with ever more unrealistic notions of what we should be and how we should feel, it, itself, creates a sense of anxiety and unrest as we fall short of its unrealistic expectations. The therapeutic sells its diseases as certainly as it sells its supposed cures; anxiety, depression, shyness, hyperactivity, and sexual dysfunction all must be "sold" before we will believe in the need for help. In the Presidential Address to the American Psychological Association, the new president, Nicolas Cummings, acknowledged the problem when he noted, "It may be that the mental health movement has promised the American people a freedom from anxiety that is neither possible nor realistic, resulting in an expectation that we have a right to feel good. We may never know to what extent we ourselves have contributed to the steep rise in alcohol consumption and the almost universal reliance by physicians on the tranquilizer."[143]

Not only has the therapeutic not managed to eradicate our feelings of there being something wrong with us as we now stand, but they are destroying the frameworks of understanding that brought solace and release. In freeing us from traditional belief systems and telling us that we alone are responsible for our lives, our happiness, and our success, the therapeutic has placed a burden on us that may be even heavier to bear than those of the religious structures that they have replaced. At least in religion, God, karma, the devil, predestination, and fate all acknowledged that life was not all our responsibility. Now, as one theoretician for the new therapies wrote, "Each of us is running her or his own life.... Once we accept responsibility for choosing our lives, everything is different. We have the power. We decide. We are in control.... If I choose everything, and if there are no accidents, then life becomes a soluble puzzle."[144]

What happens if we fail, or are not happy, fulfilled, realizing our

potential, self-aware, released from all repression, and expressing ourselves fully? Eliminating guilt in order to produce self-esteem has not eliminated our unease. There will always be times in life when we really do not
feel that good about ourselves, and if we never know that feeling, we may
be a sociopath rather than healthy.

I can sympathize with our modern abhorrence for the concept of
guilt. There wasn't anything very healthy about the amount of guilt we
carried around in the strict religious background of my youth. If the self-
esteem movement exists at one end of a spectrum, telling me how to view
myself, then at the other end was the guilt-ridden religion of my background. It was Dietrich Bonhoeffer who helped me understand why I
don't feel good about myself.

I was raised thinking that guilt was God's gift to me; if the burden of
guilt began to slip, then the church was ready to add a lot more. Bonhoeffer
helped me understand, by means of the creation story, what guilt really is.
What Bonhoeffer clarified was that "conscience is not the voice of God to
sinful man; it is man's defense against it."[145] Adam's attempt to assert himself, to eat the forbidden fruit with its offered self-godhead, had a strange
result; he looked and saw that he was naked. He discovered shame, and
his conscience was born. God did not tell Adam he was naked; Adam discovered it when he separated himself from God. As Bonhoeffer wrote,
"Here, distant from God, man plays the judge himself and just by this
means he escapes God's judgment."[146] Ever since the fall, guilt has been a
defense mechanism; by inflicting guilt on ourselves, by playing the role of
God to ourselves, we manage to avoid a confrontation with the God who
is Other. It is the nature of our fallen state that what we want and need
most—restored relationship that would free us from the burden of guilt—
is what we always hide from. Adam, and all of his children ever since, have
found themselves caught between two urges—the urge to respond to the
voice of God saying, "Adam, where are you?" and the competing voice of
our guilty conscience telling us we're naked, run and hide.

God did not cut off communication with Adam. God searched and
called out for him. Adam, however, found he had lost his ability to com-

municate with God; when he opened his mouth, only excuses and rationalizations came out. Adam could not see God's searching and calling as grace. As Bonhoeffer noted, "Adam sees this grace only as hate, as wrath, and this wrath kindles his own hate, his rebellion, his will to escape from God."[147] Once Adam could only experience God in negative terms then the separation between them was complete, and Adam had to leave the garden where he had lived in God's Presence.

When we allow the therapeutic to help us love, accept, and forgive ourselves, we are just extending the effects of the fall. We are providing grace to ourselves on human terms. Whereas conscience and guilt are the effects of man, in separation from God, playing the role of judge of himself, the obverse can also be true; in attempting to make ourselves feel good on our own terms, we are playing the role of God in extending grace to ourselves.

The philosopher Alfred North Whitehead wrote, "Religion is the transition from God the Void to God the Enemy, and from God the Enemy to God the Companion." Whether we ever know God as companion depends on what we do when we acknowledge God as Other, and standing against that Otherness, we find that our natural human response is to turn God into a projection of our fear and guilt and thus name Him our enemy. Our freedom from guilt comes not from self-imposed grace, but rather, from recognizing that it is our own projected guilt that would turn God into a wrathful, vengeful enemy. As Pascal wrote, "Jesus Christ comes to tell men that they have no enemies but themselves." In discovering God as companion, we no longer have to attempt to love, accept, or forgive ourselves. We live, rather, surrounded by love, acceptance, and forgiveness.

However, just because grace relieves us of guilt does not mean that it helps us feel good about ourselves. On the contrary, when the Old Testament characters were confronted by the holy, they would fall prostrate, overcome by the awareness of their shortcomings and inadequacies. The purpose of the new covenant is not to eliminate self-awareness or a sense of sin, but to invite us, in spite of it all, to "draw near to God with a sincere heart in full assurance of faith, having our hearts sprinkled to cleanse us from a guilty conscience" (Hebrews 10:22). A way was made available to draw near to God in spite of it all. It, however, is predicated on a life of repentance and humility. Repentance is the giving up of our Adam-like propensity to live according to our own understanding (and supported in our independence by means of excuses, rationalizations, and projections of blame) in order to see and define ourselves according to the life of God. Humility is the giving up of our inflated views of ourselves in order to live in the truth of ourselves as revealed by God.

There is an interesting progression in the Bible. In Paul's early letters, he refers to himself as the least of the Apostles. By the middle letters, he refers to himself as the least of the brethren. By the last letters, he refers to himself as the chiefest of sinners. That is not the progression of someone with low self-esteem or caught backsliding. That is the progression of someone with the courage and trust to stand increasingly revealed and naked before that radiant Light. The repentant life does not leave us feeling good about ourselves. Not only that, but we develop a real suspicion of our motives and of what actually lies within our hearts. However, as each deepening layer of our being is penetrated and revealed, it is God who has thereby been allowed to come ever nearer.

The Light of God does reveal us in a way that can shatter self-esteem. Saint Augustine noted, "If thou shouldst say, 'It is enough, I have reached perfection', all is lost. For it is the function of perfection to make one know one's imperfection." As C.S. Lewis wrote, "It is when we notice the dirt that God is most present in us: it is the very sign of His presence." Father Danielou further observed, "The sense of sin is the measure of a soul's awareness of God." Those who have no sense of sin in their lives are not the righteous; they are those who are either distanced from God or have so hardened their hearts that the reality of God can no longer penetrate. They can also, like the Pharisees, often be the most religious people of all.

The image of Light is one of the predominant images in the Bible, with good reason. Light is that which reveals. Light that is too bright, as in the case of the sun, cannot be apprehended directly, but it will light up and reveal all that lies in its path. But that is not all that the sun's light does. As it lights up the world, the sun's rays are also bringing the warmth and life-giving properties that allow for life and growth. A tree planted in the shade can hide from the light, but it will also never grow. In a similar way, by allowing the Divine Light near enough to reveal our inner life, we are also allowing its life-giving nature to be brought to bear on our lives.

As I went back through history, I realized that one of the great differences between saints and sinners lies in the fact that saints were people who didn't mind being known as sinners. The closer we get to the Light, the more we will lose our ability to say, "I can love myself, I can accept myself, I can forgive myself." However, we will also lose our guilt, anxiety, and alienation because we will have stopped being God to ourselves.

So if I have claimed that living in the Light does not allow me to feel good about myself then what is the difference between that state and the curse of guilt that we, as Adam's children, carry within ourselves? Perhaps the difference is best illustrated by a children's story.

There is a story I used to read to our children that is so true I almost think it should be in the Bible. It is the story of the sun and the wind making a wager as to who was the strongest. They decide to test it out on a traveler coming down the road. It was decided that whoever could get the traveler to remove his coat was the strongest. The wind went first. He blew his gusts with all his might and power. It was impressive, but the traveler just clutched his coat ever more firmly about himself. Then it was the turn of the sun. The sun sent down some gentle rays of warmth and the coat was soon off.

The story illustrates the two opposing forces within the church. Paul Tournier wrote, "Religion may liberate or suppress; it may increase guilt or remove guilt."[148] Every individual that attempts to turn to God will at some point know the force of that wind, and will only progress in spiritual health to the degree that they are able to differentiate the gentle rays of the sun from the oppressive power of the wind. Whether we are bowed and weighed down or freed depends on which force we respond to. The great deception of the wind lies in the fact that its purposes seem to be the same as that of the sun (after all, they were both asking for the same thing: the removal of the coat). The difference between the wind and the sun is the difference between the revelatory and the condemnatory. One leaves us wanting to discard what is heavy and bogging us down, and the other leaves us clutching and hiding under the very burdens we should be releasing.

It is interesting reading the story of Jesus' temptation in the wilderness and realizing that the devil could quote Scripture and actually asked of Jesus the same things He eventually did do (Jesus did miraculously create bread, He was miraculously rescued when about to be pushed off a cliff, and He did claim ownership of a Kingdom). As in the story of the sun and the wind, however, what Jesus had to discern before He could begin His ministry was not what was being asked but who was doing the asking. A third-world minister articulated the difference by saying, "If you feel uneasy or pushed, it's the Devil. Jesus leads, He never pushes. He gives His peace."[149] More important than the act (taking off the overcoat) is the ability to discern exactly whom one is responding to. Respond to the wind and we will become huddled inward, clutching our lives ever more firmly to ourselves, bowed down by our guilt and unease. We will hide ourselves rather than removing what weighs us down, and in our attempts to hide, we will inevitably turn God into a projection of our own inner darkness.

The wind is in full evidence in our churches and culture as many are trying to create moral societies out of guilt, law and political force. Cicero once said, "The strictest right is the greatest wrong." Guilt-induced devotion is more likely to produce fear, obsessions, and neurotic behavior than the charity and freedom that the gospel draws us towards. The removal of the offensive coat by force is not going to help if one has not learned to experience the warmth and drawing power of the Light; it will only leave one shivering in the cold.

The Bible depicts Satan as a Bible-quoting reality who seems to have the purposes of God taken to heart. The accuser coming with the full force of the wind will attempt to force us to bend under the weight of our seeing, will speak of God's wrath, will try to convince us of the need to make things right in our power, will speak of the heavy yoke God will consequently place upon us. It is for us to persist in the openness and stillness that allows us to discern the sun's rays in spite of the blowing force of the wind. The Light will reveal all that is wrong within, but if we have the courage to keep standing in the Light in spite of what it reveals, we will realize that what God reveals is what He wants to release us from. What we hide from God is what we become bound by. All will be well if we can bear seeing.

I wonder if all this talk of self-esteem, self-love, self-worth, and self-acceptance is a reaction to religious backgrounds that have burdened people with feelings of guilt and judgment. A lot of religion has also turned self-denial into self-rejection and self-hatred. However, if the Bible doesn't teach me to love myself, it also doesn't teach me to hate myself. What it does teach me is how to keep my ever-needy, all-consuming, ever-demanding self from filling the entire vista of my awareness so that I can slowly become aware of what actually lies beyond my self. What it does do is help me re-focus my attention off of myself to the wonder of a grace-filled universe. What it does teach me is how to become a being who can love.

Having been critical of our focus on self-esteem and self-love, I now have to add that our salvation also includes the healing of our self-image, and when that happens, we may eventually end up loving ourselves. Bernard of Clairvaux, a Cistercian monk from the twelfth century, is the best guide in explaining how that happens.

Bernard of Clairvaux wrote about how love grows in four stages.[150] We all, he claims, start out as beings who love ourselves for the sake of ourselves. We are the center of our own universe. To remain there is disastrous, both for us and for the people who have to live with us. Allow our self-love to become pierced by an awakened awareness of God and His love, however, and we may begin to love God—for the sake of ourselves. It is a self-centered, mercenary kind of love; we may not be easier to live with, but at least it is a stage of hope. The third stage comes by allowing our awareness and knowledge of God to continue to grow. Allow our awareness of God's goodness, love, and perfect attributes to grow and there may come a time when we begin to love God for Himself alone. That, however, is still not the end of the journey into love. Continue to pursue God and it is almost inevitable that at some point one will find oneself asking, like the Psalmist, "What is man that you are so mindful of him?" In the Light of God, we become aware of our eternal significance, of the cosmic reverberations of our life and choices, and of the high value of our life before God. With that awareness, we arrive at that fourth stage, the place where we love ourselves for the sake of God. We begin to love ourselves with an attitude of gratitude to God for the gift of our life.

The self-love that faith draws us into, however, has little in common with the self-esteem movement. The problem with allowing the therapeutic industry to teach us self-love and self-acceptance is that it will teach us to love and accept precisely what we should not love and accept in ourselves, and by applying that self-love to the beginning of the spiritual journey, it will blind us to awareness of what actually lies beyond ourselves.

Before the fall Adam and Eve "were both naked, and they felt no shame" (Genesis 2:25). Our innocence is gone; ever since our departure from Eden, we have not either individually or collectively felt good about ourselves. We have all fallen short of some sensed nebulous goal, and removing religion's external markers did not remove our sense of guilt. We just redefined it and then struggled with more amorphous feelings such as alienation, depression, unease, anxiety, and loneliness. In the end, we still ended up feeling lost. The human animal can only live with self-esteem when it has managed to blind or deceive itself.

The self-esteem movement has convinced us that it is necessary to love, accept, and forgive ourselves. That self-esteem is based on the very shaky foundation of belief that it is something that we can achieve and bestow on ourselves, rather than love and acceptance being gifts bestowed from an outside source that we need only to receive. As soon as we begin to work on our self-love, self-acceptance, and self-esteem, then we will no longer be open to the gifts that we are to receive, but rather, self-acceptance and self-esteem will become burdensome expectations that we will not be able to carry.

Wounds: Redemption versus Cure

I HAVE BECOME FOND of redemption stories. I suppose in a world where power spawns violent reaction, where evil spawns more evil, where vengeance, retribution, and justice are expected, where a gravitational pull seems to be taking our world on a downward spiral, it is so rare to see good arise out of evil that I always stop and marvel.

For a while, my favorite redemption story was that of Joseph. Joseph came from a family of twelve boys wherein he had somehow managed to assume a place of special importance. Not only was he the child of a favored wife, favored by his father, and the recipient of special clothing and attention, but also he received dreams that seemed to confirm his special nature. Needless to say, he was hated and resented by his brothers. One can almost find oneself sympathizing with the brothers who finally had enough of him and decided to sell him as a slave to the Egyptians.

Joseph, however, was a survivor. Able to pick himself up and make something of himself in Egypt, he again worked his way to a favored status in an important household, only to again be betrayed, this time by the wife in the very house where he had offered such stellar service. Thrown into prison, he was promptly forgotten. In that prison, however, he did not rot away as a victim or wallow in self-pity; instead, we are confronted with what was to become a recurrent phrase in the life of Joseph, "The Lord was with him." Under the Presence, he found the strength that allowed him to absorb all the evil inflicted on him. Again he began to rise in influence, first to a position that allowed him to serve his fellow prisoners, and then to a position where he could stand before the very Egyptians who had betrayed and misused him and, instead of retaliating, he could instead become the channel God used to warn the Egyptians of the impending famine, and also to inform them of the means whereby they could escape mass starvation. For me, however, the highlight of the story comes when, standing before the very family that had started the chain of evil in his life in the first place, Joseph found himself in a position where he could become the source of their salvation. The family that expected vengeance instead heard Joseph say, "And now, do not be distressed and do not be angry with yourselves for selling me here, because it was to save lives that God sent me ahead of you" (Genesis 45:5). The story of Joseph may have started out as a story of abuse and betrayal, but Joseph had come to see it all, even the evil, as the vehicle of God's grace. Joseph, under the Presence, had allowed all the evil in his life to get turned into a redemption story.

A more modern redemption story is offered in the life of Harriet Beecher Stowe. Harriet was the mother of seven children, of whom the most beautiful and most loved died of cholera in 1849. Harriet believed that she could only be consoled if some good could come out of the tragedy, and wrote, "It was at his dying bed and at his grave that I learned what a poor slave mother may feel when her child is torn away from her...I felt I could never be consoled...unless this crushing of my own heart might enable me to work out some good to others."[151]

As a way of working through her own sorrow, Harriet began to write *Uncle Tom's Cabin*. It was the pain of personal loss that allowed Harriet to say, "I write with my heart's blood."[152] In allowing grace to take a tragedy and buy it back from the side of evil, an event that had broken her heart got turned into a life-giving event instead. Her book had a phenomenal impact on a slave-owning society, and it caused Lincoln to later refer to her, when he met her, as the little lady who started the Great War.

I think redemption is best illustrated by looking at the genealogy of Jesus as outlined in Matthew's gospel. In the genealogy, we find Judah and Tamar, the couple who gave us the story of prostitution, incest, and betrayal. Then there was Rahab, the prostitute from Jericho. God had warned the Israelites to have nothing to do with the Moabites, as they were a people living under His judgment. It is therefore surprising to find Ruth the Moabitess in the genealogy. David had many children, but it was Solomon, the product of a murderous and adulterous relationship, who made it into the lineage. Judah had a history of faithless, rebellious kings. They, not the priestly line of Levi, are in the lineage. It is as though all that was worst in Israel's history was gathered up and absorbed to become the seed that got turned around and brought forth good. It is a story of redemption.

When bad things happen to people, there seems to be a stock number of questions that arise. However, when the disciples questioned Jesus about a man's blindness, wondering who or what had caused it, Jesus' replied, "This happened so that the work of God might be displayed in his life" (John 9:3). Basically, Jesus reduced the acceptable questions to ask over evil, tragedy, and ill fortune down to one: "What can God do with this?" God is in the business of taking evil and then turning it into a redemption story.

Evil, however, does not naturally get turned into a redemption story. In a world where the kingdom of God does not yet reign, the opposite usually happens—evil starts a chain of action and reaction that begets even more evil. In order for redemption to take place, we, like Joseph, will have to learn how to see God's Presence with us when the bad happens.

A Christian church that becomes focused on using people's gifts and best efforts misses its own message. God is interested in using our sins, our brokenness, and our wounds. A church that is focused on using its best talents and capabilities will glorify man; God uses those who acknowledge their brokenness, their poverty, and their need. God brings good out of it all in order to bring glory to Himself.

Our wounds are important to God; they are the place where God's grace can be made evident. A church that cannot teach us to meet God in our brokenness is going to become a large (but probably efficient and seemingly effective) human project. I remember the time when I was sinking deeper and deeper into a black hole of increasing darkness. By coincidence, it happened to also be the time when the minister of the church I had been attending got into the pulpit to give a testimony as to his fight with depression, which had caused him to seek a therapist. By inference, it was the therapist, not God, who was the source of healing. When my marriage seemed to have come to an end, the new president of the religious college that we had been financially supporting gave a public lecture wherein he gave a testimony as to how counseling had been necessary to save his marriage. I didn't hear any reference as to whether God had been there for him to guide him through his marital difficulties. When I withdrew our financial support, the school contacted me to explain how necessary the school was for training people who could evangelize the world. I, however, figured that if God was no longer a real and present help in the lives of our religious leaders, then we probably should not export our emptiness overseas.

Disillusioned, I found a charismatic church where people claimed to have experiences of God. What I discovered was that I had entered an unholy mess where division, bitterness, and rivalry prevailed. It was the minister who became the scapegoat for all that animosity, and eventually he was forced to leave. The last time I talked to him, his marriage had broken up, he was emotionally destroyed, and he gave me a testimony to the comfort and release he was now finding in therapy. Where was the God of those experiences? I think many of our problems in the church arise out of our mistaken belief that God wants us to serve Him, rather than accepting God's revelation in Jesus that He came to serve and save man. Our attempts to serve God out of our strengths will produce results that glorify man. However, it is rather in our need, dependence, and insufficiency that the Light of God is given a chance to shine into a dark world.

I remember the time I retreated to my special chair, ready for one more fall into a pit of darkness. There seemed to be something so humiliating about being able to weave seamless webs of self-understanding around the darkness, know the root causes, articulate exactly what triggered it, but still be unable to stop those deep falls. As I curled up in my chair, ready for the hard work of building up the mental defenses that would keep that dark from crushing me, I stopped short. For the first time in my life, I had the courage to admit what I could never have admitted before: I admitted to myself that life was never going to be fixed or made safe. As long as I lived, I knew that life, for me, was going to hurt.

With that admission, I suddenly remembered a scene from one of Thornton Wilder's plays based on the story in John 5 about the healing waters of Bethesda. Wilder depicted a physician, deep in melancholy, waiting for the waters to be stirred so that he could be healed. When the opportunity finally came, however, he found his way blocked by an angel telling him that healing was not for him. As he left the pool to be met by those needing help—only he seemed capable of helping them—it was with the words of the angel ringing in his ears: "Without your wounds where would your power be? It is your melancholy that makes your low voice tremble into the hearts of men and women. The very angels themselves cannot persuade the wretched and blundering children on earth as can one human being broken on the wheels of living. In Love's service, only wounded soldiers can serve. Physician, draw back."

By means of the play, I could see my own life reflected. I suddenly had the outrageous thought that if somebody could come and remove the broken and wounded places in my life, I wouldn't be able to give them up; too much good had arisen because of them. I actually started to feel grateful for the bad things that had happened in my life.

When I started reading the lives and works of people who had managed to live close to God, I began to notice something strange; they actually thanked God for the bad things that had happened to them. I, at first, figured that was not natural or normal and therefore it could not be healthy. I, therefore, surprised even myself as I one day found myself thanking God for the bad things that had come into my life. What I eventually discovered was that "adjustment" and "coping" are not enough for God. God wants to take us to the place where the worst that has happened to us can be turned into a good that helps the greater community. I have discovered that once gratitude seeps in, the depressive game is up. It is the highs I've become suspicious of. The dark holes come with an air of trust, of expectancy, as I wonder what God will bring out of the dark this time.

Simone Weil wrote, "The extreme greatness of Christianity lies in the fact that it does not seek a supernatural cure for suffering, but a supernatural use of it." Our wounds are important. Helen Keller, blind and handicapped, wrote, "I thank God for my handicaps; for through them, I have found myself, my work, my God."[153] Solzhenitsyn said thank-you to prison for similar reasons. Dostoevsky asked to be made worthy of his suffering.

What the preceding people all had in common was the recognition that in their suffering, they were standing on hallowed ground. Their gifts to the world arose out of the worst that had happened to them. Whenever the church stands with us in our hour of need and attempts to help us outside of reference to God, then it is getting in the way of a good redemption story.

Robert Bly once wrote, "Where a man's wound is, that is where his genius will be. Wherever the wound appears in our psyche, that is exactly where we will give our major gift to the community." The question the modern church stumbles over is whether it is God or human knowledge and understanding that offers the best solution to the problems facing its suffering parishioners. The real apostasy of modern religion lies in the fact that we don't think there needs to be a choice. Ever since Benjamin Franklin uttered his famous phrase—"God helps those who help themselves"—his quip has become the motto for modern individualism. What is frightening is that according to a study quoted in *Harper's Magazine,* three quarters of all Americans think that Franklin's adage comes from the Bible.[154] We have tried to link God with our own self-sufficiency.

The Bible is a long story telling of how God does not help those who help themselves: He instead becomes their enemy (Isaiah 31:1; Isaiah 50:10, 11). What the Bible reveals is that it is those who have the faith to seek God, to struggle with God, and to wait for God that become the vehicles of God's redemption stories. In the Bible, it is those who "wait for the Lord" who please God. Human efficiency is never applauded in the Bible; God's favor rests with those who have learned to trust and wait on Him. The therapeutic may help us with adjustment, with understanding, with intervention, and with achieving self-sufficiency, but it will never bring us to a place of redemption, a place where God takes the worst that has happened to us and turns it into a gift that can help the greater community.[155]

Redemption belongs to the realm of ultimate things, that realm where we search for meaning, purpose, and significance. One psychologist, who argued against therapeutic dependence, noted, "The care provided by counselors may be comforting, at least for a while, but it has no answers to the riddles and hazards of our time."[156] Counseling may bring temporal relief, but it cannot help us ground our adversity in that realm of ultimate meaning. That same psychologist also observed how closely the worst that has been dealt us is intertwined with what makes us most unique, writing, "Achilles is unthinkable without his vulnerable heel, as is Lincoln without his anguish and depression, Van Gogh without his outbursts of passion and craziness, Patton without his impulsiveness, and Woody Allen without his neuroses. These lives each fit together and make sense."[157] In all his examples, what cannot be argued is that their uniqueness is indistinguishable from what could be termed their "problems."

A good modern-day redemption story can be seen in the life of Nelson Mandela. Mandela bore the brunt of the evil of apartheid, but rather than getting caught up in retaliation or retributive justice, he used the power of the victim's voice to urge forgiveness and reconciliation. What Mandela tried to bring about in his Truth and Reconciliation Commission could not have been initiated by anyone in a position of power; only someone who had to first forgive great wrongs could then advise others to do the same. We can all—Christian and non-Christian alike—recognize in Mandela a transcendent power at work; we can all see how forgiveness was superior to vengeance; we can recognize when we see a reality at work that is higher than our human instincts and passions, and yet we, ourselves, choose to take our own wounds to therapists where we seek understanding and justification for our small, ego-driven lives rather than search for the grace to live transcendent, redeemed lives.

There is something about the human animal that, if left to its own devices, will fritter away its life on superficialities unless it receives a wake-up call in the form of something that is initially received as a tragedy. Tragedy, however, if used well, can clear one's vision, put life back into perspective, and help one prioritize life in a way that brings meaning. Good tragedy should never be wasted; when God is brought in, it can be the window through which we get a glimpse into a higher, transcendent life.

There is an image in the Bible that has long sat in my mind, offering an important insight if only I could learn to comprehend it. It is the image of the resurrected Jesus still carrying His wounds. Resurrection did not erase His wounds. The wounds we inflicted on Jesus became the wounds by which we were healed. Jesus, in His resurrection body, still carried His wounds, the wounds becoming the means whereby He was recognized. It was His wounds that became the mark of His glory.

Our wounds are important. Somewhere between therapeutic attempts to "fix" our brokenness and the gospel's offer to redeem our brokenness exists a clue to all the difference of eternity.

Depression: Illness versus "The Shadow of Thy Hand"

LOOKING BACK, I realize that depression has been allowed to infect most of my existence. One of my earliest childhood memories is of walking down an empty field wishing that I could die. If someone would ask me to remember all my happy childhood memories, I would be able to come up with only a few. The rest of childhood seems lost behind a grey film of unhappiness. The teenage years are too painful to even want to remember. There are no happy memories there.

Having three children gave my life real meaning and purpose for a while. Watching their zest and delight in life helped me to see life through their eyes; it was infectious. But then they grew up and became independent. Life turned very dark.

As I spent more and more time in a favorite chair, my husband would complain and ask why I would deeply sigh and gasp for air. When reminded, I would realize that I had forgotten to breathe; the gasps and sighs were my body's way of regaining its balance. The physical just mirrored my inward state; it was as though there was something in me that couldn't breathe. Finally my body began to lose its ability to feel and I would have to consciously tell my facial muscles to move to chew its food. Our home became my fortress—its main purpose was to keep everyone out. I only went out when absolutely necessary, and only invited anyone in under the same conditions.

I did at one point overcome a lifelong obsession with keeping all people at a good, safe distance and went to talk to a minister. He recommended that I read a book on co-dependency, which suggested that my problem lay in looking for something outside of myself; I needed to learn to depend on myself, to center myself around myself. Since it had taken me an entire lifetime to get up the courage to reach out to someone, I knew that wasn't my problem. I had never depended on anyone but myself; it wasn't working. Furthermore, since I had gone to the minister looking for God, it seemed strange to have my attention deflected back onto myself. The minister also recommended a good therapist, so I dutifully made an appointment and started therapy. The therapist told me I was having a mid-life crisis. I felt insulted and quit therapy. I knew that what was wrong with me lay much deeper than that. I thought Mark Twain expressed it better when he said, "You don't know quite what it is you want, but it just fairly makes your heart ache you want it so."

To struggle with deep depression in our age is to discover how much pressure one is under to get rid of it. Apparently, we owe it to the people around us to be happy. I, however, had watched too many people diagnosed and then "cured" of depression by means of drugs and therapy to want anything of their cures; some loss of humanity always seemed to come with the cure. With depression, something more than just biology or chemistry or a physical state seemed to be involved.

It was in the ecstatic highs of poets like Rilke, and it was in entering the depths of our crises and despair with writers like Nietzsche, Sartre, and Kafka, that I felt our humanity was being stretched towards its greatness. I found it increasingly difficult believing in God among "happy" Christians. But in entering the dark, brooding struggles of existentialists like Beckett and Camus, I could believe in God: I felt one could almost see the silhouette of who it was they were struggling against. I didn't want easy answers or easy solutions. I wanted to be alive, not numbed, distracted, or medicated.

Cordelia Fine, a psychologist and researcher, wrote an excellent book called *a mind of its own,* wherein she reports the numerous research studies revealing the way the mind deceives us, blinds us, distorts truth, and warps perceptions so that our ego is kept from facing difficult truths. In fact, after finishing the book, it would be tempting to think that the main purpose of the mind is to keep us from having to face reality. Fine did say, however, that there was one "category of people who get unusually close to the truth about themselves and the world….These people are living testimony to the dangers of self-knowledge. They are the clinically depressed."[158] Depression, according to Fine, could be caused by an inability to live with illusion.

Often, our best decisions are based not on cold reason, but rather on images, stories, and intuitive insights. It was the surgeon Paul Brand who gave me an image and a story that helped clarify and then gave courage for the path I chose. Paul Brand was completing his surgical residency in 1946 when a surgical procedure called a prefrontal lobotomy was being perfected by a neurophysicist named Walter Freeman. Brand described the procedure as carried out by Freeman: "He used electroconvulsive therapy to stun the patient for a few minutes and chose as his surgical instrument an ice pick, the name "Uline Ice Company" clearly visible on its handle. He peeled back her right eyelid and slid the ice pick over the top of the eyeball. Meeting some resistance at the orbital plate, he punched through by tapping on the ice pick with a little hammer. Once inside the brain, he swung the instrument back and forth, shearing off neuronal pathways between the frontal lobes and the rest of the brain."[159]

Freeman, who performed five thousand lobotomies before he had to retire his ice pick, bragged about how the procedure could help depression. He wrote eloquently "about how mental patients were better off without so much brain function."[160] When drugs came on the market, replacing the need for his ice pick, Freeman dismissed them as a "chemical lobotomy," just a variation on what he had already been doing with his ice pick.

What the lobotomy revealed was how we humans have two channels by which we perceive pain. The cerebral cortex is responsible for a clear-cut message of pain. The frontal lobes, however, are where reflection, interpretation, and analytical thought can modify our perception of that pain. The frontal lobes are responsible for abstract thinking, creativity, judgment, insight, and all our higher functions that define what it means to be fully "human." However, by means of those higher functions, we can also know emotional states such as depression, anxiety, or deep suffering that have no physical source. That is why psychiatric intervention, which creates brain damage or dysfunction, actually can help. As the psychiatrist Peter Breggin noted, "Depression requires a relatively intact brain and mind."[161]

Another research psychologist, Daniel Gilbert, also noted how the frontal lobe was the last part of the human brain to be developed. What was affected by its development was the ability of the human animal to extend its existence in time. In the words of Gilbert, "The human being is the only animal that thinks about the future."[162] Our uniqueness can therefore be the cause of our terror.

I found further reason for rejecting the idea of depression as an illness that could be reduced to a physical source by reading of the work of Wilder Penfield. Penfield was a great and important pioneer in the exploration and discovery of brain function; as a neurosurgical researcher, he spent his life studying and mapping out in great detail the areas of the brain. Penfield had come to the conclusion that there must be both a "computer mechanism" as well as a "mind mechanism" in the brain to account for human functioning, but at the end of his life he had to admit to his failure to find the source for both. Shortly before his death, he wrote: "For myself, after a professional lifetime spent in trying to discover how the brain accounts for the mind, it comes as a surprise now to discover, during this final examination of the evidence, that the dualist hypothesis [separation of mind and brain] seems the more reasonable of the two possible explanations.... Mind comes into action and goes out of action with the highest brain-mechanism, it is true. But the mind has energy. The form of that energy is different from that of neuronal potentials that travel the axone pathways. There I must leave it."[163]

Francis Collins, the scientist in charge of the research group that mapped the human genome, came to a similar conclusion, which allowed him to say, "It's true that the hardware for all that complexity—our neurons and their connections—were made possible by genetics. But that isn't the whole story. You see, scientific processes were God's plan to prepare a flesh-and blood home for the spirit to dwell in."[164] The brain may be the hardware or circuitry through which mind is able to function, but mind cannot be reduced to brain function. We were created with the capacity for mental thought that can leap the bounds of neurotransmitters and brain synapses and live on another plane entirely. I was depressed not primarily because I had a malfunctioning brain (though considering the history of depression in the family I couldn't discount that), but rather because I had a thinking mind.

Our modern enlightened attitude that has attempted to trace the source of depression to a location in the brain or to a chemical imbalance is neither modern nor enlightened. The idea of depression as having a physical source is a view that goes back to pagan times; to a certain degree we just seem to have come full circle and found ourselves back again with the ancient Greek view of emotional states as being grounded in the body. It was Hippocrates (400 B.C.) who first introduced into medicine the idea of illness being due to an imbalance in the distribution of the four humors, an idea that was still the basis of medical practice in medieval times. To the ancient Greeks, human health depended on regaining the right balance among the four humors, or substances.[165] Depression, or melancholy as it was then called, supposedly arose out of an imbalance of black bile in the spleen or gall bladder. Now, of course, being more enlightened, we have altered our view as to the location of the problem—depression is now seen as due to a lack of serotonin rather than an excess of black bile—but the thinking is essentially the same; depression has a bodily source and is due to a bodily imbalance. In medieval times, bloodletting, purges, and emetics were all ways of attempting to expel the surplus of a humor from the body. Now we add chemical substances to the body, but the thinking is the same. It is an attempt to treat depression or an emotional state as a physical problem.

Only time and life could confirm the path I chose. I lived in a world where I felt my humanity was being threatened by those who would turn me into soulless protoplasm; where science, not faith, was offered as the source for answers to what was wrong with me; where even in the church, secular humanism had set up shop, bartering its remedies for my depression. It was the hope of answers that lay beyond my physical existence that haunted me. I left the church to begin a lonely search.

I was depressed, I eventually concluded, because I was a being capable of awareness. That awareness (although inarticulate at first) came in two forms. I was increasingly aware that there was no health in me (to para-phrase the prayer book), and I was also aware that I had a need to fit my life into a larger framework of meaning than I had yet discovered.

No health in me: depression, I now know, can arise from breathing too long and too deeply the recycled air of our own poisons. Dr. Karl Menninger claimed that there was a sure-fire way for a person mired in depression to get better—just find someone else who needs help and then help him or her.[166]

Finding our life by losing it in the service of others is a secret that goes against our instinctual natures; being wounded, we instead become like porcupines, developing sharp quills to keep all danger at bay and then hiding our soft centers behind our defense systems. Curled in on our-selves, we soon lack fresh air or the ability to relate to the wider world around us. Soon, our own inner toxins become more deadly than the orig-inal threat that had us retreating from life.

There was a time when, deeply mired in depression, I felt I was being called to help a particular person. I thought that blatantly unfair at a time when I felt so needy. Since they happened to be one of the people I had most difficulty forgiving, I also thought it unjust—what about me, my needs, and what about all the permanent damage they had done to me? It was the one time I tried to pray out of the therapeutic self-understanding and jargon I had accumulated. God just needed to understand how deeply broken I was, how deep the scars were that they had inflicted. In attempt-ing to pray out of my accumulated self-understanding and self-obsession, I discovered what C.S. Lewis referred to as having "a door slammed in your face, and a sound of bolting and double bolting on the inside. After that, silence. You may as well turn away. The longer you wait, the more emphatic the silence will become."[167]

With a lot of inward grumbling, I went and started spending time with that particular person. I felt a lot worse. Listening to her was like being surgically cut open to have all my own wounds exposed and raw and bleeding. We began to meet at least once a week, and each time it was a torturous meeting where I would go home feeling personally destroyed.

I began to pray passionately for the two of us and all the injured life around us; now I knew God was at least listening and ever so close. In that attitude, I would at least go to our meetings with a sense of God's Presence with me. In fact, at times, God would be so close and real that it would make me expect that something miraculous and sudden would happen. It didn't. I kept up my inward complaining.

My attitude finally changed one day when my son came into the kitchen to say, "Mom, it's not as though you're a changed person. You're a completely different person." Startled, I looked back and realized that what I had been going through was about the healing of me. God had used my involvement with another to take me back to the places of my deepest hurt and then to make me face the truth about myself. Led through the inferno of old memories, old emotions, and given a good view of old wounds, I was then offered a chance to make new choices, to take a new approach, to form new attitudes. I found that I no longer had to struggle with extending forgiveness; having empathetically entered the world of the other person, I could finally see the other side of what had happened, and hate was no longer possible. I also discovered that forgiveness is one of the most powerful remedies; by finally being able to forgive the other person, it was me, myself, who was freed.

Only later did I realize that I had discovered the clue to emotional health, the recipe for which had long ago been revealed in Isaiah 58:10: "If you extend your soul to the hungry and satisfy the afflicted soul, then *your* light shall dawn in the darkness, and *your* darkness shall be as the noonday." (KJV; italics mine) The same chapter also promised that if one takes care of the needy, "then *your* light shall break forth like the morning, *your* healing shall spring forth speedily" (verse 8).

I think I received from the physical world an example of what had been happening to me internally. Somehow I managed to injure my shoulder. It was too painful to move my arm, so I stopped using it. Not only did that not help the pain in my shoulder, but I eventually found I had lost the ability to use my arm. I finally went to a physiotherapist, who told me to do exactly what I didn't want to do—exercise the arm. For months

I did painful exercises, slowly stretching and exercising my arm muscles. It took over a year to regain full use of my arm. Then I hurt my other shoulder. That time I ignored the pain and immediately started stretching and exercising the muscles. Within a couple of months, recovery was complete.

I think it is the same with our psychic wounds. Being hurt, our first reaction is to turn within to tend and nurture our woundedness. Soon we turn into stunted, deformed beings. The gospel offers us a different approach; it takes us outside of ourselves. The gospel way initially feels like the stretching the physiotherapist had me engage in—painful and contrary to my natural instincts it was the last thing I wanted to do, but I had to also acknowledge that it was the only way that I would regain the use of my arm.

The second way that awareness creates depression arises from the fact that we human beings have an insatiable need for purpose and meaning to our existence. I think it is more than coincidence that the rise of depression in our world has corresponded with the rise of secularism and with the declining influence of religion. Our search for biological and chemical sources for depression can be just another way we attempt to avoid the reality of soul and spirit in our lives.

The World Health Organization has claimed that depression will become the number one cause of disability in the developed countries by the year 2020.[168] This growing problem of depression has come at a time when it has gradually gone from being a problem of theology to philosophy to psychotherapy to biology to neurobiology. Perhaps our growing problem lies in the fact that we are heading in the wrong direction looking for a cure. Does depression have a biological or chemical source? That opinion has been challenged by groups such as the researchers at the University of Pennsylvania, who have shown that therapy is as effective as drugs in dealing with depression and offers longer-lasting effects.[169] The Canadian Medical Association Journal also raised the question of whether depression should be treated chemically. Reporting on a study from the United Kingdom, which looked at the effect of antidepressants (SSRIs) on children, it revealed that, "SSRIs are largely ineffective in the treatment of major depression in children and adolescents and can cause suicidal behaviour and self-harm."[170] *The Medical Post* recently reported a study out of Duke University that showed that older women who were mildly depressed lived longer.[171] The implication seems to be that depression may actually be a survival mechanism, an adaptive response helping us to avoid what is harmful and helping one deal with life.

Is therapy, then, the best approach for the cure of depression? Back when I was depressed, I came across a reported investigation showing that "improvement was greater on several psychological indexes when a troubled individual consulted with a friend who understood her than when she saw a professional psychotherapist."[172] It was community, it was having a support base of family and friends, that could be the most effective means of helping one cope with the dark times and places in life. Could the growing spread of depression have more to do with the break-up of family, community, and our fierce individualism rather than having any medical roots?

My newspaper recently ran a series of articles on depression. It included a checklist of fifteen questions that had been developed to detect depression in the elderly. A score of 5 to 9 was supposed to indicate "a strong possibility of depression," and a score of 10 was "almost always a sign of depression." The questions included the following:

> Are you basically satisfied with your life?
> Do you feel that your life is empty?
> Do you often get bored?
> Are you in good spirits most of the time?
> Do you feel happy most of the time?
> Do you often feel helpless?
> Do you feel it is wonderful to be alive now?
> Do you feel pretty worthless the way you are now?
> Do you feel that your situation is hopeless?[173]

There was a time when every one of those questions would have been considered spiritual, existential questions for which religion existed to provide the answers. I can understand why a secular society might need help, seeking drugs and therapeutic approaches to erase life's questions and the need for meaning, but why would the church become an accomplice to the attempt to medicalize life? If we had kept depression as a theological problem—a disease of the soul—could it have been prevented from becoming the number one cause of disability in the advanced world?

What I have become convinced of in my struggle with depression is that depression is essentially an existential problem. I say "essentially" because I have no problem believing that I have been "wired" to make me susceptible to dark moods. However, the therapeutic has no real answers for either suffering or for our need for higher meaning. So why has the church become dependent on the therapeutic to come to the aid of its suffering parishioners?[174]

It can be our very need for truth and meaning that causes the deepest depression. Life is an enigma and nobody can stand alone peering into its dark mysteries very long without beginning to lose one's emotional balance. The temptation will always exist to turn from the darkness that lurks at the periphery of life and escape into trivialities and distractions so that our lives finally become as rootless and immaterial as the swiftly passing days. It is faith that helps us avoid that temptation. Faith purposefully takes us into the dark so that we can exchange life-support systems.

There was a time when religion provided the ladders of ascent which were seen as the sure way of surmounting the darkness surrounding our being. As the sociologist Philip Rieff wrote in his book *The Triumph of the Therapeutic,* those vertical ladders of ascent that once connected us to a higher life have now been destroyed by the therapeutic. Rieff claimed that the great religious question was, "How are we to be consoled for the misery of living?"[175] Whereas once that would have been seen as a religious question, Rieff claims that now the therapeutic has imposed its answers on our society. Religion and its old ways of consolation have now been replaced by basically four new ways to console ourselves for the misery of being.

Freud and his analytic approach offered the first great alternative to religion. In a published letter to Marie Bonaparte, Freud wrote, "The moment a man questions the meaning and value of life, he is sick, since objectively neither has any existence."[176] The very question of meaning suddenly became a sign of sickness. Near the end of his life, Freud wrote, "I have not the courage to rise up before my fellow-men as a prophet, and I bow to their reproach that I can offer them no consolation."[177] "Consolation," for Freud, was seen as a religious notion, and it was precisely religion that he was attempting to displace. Freud's followers thought in terms of a cure, but Freud also considered "cure" a religious notion: Freud's goal was that of increasing personal capacity. If the ego was adequately strengthened, then man could improve his power of choice in life. Exactly what man would choose was irrelevant to Freud. What was important was that man could be felt to be in control.

To see the seismic shift that took place with Freud, one needs to compare Freud's goals with those of the religious faith that he was attempting to replace. Whereas faith is the slow surrender of the ego and its insistence on centrality in order to develop a life of trust, Freud, and the analytic tradition following him, developed a science around strengthening the ego's ability to make its own choices, thus rendering religion irrelevant. Whereas Jesus claimed we could not discover the Kingdom unless we became as a child (living life in trust, dependence, and obedience), Freud's goal was to produce an independent maturity that relied on nothing outside the personal ego.

Rieff claimed that Freud spawned three prophets who, unable to live with Freud's response, each tried to answer the great religious question in a new way. Refusing to revert to traditional forms, they instead created psychologies that "became modes of consolation."[178]

The first prophet, who was at the other extreme from Freud, was Wilhelm Reich. According to Reich, what was best in man was his erotic impulses. When man began to think about himself rather than follow his natural instincts, repression began. To attempt self-examination, according to Reich, was a sign of latent schizophrenia: "To stand aside, entirely logical and drily 'intellectual', and observe your own inner functioning amounts to a splitting of the unitary system which only a very few seem to bear without deep upset."[179] Instead of bearing that "upset," one could unify one's being by giving free reign to one's instinctual drives. It was no longer the Saint, but rather, the instinctual Everyman who was to be the model for the new psychological age, a new man who could unify life around his instincts.[180]

The next prophet willing to destroy religion, according to Rieff, was D.H. Lawrence. Reich and Lawrence both acknowledged an inward-outward struggle in man, but both saw that conflict not as a challenge inviting us to develop and grow towards a higher form of life, but rather, as a need to regress towards the simplicity of the animal. For both men, the answer was the same; strip man down to naked impulses, instincts, the erotic, and he will know innocence and satisfaction. The problem with man, according to both Reich and Lawrence, was his ability for self-reflection. The closer man could live to his animal nature, the less conflicted he would be. After all, an animal doesn't carry around guilt over what it killed for dinner. An animal is not tormented over whether it should remain loyal to its mate or whether it should follow the feline down the street who is in heat. An animal is not caught in paroxysms of indecision over whether to attack a weaker animal or whether turning one's back will appear to be cowardice. Forget questions of meaning and purpose, of right and wrong. If man could avoid reflection and get back to the innocence of the animal, then he would know peace and satisfaction. The more one could get in touch with one's inner feelings, desires, and impulses and live out of their life, taught Lawrence, the more unitary one would be. The darkness could thus be avoided.

I have been frustrated watching the way the church has joined the therapeutic in helping us get in touch with what is inside of us instead of helping us to believe in and live out of a Transcendent source. I have been frustrated with watching the way that the analytic attitude has been allowed to replace faith commitment as the way that we fashion our existence. But I have been most frustrated of all by the final way in which our ladders of ascent have been allowed to be destroyed: by Carl Jung and what Rieff calls his new "Language of Faith."[181]

Carl Jung was a disciple of Freud's. Their paths separated over the issue of spirituality. Jung, unlike Freud, could see that man could not live without a belief in something higher than his own transitory self. As he wrote in *Modern Man In Search of a Soul,* "Among all my patients in the second half of life—that is to say, over 35—there has not been one whose problem in the last resort was not that of finding a religious outlook on life. It is safe to say that every one of them fell ill because he had lost that which the living religions of every age have given their followers and none of them has really been healed who did not regain his religious outlook."[182]

In *Memories, Dreams, Reflections,* Jung wrote of our need to "frame a view of the world which adequately explains the meaning of human existence in the cosmos"[183] for, as he claimed, "Meaninglessness inhibits fullness of life and is therefore equivalent to illness. Meaning makes a great many things endurable—perhaps everything. No science will ever replace myth, and a myth cannot be made out of any science."[184]

Jung, however, had rejected Christianity as a viable option for modern man. Jung was the son of a Christian pastor whose religion was so troubling to him and so inadequate to meet the challenges of his world that he repeatedly ended up in an insane asylum. Jung found himself caught between the recognition of the human need for God and an abhorrence for the God of his inherited background. Jung solved the dilemma by finding his god within the self: a "subterranean God." A god who is just a part of one's own self cannot alienate one from one's self. By placing god within the self, man could again be a unitary, fully integrated being.

Jung's religious interest finally brought him back to pagan times where myths, archetypes, and pagan deities created shadow-lands. In those shadow-lands, the dark was never pierced by blinding revelation, so man could live haunted by truths, half-truths, and intimations, which he could then form into myths and archetypes. In those shadow-lands, man, himself, could interpret and form a story out of the shadows. Jung clearly expressed his intention in a letter to Freud:

I think, dear Dr. Freud, we must give psychoanalyses time to infiltrate into people from many centers, to revivify among intellectu-
als a feeling for symbol and myth. Ever so gently we want to
transform Christ back into the soothsaying god of the vine, which
he was, and in this way absorb those ecstatic instinctual forces of
Christianity for the one purpose of making the cult and the sacred
myth what they once were—a drunken feast of joy where man
regains the ethos and holiness of an animal.[185]

Jung, like D. H. Lawrence and Reich, thought the "holiness of an animal"
an acceptable goal for man. The animal, unlike the human, is a unitary,
instinctual being untroubled by the need for higher purpose and meaning.

Jung had a fascination with spiritism, the occult, and the dark side,
but he took all that and hid it behind Christian symbol and myth until
slowly, the Christian story was stripped of transcendence. Jung removed
the necessity for those ladders of ascent. God need not be feared, searched
for, encountered. When our god is a subterranean god, then dying, the
journey, the dark night of faith, and all the hard edges of the gospel can be
dispensed with.

Jungian spirituality has become ubiquitous. With its language of
soul and of spirit, it has invaded the works of even the most orthodox
writers and evangelical churches. There was a time, when I first came
across the writings of Jung, when I, too, thought I had finally found
what I was looking for. With a belief system that had gotten stuck in my
head and that had nothing real to say to a life that was fast coming apart
Jung, with his language of soul, of spirit, touched deep places of my
being that had long been lying dormant. I read his books and got a special notebook to write out favorite sayings. I read Jung until I got to his
Answer to Job, in which he describes his god, and then I stopped short.
I knew I didn't recognize his god. I realized I was standing at a place
where I needed to make a choice. To turn and choose the Christian God
would mean once again standing alone in the darkness. I chose the terror
and the darkness.

Why is it so important to lose our fear of the darkness, to accept the depression that can come when we face our true existential state? What helped me, again, was an image—an image provided by a therapist named Frederick Perls. According to Perls, we humans all live in a neurotic structure made up of four levels. He called it a "neurotic" structure because neuroses is the way we avoid misery, but it is actually life itself and reality that are the true misery. So we compartmentalize life into four layers. We learn roles, fill our lives with empty talk, and devise techniques whereby we can live our whole lives in the two surface layers. The true purpose of this neurotic technique, however, is to avoid the third layer that undergirds human existence—the knowledge that we are lost, lonely, and empty. If that third layer was ever to be pierced, then what we would find ourselves facing would be the fourth layer: "the terror that we carry around in our secret heart."[186]

Death is the surest and final truth of our human existence, but the one we least want to face. By becoming obsessed with all the broken and fractured crevasses in the surface of our existence, we can avoid the greatest and most certain truth of all, the truth that we exist perched precariously on the edge hovering over the caverns of Death and Ultimate Meaning. The one and only certainty in this life is the certainty that at some point— at a point outside of our knowing and beyond our control—we are going to fall into their boundless depths. It is in facing reality—the reality of Death and Ultimate Meaning—that the life from those depths can erupt into the top layers of our existence and, like lava erupting from the bowels of the earth, that life can begin to fill those crevasses and fracture lines in our existence that we had become so obsessed with.

First, however, we have to have the courage to face those dark depths. According to Perls, we can never know who we truly are until we find ourselves in that fourth layer.[187] It may be that the therapeutic, with all its language of in-depth analyses, exploration of the unconscious, and unmasking of repression, could itself be the greatest neurotic activity we ever engage in. It gives us the illusion of exploring depths, when in fact it keeps us neurotically fixated within those two surface levels. The therapeutic has no wisdom to help us face those two deeper levels.

Until our modern era, all cultures were built around religious assumptions. Now, with secularization and pluralism, we have lost the center that once held life together. We are bombarded with more facts and knowledge than ever before, but have no framework that allows us to unite it in some harmony. We live as fragmented and dispersed beings, constantly connecting with others according to roles, jobs, and groups, but never finding a way to bring a unity to all the pieces of our disintegrated selves. So we turn inward; alienated and isolated, we have no inherited story to gather up the broken pieces and weave them into a coherent whole. With the lack of connection and the personal strain of having to create a personal, authentic self out of all that disorder, it is small wonder that depression is becoming a major problem in our secular society.

We were created with the capacity to dream, to hope, to aspire, to envision untold possibilities, yet we live in bodies that fail, in webs of relationships that disappoint, and get caught in the cross-currents of circumstances that threaten to defeat all our higher aspirations. The greater the passion to transcend our limitations, the greater the feelings of entrapment and overload will be when forced to face disillusionment and disappointment. We cannot live without dreams and without hope, and yet we also have to face reality.

Tragedy, uncertainty, loss of control, alienation, and loneliness can all create and feed the spread of depression. Without a comprehensive story to fit our lives into, we are left to define ourselves according to how well we are doing in our ego-driven creation of a personal, self-created, and self-motivated self. The problem is, life is large and unpredictable and circumstances themselves will conspire to reveal the fragile foundations of our psychologized self. Once we have convinced ourselves that we truly can be the masters of our own destiny, then there is no way to read personal failure, loneliness, or loss of control other than as the personal failure of our mission in life.

It is faith that again helps us gather life into a coherent, meaningful whole; that grounds us in something larger than the shifting vicissitudes of life; that allows for the expansion of hope and dreams but also gives meaning to suffering and tragedy. We are not animals capable of living in a simple mode of existence, but are rather living souls before whom eternity beguiles us with its hints of significance and meaning. We are not simple or unitary organisms; our very existence is an enigma. However, in order to live before the wide horizons of eternity, we have to again recognize the reality of soul.

Depression may be the first sign indicating that we have a soul; there is something in us demanding meaning, crying out for "something more." Whereas hunger and thirst are signs that our physical bodies are in need of nourishment, depression can indicate the same for an undernourished soul. John Henry Cardinal Newman explained why, writing, "Had we no spirit of any kind, we should feel as little as a tree feels; Had we no soul, we should not feel pain more acutely than a brute feels it; but, being men, we feel pain in a way in which none but those who have souls can feel it."[188]

In the modern world, where we have been reduced to thinking animals, depression can be the cry of a sixth sense longing for a home it has not yet discovered. We were created with souls that have the capacity to apprehend God. When that correspondence is denied, then depression sets in. Depression can reveal our want of, our need of what we have as yet never found, but as such, it is a place of more honesty than the false certainties we left behind.

The higher we climb on the evolutionary ladder, the more our capacity for inner torment increases. One writer suggested that the reason why evolution has not rid us of the gene is because our capacity for madness, mental illness, and creativity are closely linked. Insanity and genius may be two aspects of the same capacity. Our torment comes from being capable of living on something higher than just a physical level. Being able to live a happy, contented life well adjusted to the visible world around us may be the sign of psychological health, but it can also be a sign of spiritual death. It was Evelyn Underhill who asked the question, "Why does full consciousness always include the mysterious capacity for misery as well as for happiness…. Why does evolution, as we ascend the ladder of life, foster instead of diminishing the capacity for useless mental anguish, for long, dull torment, bitter grief? Why, when so much lies outside our limited powers of perception, when so many of our own most vital functions are unperceived by consciousness, does suffering of some sort form an integral part of the experience of man?"[189] It is for us to discover why darkness forms such an integral part of what it means to be human.

Nietzsche wrote, "Men and women can endure any amount of suffering so long as they know the why to their existence." Depression is the place where, no longer able to live contentedly in one's former life, no longer able to bear meaninglessness, we are being prepared to live according to Ultimate Reality. It can be depression, itself, causing all the details of ordinary life to appear pointless and futile, that prepares us for God's approach. God darkens what He wants to reveal if only we'll begin to seek, inquire, to cry out. God breaks what He wants to heal, if we'll but let Him near enough. There is no room for a real God in our lives as long as our own understanding and our own self-sufficiency are adequate.

Paul Tillich considered the acceptance of despair to be itself an act of faith, perhaps even our greatest act of faith, and said, "The acceptance of despair is in itself faith and on the boundary line of the courage to be."[190] To willingly enter the dark and let it teach us may be the greatest step of faith we are ever called to:

> I said to my soul, be still and let the dark come upon you
> Which shall be the darkness of God. As, in a theatre,
> The lights are extinguished, for the scene to be changed
> With a hollow rumble of wings, with a movement of darkness on darkness,
> And we know that the hills and the trees, the distant panorama
> And the bold imposing façade are all being rolled away—
> ....
> So the darkness shall be the light, and the stillness the dancing."
> (T. S. ELIOT, "EAST COKER")

It is hard for Christians who have tried to live according to their beliefs, who have been raised with all the language of victorious Christian living, to be brought to a place of complete despair. Treating it as a chemical imbalance can be a way of trying to keep our faith in spite of the state we find ourselves in. The church attributes goodness and blessings with God, but doesn't often have the courage to face God's role in allowing darkness. However, as it says in Ecclesiastes 7:14, "When times are good, be happy; but when times are bad, consider: God has made the one as well as the other."

Not only does faith not promise us immunity from depression and despair, but also it can make one vulnerable to the deepest levels of that darkness. One cannot catch a glimpse of Ultimate Reality without also catching a glimpse of much more than we might wish to see. In the words of Ellie Wiesel, "Without God, life would be without problems, without anguish, without hope. For God is not only the answer to those who suffer as a result of questions; God is also the question to those who think they have found the answer."[191]

At the same time that the Light brings insight, assurance, and certainty, it also lights up the horizons of our existential state, presenting us with innumerable problems and questions: "But neither can a heathen be tempted to the same depths of despair as the Christian—and, indeed, as the greatest Christians and the saints. For the same flash of light that reveals to the creature the supernatural reality of grace lights up also the abyss of his guilt and his distance from God."[192]

I believe that there will be little spiritual growth, maturity, or even life in the modern church until we can again see depression, despair, and darkness not in the terms secular humanism has interpreted it—as mental illness—but rather as it has been interpreted by the saints in the centuries past—as the shadow cast by the God of Light—"is my gloom after all, shade of His hand, outstretched caressingly (Francis Thompson, *The Hound of Heaven*).

We usually start out believing in God as an idea. If God is left in the realm of abstraction, it becomes our most effective way of distancing ourselves from Him. A friend, who had moved to Japan wanting to leave behind our Western way of living and thinking, as well as our Western religion, sent an e-mail reporting some graffiti he had seen in Osaka that said, "Do you still believe God?"

This friend's response was, "I think a preposition was dropped but oh! the philosophical implications. Was the writer pissed, pithy or looking for a good english teacher?" I wrote back, reminding him that Romans 4:3 said, "Abraham believed God and it was credited to him as righteousness." It did not say, "Abraham believed in God." The graffiti artist did not eliminate a preposition; we in our Western world have added it. Right there in the missing preposition was revealed the difference between east and west, between immediacy versus abstraction. In despair, surrounded by our helplessness, meaninglessness, and futility, we are given a chance to face God as reality rather than treat Him as an idea—to believe God rather than to believe in God. As Unamuno wrote, "Those who believe they believe in God, but without passion in the heart, without anguish of mind, without uncertainty, without doubt, and even at times without despair, believe only in the idea of God, and not in God himself." We need to hear a voice from beyond if we are going to make it. We need immediacy.

We usually start out with our faith and love in God getting confused with faith and love in His goodness and blessings. In the dark, without consolation, we are given a chance to choose God for Himself alone. Darkness is the place where, feeling abandoned, we slowly turn from our narcissistic preoccupation with our own needs to ask some frightening questions about who we think lies beyond those needs. D. Martyn Lloyd-Jones noted, "People sometimes think that they are being sustained by the Christian faith when what they have is merely a psychological mechanism in operation; and it breaks down in a real crisis."[193] It is in darkness that we are forced to ask difficult questions as to what our faith is really grounded in.

Otto Rank claimed that neurosis "is at bottom always only incapacity for illusion." We cannot bear too much reality. Sometimes life destroys our illusions and we're left facing more truth than we can bear. Never is that more true than in our search for God. As St. Augustine wrote, "If you think you understand, it isn't God." Depression can be the result of the greatest struggle we will ever know—the struggle to keep our illusions of God while He, the great iconoclast, seeks to destroy them all. The God we believe in is often nothing more than our greatest illusion; we create Him out of a pastiche of inherited tradition, projected images arising out of our needs and desires, and accumulated impressions forced on us by our culture. The more passionately we believe in any false God, the more zealously we try to serve that God, the worse off we and all the people around us will be. When the God we have created doesn't dance to the tunes we play, we become depressed. Alan Bloom wrote, "God is there at the point of greatest tension, at the breaking point, at the center of the storm. In a way despair is at the center of things—if only we are prepared to go through it. We must be prepared for a period when God is not there for us and we must be aware of not trying to substitute a false God."[194]

In between our world of illusion and our encounter with God lies the darkness of that long stripping process where we've been deprived of old certainties but have not yet encountered the new.

Depression can also arise from repressed doubt. In many religious groups, doubt is seen as incompatible with faith. Doubt, however, is just a question seeking further illumination. Alfred Tennyson noted, "There lives more faith in honest doubt...than in half the creeds." Darkness, uncertainty and doubts may actually be the very sign of God's nearness: "Doubts are the messengers of the Living One to the honest. They are the first knock at our door of things that are not yet, but have to be, understood...Doubt must precede every deeper assurance; for uncertainties are what we first see when we look into a region hitherto unknown, unexplored, unannexed."[195]

A humanity that has had its awareness dulled only wants to live by simple, easy truths. I used to wonder why people who gave happy testimonies or spoke of "joy" and "peace" without any sign of depression or struggle created such a violent reaction in me. Now I understand. It's unscriptural. The Beatitudes ascribe blessedness to those who are poor in spirit, who mourn, who are meek, who are persecuted, who acknowledge their spiritual hunger and thirst. The spiritual blessings are given to those who know the dark depths of life. Jacob didn't receive his blessing from God until he struggled with Him all night. Jacob carried his blessing at the same time that he walked with a permanent limp because of the struggle.

Probably no spiritual writer has dealt with darkness more than St. John of the Cross. In his *Ascent of Mount Carmel,* he describes the three nights that the soul must pass through before it can reach its purposed end.[196] The first is a night whereby man is purged of his sensual desires. As long as we are content to live according to our five senses, we have no need or desire to nurture the life of our souls. Disaster, disillusionment, and despair may feel like small deaths, but they create the atmosphere whereby the life of spirit may be born. The second night comes as we are purged of our reliance on our own understanding. Faith leads us on paths where trust, not knowledge, is pre-eminent. Again, this difficult path will rarely be followed as long as we are capable of living under our own control. Faith teaches us to see the disasters of life that bring us to reliance on God as gift. The third night comes by means of life lived in response to God. God will always remain beyond our understanding and beyond our ability to control Him. But it is what lies in darkness, beyond our ever knowing, that is precisely what we can become most certain of.

Our spiritual acuity and depth will probably be more closely tied to our ability to suffer and to endure the darkness than to all the religious highs we experience: "There is nothing spiritual or even human about a completely happy and contented creature, impervious to evil, suffering, pain and tragedy. A sensitive awareness of evils and a capacity for suffering are one of the attributes of the spiritual man."[197]

Baron von Hugel wrote, "Wherever there is the fullest, deepest, interiority of human character and influence, there can ever be found profound trials and suffering which have been thus utilized and transfigured." The tradition of linking suffering to divine wisdom is an old one. Aeschylus (about fifth century B.C.) observed, "We must suffer, suffer into truth," and in "Agamemnon," he wrote,

Hour by hour, drop by drop
Pain falls upon the heart
And against our will
And even in our own despair
Comes wisdom from the awful grace of God.

Joseph Campbell, the man who studied myths and recognized their universality of themes, wrote, "One thing that comes out in myths, for example, is that at the bottom of the abyss comes the voice of salvation. The black moment is the moment when the real message of transformation is going to come. At the darkest moment comes the light."[198]

Bernard Smith, one of the early Trustees of A.A., noted, "The tragedy of our life is how deep must be our suffering before we learn the simple truths by which we can live."[199] We gain our wisdom, strength, and develop our character through suffering and adversity.

Perhaps we can only be trusted with the highs of life to the degree that we have been faithful in the dark lows. Our choice in life is to live in the surface layers of life and experience pleasure surrounded by futility and meaninglessness, or else experience the dark and suffering that goes with entering the heart of life and encountering the "joy unspeakable" and the "peace that passeth understanding." We were offered the gift of eternal life, but that life needs to be expressed in a body of death. That is why we can know the "peace that passeth understanding" while depressed, we can discover "joy unspeakable" while traveling through the heart of darkness, and we can discover the giftedness of life while our own lives are disintegrating. If it is mere happiness that we covet, then therapy is much better than religion. But if it is eternal life—that life that exists on a deeper plane than mere happiness—then we need to be prepared to enter the depths and darkness of life.

The therapeutic exists to help us rid ourselves of suffering. Christianity, however, is a religion that places suffering right at its very center. In 1Corinthians 1:8, 9, Paul wrote, "We were under great pressure, far beyond our ability to endure, so that we despaired even of life… But this happened that we might not rely on ourselves." We humans are usually

186 THE ALTARS OF AHAZ

content to live small lives cramped and turned into ourselves. We need darkness, adversity, and despair to draw us out of ourselves to face the large horizons of eternity. It is in and through darkness and suffering that the human capacity for God is born and grows.

Kierkegaard was a teacher who helped me see despair as the place where the life of spirit is born. Kierkegaard considered the greatest despair to be that of those who, thinking to escape it, devised for themselves lives of contentment and seeming security that allowed them no consciousness of being characterized as spiritual beings. Our only hope, however, is to enter despair so thoroughly that we can finally arise reborn as spirit. Like a caterpillar withdrawing inside its cocoon to emerge as a butterfly, despair can be the protective cover that causes us to withdraw from meaningless-ness and futility so that new life can be born.

Before I was ready for new life, however, there was a problem I needed to sort out. In my mind, it was somber faces, pursed lips, life-denying practices, and joyless living that I would have associated with Christianity. After all, did Jesus not say, "The man who loves his life will lose it, while the man who hates his life in this world will keep it for eternal life" (John 12:25)? I was certainly obedient; as a depressive I hated life. How could I, a depressive, learn to accept the goodness of the world and of life when its rejection had been glorified? In retrospect, my attitude to life may have been more Buddhist than Christian.

Chesterton noted that the difference between Christianity and Eastern religions lay in that, "Christ said 'Seek first the kingdom, and all these things shall be added unto you'. "Buddha said 'Seek first the kingdom, and then you will need none of these things.'"[200] Having encountered the suf-fering of life, the reaction of the Buddha was renunciation; he wanted to be free of the world of desire and disappointment and meaninglessness and struggle. In Christianity, however, the joy and peace and the secrets of life are the pearl of great price found in the midst of the roiling mess of it all; they are the prize mixed in with the pain and the toil of it all.

What I eventually came to see was that peace and joy cannot be made synonymous with happiness and feelings of well-being—they are instead the gifts and power of another age breaking into time to counter and meet the worst that our world can do to us. Perhaps that is what Dorothy Sayers was trying to say when she wrote, "The capacity for joy and the capacity for something like despair tend to be found together... people of a happy temperament are seldom capable of joy—they are insufficiently sensitive."[201]

The very purpose of the darkness of life may be ultimately to prepare us for joy. Elisabeth Elliott, whose husband died as a missionary martyr, said, "God's ultimate purpose in all suffering is joy." The gospel does not offer us happiness but joy—and it leads us along paths that make us realize they are not the same thing. The gospel does not offer us well being but peace, and often we need to discover that the one can only be discovered at the expense of the other.

Spiritual life and growth will always include darkness and pain; they are "the grave but kindly teacher[s] of immortal secrets."[202] The alternative is a numbed existence, as Aldous Huxley so presciently described in *Brave New World*. Huxley's novel ends up being more prophetic than futuristic when it describes a society where the drug soma is prescribed for the entire society. Soma, according to the head of the society, was, "Christianity without tears—that's what soma is."[203] As Mustapha Mond, the head of the society, admitted, "Every soma-holiday is a bit of what our ancestors used to call eternity."[204] A soma-holiday was peace and happiness achieved by means of drugs. According to Mustapha Mond, "It hasn't been very good for truth, of course. But it's been very good for happiness."[205] "Happiness," of course, meant numbness and distraction rather than anything particularly human.

Our attempts to avoid suffering and pain by means of soma or Prozac may alleviate our need to face the darkness that surrounds existence, but they will rid us of much more; they will rid us of the wisdom and depth and joy that we can only acquire by allowing ourselves to be willingly led through those dark depths.

There is a powerful image in the Bible of God calling out a people whom He had chosen to become the visible manifestation of how life was to be lived in response and in relationship to a Living God. The Scriptures give us two responses to the divine call, saying, "The people remained at a distance, while Moses approached the thick darkness where God was" (Exodus 20:21).

Our choice is to, like the Israelites, create a safe distance in order to escape the dark, or else to allow an appropriate fear to guide us through the dark to where God is. It is those who run from the darkness, creating safe structures in which to hide from God, which will be the ones most capable of doing damage to our souls. The health of any community is dependent on those who brave the dark in order to encounter God. Without their leadership, we tend to spend our days, like the Israelites, living on the plateau and creating idols.

Is depression a physical or a spiritual problem? Our confusion may be symptomatic of our inability to any longer see how the body and soul interconnect. There is nothing in life that can be reduced to the merely physical. Everything in life reveals and points to the world of spirit. As Paul Tillich wrote, "In man nothing is 'merely biological' as nothing is 'merely spiritual'. Every cell of his body participates in his freedom and spirituality, and every act of his spiritual creativity is nourished by his vital dynamics."[206] Man is actually the focal point wherein two realities—the physical and the spiritual—meet.

In Luke 13, Jesus healed a woman who had been bent and crippled for eighteen years. Jesus then goes on to describe the woman as one "whom Satan has kept bound for eighteen years" (Luke 12:16). Her deformity seen as evidence of Satan? The woman was obviously physically handicapped! There is a spiritual aspect to all reality, however, and that is what Jesus chose to focus on. There is nothing in either our nature or the world in general that can be reduced to the merely physical.

Depression—is it a mental illness or is it the shadow cast by the nearing of the Light? How can those two views coexist in one church? A church that has allowed life's deepest forces to become medicalized is not going to have spiritual depth. A church that stands at our places of darkness, serving as accomplice to those who would pathologize and then medicate away our pain, is a church that is going to have few, if any, stories of God to pass along to its children. It will be a church that may have helped us avoid depression and anguish, but it will have simultaneously erased the "peace that passeth understanding" and the "joy unspeakable." They come together.

Spirituality: Holy Spirit versus Universal Spirit

I FIND THE IRONY of our present situation to be incredible. First, we allowed psychology to make our inner workings a matter of science and thus destroy the reality of soul and spirit. Then we allowed psychology to "discover" the soul and to make it the domain of its new interest and research. "Spirituality" thus became the place of its new "insights," but in the process, few seem to notice that a sleight of hand has taken place. The spiritualities that are filling our world and our churches are unlike those from our Christian heritage.

There was a time, almost a decade ago now, when the new "Spirituality" sections that opened up in secular bookstores intrigued me. I would gravitate to those sections first to read the back covers and see who was writing those books. I stopped when I found it too upsetting. Instead of being written by people who arose out of established traditions of religious belief they, instead, seemed to mostly be written by people who had once been in the therapeutic industry. An example is Robin Norwood, the psychologist who added words like "co-dependency" and "relationship addiction" to our vocabulary. As Norwood said, "I knew that for me, the whole field of psychology just didn't hold the answers."[207] Wishing to leave behind "all these people who thought I could fix their lives,"[208] she quit her counseling practice to pursue and offer advice on the area of spirituality and "such New Age concepts as karma, etheric bodies and soul evolution."[209]

The sections in the bookstores labeled "Spirituality" didn't last very long. Soon, labels such as "New Age" and "Occult" replaced them. Unfortunately, the spiritualities now being offered in our churches and religious schools do not come with such warning labels.

"Spirituality" is the new hot commodity in our modern world. According to my national newspaper, the fastest-growing religious group in North America at this time is the "spiritual-but-not-religious" group. This group comprises approximately thirty million people in the US, and if they were actually classified as a religious group, they would trail only the Catholics in number.[210]

The area of spirituality has become a potpourri of everyone's influence. The Canadian sociologist Reginald Bibby has been asking Canadians what they mean when they speak in terms of "spiritual needs" or being a "spiritual person." Roughly half, he found, still think in traditional terms using words like "God" and "prayer." The other half of the population offers highly subjective and individualistic responses, using terms such as "a feeling of oneness with the earth," "inner awareness," or "peace of mind."[211]

I thought our fascination with non-traditional spiritualities was a modern phenomenon until I began to read history and discovered the roots of our current spiritualities—pre-Nazi Germany. In pre-Nazi Germany, as in our time, the language of "spirit," had come to the fore. In their time, as in ours, a reaction against reason had set in. The Nazis, instead, trusted in their intuitions and in "the glorification of the subrational vitalities of life."[212] Although we would now condemn their trust in irrational intuition and their freedom from reason, sense, and decency, we have still taken three of the formative figures who helped form their vocabulary of "spirit" and have allowed them to influence and form our own understanding of spirituality. Pre-Nazi interest in "spirit," as in our time, was formed by that German triumvirate of Schleiermacher, Jung, and Hegel. Schleiermacher, the father of modern liberalism, was a minister who made "spirit' synonymous with "world spirit." Carl Jung, the psychoanalyst, made "spirit" synonymous with the collective unconscious. Hegel was a philosopher who seemed to define spirit in much the same way as Jung, making it universal spirit, but with a historical, dialectic emphasis. What all three had in common was a detaching of spirit from a Transcendent source to make it a universal spirit synonymous with the spirit of man, of the world, and of the world's processes.

It was in reaction to that German triumvirate and the growing attempt to make Spirit synonymous with the spirit of man or universal spirit that caused Karl Barth's to write, "Indeed, the Spirit of the Good, the True, and

Beautiful, or even the Spirit of Love, or the Spirit of Goodness married to Holiness, in which man has a share more or less, is certainly the Evil Spirit when taken as a substitute for the Holy Spirit. To make that other spirit the conqueror over sin is to put a Fox in charge of geese!"[213]

It is not enough to allow for an awakened awareness of the spiritual realm; we need to choose the object of our devotion and decide how we choose to relate to it. As we can see from history, an awareness of the spirit realm is not enough; that awareness needs to be grounded in something life affirming and healthy.

Of that German triumvirate, it is Carl Jung who has had the most profound influence on our culture. Richard Noll, a clinical psychologist and Lecturer in the History of Science at Harvard, has written two books showing how, when Jung broke off relations with Freud, it was essentially to start a new religion. Noll showed how theories of the "collective unconscious" came as much from neo-paganism and occultism as from science.[214] By being able to hide behind the patina of a science, however, Jung's influence has permeated our culture and has become an insidious and ubiquitous force in modern spiritual movements and therapies.

Perhaps the first to popularize the Jungian concept of spirit in North America was the psychiatrist Scott Peck. In his book *The Road Less Traveled,* he wrote, "Since the unconscious is God all along, we may further define the goal of spiritual growth to be the attainment of godhead by the conscious self. It is for the individual to become totally, wholly God."[215]

Whereas the Biblical account makes eating the fruit of the Tree of Knowledge with its offer of self-godhead the original sin, Peck turns it around and makes the attainment of self-godhead the goal of spirituality; he writes, "It is one thing to believe in a nice old God who will take good care of us from a lofty position of power which we ourselves could never begin to attain. It is quite another to believe in a God who has it in mind for us precisely that we should attain His position, His power, His wisdom, His identity .... We don't want God's responsibility."[216]

It is interesting living in a time when, thanks to those in the therapeutic industry such as Jung, Peck, Rogers, and Fromm, our world is increasingly being infiltrated by those convinced of their own Divinity, convinced that god is to be found and defined as the ground of their own being. They all want to become God, but without first becoming like Jesus Christ. We live in a time of encroaching pantheism; at the same time that belief in a Transcendent reality is being eroded, we are increasingly becoming convinced of our own Divinity, of the Divinity of creation and of the world's processes.

Now the greatest error will always be that which flies the closest distance from truth. The Apostle Peter did say that Jesus' promises were given "so that through them you may participate in the divine nature" (1 Peter 1:4). Origen, (born about 185 C.E.) did write, "For Christians see that with Jesus human and divine nature begin to be woven together, so that by fellowship with Divinity human nature might become divine, not only in Jesus, but also in all those who believe and go on to undertake the life which Jesus taught."[217] St. Athanasius (about 296-373) wrote that God "became man that we might become divine."[218] Basil of Caeserea—a church father writing from the fourth century—did write, "The human being is an animal who has received the vocation to become God."[219] John of Damascus (the seventh century) wrote, "By surrendering his godhead to our flesh, God has deified our flesh." St. Thomas Aquinas (1225-74) wrote, "The only begotten Son of God, wishing to enable us to share in his Divinity, assumed our nature, so that by becoming man, he might make men gods."[220] The Psalms do say, "Ye are gods." In the Roman mass, the communion is accompanied with the words, "May we come to share in the divinity of Christ who humbled himself to share in our humanity." A more modern writer observed, "It is not enough to contemplate God, humanity must be divinized by its contemplation: The new religion cannot be simply a passive reverence for God (*theosebeia*) or an act of worship (*theolatreia*) but must be activity in and with him (*theourgia*), a common movement of God and humans to transform natural humanity into a spiritual race, a divine people; it is not a matter of creation out of nothing but of transformation, a transubstantiation of matter into spirit, of the life of this world into the life of God."[221]

The Christian writers, however, claimed that we became divine through grace. The life of God is given at those places where we lose our-selves, empty ourselves, die to self, or where the cross has left its imprint in our nature. For Peck, however, and for the others from the therapeutic industry who are spawning our new spiritualities, our Godhead comes through self-awareness and self-assertion. We just need to actualize our inherent Divinity. As Peck wrote, "So original sin does exist; it is our lazi-ness."[222] It is the responsibility of man to make himself God.

Not long ago, the words "soul," "spirit," and "spirituality" were so con-spicuously absent from religious life that I could facetiously claim that I went to a church that believed in God the Father, God the Son, and God the Unspeakable Other. We had become so rational, so science-based, and so cultured that even the Holy Spirit had been turned into a theological concept rather than an experiential reality. That barrenness is what caused the theologian Paul Tillich to speak of "the almost forbidden word 'spirit' as 'lost beyond hope'."[223] That, however, was a few decades ago. It was before the Enlightenment experiment of trying to turn man into a thinking animal with no soul finally backfired. Those suppressed regions re-emerged with a vengeance, often with no desire to be held back by reason, tradition, or submission to a higher authority.

It was Carl Jung who initially laid the groundwork for the modern growth of spiritual interest. What Jungian spirituality does is allow man to acknowledge latent spiritual longings, desires, and forces without having to acknowledge a Transcendent source or submit to a traditional religious form. The God of traditional Christianity is seen as both Transcendent and immanent. Jung, and the modern spiritualities that follow him, acknowl-edge immanence, but then cut off the spirit from its Transcendent source. Jung did not overtly attack the traditional forms of religion—he even went so far as to acknowledge their necessity in human emotional health—but he redirected attention from the truth claims of those traditional forms of religion to focus on the inner experiential and emotional validation of the religious experience. In the words of Carl Jung, "To gain an understand-ing of religious matters, probably all that is left us today is the psychological approach. That is why I take these thought-forms that have become historically fixed, try to melt them down again and pour them into molds of immediate experience."[224]

What religion did, according to Jung, was give us archetypes or images that were concrete manifestations of the inner life of the collective unconscious. Truth was not external to man, according to Jung, but was a projection of his own inner truths, so Jung redirected attention away from traditional forms back into the inner life of man.

The spiritual foundations laid by Jung have blossomed in North America. The psychoanalysts Erich Fromm and Carl Rogers both went even further than Jung in redirecting our attention away from traditional authority to belief in our own inner wisdom and ourselves. For Carl Rogers, the "higher power" of religion to which one surrendered was actually part of the unconscious self. For Erich Fromm, that was a position still too obsequious; religion was meant to serve the self; it was a utilitarian aid to self-realization and should be seen, paradoxically, as a means towards man's autonomy. God, according to Fromm, was actually a symbol for human capacities and powers.[225] Fromm acknowledged the human need for religion; he saw that the human being needed a "frame of orientation and an object of devotion,"[226] but he reasoned that in man, himself, lay the inner *telos,* the self-actualizing powers that would drive him to ideal and ethical ends. Both Rogers and Fromm wished to free the individual from external authority, from legalism, and from societal and institutional structures so that the "true" self could be realized and fulfilled. What I find interesting is that although both were part of a movement that produced humanistic religion (religion without God at its center), their work was taken up with relish by the pastoral counseling movement and has become an integral part of the spiritual landscape of North America.

Moses, the man who reportedly came closest to God, repeatedly referred to God as "God of the spirits of all mankind." The awareness of immanence has always been in the Gospel, but so has the temptation to therefore look for God and define Him according to the life we find within. That is why, in going through history, one hears repeated warnings against understanding God according to our own inner life:

Saint Augustine said, "I sought the substance (of God) in myself, as if it were similar to what I am; and I did not find it."

Dionysuis the Areopagite said, "It may be true that the divine principle is present in every being, but not every being is present in him."

The author of Cloud of Unknowing wrote, "For he is your being, and you are what you are in him…preserving always this difference between you and him, that he is your being and that you are not his."

Jan van Ruusbroec, a Flemish mystic from the 14th Century, complained of those who "think themselves to be God in their simple ground; for they lack true faith, hope and charity."[227] As to a trust in immanence without an attending fear of God as Other, God's response was, "'Am I only a God nearby', declares the Lord, 'and not a God far away?'" (Jeremiah 23:23).

When spirituality is allowed to be formed and understood subjectively rather than by traditional forms or eternal quest, three things happen. First, pragmatism reigns supreme. It is what works rather than what is true that defines spiritual life. For example, since religious belief and prayer have been shown to significantly improve one's health, medical schools are now incorporating spiritual studies into their schools as an area of study.[228] In the US, 122 medical schools have begun spiritual training.[229] Those spiritualities will obviously be designed according to pragmatic value and according to universal appeal rather than according to pre-existent forms. In Healing Words, a book written by a former internal medicine specialist named Dossey, it was reported, "Experiments with people showed that prayer positively affected high blood pressure, asthma, heart attacks, headaches and anxiety."[230] He also wrote, "It is not necessary to be religious or even to believe in God for the prayer to work."[231] As Aldous Huxley aptly noted, "Men who turn towards God without turning away from themselves do not, of course, reach God; but if they devote themselves energetically enough to their pseudo-religion, they will get results."[232]

Secondly, spiritual disciplines are changed. Whereas prayer, meditation on the Word, and spiritual readings formed the core of spiritual life in the past, now techniques for centering the mind, breathing techniques, body positioning, etc., become the new way of establishing an acquired state of peace and health. The spiritual life becomes simply a tranquilizer. The more well-being it gives, the better it "works."[233] In reaction to that attitude, Evelyn Underhill observed, "The devotee who is content to be shut up inside his or her own enjoyable, pious practice and nice religious feelings, is the mongrel of the spiritual world. One of his parents may be Spirit, but the other is Self."[234]

Thirdly, external, objective realities are slowly melted down into a pantheistic, subjective blend of personal experience. Jesus, repentance, the cross, and all the symbols that mediate a higher life are stripped of their meaning and power. Religion's ability to draw one out of oneself or to affect inner transformation is lost.

True Christian spirituality, in contrast, foregoes subjectivity in order to align its life with an objective order. In Christianity, the Spirit and Word are always linked. Spirit, in Christianity, is never allowed to remain as impersonal spirit or as a subjective force. There is always an end towards which it moves; there are always purposes to be accomplished; change and transformation are the signs of its Presence. It is the Word that reveals the purposes and ends to which God's Spirit would lead us. When Jesus came as revealed Word, he revealed the personality of the Spirit. Jesus became the archetype or the visible shape of the end towards which the Spirit works.

My Bible never speaks of spirituality, but rather, of the Holy Spirit. The Holy Spirit is the personal manifestation of a personal God. Christian spirituality starts with the acknowledgement that our completion will never be found within ourselves. That which we long for, that which we have been cut off from, lies outside of ourselves. Our search is for the Other.

I find it significant that when Jesus taught his disciples to pray he asked them to start with, "Our Father who art in Heaven." The God who is "in Heaven," who is Transcendent, is also the God whose Presence fills the earth, but it is in, and only in, our acknowledgement and recognition of the Otherness of God that we can safely begin to separate the God within from our own subconscious, our own wish-fulfillment fantasies, our own blind projections. God cannot be made synonymous with our own inner depths, for the "heart that is not purified is a dark abyss, an immensity of the subconscious, that is not merely individual but pan-human, even cosmic, containing all the dark side of the world."[235]

In Christianity, therefore, where "spirit" is not defined subjectively, one cannot speak of Christian spirituality too long without touching on the fact of "religious experience." Perhaps it is the fact of ecstatic experience itself that turns people away from Christian spirituality. It is an embarrassment to the secular rational mind. It is a threat to our modern concepts of self; we cannot be filled with the Holy Spirit if we are full of ourselves. An experience of the Holy Spirit is also an affront to modern spiritualities; someone who has been "touched" by the Holy knows that they have encountered the Other. As Albert Einstein acknowledged, "Everyone who is seriously involved in the pursuit of science becomes convinced that a Spirit is manifest in the Laws of the Universe—a Spirit vastly superior to that of man, and one in the face of which we, with our modest powers, must feel humble."[236] Humility is a pre-requisite for knowledge of the Spirit – an attitude which is currently in short supply.

At the center of Christian spirituality, then, is the reality of the Holy Spirit. The Holy Spirit is the member of the Trinity that creates the bridge between us humans living confined and diminished to our time-bound physical existences, and the reality of another Kingdom. The Holy Spirit provides the experiential knowledge and validation of that other parallel plane that co-exists with and permeates our visible world. It is the Holy Spirit that keeps religion from degenerating into just another human project and turns religion into a passion, a fire. According to Abraham Joshua Heschel, "A pious man is usually pictured as a sort of bookworm, a person who thrives among the pages of ancient tomes, and to whom life with its longing, sadness, and tensions, is but a footnote in a scholarly commentary on the Bible. The truth is that a religious man is like a salamander, that legendary animal that originates from a fire of myrtle-wood kept burning for seven years. Religion is born of fire, of a flame, in which the dross of the mind and soul is melted away. Religion can only thrive on fire."[237]

Pascal, upon his conversion experience, wrote on a piece of paper—"From about half past ten at night to about half an hour after midnight, FIRE"—a testimony he sewed into his clothes and always carried with him. The evangelist Dwight L. Moody had an encounter with the Holy that he described as being consumed by a fire of love that he asked to have stayed for fear of his survival. Simone Weil was surprised to be possessed by a manifestation of love, which she described as "a presence more personal, more certain, more real than that of a human being, though inaccessible to the senses and the imagination."[238] Alcoholics Anonymous was started by an alcoholic named Bill Wilson, who described his conversion in the following way:

My depression deepened unbearably and finally it seemed to me as though I were at the very bottom of the pit. I still gagged badly at the notion of a Power greater than myself, but finally, just for the moment, the last vestige of my proud obstinacy was crushed. All at once I found myself crying out, "If there is a God, let Him show Himself! I am ready to do anything, anything!" Suddenly, the room lit up with a great white light. I was caught up into an ecstasy, which there are no words to describe. It seemed to me, in the mind's eye, that I was on a mountain and that a wind not of air but of spirit was blowing. And then it burst upon me that I was a free man. Slowly the ecstasy subsided. I lay on the bed, but now for a time I was in another world, a new world of consciousness. All about me and through me there was a wonderful feeling of Presence, and I thought to myself, "So this is the God of the preachers!" A great peace stole over me and I thought, "No matter how wrong things seem to be, they are still all right. Things are all right with God and His world."[239]

Christian spirituality is not a quiet we achieve, but rather a place where we are possessed by God.

Celtic spirituality speaks of "thin places"; it acknowledges that we live immersed in two realities, the physical being interpenetrated by the spiritual. In "thin places," the boundary between those realities becomes permeable, allowing us to get a glimpse of that which transcends our limited existence. Christian spirituality is about living so close to the grain of the universe that it begins to be made visible in the world that denies and lives in rebellion to it.

I remember telling the story of a miracle to someone only to hear them say, "That's freaky." We go to churches where we affirm the Gospel stories of angels, miracles, walking on water, and God's mighty intervention in history, and then leave the sanctuaries to enter a world where we find any sign of that Kingdom being made visible here below to be "freaky." It is as though we lived in a dry creek bed and told ourselves stories of how it was once a raging river, and how after our death we were again going to join its swift currents taking us to another shore, but in the meantime we are content to live without any sign of water in the here and now.

Harvey Cox, the man who wrote *The Secular City*, in which he predicted the death of religion, was approached several decades later and asked to write another book on why religion was not dead but growing. Cox went to study the charismatic movement, the one area where the church was growing the fastest, and reported, "What Pentecostals call 'speaking in tongues', or praying in the Spirit, has appeared in history before, and it is always a sure sign that the available religious idiom has become inadequate. Glossalalia is a mystical-experiential protest against an existing religious language that has turned stagnant or been corrupted."[240]

The theologian Henry P. Van Dusen, once President of Union Theological Seminary, made a similar observation, writing,

> A review of the "biography" of the Holy Spirit through Christian history discloses that it has been at the heart of Christian experi-

ence and Christian proclamation whenever they have been vital and dynamic. But the Holy Spirit has always been troublesome, disturbing, because it has seemed to be unruly, radical, unpredictable. It is always embarrassing to ecclesiasticism and baffling to ethically-grounded, responsible durable Christian devotion. And so it has been carefully taken in hand by Church authorities, whether Catholic or Protestant, and securely tethered in impotence. But—the Spirit will not long be silenced. When neglected or denied by the prevailing "churchianity," it unfailingly reappears to reassert its power, often with excesses and aberrations, beyond the bounds of conventional Church life.[241]

I spent several years attending churches that would have been identified as charismatic. I have to admit that at one time, the branch of the church that I would have felt least comfortable with would have been that which most closely identifies itself with the work of the Holy Spirit. I was a rationalist. I loved control. But at the same time, when life came apart, I also complained about how the church had become a human institution. Human reasoning and theological arguments had created its institutional walls. Therapeutic systems covered for God's missing power. Minds formed to think according to business models were creating the vision and agendas of the church. We were being soothed, not challenged; comforted, not stretched; entertained but not transformed. I eventually realized I needed to stop complaining and go check out places where people at least claimed God was experientially present.

My worst fears were confirmed; my mind was stretched beyond my comfort levels as I searched for the understanding to accompany experience. Religion, I discovered, that focuses on experiences will get itself into trouble. It is not enough to have an experience of God; one has to be able to place that experience within a framework of understanding. Genuine religious experience is not an encounter meant to leave us sunning ourselves in its warmth; it draws us beyond ourselves and sets us on a journey to some place completely new. It is tempting to think that ecstasy and religious experiences are states granted to us for our personal fulfillment or enjoyment. As such, it becomes a dangerous seduction, another of our narcissistic activities, and it eventually causes God to withdraw from us. As E.M. Forster wrote, "Ecstasy doesn't last, but it cuts a channel for something lasting."

What religious experience does is open up our awareness to the reality of another whole plane of existence and then presents us with its innumerable questions. Who have we encountered and why? How can we understand what approaches us on a different epistemological plane than all our other realities? How can a human be trusted to comprehend and carry the mysterious and holy? It is for failure to answer those questions adequately that Spirit-led movements run aground or fall into disrepute.

It was Kierkegaard who gave me illustrations to explain the "why" of religious experience. He asked that we imagine the most difficult dance maneuver. No one could do a perfect pirouette, for example, without years of practice. In the world of Spirit, however, one might be surprised by the ecstasy of a flawless pirouette without ever having gotten blisters practicing. The purpose is not to eliminate effort, but rather, to entice one to learn to dance. The Christian life is a difficult life. It is actually a supernatural life, capable of being lived only with divine help. If we manage to follow the Way to the end, it will be because we have known the Presence of God with us, helping us. Perhaps the reason the world has so few dancers is because it is divided up into those who think that to have all the book knowledge about dancing is to be a dancer, or those who think that to sit enjoying the inner emotion of the music is to be a dancer, or those who have fallen or crashed after their pirouette, thinking that they were dancers instead of realizing they were only being invited or enticed to join the dance.

History has shown that my wariness over Spirit-led movements is warranted. Although we humans need divine help in living as members of another Kingdom, we have a long history revealing how we abuse the divine aid when given. Saul was "slain in the Spirit" so often it was being rumored that he was one of the prophets. It did not, however, transform or mold his life, and he would just rise from another ecstatic trance to go and continue his murderous and paranoid pursuit of David. What is more ominous is that Saul's experiences actually created a dependence on the supernatural, and when God withdrew, Saul just went off to find a witch in order to get guidance. The story of Samson is another story that serves as a warning. Samson had a special anointing of the Spirit of God, which he used to increase his capacity for lust and vengeance. In the story of Simon the magician (Acts 8), we see another example of the Spirit being sought in order to accommodate and exacerbate all that is worst in fallen humanity. There has been a long human history of people proving that we are not yet ready to be carriers of the power and goodness of God. And yet, the Spirit is imperative to effect the ends toward which creation moves. According to the Bible, the ends to which God gives His Spirit are two-fold: the creation of sons of God and to initiate the coming of the new Kingdom.

Christian spirituality is about Immanuel—God with us. It is the Holy Spirit that turns that knowledge from a theological idea into an experiential fact. We are told that the creation groans waiting for the sons of God to be revealed; it would seem that the whole purpose of creation was the creation of those sons of God. "Sons of God," however, are defined in the Bible as those who are led by the Spirit of God. The purpose of God is the creation of a humanity that can carry His life, His power, and His goodness; it is for a people who are born into and become participants of the New Kingdom, bringing its power and goodness into the earthly kingdoms of man. If the touch of God results in abnormal behavior, it is because we have not yet achieved the maturity that can carry that glory. Christianity without the experiential knowledge of the Holy Spirit is fraudulent. But knowledge of the Spirit without the wisdom and maturity to know the ends to which God gives His life will be dangerous. However, as much as human beings may seem to be incapable of becoming carriers of the life of God, it is nevertheless still the end towards which creation strains. Ever since Jesus was named the firstborn son of God, the implication has existed that further sons of God are yet to be revealed, the "sons of God" being those who have followed in Jesus' footsteps and have discovered how the divine and human meet to be melded into one harmonious whole.

The greatest clue, therefore, as to the ends for which God gives His Spirit lies in the reality of the Incarnation. In Jesus, two natures reached their completion and lived in perfect harmony: the fullness of God and the fullness of man. By placing his will within the will of God, Jesus showed us a "wholly new way of being human."[242] Jesus became human to show us that "God is more human than man himself."[243] Never again can we claim that the soul needs to escape either life or its body in order to become spiritual. Early secularists such as Spinoza had placed Divinity in nature itself because they believed that a Transcendent God would alienate man from the world and his own nature.[244] By being God, however, the humanity of Jesus was not neglected or reduced, but rather, reached its fullness and perfection.

One of the great paradoxes of our creaturely state lies in the fact that in order to become human we need supernatural help. As Teilhard de Chardin noted, "We are not human beings seeking a spiritual experience, we are spiritual beings seeking a human experience." It is our humanity that we have lost. That is why Elie Wiesel, a Holocaust survivor, could say, "Man is not human."[245] George Bernard Shaw could quip that it was probable "that some who achieve or aspire to sainthood have never felt much the temptation to be human beings."[246] According to Nietzsche, "Man is the sick animal." There is something in the human animal that if left to his own devices will always destroy himself and all around him. We need to find God in order to be taught how to become human.

We humans can stand in the midst of all that God created and declared to be good and then slowly and methodically destroy it all. We may be dying inwardly of loneliness, but respond by accumulating more wealth, more honors, and more experiences to create walls of supposed security that distance ourselves even further from our neighbor. We are incapable of the forgiveness that would finally set us free, but rather nurse, nurture, and tend to all our wounds until we grow into the twisted, deformed shape of our woundedness. We lust for power and control, and then use it to spread our inhumanity over ever-widening spheres. All our attempts to love get hijacked by our possessiveness, our neediness, our passions, until they reflect our animal-like instincts rather than that Transcendent Love that is God. We need supernatural help in order to recover our lost humanity. The Holy Spirit is not only given to make us spiritual beings, but also to turn us into human beings. The power of Jesus had its basis in "the power of an indestructible life" (Hebrews 7:16).

Maximus the Confessor wrote that the life of Christ revealed God because "it carried within itself a new energy of one who lived in a new way."[247] Christian spirituality is about taking the power of another age and making it concrete and visible now in temporal history. True spirituality is about learning to forgive, turning the other cheek, being able to mourn with those who mourn, becoming peacemakers, and being merciful. In other words, it is about living out our humanity in a supra-human way that is impossible without divine help.

That is why, when evaluating movements of the Spirit, it is important to separate what is of God and what is evidence of humanity's weakness. There is no report of Jesus speaking in tongues or being "slain in the Spirit." There is no example of Jesus trying to work up the crowds by means of emotional manipulation, or else stoking the fires of enthusiasm or ecstasy. It is easy to dismiss movements of the Holy Spirit, or of "enthusiasm," in history when one only looks at the aberrations in human response. For example, modern Pentecostalism was born in Azusa Street under the leadership of a man named William Seymour, who originally believed in speaking in tongues as the sign of being a Christian. However, the more Seymour was confronted with human sinfulness and intrigue, the more he came to see that the most important sign of being a Christian was not tongues but rather manifesting the fruits of the Spirit, the fruits of love, longsuffering, joy, and peace.[248] In historical movements of the Holy Spirit, such as at Azusa Street, society's strictures disappeared: blacks embraced whites, women were freed from their servile roles, the distinctions between classes disappeared, and denominational differences were abolished. On the personal level, people were transformed, relationships were healed, and problems in living were overcome. Usually, unfortunately, the movements proved to be too frightening and controversial for some and were quickly squelched.

We were created with souls that have the capacity to apprehend God. Christian spirituality is first and foremost about returning to that awareness. We were created to be amphibious beings, beings able to live in two time zones—temporal and eternal—simultaneously. Christian spirituality is about learning to live in temporal time as though it were eternal time. We were created as hybrid creatures. Christian spirituality is about the growing awareness that if our souls are nurtured, it is our human nature that is redeemed. In the words of Jesus, "They will all be taught by God" (John 6:45). True spirituality is about being awakened into awareness of the Presence of God and then living in response to God and to His purposes.

Both the therapeutic and the church are now involved in the area of spirituality, designing new offerings and competing in what has become a hot new market. All spiritualities recognize that it was a mistake to reduce man to his brain, biology, and chemistry. Basically, the spiritualities that are competing for our loyalties can be divided into those that rely on revelation, and those that have the therapeutic as their base and use the knowledge we have gained in our introspection to design a soul according to our own observations. The former is based on the work of the Holy Spirit; the latter reduces spirit to a universal spirit. The former is concerned with the perfection of our humanity, while the latter offers Gnostic theories of the spiritual realm. The former claims that it is losing and dying to self that leaves room for the God-life to be formed in us, while the latter helps us to actualize the god within. The former breaks down our personal boundaries in order to create community. The latter augments our individualism. The church has a rich and deep heritage in the awareness of the soul and in the work of the Holy Spirit; unfortunately, much of what is now creeping into its midst has its source elsewhere.

Sin Versus Pathology

IT IS THE MANDATE of both the church and the therapeutic to meet us at those places of our unease and then help us to articulate, understand, and then wisely choose what to do with what we feel is wrong within ourselves. The church has had a rich concept that they called sin to explain the nature of our unease. The concept of sin, unfortunately, has fallen into disfavor these days. Being enlightened and modern, we now prefer the more acceptable terminology offered by the therapeutic; we now articulate and understand ourselves in terms of pathology, illness, dysfunction, and the medical diagnoses.

I have long felt a sense of unease at hearing of people who had just been diagnosed with "depression," "bipolar disorder," "personality disorder," or who were "manic-depressive," had an "anxiety disorder," a "narcissistic personality," were suffering from post-traumatic stress syndrome, or had any number of other "illnesses." There has been such a proliferation of these "diseases." It seems that we, in our society, are being turned into a walking collection of personality disorders. I can't help but ask myself—who is more human or healthy, the person who can go to a war-torn area like Bosnia, enter the heart of horror and darkness, and come back emotionally unscathed, or the one who is traumatized by the horror of it all and is therefore diagnosed as having Post-Traumatic Stress Disorder? Why do we consider the first one healthy? Why is it the latter one and not the former one who is given a label of "illness"?

It has been sad for me to watch acquaintances and friends being persuaded that their inner suffering is an "illness" and then begin the search for the right chemical to alleviate their pain, as though the richness of their humanity could be ignored and they could be reduced to the level of a biological organism. Why this insistence on organic or physicochemical views? Why are we becoming a people obsessed with trying to describe the fullness and richness of life with its full array of diverse experiences in pseudo-medical terms?

The British Government did a study that showed that between 1985

208 THE ALTARS OF AHAZ

and 1996 the number of people who regarded themselves as disabled increased 40%. When they surveyed the 16–19 year olds, the increase was 155%.[249] The change was obviously not one of objective state but rather in the way individuals were learning to perceive of themselves. Why is the primary way we see and define ourselves increasingly becoming in terms of illness?

Perhaps one of the reasons is because in a world that has lost its external reference points, the assigning of a diagnosis can give definition, recognition, and identity. When problems arise, we want them reduced to one-word labels that encapsulate the problem. A diagnosis can become our new identity, simplifying the complexity of life; it can be the new idiom that explains all that is wrong. In our day, an "illness" can also place one in a community of support; in an age where our fierce individualism has destroyed traditional communities, the support groups that rally around each specific diagnoses can become our new communities of understanding. But how healthy is the problematization of life?

In 1976, Ivan Illich wrote a book called *Limits to Medicine* in which he argued, "The medical establishment has become a major threat to health." His argument was that death, pain, and sickness are parts of our humanity. In the past, our cultures taught us how to deal with those realities, and health was defined according to our success or failure. Now, however, "Medicine has unfortunately destroyed these cultural and individual capacities, launching instead an inhuman attempt to defeat death, pain, and sickness. It has sapped the will of the people to suffer reality."[250]

Now, more that a quarter century after Illich's book was published, the *British Medical Journal* (BMJ) has taken up the questions Illich raised. As the accompanying editorial in the *Journal* pointed out, creating new diseases out of the normal processes and states of life—such as unhappiness—can be easy, but it can also do harm and be of benefit to the wrong people. Pharmaceutical companies clearly gain whenever a new portion of life is medicalized. It allows them to create one more pill. Doctors can create a wider area of influence and income when more of life is medicalized. There are personal reasons, not always good or healthy ones, why we can benefit from having our condition bestowed with the label of a "disease." So the normal challenges of life are being categorized as medical "conditions," the normal ups and downs of life have been turned into mental disorders, and the ordinary populace is being turned into patients. *BMJ* observed, "Beyond a certain point every penny spent may make the problem worse, eroding still further the human capacity to cope with reality."[251]

It is psychiatry, especially, that has tried to link mental disorders to physical sources. After all, if mental illness is not due to genetic predisposition or biochemical imbalance, then all their years of medical studies, their scientific philosophy, and the authority and power they wield because of their greater medical education has been wasted. It is only psychiatry, in the therapeutic field, that is licensed to offer drugs, psychosurgery, and electroshock. It is, therefore, imperative for them to keep mental illness tied to physical sources. However, we, the non-medical community, have become accomplices to their efforts. We must have our own reasons for wanting to believe our problems in living can be reduced to a matter of biology and chemistry. What we haven't done is stop and ask ourselves what is being lost in the bargain.

In the first place, one of the things we have lost is a sense of responsibility for our lives. If our problems are due to medical pathology or the biochemistry of our brains, then obviously we can take a passive role as pills, appointments, and rest are prescribed; we are no longer in charge of our lives—experts are. The psychiatrist Garth Wood, in his book *The Myth of Neurosis: Overcoming the Illness Excuse,* wrote, "There are no easy transports to delight, no shortcuts signposted by 'experts'. Instead there is toil and sacrifice, hard work and struggle, self-discipline and denial—that is the only road towards satisfaction. The hardships are necessary and valuable, providing obstacles in the overcoming of which we learn to like ourselves more. Never should we underestimate the importance of difficulty."[252]

That is not an opinion that most people are going to pay good money to hear, so we choose instead to subject our humanity to an "illness" model that relieves us of much of our responsibility.

Another thing we lose by medicalizing life is our full capacity to face the challenges that life presents us with. Our humanity and character are formed out of struggle and the overcoming of impediments. Not only do medical interventions impede personal growth, but also they can reduce the human organism's ability to react to its environment. Psychiatrist Peter Breggin observed, "All of the major psychiatric treatments work by producing brain dysfunction, and too often they result in lobotomy-like effects and permanent damage."[253] The impairment of normal brain function is not a side effect of psychiatric treatment; it is, rather, its intended clinical goal.[254] Life itself is a question and a challenge; rather than rising to the challenge, we can instead use medical intervention in order to limit our ability to perceive the full game. The operative word then becomes "coping" rather than the "becoming," which uses the challenges of life in order to rise above them, and in the process, become more fully human.

Medicalizing life also helps in the secularization of our views of life and its purpose. Psychiatry and its influence has been slowly bringing the entire therapeutic field closer to a lab science rather than a humanistic field, and it offers us a scientific focus rather than a spiritual understanding of the human creature. In the 1856 edition of Webster's Dictionary, psychology was defined as the study that examined "the human soul or the doctrine of man's spiritual nature."[255] By 1999, my Oxford Dictionary defined psychology as "the scientific study of the human mind and its functions." Now, under the influence of psychiatry and neuropsychology, "mind" is being reduced to "brain," and awareness of soul and spirit are being forfeited to our preoccupation with the scientific manipulation of human emotional states. Inner struggle, psychic upheaval, acute sensitivity, and existential angst—all at one time seen as signs of spiritual acumen—are being given labels of disease and are being blunted by drugs in the name of "health."

Having already held a skeptical attitude over our attempts to view life pathologically, I was delighted to come across the work of a psychiatrist named Thomas S. Szasz who, in his book The Myth of Mental Illness, wrote, "Mental illness is a myth. Psychiatrists are not concerned with mental illnesses and their treatments. In actual practice they deal with personal, social, and ethical problems in living."[256] Szasz himself had reached the conclusion, "The notion of mental illness is used chiefly to obscure and explain away problems in personal and social relationships…. We now deny moral, personal, political, and social controversies by pretending that they are psychiatric problems; in short, by playing the medical game."[257]

A human being cannot be reduced to the organic. Even those who professionally ascribe labels of disease still spend their time with their clients not explaining genetics, chemistry, or biological structures, but rather listening to clients talk about their lives, their emotions, and their attitudes. Why then this pretense over the scientific and medical basis for mental and emotional dysfunction?

Szasz traced the historical development of the concept of mental ill-ness and concluded that its basis and roots were not in science at all, but rather in expediency; linking itself with science was an attempt to free itself from association with quackery and charlatanry.[258] He concluded, "So-called mental illnesses share only a single significant characteristic with bodily diseases: the sufferer or 'sick person' is, or claims to be, more or less disabled from performing certain activities."[259] The language of "ill-ness" is therefore used metaphorically; it as an attempt to borrow the lan-guage and respectability of science and apply it to the processes of life. Szasz claimed, "This sort of search for the biological and physical causes of so-called psychopathological phenomena is motivated more by the investigator's craving for prestige and power than by his desire for under-standing and clarity…patterning his beliefs and behavior on the medical model enables the psychiatrist to share in the prestige and power of the physician."[260]

If psychoanalyses and the whole therapeutic field has attached itself to science in order to gain intellectual credibility, then the next question that needs to be asked is why we as a populace have been so gullible, so "co-dependent," so willing to play their game according to the terms that they have designed. Again, I believe the answer lies in the benefits accrued by our "co-dependency" or culpability. We humans have much to gain by seeing ourselves as "ill" rather than morally falling short or having a faulty philosophy of life. The philosopher Immanuel Kant claimed that mental disorder was due to delusion or false beliefs. How much easier it is for us to see it in organic terms. A label of "illness" can justify offensive behavior, it can release one from responsibility, and it can help rationalize or aid one in avoidance of facing the roots of one's problems in living. But perhaps most significant of all for our day, medicalizing life can help one avoid issues of moral order.

Szasz concludes his book by saying, "Human behavior is fundamentally moral behavior. Attempts to describe and alter such behavior without, at the same time, coming to grips with the issue of ethical values are therefore doomed to failure."[261] It is perhaps our desire to free ourselves from the moral imperative that has us so readily submitting to the attempts to medicalize life. In refusing to acknowledge a reality other than and higher than our ego, and in refusing to bow before anything that would thwart our drive towards self-determination, the weight of the moral imperative can be bypassed by running to hide underneath the umbrella of science. We can thereby hope to justify ourselves by saying, "It could not be otherwise."

If the therapeutic were really a science, then it would have to demonstrate objectivity and moral neutrality. Freud made much of his moral neutrality. His claimed moral neutrality, however, was a sham; it just became another moral position. Freud didn't just study sexuality in children; he advocated their sexual enlightenment. He found homosexuality to be a "perversion." He was a misogynist in his views on women. With regard to human relationships, he was patronizing and undemocratic, believing human relationships to be based on domination and submission.[262] Unlike real science, where a cancerous tumor will be discovered to have the same qualities regardless of whether it is studied by a righteous man or a bigoted philanderer, the therapeutic always comes with a human point of view and from a particular moral stance.

All claims of moral neutrality on the part of the therapeutic are basically fraudulent. As the psychoanalyst Jeffrey Moussaieff Masson concluded, "I think by now there is general agreement that no psychotherapy can be value free, and that no psychotherapist can avoid instilling or attempting to instill his or her values in patients."[263] There is no such thing as a morally neutral human being or a morally neutral space. The very setting, approach, and questions of each and every therapeutic encounter are determined according to training in some school of thought; they are not ever free from a particular point of view or moral stance. We live in a moral universe, and to provide a supposed morally neutral space is actually to free a person from the constraints of the moral order. What is more, since clients are usually at a crisis point in life and in a position of vulnerability, it is easy for therapists to subtly instill their own values and beliefs in their clients. David Rosenthal, after doing research in the area, concluded that patients, not surprisingly, tended to accept the values of their therapists.[264] Those values never need to be stated; every detail of the therapeutic encounter, from the counselor's attitude, responses, questions, and even the set-up of the space, has unstated implications.

No therapeutic encounter is a morally neutral act. To begin with, one major way in which the therapeutic frees the individual from the moral imperative is by positing the self as the center of moral authority. By shifting the center of our universe away from a transcendent source and making the knowing ego the center of its own world, one is therefore helped to individualize one's own moral universe. In the past, moral cultures provided us with a moral compass, which we internalized. The therapeutic loosens the influence of that external compass and framework. Much of modern therapy is based on the work of Carl Rogers, who taught that clients could be guided to find and make decisions based on their own set of values. We humans apparently have an innate goodness imbedded in us; we just need a facilitator who will, with the right tools and techniques, help that goodness to become actualized. Right, wrong, good, and evil are all useless categories—what is significant are the methods we use to actualize our chosen values. According to Kohlberg, it is not important what we decide but how we make our choices that determines our moral development level. The goal of therapy is to increase our capacity to problem solve, to create our own values. What all therapies have in common is the belief that, according to sociologist James Davison Hunter, "Moral reality is, finally, a subjective reality; that moral authority is, finally, a subjective authority; that moral norms are the aggregate of rudimentary subjective sensibilities."[265] The therapies may disagree over how we come to our subjectively chosen and achieved destinies, but those destinies are subjectively chosen.

What all the therapies refuse to recognize is the fact that we human beings are "instinctually deprived."[266] As Hunter observed,

> We don't innately know what is socially acceptable to eat or when to sleep, what clothes are appropriate in what circumstances, or how to act toward others. Our sexual instincts area not reliable guides to how, when, where, or with whom sexual intimacy might be appropriate. We have no sense of what our obligations are toward the environment or toward other species, much less how to treat strangers, how to express empathy with those in need, or even that empathy toward the needy might be a good worth pursuing. We are not born with moral obligations to stabilize life, a worldview to give coherence to life, or ideals to guide our lives.[267]

We, unlike the animal kingdom, need to be socialized into appropriate behavior. We need an external authority to guide us into knowledge of what our potential as a human being really consists of. We are the only animal that will self-destruct if we follow only our own inner gyroscope and instincts. When counseling becomes client-centered, focusing on the client's "inner wisdom," then it lacks religion's ability to provide a vision and transformation. Compare the therapeutic approach to the advice offered in Proverbs, which says, "He who trusts in himself is a fool, But he who walks in wisdom is kept safe" (Proverbs 29:26). In Biblical terms, wisdom is always externally revealed knowledge; it is that which we accept in faith rather than coming to by means of subjectivity or by our own understanding.

By claiming the status of a "science," not only has the therapeutic managed to free us from the moral imperative, but it has also managed to free us from the web of commitments by which we, in the past, were socialized into society. The therapeutic makes much of the unencumbered self, the fully individuated self, and the autonomous self. It posits a self freed from the institutions, society, and the cultures that have traditionally been seen to form the individual. Relationships, commitments, and obligations are all consigned to subservient status; they are seen as secondary to the need to serve the self. By placing professional encounters where family, friends, spiritual director, and church community used to provide support, the therapeutic has actually freed the individual from the very support systems that would once have drawn the individual outside of himself to find meaning in a larger system of understanding.

By claiming the status of a "science," the therapeutic has also claimed the license to treat the human being outside of reference to his soul and spirit. Since the "soul" is not a term considered relevant in science, it can be ignored by the therapeutic, resulting in aberrations in vision as this "science" tries to come to grips with the human entity stripped of precisely what makes it most unique.

The advantage of defining ourselves in terms of "illness" or "pathology" may lie in the fact that they are morally neutral terms, but by viewing ourselves medically outside the purview of religion, has our more "scientific" terminology allowed us a more progressive view of our humanity or has it just created illusive pseudo-scientific bubbles behind which we can hide?

Certainly there are some, it can and has been argued, who are truly ill, for whom the language and understandings of religion prove inadequate. With that view in mind, it was interesting coming across the works of Anton Boisen and R. Frederick West.[268] Both were written by men who had been committed to mental institutions and had been pronounced to be beyond hope. Both men made remarkable and quick recoveries. Both came to see mental suffering as remedial and a sign of hope. For both men, their period of "illness" became like a "religious conversion" experience, allowing for a breakthrough to a new way of seeing life. Boisen eventually became a chaplain in a mental institution and started a program whereby members of theological schools could be trained to see the religious side of mental "illness."

Anton T. Boisen came to his religious view of mental illness after studying the conversion experiences of religious figures of the past and then comparing them to his own experience and also to the experiences of the inmates of a mental institution. Boisen, like Szasz, concluded that functional mental illness was about one's philosophy of life, saying, "Acute upheavals are really attempts at reorganization which are closely related to those eruptive solutions of inner conflicts so familiar to the religious worker under the name of 'conversion experiences'."[269] It was what one did with those "acute upheavals" that was crucial. To counsel one suffering, Boisen therefore claimed, without reference to the sufferer's religious outlook, is not an impartial, "scientific," act, but is rather an attempt to reduce man to a non-spiritual being; it is not a "science" so much as an elimination of the soul and spirit as significant reference points for the patient.

Although seeing mental "illness" as a religious issue or due to an inadequate philosophy of life might seem regressive to those who have become accustomed to seeing the human being only in scientific terms, the spiritual side of mental health does occasionally surface. In the 1971 *Archives of General Psychiatry,* for example, one author referred to the schizophrenic as a failed mystic, writing, "Both mystical and psychotic states have arisen out of a situation in which the individual has struggled with a desperate problem, has come to a complete impasse, and given up hope, abandoned the struggle in despair. For the mystic, what emerges from the "cloud of unknowing" or the "dark night of the soul" is an ecstatic union with God or Reality. For the psychotic person, the world rushes in but does not become integrated in the harmony of *mystico unio* or *satori.* Instead, he creates a delusion to achieve a partial ordering or control."[270]

The "failed mystic," or those who become mentally ill, are those who, instead of living in reality or in harmony with the whole instead withdraw into an inner world where they can construe their own reality. When we decide to ignore the moral nature of the universe and of ourselves, then guilt, anxiety, alienation, depression, and finally, inner disharmony and delusion are the result.

A while back, I attended a secular medical banquet where a doctor at our table who had spent a year working in a mental institution talked about how religious language was so prevalent among the inmates that she had finally gone to the medical director in charge of the hospital and asked whether there could be something such as demon possession. My daughter is a nurse who in her training rotated through the psychiatric ward. She told me it had struck her that the one thing that made the people on her ward unique was their interests and preoccupations; unlike the general public, they seemed to be more interested in religion, in the spirit world, and in otherworldly issues. The patient she had been assigned, for example, had been a perfectly healthy boy until he started playing with a Ouija board, whereupon he started to hear voices, was hospitalized, diagnosed as a schizophrenic, and placed on heavy medication. In our desire to see the human in purely scientific categories, are we missing something that is essential to what it means to be human?

If mental illness is essentially about "the disorganization of the philosophy of life,"[271] and if it has to do with "the sufferer's attitude toward his world and his conception of his own place therein,"[272] then suffering can actually be seen as remedial; it can be seen as the soul's attempt to reorganize. The "illness" gives one the opportunity to either succumb to the forces of disarray, or else to break through to a "conversion" experience where one manages to reorder life around a new and higher order of seeing and living.

The therapeutic claims that a new integration is exactly what they are about; the most they can offer, though, is a new human way of seeing. It is still the old ego, which got one into trouble in the first place, which is in charge of the new formation. That is why if change actually happens in the therapeutic encounter, it is extremely slow. Nature cannot really overcome nature. In religion, however, the breaking up of old ways of seeing allows one to reorder on a completely new, higher plane. Suffering opens the door to the supernatural; if man is going to radically change, then it can only be by means of the help of something higher than his own limited nature.

In our attempts to avoid the moral order, our failures in life, and the persistent awareness that we have fallen short of what we were meant to be, we have run to the sheltering umbrella of science, which is increasingly finding labels of pathology to attach to all our shortcomings and unease. In spite of all of psychiatry's claims to be a science, perhaps nothing discredits those claims more than looking at the way it determines those labels of pathology. Scientists "discover" pathology. The therapeutic "creates" categories of pathology. Paula Caplan, a clinical and research psychologist, likens the ascribing of diagnoses to the labeling of constellations in the sky. We cannot say that there is such a thing as the Big Dipper or Orion in the same way that we can say that we see a table, a tree, or a cancerous tumor. The constellations are a human construct. Constructs serve man's needs for labels, definition, and reduction rather than any need for truth. There is no such thing as the Big Dipper or Orion that exist in their own right; we humans have lumped certain stars together and given them those names. They are constructs.

The labels that are created by the therapeutic industry are also constructs. It is deceiving to present them as diagnoses similar to that of, for example, cancer. As Caplan noted, professionals in the therapeutic industry often make diagnoses "as though they have simply discovered what is there and where it should be classified instead of deciding what is there and how to pigeonhole 'it'."[273] Psychiatric categories are created, not discovered. In order to see how pathology is "created" by the therapeutic, one needs only to study the history of the creation of the *Diagnostic and Statistical Manual of Mental Disorders* (DSM).

The *DSM* is the inspiration of the American Psychiatric Association (APA). Because the APA has the authority and respectability that comes with their higher medical education, their publication, the *DSM,* is the diagnostic manual that influences the whole therapeutic field. The mental illnesses listed in the *DSM* are constructs. That is why, unlike a true science, they are open to such varied interpretation. One psychiatrist, who in disillusionment left her orthodox training behind, spoke of how on the ward, she had noticed how "those darn patients refused to fit neatly into any one category, as witness the emergence of ten different diagnoses when ten different staff members examined the same patient!"[274] Since the diagnoses are humanly created constructs, their interpretation and application can be as variable as the humans that use and abuse them and as variable as the humans to which they are applied. Because the DMA deals with constructs as opposed to hard science, the APA can also decide that hundreds of thousands of people have a type of mental illness, and then reverse their position, a practice they have accomplished more than once

When Paula Caplan, who once worked as a psychotherapist, became aware that the APA was about to label certain female problems as "illness" and then attempt to include them in the *DSM*, she found herself objecting, and soon got caught in a battle that would eventually see her working on the very work groups that create the *DSM*, a position from which she got a good inside look at how the *DSM* is actually created. What she discovered is revealed in her book *They Say You're Crazy: How the World's Most Powerful Psychiatrists Decide Who's Normal.*

Caplan's campaign against the APA began when she discovered that the APA had decided to create a new category of mental illness called "Masochistic Personality/Disorder" (MPD), a label they later changed to Self-defeating Personality Disorder (SDPD). Caplan objected because she could see that the labeling could be abused by attaching it to women in traditional roles and to those in abusive situations. It was called the "good-wife syndrome" because it meant putting another's needs before one's own.[275] Could that really be considered pathological? According to the APA the people with MPD were apparently "sick" because, since they were in positions that caused them suffering, it was concluded that they must have a need to suffer, or else at least enjoyed suffering. Caplan had herself done studies revealing no evidence to back those claims. However, if the women in therapy denied the desire to be hurt, then they were called "unconscious" masochists.[276] In fact, one of the stated characteristics of people with MPD was that of a "negative therapeutic reaction." What that meant was that when undergoing therapy for this condition, they actually got worse.

Caplan's opposition to the APA and the *DSM* grew when PMS was turned into a disorder—Premenstrual Dysphoric Disorder (PMDD), later renamed Late Luteal Phase Dysphoric Disorder (LLPDD), a much more scientific sounding name. Conservative estimates showed that 500,000 women would immediately be pathologized. The potential for harm was quickly revealed by a legal battle in which a husband was claiming custody of his children because his wife was "premenstrually mentally ill."[277]

The third battle was over the label Paraphelic Rapism, later relabeled Paraphilic Coercive Disorder. Even before that category was listed in the *DSM,* therapists were already being hired in court battles to show that rapists were not actually evil, but rather emotionally disturbed and therefore in need of therapy, not jail. This claim was made even though therapy had not been shown to help rapists.[278]

In order to show that excessive diagnostic labeling can do harm by masking or deflecting attention from where harm actually occurs, and to show that the diagnostic categories of *DSM* are biased according to the few dozen people who control the process—a few who are "mostly male, mostly white, mostly wealthy, mostly American psychiatrists"[279]— Caplan submitted a proposal for a new diagnostic category: the Delusional Dominating Personality Disorder. The criteria she included were many of the attributes we would associate with, find most annoying, but have learned to accept as part of the "male" personality. It was turned down, but not because it was less scientific than the other diagnostic categories of illness that were being decided on, but rather because she was not in the dominant power group that got to decide who to categorize as "ill."

What Caplan discovered in her involvement with the *DSM* was how shallow its claim to scientific objectivity really is. Much of what Caplan discovered has been reinforced by others who have looked into how the *DSM* is actually created, and they have offered comment; "To read about

the evolution of the *DSM* is to know this: It is an entirely political document. What it includes, what it does not include, are the result of inten-
sive campaigning, lengthy negotiating, infighting, and power plays"
(Louise Armstrong *And They Call It Help: The Psychiatric Policing of
American Children*),[280] and, "In the world of modern psychiatry, claims can
become truth, hopes can become achievements, and propaganda is taken
as science." (Peter Breggin, *Toxic Psychiatry*)[281]

As one psychologist who participated in the work of *DSM-III-R* said,
"The low level of intellectual effort was shocking. Diagnoses were developed by majority vote on the level we would use to choose a restaurant.
You feel like Italian, I feel like Chinese, so let's go to a Cafeteria. Then it's
typed into a computer. It may reflect on our naiveté, but it was our belief
that there would be an attempt to look at things scientifically."[282]

Because of the weight of influence that psychiatry and the *DSM* carry
in our world, their influence is pervasive in teaching us to view human
beings in terms of pathology. Whereas the original *DSM* (1952) had 60
types and subtypes of mental illnesses listed, by the third edition of *DSM*,
there were 297 ways to be listed as mentally ill. The *DSM-IV* has 374 list-
ings. Whereas in 1968 the DSM consisted of 119 pages, it has now grown
to 886. Between 1980 and 1990, the listed disorders increased by almost
300 percent:[283] we are ever-increasingly becoming pathologized. Why? In
the March 1994, *DSM-IV* Update it was reported that a new category—
Bipolar II Disorder—was added—"because it increases diagnostic coverage."[284] A psychiatrist running for APA president said in his candidacy
statement, "It is the task of APA to protect the earning power of psychiatrists."[285] No wonder that the psychiatrist Breggin wrote, "Organized psychiatry is big business more than it is a profession."[286]

What has also become alarming is the degree to which the pharmaceutical companies have been actively involved in "helping" the medical field to
find, label, and then "cure" diseases. Finding new illnesses and disorders has
truly become big business. *The Reuters Business Insight* reported,
"Pharmaceutical companies are searching for new disorders, based on exten-
sive analysis of unexploited market opportunities (whether recognized

today or promoted as such tomorrow). The coming years will bear greater witness to the corporate sponsored creation of disease."[287]

An example of a disease largely created by the drug industry is "female sexual dysfunction" or FSD. It was claimed that 43%[288] of women suffered from this "disease," although there was some difficulty defining exactly what it was. Although a definition had existed in the *DSM*, in 1999 a group of nineteen participants gathered in Boston to produce a classification and definition that could be used by the medical community. What few in the medical community were aware of was the complicity of the drug companies. Eight drug companies sponsored the meeting in Boston, and it was revealed that eighteen out of the nineteen authors had financial ties or relationships to a total of twenty-two drug companies.[289] Of course, those drug companies already had drugs to provide answer to the new disease.

Other "diseases" in which drug companies have played a significant role, both in their creation and also in the massive advertising campaigns needed to raise public awareness and desire for their drugs, have been those of "social anxiety disorder," PMDD, and depression. The "symptoms" for ADD have been expanded so greatly into the terrain of common behavior that between 1980 and 1987 the children who could thus be labeled "sick" had expanded 50%.[290] Of course, that has allowed the stimulants to treat this "disease" to become one of the fastest growing group of drugs.

The pharmaceutical industry in America spends more than three billion dollars a year on advertising targeted at the consumer, much of that being aimed at convincing us that our quality of life would be improved if we just tried their drugs. Recently two doctors out of Dartmouth Medical School analyzed the ads that drug companies had placed in ten popular US magazines. What they found was that almost half were an attempt to impute medical causes for the normal experiences of life.[291] Since it is the psychiatrists, in the therapeutic field, who have the authority to prescribe drugs they, especially, have become the targets and accomplices in the drug companies' campaign to turn normal life into categories of illness.

Psychiatric labeling has a long history of serving purposes that are not very noble. Not only does labeling serve financial ends, it can also be used to mask social causes and personal helplessness. Benjamin Rush, one of the signers of the American Declaration of Independence and the one who was regarded to be the father of American psychiatry, was known to invent diagnoses for behaviors that he found troubling. An example was "anarchia," which was the term he applied to people who were not satisfied with the present political structure and wanted more democracy.[292] In the 19th century, the psychiatric profession "discovered" a mental disorder that it called "drapetomania," that being a label of disorder given to slaves who wanted to escape from slavery.[293] Native people who drink too much are said to have "psychoactive substance use disorders."[294] A label allows the internalization of problems; it deflects attention from the real sources of problems in order to place blame on the victim. Thus, wrongs such as slavery and the long history of the marginalization of the native people can be masked by hiding behind the labels of "science." That is what has caused Louise Armstrong to argue that the power to bestow a "name" has been used as a powerful tool for social control, saying, "Whatever validity there may be to the concept of psychiatric illness, naming, in the psy world, has always been an expression of social opinion."[295]

In the 1960s, Bruno Bettleheim declared that the protesters of that decade did not have a political agenda but rather unresolved Oedipal complexes and were attacking institutions as surrogate fathers.[296] In the Los Angeles race riots of 1992, the city's response was to spend $6 million on counseling.[297] When overcrowding in New York City caused the eruption of conflicts the city did not look into the problem of housing but rather trained therapists in conflict resolution to help the people cope.[298]

When a child has had its stability threatened by a bitter divorce, is caught in the messy crossfire of a custody battle, acts out in class, and is therefore referred to a professional for help, where the child is diagnosed as having ADHD and is placed on Ritalin, is the diagnosis and medication an answer to the problem of the child or is it a way of policing and of social

control? Does the real problem lie with the child or with his life framework; is it a medical health issue or a life issue? Studies have shown a
direct relationship between the number of hours children watch television
in the preschool years and their chances of being diagnosed with ADHD
in later years. Apparently, doctors in Pennsylvania claim they have seen no
cases of ADHD among the conservative Mennonites (who have no television). Could our penchant for diagnosing be an attempt to avoid moral
and social issues?

I was raising my children at a time when the people around me were
using the current therapeutic jargon of emotional separation, individual-
ization, fostering independence, and parental disengagement to explain
the need for the parent to loosen ties with one's children at an early age.
Yesterday I opened the newspaper to discover a new disorder—"peer-
attachment disorder"—created. Apparently the youth who were separated
emotionally from their families too early became harmfully bonded to
their peer group. Also, apparently racism is now being considered as a
potential disorder. Does that mean that hate crimes will be excused
because they are only indicative of a mental disorder?

Christopher Lasch wrote that the narcissistic personality has become
"the dominant type of personality structure in contemporary society."[299] To
what degree has that narcissism been caused by the self-absorption fos-
tered by the therapeutic? Who taught us to turn into ourselves and place
the self at the center of all concern? Is it not time we recognize that the
therapeutic itself is creating some of the pathology that it is now attaching
all those labels to?

What the preceding examples reveal is an attitude that attempts to
place the source of suffering within the individual and not in the external
world. However, as can be seen, the therapeutic itself can thus become an
"avoidance mechanism," helping one avoid responsible action. It is easier
to internalize the problem and ascribe a label of mental illness than to look
at the consequences of oppression, poverty, and societal breakdown. It is
easier to accept the label "depression" and take Prozac than to face our anxiety, fears, the consequences of bad choices, or just the problems of living.

Is it not time that we ask—when labels of pathology and drugs and therapy mask larger or deeper problems, are they not morally wrong?

It is the needs of the professionals that are being served by our excessive labeling. As one therapist wrote,

> I often see patients with complaints whose origins are largely sociogenic: unresponsive institutions, alienating work circumstances, occupational stress, arbitrary job displacements …. Yet many times, I'm required to award "courtesy disease labels" myself, either to enable clients to receive insurance benefits, and get reimbursed, or provide easily decodable data for colleagues…our lives as professionals sometimes quarantine us from the "contamination" of that larger world where we and our patients ultimately have to cope, as best we can, with the apocryphal issues we face as parents, citizens, teachers, dreamers, and friends.[300]

Being fitted with "courtesy disease labels" has become a way of, in despair, withdrawing from the world and its challenges in order to allow ourselves to be fitted, instead, into bureaucratic and managerial frameworks.

The psychiatrist Peter Breggin observed, "Psychiatry is the institution socially mandated to respond to personal helplessness and failure."[301] That also happens to be the mandate of the church. An alternative to allowing ourselves to be defined in terms of illness and pathology would have been to reconsider issues of moral order and the unfashionable notion of "sin." I know the word "sin" causes a reaction of revulsion within us, but that is because it has, in fault, been made synonymous with morality. Before we can understand the richness of the concept of sin, we need to first separate it from morality.

There was a time when morality had been seen as a byproduct, as "one reverberation of man's encounter with the terrible sweetness of Divinity."[302] It was one of the side effects of falling in love with God. That, however, was before the Enlightenment thinkers had managed to relegate God to some Deistic sphere and had destroyed the relevance of God to life here below.

In early Latin and ancient Greek—the two languages from which our Bible is translated—there is no word that is directly translated by our word "moral."[303] Morality was once seen in holistic terms, as the set of character that determined one's approach to life rather than in terms of individual acts.[304] The history of the word "moral" is a history of the narrowing of its meaning until by the late seventeenth century it became used in the most narrow sense of all, as to do with sexual behavior. Now we almost never hear the word "immoral" applied to those perversions in character such as pride, greed, envy, or bitterness, which destroy human community, but only to sexual indiscretions.

For the ancients, such as Aristotle, morality meant "the fulfillment of human nature; virtue means excellence."[305] Medieval Christianity essentially saw morality the same way. They believed in a God who had created a universe that was a compatible home for our essentially moral natures, a universe in which we were meant to live in harmony with the natural order and with others. The loving God who had created that natural order had also implanted in our hearts a longing for Himself, a longing that would not be stilled until it found its way back into harmony with both God and, by implication, with the natural moral order of the universe in which we had been planted.

The Enlightenment separated the idea of morality from the idea of a divine ordering where community and harmony reigned. The Enlightenment thinkers chafed at the idea of a morality that had been handed down from some divine being on high; they thought that morality could be grounded in a study of human nature and society. Morality, they thought, could be understood from a philosophical perspective separated from the theological framework that had once given it form. With the increasing separation of the moral from its theological base, a narrowing of the concept of morality ensued.[306]

Once morality had become separated from relationship to God, it then became the Enlightenment project to justify morality on rational terms. Kierkegaard, Kant, Rameau, Hume and Diderot all tried to philosophically justify, explain, and define moral behavior. The basis for morality seemed to erode a bit more with each attempt.[307]

At the same time, the church, increasingly losing its significance in society, was not going to be consigned to irrelevance without a fight. The more our reliance on God shifted to become reliance on ourselves and our own rationalistic tendencies, the more the church needed a new project to justify its existence. Morality provided the answer. Morality, after all, could be thought to be its rightful jurisdiction. The historian James Turner noted, "As spiritual realities thinned, the temptation thickened to seize on something as solid as morality."[308] It was in the management of morality that the church thought to build a bridge that could connect itself to and could provide common ground with the Enlightenment. What the church seemingly failed to recognize was that by preaching morality, the church was no longer mediating God's Presence in the world, but was rather taking over in His absence.

Morality was an area where God and man were seen to have common interest, so becoming custodian of morality allowed the church to feel a little closer to the God that the Enlightenment thinkers had pushed out of the universe. By becoming society's moral guardian, the church felt it could remain buddies with the God who was increasingly becoming silent and absent. Moralism justified the church's existence in a world where it was becoming increasingly irrelevant; it took care of the question of what to do with God's absence. One could throw up one's good behavior like a sop to the Eternal One while at the same time avoiding the need to seek for the missing God, develop a relationship with God, and consequently for the need to relinquish control of one's heart and life. What the church failed to realize was that moralism never brings salvation to either individuals or to a society; when the church no longer mediates God's love and Presence to a society, choosing instead the role of moral policing in God's absence, then it becomes a stench in the nostrils of society and brings not health, but rather causes a violent backlash.

History has shown that once morality becomes separated from relationship with God, then the battles begin. As our modern world increasingly demanded that morality not be pegged to religious notions but to rationalistic thinking and human common sense, the church was ever-increasingly thrown into a reactionary pose. Our secular society's increasing ability to live without God is coincident with increasing conflicts over issues of morality.

Religion can do its most harm when estrangement from God causes one to react to that abandonment by taking up God's cause of morality. Moralism does not express a zeal for God or for the kingdom of God, but rather a zeal for the maintenance of the status quo. Obsession with morality often arises less from faith than from a reaction of fear to the shifting structures of society. Morality in itself does not restore harmony with either God or the larger universe in which we are consigned to live. Focus on morality, instead, consigns us to cycles of addictive or habitual behaviors, repentance or confession, and then a return to those guilt-producing behaviors. Moralism may improve conduct, but it does not transform hearts or character. Moralism instead instills guilt, which, even if it causes the individual to submit to societal structures, does not result in one opening up one's life to a loving God. Perhaps one of the worst effects of allowing moralism to replace a larger vision is that moralism inevitably destroys compassion in a society and replaces it with judgmentalism. Moralism thus strains even further our relationships with God and with society. A focus on morality is healthy only when we know it to be a byproduct and not the main purpose of religion. Karl Rahner writes, "Where someone has not had an initial experience of God and of his Spirit, liberating him from his deepest fears and from guilt, there is no point in announcing the moral norms of Christianity to him. He would not be able to understand them; at best, they might seem to him to be the source of still more radical constraints and still deeper fears."

Jesus told a story which I find applicable to our moralizing tendencies: "When an evil spirit comes out of a man, it goes through arid places seeking rest and does not find it. Then it says, 'I will return to the house I left.' When it arrives, it finds the house unoccupied, swept clean and put in order. Then it goes and takes with it seven other spirits more wicked than itself, and they go in and live there. And the final condition of that man is worse than the first. That is how it will be with this wicked generation." (Matthew 12:43–45).

Moralism is like the scrupulous housekeeper who cleans out a room only to find her efforts bedeviled by forces that only grow in strength from the attempt to have them eliminated. If moralism was sufficient to cast out our demons, then the work of Jesus was superfluous; the Pharisees had already developed a moral code that took care of all of life. Christianity is not about how to clean out rooms, but rather about what can fill those rooms so that all our demons can be kept at bay.

In a time when "values" language has been politicized, providing the rhetoric for partisan politics, we need to again hear the message of Jesus; moral order is not synonymous with transformed hearts. In fact, an obsession with morality and with external works can be the judgment of a people who would not accept the rest that God desires to bring: "Do and do, do and do/rule on rule, rule on rule" (Isaiah 28:10, 13). A focus on ethics and values can be a human attempt to impose the shell of religion without offering the life-giving kernel. Jesus claimed, "The good man brings good things out of the good stored up in him, and the evil man brings evil things out of the evil stored up in him" (Matthew 12:35). True religion is about transformed hearts, not morality.

The history of morality is interesting because the words "moral" and "morality" are conspicuously absent in my Bible. The Bible instead uses the language of sin. Sin is a state of being before it results in moral lapses. Whereas moralism is about submission to something static—rules, law, societal strictures—sin is about lost relationship. "Sins" as lapses in moral conduct are a result of "living in sin"; that is, life lived away from God. Sin is the orientation of the will away from God and the harmony of the whole in order to carve out a private universe where the personal ego, not God, can reign supreme. Sin is the creation of a life that does not measure up to the glory of what God had intended us to be—"All have sinned and fall short of the glory of God" (Romans 3:23)—but to re-orient our lives around God would mean surrendering lives that we clutch tightly to ourselves. Sin is about impediments that keep us from the fullness of personal relationship with a personal God. The original sin was succumbing to the tempting promise of fruit that would allow us to function as god and decide good and evil for ourselves. Sin is all of the above. Sin in the past was seen as something much larger and all encompassing than mere morality; it was a state of being that could only be overcome by becoming reconnected to God. H. Wheeler Robinson claimed that the "judgment of moral evil as 'sin' is possible only in the light of grace."[309] We all are aware of the presence of moral evil and our own moral lapses, but as long as we view those lapses in terms of morality, we feel judged and long to hide. When our lapses are seen as sin, we are left yearning for the glory from which we have fallen and for a return to the relationship that we have lost.

Morality is appealing precisely because it deflects attention away from the issue of sin. In the past, Martin Luther had defined sin as "man turned in upon himself." Now we have filled our churches with those who help us turn in upon ourselves and have turned it into a laudable activity. In fact, if we don't spend a lot of time and energy examining ourselves, we are accused of repression or denial. If, on the other hand, we express too much interest in God and religion, we are suspected of trying to escape reality, or of having a "religious addiction."

Whereas sin was once understood as the attempt to usurp God and take control of our own lives, we now have filled our churches with therapists whose purpose is to help us take control of our lives and live them on our terms. We have turned what was once understood as "sin" into the state we now call "health." We may go to church and confess that we "have followed too much the devices and desires of our own hearts (*The Book of Common Prayer*), but our next stop is the therapist who teaches us to get in touch with the feelings and desires of our own hearts and urges us towards their full expression. When we hear the voice of the tempter saying, "Did God really say...?(Genesis 3:1) we now have experts with the expertise of "science" telling us that God and His laws are culturally specific and can be superseded by further "knowledge" from the realm of "science." Of course psychology provides the "science" that helps us see in new, enlightened ways. Whereas the Bible once told us to "lean not upon thy own understanding," we now have therapists who help us with self-understanding. Whereas sin was once understood as the state of living outside of reference to God, we have now developed theories of individuation and autonomous being that have turned that state into a virtue. If one returns to the earlier perceptions of sin, then one has to admit that what the therapeutic does is help us live in sin.

When we substituted the language of sin for morality, something important was lost. We lost an awareness of how all our problems are connected to our loss of harmony with God and with the higher universe of meaning. We now exist as individualistic, isolated atoms, our problems no longer being seen in holistic terms. Instead of catching a vision of the glory towards which we were meant to live, we define our falling short in terms of personal pathology, illness, and in terms of biology, genetics, chemistry, and brain function. It is in that process that our humanity is increasingly being reduced and destroyed.

Both religion and the therapeutic meet us at that point where we become aware of our inner unease. When we rid ourselves of God and the notion of sin, we did not eliminate the questions that are basic to and form the root of all religion, the questions of: *Who are we? What is wrong with us? What shall we do about it?* We just began to answer those questions in a way that does a disservice to our humanity. We allowed ourselves to be objectified and seen through the lens of *DSM* categories. We submitted to being placed into the deforming mold called a diagnosis. We allowed the quest for Truth and Ultimate Reality to be replaced with psychological effectiveness.

Who are we? The Biblical answer is, "You are 'gods'; you are all sons of the Most High" (Psalm 82:6). It teaches us to say, "I praise you because I am fearfully and wonderfully made" (Psalm 139:14). The problem is that we, in actual fact, do not feel that good about ourselves. That is why we need to ask the second question. What is wrong with us? Christianity tells us that we have been infected with a fatal flaw. Live on our terms according to our own understanding and we will self-destruct. To the next question—What shall we do about it?—the answer is that self-surrender and reconnection with God will help us overcome what is wrong.

Living in the Light of God will reveal more than we initially feel comfortable knowing. That is why we keep running from God. But before God, the truth of ourselves will be combined with the truth of God—the truth of His love, acceptance, and forgiveness. It is that truth that will have us wanting to shed all that prevents us from getting closer. True morality is a byproduct of divine relationship.

If the therapeutic seems to be an ally of religion, then it is because the church has lost its orientation. It has allowed sin to become reduced to morality, and once sin became morality, we could design a personal moral code that allowed us to feel righteous while living in our chosen state of sin—sin understood as a life lived as an autonomous being relying on self-understanding and self-realization.

As long as we reject religion's answers to the question of our unease, we will live without a vision sufficient to draw us towards our God-given potential. Answering the question of what is wrong with us in terms of sin, I find, is much more constructive and hopeful than seeing the answer in terms of illness and pathology.

Science Versus Faith

PERHAPS THE GREATEST LEAP of blind faith being required of us in the church today is that which asks us to entrust our lives to trained counselors because, after all, their special training allows them special insight into the reality of our lives and our problems. The theories of psychology are presented to us as though they were provable dogma, its observations are offered as "hard" knowledge, its beliefs are presented as "science," and its prejudices as "facts." Just because the therapeutic has invaded the church, however, does not mean we should take what it offers in blind faith. Where is the basis for its authority? The therapeutic has gained our trust precisely because it has been presented to us as a science. Since science, by implication, is that which is true because it has been proven by means of scientific method, as opposed to faith, which cannot be proven, it is interesting studying the attempts made to "prove" therapeutic effectiveness.

I personally have seen little anecdotal evidence as to the effectiveness of the therapeutic approach in significantly changing lives for the better, even though I live in a culture where turning to the therapeutic for help with the problems of living has become almost a reflex action. On the contrary, it was watching the effects of counseling on those lives around me that raised my suspicion as to whether it couldn't actually be seen as a malevolent force. Perhaps that is why I became intrigued as to whether scientifically-based trials had ever been done to confirm the effectiveness of psychological counseling.

What I found is that there is a long history of studies that were set up using science-based research methods that had hoped to validate the claims of the therapeutic, but had instead only ended up proving the opposite, revealing instead that research cannot prove the claims of the therapeutic.

One of the early studies showing that perhaps psychotherapy might not be as effective as it was purported to be was done in 1952 by Dr. Hans Eysenck, a professor at the Institute of Psychiatry, University of London.

Eysenck had looked at two separate studies of neurotics that had been hospitalized but had received no therapeutic care—only custodial care. The first study, published in 1938 by Landis, looked at those discharged from state hospitals in New York between the years of 1917 and 1934. Upon discharge, 72% were symptom-free or much better. In the second study, done in 1946 by Denker, five hundred consecutive clients who made insurance claims due to "psychoneurosis" were followed up. They, too, were seen by general practitioners, but not therapists. Within two years, 72% of the patients were recovered, and within five years, 90% were recovered. Eysenck figured that if there was a consensus between the two studies that showed that 72% of neurotics got better just with the passage of time, then what happened when they were offered psychotherapy? Eysenck looked at nineteen studies and found, surprisingly, that only 44% had improved that were in Freudian analysis, and among those who were in eclectic forms of therapy, 64% improved.[310] It appeared that healing was actually slowed by therapy. As he wrote in the *Journal of Consulting Psychology,* "There appears to be inverse correlation between recovery and psychotherapy; the more psychotherapy, the smaller the recovery rate."[311]

Eysenck's studies produced a critical backlash that provided the impetus for further studies, but as studies by other researchers began to follow suit, they repeatedly confirmed what Eysenck had found; they revealed that psychotherapy was no more effective for cure than the simple passage of time. As a distinguished psychotherapy researcher named Hans Strupp wrote in 1973, he had "become increasingly skeptical that psychotherapy has anything 'special' to offer, in the sense that its techniques exceed or transcend the gains that may accrue to a patient (or should we say learner?) from a highly constructive human relationship."[312]

Now the studies and the conclusions that arose out of them created a problem, for people tended to have great confidence in the effectiveness of the therapy they were receiving. The scientific research seemed to fly in the face of anecdotal and testimonial evidence that showed that both therapists and clients claimed effectiveness in the therapeutic encounter. Why the discrepancy between personal testimony and scientific evidence? The clue lies in more studies done.

In one such study, Dr Ernest Gruenberg and Dr. M. Shepherd studied those with severe anxiety who were enrolled with the Health Insurance Plan in New York. They discovered, "Neuroses have a limited course even if untreated."[313] Any improvement in therapy, therefore, had been a placebo effect. Other studies done in England and the US also showed the same thing, concluding, "About 70% of neurotics improve within two years; within five years, nine out of 10 show marked improvement."[314] When the comparative studies were strictly controlled, the success results came up as "zero for psychotherapy: the rates of improvement in the treated and untreated individuals remained identical."[315] What the studies showed was that what was actually effective was the human's propensity towards healing. As Eysenck stated, "All methods of psychotherapy fail to improve on the recovery rate obtained through ordinary life experiences."[316] Simple passage of time allowed healing to take place. Left alone, patients tended to improve at exactly the same rate as those in therapy. The patients, however, continued to believe in their therapies even though the studies could not verify their effectiveness.

What is more, what other studies also showed was that even when change occurred with therapy, it was questionable as to whether that change became permanent. Three researchers who had perused relevant studies and clinical reports concluded, "In the large majority of psychotherapeutic endeavors—be they psychodynamic, behavioral, existential, or otherwise—patient improvement neither persists nor generalizes to new settings."[317]

One even earlier and famous study, which should have provided early warning as to therapeutic effectiveness, was done between 1937 and 1945 in the Cambridge-Somerville area of Boston. Teachers, the police, and settlement workers were asked to submit a list of 650 boys between the ages of six and ten who were thought likely to be in danger of delinquency. The boys were then placed into two groups: one group would receive therapy and the other would not. Great pains were taken to match two groups according to all significant variables. In the group that received therapy, the average length of psychotherapy was four years and two months. What follow-up study showed was that of those who received therapy, 96 ended up in court, while only 92 of those untreated ended up in court. The number of offenses noted were 264 for the treated boys and only 218 for the untreated. Surprisingly, the treated boys were actually more likely to commit further serious crimes. A follow-up study done thirty years after the original study reported, "On a number of other measures—including alcoholism, mental illness, stress-related diseases, and job satisfaction—the treated group was worse off than the control group."[318]

In another study done during the war, a psychiatrist and a statistician teamed up to find out what happened to those who had nervous break-downs related to combat. The government had become interested in the most effective way to return men to combat as quickly as possible. When they recorded the number who could return to combat they found that 56% returned who had received no treatment, 48% returned who had been submitted to hospital routine, 62% returned who had received indi-vidual therapy, and 68% returned who had only rest and sedation. Therapy was less effective than just rest and sedation and little better than other treatments.

The psychologist Dr. Eugene E. Levy at the Illinois Institute for Juvenile Research did another famous study. A group of 469 emotionally disturbed children were studied. The group was divided into 327 children who were treated with psychotherapy and then compared to 142 who received no treatment. What was found was that five years later there was "no difference at follow-up between the adjustments made by treated and untreated child patients."[319] Dr. Levy then went through thirty-seven investigations that involved 8,000 patients given therapy through various clinics. What he discovered was that the differences between treated and untreated groups was negligible.

Perhaps just as interesting as the previous studies are the studies that show "untrained lay people do as well as psychiatrists or clinical psychol-ogists in treating patients."[320] Hans Strupp and his associates undertook one such study at Vanderbilt University. In the study, clients were divided up to be seen by either professionals who were chosen for their clinical expertise (their average history of experience was twenty-three years) or else were sent to non-professional college professors who had no experience or training in therapy but who were chosen for their warm personalities. Those going to the non-professionals showed as much improvement as with the other group.[321]

In 1979, Durlak reviewed forty-two studies that compared the effectiveness of professional versus paraprofessional (college students, adult volunteers, or psychiatric aides) helpers. He concluded, "Findings have been consistent and provocative. Paraprofessionals achieve clinical outcomes equal to or significantly better than those obtained by professionals…. Moreover, professional mental health education, training, and experience do not appear to be necessary prerequisites for an effective helping person."[322]

In 1990, as reported in *Psychological Science,* F. Scogin and his colleagues looked at forty studies that compared treatments by therapists for a large range of issues ranging from phobias, depression, and habit control to parenting difficulties, and then compared their effectiveness to that of those who used self-help programs, and found that the difference was not significant.[323] Of further interest were studies referred to as the Rosenham studies, which presented mental hospital staff with both normal and disturbed people, and discovered the "mental hospital staff could not even tell normal people from genuinely disturbed ones."[324]

For years, therapists have been turning us into our pasts, attempting to discover the roots of our problems in living, and yet the many tests done to determine a link between early upbringing and later emotional health may suggest that there is little connection. One such study took 100 Air Force officers who were considered to have excelled in both their personal lives and also on the job. Assuming that they would be revealed to have come from exceptional families, the researchers were surprised to discover that their backgrounds were as pathological as their psychiatric patients.[325] Another study observed 200 children from infancy through adolescence, thinking that those from troubled homes would later have problems and that those from happy homes would end up being well adjusted. When the children were reassessed at the age of thirty, the researchers were surprised to find that their predictions were wrong two-thirds of the time.[326]

Rather alarming are the studies that show that therapists have a tendency to discover pathology where there is none. In one study, eight very normal people complained of nonexistent symptoms and then managed to gain admission to psychiatric wards, where they proceeded to behave normally. They all got out, eventually, on good behavior, but each was diagnosed as a schizophrenic in remission. In another study, therapists and therapy students were presented with what was supposedly a recorded first therapy session. Actually, it was a recording by an actor who was playing the part of a competent, productive, relaxed, and confident man. Among the therapists and students, 43% diagnosed him as psychotic or neurotic and 19% rated him as having adjustment problems. The minority—38%—perceived him as healthy.[327]

Even more alarming has been the "repressed memory" fad, whereby countless therapists have "discovered" repressed memories. A 1995 study in *Psychological Medicine* reported, "Laboratory studies over the past 60 years have failed to demonstrate that individuals can 'repress' memories."[328] On the contrary, there is a lot of evidence revealing that therapists can implant false memories in patients, resulting in false blame, family break-up, and untold anguish. By 1993, the False Memory Syndrome Foundation, composed of people who claimed to be victims of false blame after relatives had "discovered" repressed memories in therapy, had 4,600 members.

I have become used to seeing articles in our national newspaper revealing still another study that exposes the inability of the therapeutic to produce the results for which it purportedly exists. For example, a recent report in the press revealed a study in which marriage therapists, graduate students in clinical psychology, religious counselors, professors in the area of marriage, and those who had been married for various lengths of time were shown a video of couples discussing conflict in their relationships. The videos had been made between six to thirteen years earlier. Being asked to identify and rate the marriages, those who were most competent in detecting a happy marriage were not any of the professionals but rather first, those who were long and happily married themselves, secondly, those who were long but unhappily married, and thirdly, the newlyweds.[329] The professionals scored last. Perhaps that is why in a study of seven medical specialties, it was found that the psychiatrists had more marital problems than that of any other specialty.[330]

The most recent press release to raise questions about therapeutic effectiveness was a new study done with Canadian sex offenders. As of the 1980s, all sex offenders had been required to participate in treatment programs. That requirement allowed a base to be formed that allowed for the study of success rates. The findings, which were taken from the *Canadian Journal of Behavioural Science,* reported, "Unexpectedly, the treated offenders were at higher risk to re-offend than the comparison offenders, as indicated by the number of prior sexual offences."[331] The study seemed to reveal that treatment is virtually worthless.

One of our unquestioned cultural myths is that of the relationship between self-esteem and personal achievement and social cohesion. Speakers and media that link lack of self-esteem with societal and personal problems bombard us, and I have never yet heard that association challenged. That is why I was intrigued to come across studies that failed to prove the connection.[332] Although reported earlier, it is worth repeating. In California, where the need for self-esteem initiatives were mandated into legislation and then after the fact testing was put in place, what was actually found was that the expected association between low self-esteem and social problems could not be found. Instead, what was found was an inverse relationship between self-esteem and SAT scores.[333] Violence was found to be more likely to occur among those who had a high opinion of themselves.[334] Illegal drugs were found to be more prevalent among those adolescents with high self-esteem than with those who had low self-confidence.[335] Adolescents with high self-esteem were found to be more likely to break the law and engage in anti-social behavior.[336] The huge self-esteem movement seems to be based more on faith and hope than on any provable evidence.

The therapeutic provides the language and framework for the self-esteem and moral education programs provided in schools. The efficacy of those programs has been researched by a host of social scientists. One estimate places the number of studies at 10,000.[337] What the studies reveal are conclusions that have been called, "As unambiguous and indisputable as any body of social scientific analysis can provide."[338] They reveal, "There is little or no association, causal or otherwise, between psychological well-being and moral conduct, and psychologically oriented moral education programs have little or no positive effect upon moral behavior, achievement, or anything else."[339] The myriad of studies, however, have not been sufficient to shake our confidence in the ability of psychology to provide the frames of reference for the development of personality and moral character of school children.

In the last year, coverage has been given to studies that show that trauma counseling (CISD or critical-incident stress debriefing) is ineffectual and can actually be harmful. It was an article in the *Lancet* that first reported that CISD, which has become a popular way of dealing with tragedy, showed no positive results and showed, in fact, that its effects could be detrimental.[340] According to one psychologist, "This intervention shows up as being an irritant at best, potentially harmful to some and less effective than doing nothing."[341] It seems that the imputing of pathology to the normal processes of life can raise negative expectations that then become realized. It can also get in the way of community—the normal reaching out of those in distress to family and friends who have traditionally formed the support base. Every time I hear trauma counseling still linked to our modern tragedies, I am in awe at our gullibility.

Recently, the pharmaceutical companies have become so closely allied with psychiatry that the question of scientific collusion and compromise has become an important one. For example, when it became evident that the use of anti-depressants in children actually increased the risk of suicide and suicidal thinking, the regulators were forced to go back and systematically review the drug-company-funded trials. What they found was that antidepressants had not been shown to be more effective than placebos. And yet, in just the US alone, each year five million prescriptions were being made, allowing Zoloft and Paxil to be given to those who were under eighteen.[342] Incidentally, in the area of depression, almost 100% of the biomedical research and development done in the area had been funded by private sources such as drug companies.[343] That certainly does not make for scientific integrity.

My suspicion over whether the modern therapeutic industry could justifiably be called a science increased when I read the work of Frank Furedi, a British sociologist, who reported a survey done among counselors in Britain, which found that not only do therapists not become actively involved in research, they actually hold negative views about it. The study concluded,

> There is a widespread anti-science, anti-research feeling in the therapeutic community. The authors of this study characterize counseling as an 'anti-intellectual movement' where 'feelings are more valued than thoughts and where there is little emphasis on "book learning."' They also claim that 'research is invariably rejected in favour of emotionally held principles'. The social psychologist Carol Tavris believes that 'the split between the research and practice wings of psychology' in the US has become so wide that 'many psychologists now speak glumly of the 'science-practitioner gap'.[344]

Not only did I not find convincing scientific validation for the effectiveness of modern therapy, but also I came upon reports that revealed the more sinister side of the therapeutic. One journal reported, "The concept that psychotherapy may also be harmful is supported by rather a large body of clinical experience."[345] An example is that of a woman who went to a psychologist for minor problems in regards to her son. By the time she finished her therapy, she had become incapacitated. What had happened?

An analyst who was later asked to see her wrote, "Enjoyment in public was examined for an exhibitionistic taint, and in consequence disappeared. Constructive activity with underprivileged children was viewed as self-ishly ego building, and in consequence stopped completely. Warmth to her friends was examined with a jaundiced eye for neurotic motivation, and almost completely vanished. The patient began to believe that only through meditation and 'understanding' could she become truly aware of herself. So, paralyzed, she waited at home for a miracle—which never came."[346]

An extreme example, no doubt, but one that raises questions about the blind faith we have been willing to place in the therapeutic. In my own circle of acquaintances, I can give numerous examples of abuses, some almost as destructive as in the example given above. One review of studies of family and marriage therapy found that five to ten percent of relationships being treated actually got worse.[347]

Can therapy do actual harm? Studies that look into that question are hard to come by; a study by Hadley and Strupp in 1976 found that in spite of psychotherapists thinking themselves based in science, they seemed reluctant to participate in their studies. However, in 1981, Buckley et al. investigated a small sample of ninety-seven psychotherapists who, themselves, had submitted to therapy. Twenty-one percent admitted to having been caused harm by their therapy, admitting to "bad effects on their marriage, destructive 'acting out' and withdrawal from the ordinary world."[348] Scientific studies, however, seem incapable of shaking our faith in therapeutic effectiveness.

Yes, there are also studies that seem to confirm the effectiveness of therapy. In 1995, *Consumer Reports* published an article called "Does Therapy Help?" in which it reported that in a study of 2,900 people who had undergone therapy, they had found remarkable improvement among many who had originally been feeling bad. After years of being confronted with marginal or even negative results, the therapeutic industry was jubi-lant. However, it is interesting looking at the scientific basis of the report. There was no control group. Even the president of the American

Psychological Association had to admit, "Because there are no control groups, the CR study cannot tell us directly whether talking to sympathetic friends or merely letting time pass would have produced just as much improvement as treatment by a mental health professional."[349] There was no external verification of improvement. People were asked how they had felt before therapy and after. Personal memory, especially of emotions, which we all know to be unreliable, was taken at face value. That is hardly a scientific study.

The therapeutic field is now becoming splintered as different groups, all acknowledging the ineffectiveness and problems in other areas, attempt to solve the problem and enigma of our humanity. The psychosocial group focuses on the mind; it is memory and what we do with our consciousness that is their area of interest. Psychiatry focuses on our physical make-up—biology, chemistry, and the brain can all be studied as to our make-up and how we malfunction, and drugs quickly become the answer to all our problems. Populist therapies focus on the heart; our emotions define us, and they need to be understood and managed. Recent therapies acknowledge the soul; it is the spirit of man that can supposedly explain our uniqueness, but with no firm tradition to give form to that uniqueness it is the branch that wanders farthest from science and degenerates into mindless speculation and wishful thinking. It was watching each branch criticize and denigrate the effectiveness of the other branches of the therapeutic that fueled my cynicism. What was noticeably absent was a holistic view that could see the human as more than its individual parts. It is as though the heart, mind, soul, and body of man could be divided up to be possessed by the competing sections of the therapeutic. It is precisely that conflict that best reveals the inability of any branch of "science" to adequately define and illuminate the illusive and complex enigma of our identity.

As interesting as all the studies are showing that the claims for therapeutic effectiveness cannot be proven, what I find even more interesting are the number of attempts being made to show that spiritualities, faith, and prayer can be scientifically validated. The *American Academy of Pediatrics* printed an article recently in which it was revealed,

A number of studies suggest that spiritual/religious beliefs and practices may contribute to decreased stress and increased sense of well-being, decreased depressive symptoms, decreased substance abuse, faster recovery from hip replacements, improved recovery from myocardial infarction, and enhanced immune system functioning, A recent meta-analysis of 29 earlier studies involving nearly 126,000 patients argued that the odds of survival were significantly greater for people who scored higher on measures of religious involvement than for people who scored lower.[350]

In 1988, a respected medical journal published a study on prayer that showed that patients who were prayed for required fewer treatments and had fewer complications. It is interesting that an epidemiologist from a medical school in Virginia declared that the study "was no less rigorously conducted than a drug trial."[351] Perhaps that is why an article written in 2001 reported, "72 medical schools—well over half of those in the United States—have offered some kind of course on spirituality and healing."[352]

I am not advocating attempts to prove faith issues by means of using scientific method. To do so would be to try place faith in an unnatural mode. What I am convinced of, however, is that the arguments for the blending of the therapeutic and religion on the basis of their compatibility—after all, one is based on faith and the other on science—are just not capable of standing any scientific scrutiny.

God versus gods

AS I, AS AN ADULT, began to read my Bible, as I allowed my twentieth century blinkers to slowly fall off, and as I began to get over my hang-ups over the male imagery and power portrayed therein, I have to admit I grew fascinated by the God revealed in those Scriptures. And the more I became fascinated with the God of the Old Testament, the more I became frustrated with the Israelites, wondering why, when they had such an amazing God, why could they not keep their hands off their neighbors' gods? As I began to research those pagan deities, as I began to discover what they were, I slowly began to understand. I also became aware of how little has changed since Old Testament times.

It was the prophet Jeremiah who had asked the rhetorical question, "Do men make their own gods?" He then answered his own question, "Yes, but they are not gods!" (Jeremiah 16:20). The philosopher Feuerbach seems to have been right when he declared that gods were nothing but projections of man writ large on the heavens. At least he was right when it came to describing the gods of idolatry. Joseph Campbell noted, "Deities are the symbolic personifications of the very energies that are yourself,"[353] which is why Voltaire could say, "In the beginning God created man in his own image, and, ever since, man has been returning the compliment." God had already revealed that god-making process to the prophet Isaiah when he said, "You turn things upside down, as if the potter were thought to be like the clay!" (Isaiah 29:16).

Becoming aware of the pagan gods helped me to understand how it was that they were described in the Bible as having been created "in the form of man, of man in all his glory" (Isaiah 44:13). They did not necessarily look like man, but they were projections of what man had found within himself. The human being, I realized, has always been a god-creating machine, and the gods that we create are gods that inevitably reflect one's self and one's own personal needs.

With that in mind, it was interesting studying the pagan deities. I could see they represented the divinizing of life and life's processes. The

Baals and Ashtoreths revealed the fertility and sexuality inherent in life. Man, after all, knows himself to be a sexual being. What could be more natural than to have his sexuality expressed, celebrated, and even hallowed? Molech was a vengeful deity, demanding the life of firstborn sons and then devouring them in his fires. However, has history not shown that man has always allowed his unpurified rage and anger to be projected out and then go parading behind the forms of religion? Jeremiah depicts the Israelite women making cakes to the queen of heaven, and yet why shouldn't they? We can see that the "heavens declare the glory of God" (Psalm 19:1), so why not divinize creation? And wouldn't it only be natural for women to prefer a female deity, a god representing our feminine side, making her easier to identify with?

After a while, the golden calf began to make sense. Pagan deities were often depicted astride bulls or calves, the calf symbolizing the god's strength. By avoiding the depiction of a god astride the calf, the Israelites could claim obedience to God's command to make no physical image representing Him. It is our very needs, however, that can be divinized. To a foot-weary people carrying all their belongings over the dry, dusty desert, that calf could represent the need for strength to endure and their need to have their burdens carried. It was not the image of the calf that was wrong. When God gave orders for the temple design, He had twelve oxen carrying the bath, oxen in the relief work—God obviously understood what the neighboring peoples were trying to express with their images of bulls and calves. However, the most seductive idolatry will always be that of gods forged in the fire and according to the currency of human need.

I must say that by the time I visited Greece, I had become quite fond of the Greek gods and Greek mythology. They gave me stories that helped with self-understanding, self-articulation, and self-expression. They spoke of eternal verities as man could discover them within and without the aid of special revelation. They offered archetypal images that resonated deep within. Slowly, however, I also saw that their truths were not about transcendence, but rather about man. I began to see why early Christians were called atheists. A god who was not a reflection or a projection of man but rather said that man would have to leave himself behind in order to find Him—belief in that God was akin to shattering that canopy of mirrors that the pagans had come to call gods and then being invited to travel into some cosmic black hole.

The real uniqueness of Judaism was not its belief in one God— intimations of that were already around—but in its understanding of the character of God.[354] The Hebrew God was understood, first and foremost, to be completely different than man. He could never be understood by studying His creation. According to Karen Armstrong, the word "holiness" for the Hebrew mind did not have its modern connotations of morality; it meant separateness. Isaiah's seraphs—crying, "Holy! Holy! Holy is Yahweh Sabaoth"—would have registered to the Hebrew ear as a warning, saying, "Yahweh is Other! Other! Other!"[355] One could not understand God by looking at man or by studying creation.

The Bible claims that only the pure of heart will see God; those without purity of heart will look for God and see only themselves reflected. Outside of purity of heart, we create gods who are a pastiche of our hopes, needs, fears, and our lust for some magical power that will allow us some control of our world. Outside of purity of heart, we never want a real God, but rather, some power and an extension of ourselves.

We live in a world where our gods are once again becoming anthropomorphic and polytheistic. Now, scant decades after we followed Nietzsche's lead and wrote, "God is Dead" on billboards, it has again become fashionable to believe in god. Why? Because those who study man have discovered that the human being has need of a transcendent dimension in his life. Freud had called God an infantile projection of man's needs. His disciple, Carl Jung, however, discovered that ridding man of his belief in God did not rid man of his problems; the human animal was actually worse off without its ability to believe in God. As Jung wrote, "The idea of God is an absolutely necessary psychological function of an irrational nature, which has nothing whatever to do with the question of God's existence."[356] For Jung, religion was not about God, it was about man. According to Jung, the real issue for religion was what kind of gods to create that were best for the human being.

What man really needed, according to Jung, was to be taken back to pagan times of myths and archetypes wherein man had gods that were good for man, himself. In order to regain those gods and the supposed innocence of those primitive times, Carl Jung, and countless modern disciples, have been filling our world—and our churches—with gods designed for man, by man, according to the study of man—designer deities individually crafted according to human specifications.

We now live in a world where spirituality has become the new "in" thing because those who study man have discovered that the human animal has a need of Transcendence, of what Abraham Maslow called "peak experiences." Erich Fromm argued that we humans have need of religion, but of a religion that served the personal self. God, for Fromm, was a symbol for the capacities and powers latent in the human being. For Carl Rogers, probably the most important guru for the modern pastoral counseling movement, the "higher power" to which one surrendered in religion was actually part of the unconscious levels of the self. For the psychotherapist Rollo May, transcendence was not a state achieved by connecting with a reality outside and greater than the personal self, but was actually a state achieved within the self by means of personal development and by personal movement towards higher levels of actualization within the self. Maslow, Rogers, May, and Fromm did not work from a base of knowledge of God—they were all essentially atheists—but according to their studies of man they have brought forth spiritualities created by and for man, spiritualities that lead us nowhere safe or sure but, rather, leave us trapped within the parameters of our own limited selves.

We live in a world where it is no longer enough to believe in God. One actually has to choose a god. All of our gods are not created equal, and only one was not created at all; to the degree we risk it all in the venture of faith, He comes alongside and reveals His reality to us.

The single most defining issue of our lives will be that of who we think God is. That single issue itself will ultimately set the course of our lives and determine how we live out the details of our days. In our culture, God seems to be mostly used and abused for human ends. God is seen as a tool to be used towards self-realization. He has become consigned to the role of mascot of political parties. His name is used to stamp a seal of approval on human plans. Noticeably absent is a fear and reverence of the God who is Other and the realization of that God as a Living Reality before whom we are living out the moments and details of our lives.

The more I became aware of pagan deities, the more I became aware of how little has changed since Old Testament times. We no longer cover our gods with gold, wood, or stone; they are all reduced to intellectual constructs. We no longer differentiate by name; they are all called gods. We are still, however, surrounded by neighbors who—to use the image God uses in Isaiah—can't tell the difference between a god created by studying the lump of clay, and a God who is found by seeking the missing potter. We are still surrounded by neighbors who design their gods according to their study of the fears, needs, desires, and shape of man. We are still surrounded by neighbors who create gods as projections of what man finds within himself. We are still surrounded by neighbors who find their gods by scratching beneath the surface of man, and we still haven't kept our hands off of our neighbors' gods. What I mind most of all about the way we have tried to integrate the therapeutic into the church is what we have allowed them to do to the image of our God.

Well-adjusted versus Transformed

IN OUR CULTURE, it is not unusual to see the kingdom of God being promoted by using the currency of this world. The rich, the brilliant, the beautiful, the successful, and the famous have all been utilized to advertise the Kingdom of God. The hidden message seems to be: (1) true faith cannot sell itself so it needs to come camouflaged by the allure of the world; (2) God is interested in turning out prize specimens of our culture, or (3) faith will help us achieve what our culture deems praiseworthy.

Recently, it seems to be political power that has been chosen as the preferred means of choice for the furtherance of the kingdom of God. Religion has been linking itself to the power structures of society in order to further its causes, and in return, the political powers have leaned on the religious establishment to support, justify, rationalize, and to turn their human platforms and plans into something sacrosanct. Doug Coe, the principle instigator behind the popular Presidential Prayer Breakfast in Washington, D.C., claimed he had discovered, "the best way to get religious leaders together was to invite them to a meeting with a powerful political leader."[357] Trying to bring in the kingdom of God by using the currency of the world is a constant temptation.

It is therefore of interest going through the Old Testament and seeing who God actually did use as His spokespersons. They were not the famous, successful, or even prime specimens of the society. By faith, Abraham chose to live "like a stranger in a foreign country" (Hebrews 11:9), considering himself and his people to be "aliens and strangers on earth" (Hebrews 11:13). An inability to identify or relate well with those around him would not have looked good on his evaluation form. Moses, who "chose to be mistreated along with the people of God rather than to enjoy the pleasures" (Hebrews 11:23) of Egypt, would, in our day, have been diagnosed with either a MPD (Masochistic Personality Disorder) or a SDPD (Self-defeating Personality Disorder). Jeremiah, living in our day, would certainly have been labeled a depressive. A bit of Valium, Paxil, or Zoloft could have certainly softened his jeremiads. Ezekiel had no ability to define his boundaries, and as he took upon himself all the sin of Israel, he lay immobilized for years (cooking his food over excrement being his one constructive act). Perhaps a bit of shock therapy could have returned him to the real world. Hosea was relationally addicted to a prostitute. Not only that, but he claimed his addiction was ordered by God. Ezra exhibited masochistic tendencies, engaging in self-mutilation as he tore his clothes and pulled the hair from his head and beard. Nehemiah, in contrast, was an abusive extrovert; he beat the men before him and pulled out their hair. Certainly the *DSM* could be enlisted to classify their disorders. Isaiah was an exhibitionist, walking around naked for three years; living in our time, he would certainly have been consigned to a mental institution. From Moses, the outcast with his stutter, to David, so insignificant that his family did not even invite him to Samuel's king-choosing ceremony, to Jesus being ignored by the religious of his day—"Nazareth! Can anything good come from there?"—God seems to have consistently used history to prove that He does not view us humans in the same way that we see ourselves. Rather than condemning the biblical characters for their lack of adjustment, God, instead, revealed that from His point of view, "The world was not worthy of them" (Hebrews 11:38).

A friend of mine phoned me in order to repeat a conversation that she'd just had with the leader of a religious college. This friend had complained to the leader about the way the school used the therapeutic as a crutch. Since the school was training future ministers should they not, she asked, be taught how to see life through a different lens? In the conversation that followed, the leader admitted that when he interviewed pastoral candidates he asked them about their prayer life—he acknowledged that religion was necessary—but at the same time he also wanted his wife by his side (his wife was a therapist) to determine how well-adjusted they were. I could not but help but be aware that if that was the approach he used in choosing future pastoral candidates, then when presented with the Biblical prophets, he would, in every case, have missed the voice of God.

Before one tries to relegate all the eccentricities of the biblical characters to the time of the canonical scriptures, one should look at the history of the Christian saints. The early monks who fled to the desert were certainly known for many eccentricities. Saint Francis of Assisi defies all categorization. George Fox, a good example of how eccentric the reformers could be, would rather receive "blows, punchings, beatings, and imprisonments"[358] than remove his hat. Richard Lovelace has noted, "Luther, Bunyan and the Apostle Paul would be referred to psychotherapists if they appeared in the evangelical community today."[359] Would the Reformation have ever become a reality if Luther would have had Paxil and shock therapy for his psychotic breaks?

Many years ago, my children, who rode the city buses, came home to report on an advertisement they had seen on the bus. The advertisement asked, "What do these people have in common?" The answer was, "Mental illness." My children knew it would make me upset, because the names they remembered were all Christians and they were all people who had become spokespersons for the faith. The advertisement was for therapeutic intervention, and I suppose its purpose was to make people at ease with being mentally ill, but in the examples they used, the bouts of depression and inner torment were not incidental to the faith of the individuals, but rather their faith was forged in the darkness of depression and inner torment. If T. S. Eliot, Kierkegaard, Dostoevsky, C.S. Lewis, St. John of the Cross, Catherine of Genoa, and a long host of others would have had drugs and therapy available to help them through their bouts of depression, they certainly would have been "happier" and more "well-adjusted," but they would also have had little to say about faith and the spiritual realities that they had became increasingly certain of. It was the darkness in their lives that caused them to reach out and cling to a reality that existed outside of our world and our small human understanding.

Not only can eccentricity and pathology not be separated from the biographies of the prophets and Christian saints but also, as Kenneth Leech has noted, "This crazy wilderness eccentric element is more important than is sometimes realized. For these were people who were straining at the boundaries of consciousness where mysticism and madness meet, where sanctity can threaten sanity."[360] Even Jesus' family tried to rescue him because they perceived him to have gone mad.

There seems to me to be a growing confusion in the church as to what its ends should be; should it work towards the emotional well-being of its parishioners or should it keep its focus on spiritual salvation? Obviously, wholeness and healing are byproducts of salvation, but when they are approached directly, something else of greater importance may be lost. The difference between the two goals was well articulated by Viktor Frankl, a psychotherapist who was interested in and argued persuasively for the need of religion in the life of the human being. He also, however, argued against trying to blend medical therapy with pastoral ministry, saying,

> Although religion might have a very positive psychotherapeutic effect on the patient, its intention is in no way a psychotherapeutic one. Although religion might secondarily promote such things as mental health and inner equilibrium, its aim does not primarily concern psychological solutions but, rather, spiritual salvation. Religion is not an insurance policy for a tranquil life, for maximum freedom from conflicts, or for any other hygienic goal. Religion provides man with more than psychotherapy ever could—but it also demands more of him. Any fusion of the respective goals of religion and psychotherapy must result in confusion.[361]

The birth of new life, not better adjustment to the old ways of life, is what true religion is about. Perhaps that is why the Bible does not speak of "adjustment," but rather of transformation. The kingdom of God is so radically different from the kingdom of man that change and adjustment are not sufficient; one needs to become attached to a completely new otherworldly life source. C.S. Lewis articulated that difference best when he wrote,

> God became man to turn creatures into sons: not simply to produce better men of the old kind but to produce a new kind of man. It is not like teaching a horse to jump better and better but

like turning a horse into a winged creature. Of course, once it has got its wings, it will soar over fences which could never have been jumped and thus beat the natural horse at its own game. But there may be a period, while the wings are just beginning to grow, when it cannot do so: and at that stage the lumps on the shoulders—no one could tell by looking at them that they are going to be wings—may even give it an awkward appearance.[362]

Not only will those appearing wings not be functional at first, but their appearance might seem like a deformity, their weight potentially unbalancing one and making walking difficult.

Edwin Starbuck was a psychologist who tried to bring science into the area of religion in an attempt to find a natural basis for the religious conversion experiences of young people. When he studied the religious conversions of adolescents, he reported that those adolescents who had claimed to have experienced a religious conversion actually went on to experience 10% more "storm and stress" than those who had not experienced conversion. Now that is interesting, for if the church is really interested in psychological health, should it not warn those interested in conversion of the possible health risks involved? Starbuck's explanation for the increased psychological disturbance was that the conversion group had been confronted with an ideal that brought into clearer relief the difference between their higher and lower selves.[363] The divine call disturbed one's psychological balance.

Our "adjustment" was meant to be towards a foreign Kingdom. If we were to look at the requirements of the new Kingdom—humility, gentleness, turning the other cheek, poverty of spirit, loving one's neighbor as one's self, forgiveness—then one would have to admit that they require a transformation of the human personality. They are attitudes that in fact handicap one for life in this world; becoming a Christian is a counter-cultural move. The church was meant to exist as the beachhead of another kingdom seeking to become implanted on earthly, visible soil. So why are our churches so interested in helping us to become adjusted to this world and to the categories of health that our secular society has devised?

Perhaps the best way of comparing the well-adjusted life to the transformed life is by means of the Beatitudes.

"Blessed are the poor in spirit, for theirs is the kingdom of heaven." Poverty of spirit does not come from learning to think less of ourselves; it comes from seeing ourselves as we truly are. The need to feel good about one's self is one of the major premises of the therapeutic. It is those who are poor in spirit, however, who are standing on the doorstep of grace and redemption; that Kingdom remains closed until we can see and acknowledge the vulnerability, the dependence, and the neediness that is the true state of the human creature. That Kingdom can break through to the degree that we are capable of acknowledging our true state. In the upside-down way of that other Kingdom, it is precisely those who are most broken and needy that are blessed, for they will know their need and thus have the greatest capacity for God.

"Blessed are those who mourn, for they will be comforted." This is not a glorification of the state of feeling bad. After all, the fruits of the Spirit are said to be joy and peace. God, however, is said to come to those who are broken and contrite in spirit. As long as we are masters of our own life and destiny (in other words, playing God to ourselves), then there is no room for a real God in our life. It is the self-satisfied, well adjusted, well integrated that are most to be pitied; they do not yet have a need for a real God in their lives. It is autonomy and control, not surrender, which is the therapeutic project. However, it is in surrender that we discover God's comforting Presence.

"Blessed are the meek, for they will inherit the earth." I believe that the word for "meekness" is the same word used to describe Moses. Moses was not called meek because he was a doormat; he was, in fact, a murderer. Eugene Peterson defined biblical meekness as "sanctified energy." The explosive anger that once caused the violent slaying of an Egyptian was tamed and channeled under obedience to God to become the energy used for divine purposes. Meekness obviously had more to do with learning one's relationship to God than one's standing before man. Those who learn to be meek, humble, and submissive before God are given the courage to

stand straight and strong before man on earth. In the words of Thomas
Merton, "Humility is the surest sign of strength."[364]

Perhaps meekness is best exemplified by the life of David. In the story
of David and Goliath, we are given a small glimpse into the dynamics of
David's family. Eliab, David's older brother, greeted David's arrival on the
battlefield with a sneering insult. David returned the jibe with a soft, truthful answer. The famous preacher F.B. Meyer once preached a sermon
claiming that in that exchange was the real secret to the battle's victory. It
was David's victory over himself in allowing meekness to counter malice
and envy that allowed for the victory over Goliath, for a "marvelous exhi-
bition was given that day in the valley of Elah that those who are gentlest
under provocation are strongest in the fight, and that meekness is really
an attribute of might."[365] We, however, would be hard pressed to find
meekness listed as an acceptable attribute in any therapeutic literature.

"Blessed are those who hunger and thirst for righteousness, for they
will be filled." To know eternal life, one first has to be aware of the hunger
and thirst that keep us from being satisfied with earthly life. It is the longing for "something more" that drives us heavenward. The therapeutic will
help us articulate those longings in terms of transference or sexuality or
pathology, but it does not have the vocabulary by which it can articulate
those longings as the very call of the eternal God drawing our souls
beyond ourselves.

"Blessed are the merciful, for they will be shown mercy." Mercy cannot grow where therapeutic boundaries have been allowed to define our
parameters. Mercy, after all, requires that something of my self, my rights,
my perceived sense of justice is given up and where forgiveness and mercy
are offered instead.

Years ago I was embroiled in a conflict that saw me reach the full
extent of my moral outrage and righteous indignation. At the height of
tension, a Bible verse that I didn't even realize I knew suddenly popped
into my mind, "Be merciful, just as your Father is merciful" (Luke 6:36).
Like an animal caught and immobilized by the sudden appearance of
headlights, I, too, felt blinded by the concept of mercy. I found that I

lacked the capacity to accept the implications of mercy. It was only much later when I began to accept how dependent I, myself, was on mercy that I began to struggle to extend it to others. What I had developed instead was an overweening sense of justice. Only later did I realize that the New Testament speaks less of justice in order to stress mercy, saying, "Mercy triumphs over judgment!" (James 2:13). That does not mean that we should not fight for justice in this world; but justice is just the beginning of the journey, not its end. The mercy that we will require as we stand before God is to be dispensed as a foretaste here below; those who count on God's ultimate mercy are asked to be advance agents of its dispersal here below.

"Blessed are the pure in heart, for they will see God." Purity of heart cannot exist alongside modern therapeutic conceptions of the self; we end up seeing only ourselves, not God.

"Blessed are the peacemakers, for they will be called sons of God." Peacemakers are never those who have been taught how to focus on their personal needs and rights. As long as a society is viewed as a conglomerate of individuals all seeking personal rights and personal fulfillment, then not only will there be increasing friction, disorder, and disunity, but personal peace will also be destroyed. Peace can only exist where there is a belief in a reality higher than the personal ego and its needs and rights.

"Blessed are those who are persecuted because of righteousness, for theirs is the kingdom of heaven." Persecution is the means whereby God-like character is formed and tested. Paul wrote of how our troubles "are winning for us a permanent and glorious reward out of all proportion to our pain" (2 Corinthians 4:16). God-like character, however, is nowhere on the radar screens of therapeutic understanding. In the therapeutic, there is also no redemptive purpose for pain—the therapeutic exists to help us get rid of it all.

Therapeutic self-understanding exists as an antithesis to the Beatitudes. Christianity is not about becoming well-adjusted, but rather about transformation. Spiritual life is predicated on our ability to change life support systems from the lower (visible) to the higher (invisible) realms. In the process, a lot of inner chaos and uncertainty can result.

Evelyn Underhill likened the growth of spiritual life to adolescence. Having been the mother of three children who all went through adolescence, I have wondered whether, if we were given the chance, we would allow our children to grow beyond the sweetness of childhood. In the realm of spirit, that is not just an academic question; growth is a matter of choice and is optional.

It is interesting that Jesus, who was the only perfectly human and perfectly sane being ever to live on our earth, has managed to accumulate so many "holy fools" among His followers. Why? What did the writer of 1 Corinthians 3:18 mean when he wrote, "If any one of you thinks he is wise by the standards of this age, he should become a 'fool' so that he may become wise"?

In the first place, as already mentioned, what the biblical characters and saints made evident was that spiritual and psychological health are not synonymous. If one would have refused to listen to the prophets because they were not "well-adjusted" or "well-balanced" individuals, then one would have consistently missed the voice of God. Anyone attempting to initiate a new worldwide movement should have known that the disciples were not good candidate material—they were "unschooled, ordinary men" (Acts 4:13). Any personality test would have revealed Peter to be unstable and unsuitable. God, however, repeatedly chooses individuals who are rejected by society in order to reveal that the kingdoms of God and of man do not run according to the same rules or values.

In a society that has lost its bearings, "The prophet is considered a fool, the inspired man a maniac" (Hosea 9:7). It is the society, however, that is being thereby judged, not the individual that it considers deviant.

Martin Luther King, Jr. wrote, "Human salvation lies in the hands of the creatively maladjusted."[366] He called for "transformed nonconformists," or for people who had become transformed into new creatures in Christ so they could resist the pressure to become adjusted or socialized into the evil and dysfunction of a society. "Transformed nonconformists" are those who can resist social climbing in order to identify with the downtrodden and neglected, who can resist power in order to become

servants of all, who can deny the self but promote the good of their neighbors, and who can see beyond the distorting labels we attach to people
and see the eternal spark that lies within. It is in forming our lives around
Jesus that we can hope to be freed from the distorting pressures of a society that would tempt us to become less than what we were created to be.
In Jesus lies our hope to become truly transformed, not well adjusted to a
lesser light.

Perhaps another reason why Christ's followers have been known as
"holy fools" is because they deliberately choose a more difficult path, and
then stumble, doubt, and grow weary as they persist in taking the hard
way. Our one and only true North Star is Jesus, the only perfect and sane
human that ever lived. In Jesus we get an image of what humanity was created to become. And yet the life of Jesus is enigmatic; to follow him we
work from "hints and guesses,/ Hints followed by guesses; and the rest/ Is
prayer, observance, discipline, thought and action" (T.S. Eliot, "The Dry
Salvages").

"Holy fools" believe there is another whole reality surrounding and
penetrating the visible world and they attempt to tune their hearing to that
other world. In so doing, they make their way through the devil's territory,
a territory marked by the occult, superstition, magic, mental illness, and
distorted images of God's true realm. As Coventry Patmore noted, "The
frontiers between sense and spirit…are the devil's hunting grounds." As
they try listen with their spiritual ears, the "holy fools" discover that, like
any person living in any foreign country, they misunderstand, they make
mistakes, and they fail to comprehend. So the "holy fools" stumble on, an
enigma in our material world.

The followers of Jesus are "holy fools" not only because they follow a
vision that most of us cannot see, but also because they dare to live transparent lives. We humans spend much of our lives creating false selves, glittering external surfaces to camouflage the brokenness, the insecurities, the
immaturity, and the darkness that lie in the heart of our being. There is
much within all of us that we feel needs to be hidden. Those who follow
Jesus shift their focus from external impressions in order to find and live

out of new life within. If our inner hearts and spirits are to be allowed room to grow and be revealed, then in the process our outer defenses, the illusionary self we hide behind, is going to have to be destroyed. That process can create or be triggered by crisis whereby we lose our psychological balance for a while.

Once one begins to live out of one's center, however, it becomes less important to hide behind the masks that we have created. We become free to live genuine and revealed lives. Only a "fool," however, would make themselves vulnerable and open in a society where everyone else holds their cards close to their chests and where most bluff their way through the game of life. One who no longer lives for societal approval, for competition, who ignores the games of power, who refuses to be masked for a society where masks are part of the dress code, is going to appear as a fool. The world will never understand chosen vulnerability and weakness.

Perhaps another reason why the Kingdom has so often been associated with "holy fools" is because it takes an act of humility to enter God's Kingdom. In the New Testament, God came in a form so humble that He became easy to reject and despise. If we are going to know God, then we are going to have to share in His humility and stoop a bit to enter the Kingdom. As Paul wrote, "God chose the foolish things of the world to shame the wise; God chose the weak things of the world to shame the strong. He chose the lowly things of this world and the despised things— and the things that are not—to nullify the things that are, so that no one may boast before him" (1 Corinthians 1:26–9). It is the broken, the downtrodden, the neglected, the rejected, and the passed over that find it easier to enter the Kingdom. They are already so far down they don't have to stoop much farther. Before God we are all supplicants; we are never in charge. Recognizing that takes an act of humility that only the desperate seem capable of mustering. That is why Jesus could say to the religious people of His day, "I tell you the truth, the tax collectors and the prostitutes are entering the kingdom of God ahead of you" (Matthew 21:31). God just keeps choosing to associate with and identify Himself with people we would normally have little time for. If we do not know God, then it will not be because we were not smart enough, or not strong enough, or not holy enough; it will be because we could not stoop low enough.

There will always be those in religion who try to bypass the cross, the disgrace, and the humility inherent in Christianity. The cross is the key to life—those who pass through come out looking like Jesus. Jesus, however, was not a hero. Christianity is full of examples of those who have tried to eliminate the humility and the stigma of the cross and have instead attempted to restore some cult of hero worship. We are inherently attracted to those who exude an aura of confidence, competence, and power. We feel more comfortable with those who seem to have understood the mystery with no inner struggle, who don't have doubts, who are self-assured. The Apostle Paul came up against people like that—the "super-apostles"—in Corinth and found himself unable and unwilling to compete on their terms. Paul, instead, chose to glory in his weakness and suffering. By means of adversity and need, he had learned the dependence that is the sign of a true follower of Christ. In the words of Paul, "I delight in weaknesses, in insults, in hardships, in persecution, in difficulties. For when I am weak, then I am strong" (2 Corinthians 12:10). Those are the words of a "holy fool."

I think one of the saddest endings to an autobiography has to be that of Carl Jung's. As he wrote, "When people say I am wise, or a sage, I cannot accept it. A man once dipped a hatful of water from a stream. What did that amount to? I am not that stream. I am at the stream but I do nothing…I stand and behold. There is a fine old story about a student who came to a rabbi and said, 'In the olden days there were men who saw the face of God. Why don't they any more?' The rabbi replied, 'Because nowadays no one can stoop so low.' One must stoop a little in order to fetch water from the stream."[367]

Jung's story stuck in my mind as I discovered my first charismatic writer in the Vancouver Public Library. Both Jung and the charismatic writer had had experiences of the supernatural in their lives. The charismatic writer spoke of the peace, joy, and freedom in the Holy Spirit. That seemed to be an element missing in Jung's life.

It would seem that an Eternal River with ever-widening, glorious flow beckons us towards ever-expanding awe, wonder, mystery, but few if any seem to be invited to enter in at its point of glory. At the point of our entry, it is more likely to appear as a narrow, muddied, parochial creek bed. Jung's prideful loneliness and the charismatic's joy—the difference seemed to lie in an act of humility. The choice seemed to be between intellectual superiority and the chance to remain master of one's own life pitted against giving up control and accepting a gospel that had faith, not mind, at its center. In the writings of the charismatic, I had discovered a gospel that had been simplified and reduced to below my normal comfort levels. Pride did not make it easy stooping so low. However, I also discovered that if we are having difficulty stooping, God can sometimes help by removing the props from our lives; knocked flat on our backs, we may discover we're in a perfect position to drink from the stream we once found too lowly.

I once recommended the book I had been reading to a friend. She let me know she had considered me intellectually beyond that. I told her the story of how Naaman had gone to Elisha to be healed of his leprosy. Elisha asked him to dip himself in the river Jordan. Naaman stomped off in a rage. Damascus had better waters; there was no swimming in the lowly Jordan for him. His servant, however, asked him why, if he would have complied with a great and glorious request, could he not do something lowly? Naaman acceded to the lowly and was healed. I decided I could learn to stoop. If God chooses to reveal Himself not through the high and mighty or through intellectual giants but rather through those who are willing to be transparent and humble before Him, then that is where I would need to look for Him.

Perhaps an act of humility is required because outside of a significant act that separates us from all our old communities and ways of thinking, we just adjust our lives to the shifting and passing vagaries of the inconsequential world around us. Our ideas of "adjustment" can be put in perspective by turning to David Riesman, a social scientist, who wrote of the successive stages all societies pass through. Societies, according to

Riesman, are originally organized according to "tradition-direction"; the culture, itself, provides the over-arching canopy that gathers and forms its members. Religion, rituals, and routines all provide a framework that gathers and forms individuals into a cohesive social group. With societal changes, however, the canopy holding a society together splinters, forcing the individual members to become "inner-directed," developing inner gyroscopes in order to find their bearings. The responsibility inherent in forming one's own life according to the myriad of choices now available proves to be too much for the individual, however, so once again society becomes "other-directed." The canopy holding a society together has irrevocably shattered, however, so one's reference points now come from whatever flits across the radar screen of one's vision. Reisman writes,

> What is common to all the other-directed people is that their contemporaries are the source of direction for the individual—either those known to him or those with whom he is indirectly acquainted, through friends and through the mass media. This source is of course "internalized" in the sense that dependence on it for guidance in life is implanted early. The goals towards which the other-directed person strives shift with that guidance: it is only the process of striving itself and the process of paying close attention to the signals from others that remain unaltered throughout life.[368]

The "other-direction" of the first stage was stable; traditions, cultures, and religions can last for a long time, or even forever. The "other-direction" of the third stage is only as stable as the chosen human idols, such as pop stars, actors, sports entities, or whatever flits across one's radar screen. Riesman concluded, "Men are created different; they lose their social freedom and their individual autonomy in seeking to become like each other."[369]

What Riesman's three stages of social character reveal is that we always adjust our lives according to some goal, whether internal or external. What we, as human beings, find most difficult is freedom. The freedom of our salvation includes the discovery that by adjusting our lives to God's Transcendent Kingdom, then the God for whom each individual is a unique thought saves us from the dehumanizing forces of mass humanity.

"Well-adjusted" and "transformed" are two words that have become the linchpins around which completely different worldviews are formed. One orients us to the temporal world that we live in, and the other invites us to live according to the invisible realm. One defines health according to the demands of the psyche, and the other according to the life of the spirit. One uses the "number of man" to determine what is "normal," and the other uses Jesus to reveal what humanity was meant to look like. We cannot blend those worldviews—trying will only destroy our ability to see and understand that otherwise invisible Kingdom.

CHAPTER FIVE

HOW ARE WE TRANSFORMED?

Our Transformation: External versus Subjective Vision

THERE WERE SO MANY INCIDENTS that contributed to my final exodus from the institutional church that I cannot claim any one defining incident, but certainly one of the minor revelatory moments was a church dinner where I sat beside a psychologist and social worker who were discussing a human being's capability to change and coming to the conclusion that people do not nor cannot really change. Considering we were part of a Christian church where the central message was about transformation, redemption, salvation, being "born again," and being made into new creatures, I was initially incensed. How could we continue to give lip service to a gospel of transformation when we had lost all belief in its efficacy and power?

In retrospect, I realize I should have seen that cynicism as a sign of hope. Our problems have largely come about precisely because of our naïve optimism in our ability to change and improve. The belief in human malleability is what has spawned over 200 therapies offering happiness, healing, fulfillment, the achievement of our human potential, great sex, the overcoming of our personal pathologies, and the release from anxiety, depression, fear and all other problems, many of which we didn't even know we suffered from until the therapeutic kindly alerted us to their presence in our lives. Perhaps disillusionment with all our own human efforts is precisely what is needed before we can again be ready to hear the gospel of grace.

It is precisely because there has been so little sign of personal transformation and new life within the church that I have been chagrined to hear of ministers and therapists being supported by the church to go on "missions" to Africa and Eastern European countries, not to spread the gospel, but rather, to bring them counseling knowledge and techniques. Exactly what are we trying to export? My consolation lies in the fact that the North American soil seems to be unique in the degree to which it has been able to spawn the therapeutic mentality. My hope is that other continents with other cultural biases will be able to discern and reject what we are trying to export.

There have been many factors that have prepared the North American soil to make it peculiarly hospitable to the growth of the therapeutic mindset, but perhaps first and foremost is a blind optimism that allows us to believe in our ability to master all circumstances. The American Dream has instilled in us a belief in the individual's ability to overcome all obstacles in order to achieve whatever one dreams. We believe we are the masters of our own destinies. Death, disease, starvation, and oppression are not our constant companions as they are in other parts of the world, so we have fewer opportunities for reality checks. We have the option of turning our attention from survival to achieving our potential.

We have also been fiercely individualistic. The therapeutic emphasis on autonomy and self-fulfillment suited a people already used to thinking in terms of individualism, not in terms of obligation or community. When the therapeutic offered us power through assertiveness, wholeness through self-understanding, the keys to reaching our potential, and fulfilling relationships through therapy, we were prepared to accept it all at face value.

Another factor contributing to our gullibility has been our belief in the limitless possibilities for technology. If, on our continent, every physical problem could be solved with a technological solution, then why could we not tackle problems in living in the same way? Much of therapy is just taking that technological mindset and transferring it onto the human being. Along with our growing trust in technology has also come a growing dependence on experts. In simpler societies, people still need to survive by their own wits and capabilities. In our complex society, however, none of us can survive according to what we, ourselves, can understand. We need experts for everything from fixing the car or the computer to fighting our cancer or knowing what to eat. Why shouldn't we expect that experts could also help us fix, tune up, and help us maximize the potential for our inner life, as well as solve all problems with living and with relationships?

There seems to be a close relationship between affluence and a preoccupation with our inner emotional states. We have to have achieved a high level of development before we can afford the luxury of thinking about happiness, anxiety, and depression. Since the Constitutional right to the pursuit of happiness seems to have subtly been changed over time into our Constitutional right to be happy, why not also trust that technology and experts can help us achieve what we have come to perceive as our God-given right?

Perhaps the cynicism expressed at that church dinner is precisely what we need in order to go back and re-examine the frameworks and assumptions we have been living with. We are living in the era of psychological man. We look to Jung, Rogers, and Fromm instead of to God for our salvation. The *DSM* has replaced the Ten Commandments as the book of law revealing what is wrong with us. The testimonies in churches ring out to the glory of their therapists, not the Presence of Christ, and the source book for the stories of success is not the Bible, but rather whatever new school of personality change is now in vogue.

Disillusionment may be exactly what we need in order to re-assess our notions of human malleability, the need for personal change, and how that change comes about. If there are few examples of transformed lives on our continent, then perhaps that is because we have shifted our beliefs from religion to the therapeutic gospel and its alternative systems of belief.

In actual fact, personal transformation and change are not central to many of the therapies that have brought their influence into the church. Psychotherapy is based on the recognized need for personal insight; it turns us into the past and the deep regions of the unconscious, where we are helped to mine for the clues that will grant us that insight, and then it offers frames of reference by which we interpret our gained insight. It is insight, however, not change, that is central. How we use our achieved insight is supposedly up to the individual. As long as we can feel that we have control of our lives, then the way that we decide to shape those lives is inconsequential. Psychiatry, on the other hand, is based on a medical model where biology and chemistry, not character and personality, are central. It was not until Carl Rogers and his humanistic psychology came onto the scene that personal change was placed at the center of therapy. However, although Rogers admitted the need for personal change, he also destroyed the belief systems and referential structures that gave the individual an external ideal of what one should be transformed into.

Carl Rogers had originally planned to be a minister, and to that end entered Union Seminary in New York. While in Seminary, he decided that what he had hoped to accomplish could be better brought about through counseling rather than through ministry. That was a fateful decision for both the future of pastoral counseling and for the church at large, for the work and influence of Carl Rogers has permeated the entire pastoral counseling industry, as well as instigating the plethora of self-help and pop psychologies that fill our world.

Rogerian counseling is about change, and Carl Rogers had definite ideas about how that change comes about. In his book *On Becoming A Person,* Rogers claimed that if three specific conditions were put in place, then "therapeutic movement ensues."[370] First, the therapist had to be genuine, real, or in Roger's terms, "congruent." To quote Carl Rogers: "Change is facilitated when the psychotherapist is what he is."[371] Secondly, the psychotherapist needed "a warm, positive and acceptant attitude toward what is in the client."[372] Or, in other words, they needed to be accepting and positive. Thirdly, the psychotherapist needed to be empathetic, able to reflect understanding back to the client. If those conditions were met, then, according to Rogers, "No other conditions are necessary.... The process of constructive personality change will follow."[373] Since Rogerian counseling has become so widespread in its influence, it might be constructive to look at those premises.

Rogers was certainly on to something when he linked personal healing and change with the ability of the individual to connect with another human being who was compassionate and empathetic. The Christian church has a long heritage of spiritual directors who understood and offered that. The Reformation idea of the priesthood of all believers stressed that we all have responsibility for the nurturing of our neighbor's body and soul. A mutuality is built into the gospel; we are the means by which God brings His life to our neighbor. Thus, the covenant of one American Baptist church (1818) stated, "We will watch over each other in brotherly tenderness, each endeavoring to edify his brother."[374] St. Basil of Caesarea (d. 479) advised that no one keep the agitation of soul secret, but that all should be confessed to those who were trustworthy and sympathetic with the weak.[375] In that regard, he was reflecting the Biblical injunction to "confess your sins to each other and pray for each other so that you may be healed" (James 5:16). St. Ambrose (d. 397) was said to have so empathized with the penitents who came to him that he wept as they offered him their confession, and in the fifth century, one bishop was said to have so identified with his penitents that both before and after the penance he would share their tears and their prostrations.[376]

However, aside from the acknowledged need for human empathy, Rogerian counseling has little else in common with traditional spiritual direction. Although Rogerian counseling acknowledges that empathy and relationship are what lay the foundation for change, it was Carl Rogers who turned the "patient" into a "client," thus underscoring the financial basis of the relationship. Since it was Rogers who made counseling egalitarian, opening it up to those who showed talent rather than those who held professional degrees, it was therefore the ability to establish relationship and the capacity for empathy of the therapist and not primarily some scientific theory that established the identity and the credibility of the therapist. However, how can one ascertain the genuineness of the therapist and their empathy when finances form the basis of relationship?

For spiritual directors, it was their love of God that caused them to pour out their lives in service to their neighbor. The traditional spiritual directors of old did not see the source of healing as lying within themselves. They considered themselves fellow pilgrims who were acting as channels for a power that came from another source and brought healing. Rogers, in contrast, replaced the Transcendent vision with the personality and knowledge of the counselor.

Rogerian counseling is inner-directed and client-based. It is the client's inner wisdom, their "internal frame of reference," that is the required focal point of attention; it is the universe of the client that needs to be entered and understood. Traditional spiritual direction, in contrast, begins with the assumption that there is a large cosmic story being enacted into which our lives needed to be fitted. We live best when our lives find their harmony in that larger story. It is the experiential knowledge of that transcendent story, therefore, that provides the authority of the spiritual director.

Rogerian counseling is deliberately non-directive. It offers human support separated from higher authority. Rogers believed in the need for personal change and also in the ability of the individual to affect change under the right circumstances, but he also believed that the individual, in order to change, needed to grow beyond the traditional structures and traditions that gave a vision for what we should be. It was up to the person to create themselves anew according to their own personal vision of what the new should be. To that end, the personal judgment and interpretations of the therapist needed to be foregone. The prevalent attitude was that people are what they are and act as best as they know how. Rogerian counseling had no intention of imposing a vision of the new and neither did it have a vision of what the new should entail. Therapy was not designed to awaken one to the kingdom of God and its inherent judgment of broken relationships, personal failure, social inequality, wrong attitudes, lack of responsible living, and shortcomings in character. Its non-judgmental stance insured that those issues would not be broached, or only in ways that would stay within the client's comfort zone. Perhaps that is why Rogerian counseling was said to be "only suited to middle-class, mildly unhappy Americans."[377] It did not have a radical vision that could engender radical change.

Most therapies, including Rogerian counseling, are attempts to remove the cure of souls from the realm of religion and place it in the domain of the secular. Basically, the psychological strategy has been to create an "individualism oriented toward liberating the self through autonomous decision making and reforming the self through personal understanding."[378] There is no room for a Transcendent God in that vision. The humanistic psychologist eschews religious vision in order to help the client come to his or her own inner resolution according to individual achieved understanding. What Rogers would do was repeat back to the client whatever he or she said, but in new words, hoping to therefore provide a mirror in which the client was reflected.

Rogers admitted in an interview that therapy was "basically subversive since it opposes what society stands for…. Therapy theories and techniques promote a new model of man contrary to that which has been traditionally acceptable."[379] What Rogers advocated was an "open self" that could live without traditional and fixed belief systems (the lot of the "closed self"), a self that could rather focus on expressiveness, freer communication, and spontaneity. It is of interest noting a study that showed that in adverse conditions those under a "closed self" had better survival characteristics.[380] A fixed belief system offers a firm reference point around which to orient life, it offers meaning in adversity, and it offers security. Rogers acknowledged that his theories did not offer the individual security, and yet he still advocated a life lived in open process rather according to anything fixed.

On the one hand, Rogers turned the therapist into a good friend, but

then, while admitting that a good friendship itself could fulfill the conditions he had outlined for change in the client, he also said that, in friendship, "This is only momentarily, however, and then empathy falters, the
positive regard becomes conditional, or the congruence of the 'therapist'
friend becomes overlaid by some degree of façade or defensiveness."[381] In
other words, in real life, people do not act in ways the counselors are
trained to act. In real life, people are not always accepting, empathetic, and
positive. In the messiness of real life there will always be some people we
like more than others, our attitudes are influenced by personality and
behavior, and relationships are mutual.

While Rogerian counseling offered "unconditional positive regard,"
"empathetic understanding," and a non-judgmental environment in
which clients could examine their lives, it has to be asked whether that is
how we humans realize the need to change. It is certainly an attitude that
runs counter to the Biblical view of how we gain wisdom:

> "Rebuke your neighbor frankly so you will not share in his
> guilt"(Leviticus 19:17).
> "He who listens to a life-giving rebuke will be at home among the
> wise" (Proverbs 15:31).
> "Rebuke a discerning man, and he will gain knowledge"
> (Proverbs 19:25).
> "It is better to heed a wise man's rebuke than to listen to the song
> of fools" (Ecclesiastes 7:5).
> "Rebuke a wise man and he will love you" (Proverbs 9:8).
> "Correct, rebuke and encourage—with great patience and careful
> instruction" (2 Timothy 4:2).
> "Those whom I love I rebuke and discipline" (Revelation 3:19).

According to the Bible, it is a loving encounter with truth that causes
us to change, not "non-directive" encounters with "unconditional positive
regard." I am reminded of Shakespeare's King Lear, who banished the
daughter who told him the truth and then gave his kingdom to the two
daughters who gave him "unconditional positive regard." The disaster that

ensued reveals that truth, though painful, is always better for us.

Rogers' client-centered counseling is escapist and unreal. No real person in real life is non-judgmental, accepting, and empathetic regardless of how we behave, and neither would it be healthy if they were. No real friend remains non-directive, withholding opinions and criticisms, and neither would it be healthy surrounding ourselves with people who behaved like mirrors, only reflecting ourselves back to us. In real life, people who care about us do not reflect compassion and acceptance as we engage in destructive behavior.

Religion once offered us a vision. It was the vision we caught sight of and the Presence of God revealed by that vision that produced change. Paul wrote, "And we, who with unveiled faces all reflect the Lord's glory, are being transformed into his likeness with ever-increasing glory, which comes from the Lord, who is the Spirit" (2 Corinthians 3:18). Proverbs 29:18 (The Message) says, "If people can't see what God is doing, they stumble all over themselves." We need a new vision in order to engender movement. The Bible is brilliant in its revealing of how we humans actually work. We eventually become what we focus our attention on. That is why, in Philippians 4:8, it tells us what to focus our minds on.

If our churches are no longer producing transformed lives, then it is because they have lost their vision. What psychology has purposely eschewed is any external vision of who we should be or what we were meant to become. The therapeutic instead teaches us to see ourselves in terms of subjective states: suppression, anxiety, obsessions, unconscious urges, repressed hostility, depression, self-esteem, emotional trauma, and the list goes on endlessly. It claims to be objective, but in actual fact, our lives are always being fitted into frameworks created according to the latest shifting theories of understanding. According to one psychiatrist, the therapist not only listens to the patient but is also "listening to formulas—and word by word, step by step, they are fitting patients' words and actions into the categories they themselves have been taught and trained to respect, perhaps to worship."[382]

There are many schools of therapy, all decrying the weakness of other groups and expounding the superiority of their own approach, but they are all temporary and human frameworks created according to human understanding. According to one sociologist, "To seek out therapy today is to stick your hand into a grab bag of theories that often utterly contradict each other in their specific assumptions but that agree on a more general unproved assertion that the therapist has the knowledge and techniques allowing him or her to see into the most fundamental and hidden motivations of the mind."[383] It is the subjective orientation of the counselor that establishes the framework for the counseling session.

The objective vision once offered by religion has been lost. The foremost achievement of Freud, according to one psychotherapist, was "in getting two people into the same room to talk about the anguish of one of them without the intervention of religious dogma."[384] Freed from any fixed religious framework, the analysts instead turned to free association, to dream analyses, to plumbing the unconscious with a lexicon of symbols and myths that would supposedly bring clarity to those inner regions. Therapy is still "a method for coming to any conclusion the therapist would like to form."[385] Modern therapists have not been able to give up the belief in their own intuitive ability to unlock the inner secrets of their clients. They still come to the therapeutic encounter with preconceived beliefs and then feel confirmed when they discover what they have already decided they were looking for. What exactly they find depends entirely on what school they come from. Since therapists work in private quarters without observation, with no external checks or controls, with no scientific testing or required results, they have few occasions for reality checks. However, rather than our society becoming disillusioned with the subjectivity of therapy, our dependence on their "insights" has just grown. Between 1975 and 1990, the numbers in America of those working in the therapeutic field more than doubled, the alarming point being, "By far the greatest growth in the profession was among the category of therapists with the less rigorous degrees that incorporated little or no exposure to scientific method."[386]

It is our ability to believe in "truth" that is being sacrificed. One psychiatrist noted, "Insights can be curative regardless of whether they hold any truth at all."[387] Another therapist claimed, "There is no necessary relationship between the truth or falseness of insight and therapeutic results."[388] It is not what is "true" that is sought in therapy as much as what is "meaningful" or what "works." What is "meaningful," however, is just a shifting cultural perception. Therapeutic "insights" reflect the current society's preoccupations more than they reflect the truth of the individual client. Take the idea of the unconscious, for example. Freud's "unconscious" is a shell of an idea that has lingered; what the unconscious hides, however, has shifted with each age. At one time, therapists found "penis envy" in its depths. In the 1990s, it was sexual abuse that lurked there. Now it is Multiple Personality disorders or sexual identity. One therapist presciently noted, "Patients and analysts are living in the same culture, and are being formed by similar trends. They may collude in what they believe is an accurate diagnoses of the patient's problems. But because they are both culture-bound, the truth may elude them both."[389]

It is because of that subjectivity that I became frustrated watching attempts made to integrate therapeutic thinking into the church. The church was meant to be the one place where a transcendent vision that was greater than our subjectivity and our attempts to lean on our own understanding was offered. When we brought the therapeutic into the church, we introduced subjectivity into the one place where we had hoped to discover truths that were greater than human understanding and that were not first filtered through the lens of subjective orientation. The church that has become dependent on the therapeutic is a church that is going to be caught floundering, lost without a North Star to guide it.

I remember going to a church weekend retreat where the main speaker was a therapist who was giving us theories of birth order to help us understand ourselves. In looking at our various families afterwards, it seemed that reading our horoscopes or reading tea leaves would have given us a truer picture of our personalities.

For a while, I attended a church that "blew up" when a pastoral counselor who had studied systemic family systems had "learned" that in groups that are dysfunctional, it was reasonable to "blame" one member of that group. Applying that "knowledge" to the church, she decided that it was reasonable to blame the minister for a dysfunctional church and the result was a very unholy mess. I later tried to talk to the individual and question her as to whether it was appropriate to bring the latest theories she had just learned into the church; I asked whether the church should be getting its bearings by something a little more reliable and firm than just the latest shifting theories of family dynamics—such as, for example (I dared to suggest), the Bible. When I was told that it was using the Bible that way that brought abuses, it became one more reason for my eventual exodus from the church.

I remember sitting in a psychiatrist's office giving my version of family dynamics and wondering why I thought the psychiatrist would have the wisdom to sort through all the truths, half-truths, rationalizations, and misunderstandings that had brought our family to a place of crises. A sense of helplessness washed over me as I realized the degree to which the psychiatrist would be working from what we chose to reveal. He had no true objective view from which he could see us and mediate reconciliation. As individual members of our family were to see him separately I knew he would get as many different stories as there were family members. Since I was married to someone who was highly successful, a noted physician, brilliant with words, and male, I began to wonder why I thought the psychiatrist, chosen by my husband, also a physician, and also male would have the objectivity to be able to help us. Since religious belief had become a growing issue in our problems I also felt increasingly defensive about placing family problems in an environment where faith issues would be seen as irrelevant, a sign of pathology, or never more than a side issue. Suddenly I had a deep longing for someone who could get past our family's various abilities with words and just see what was in the heart of each one of us. I believe that longing was heaven-sent and I believe it was following that longing that brought final resolution and peace in our family.

If we think that subjective awareness and self-consciousness is what will procure our freedom, then when we have our lives all wrapped up by the latest theories of knowledge, all "discovered" by plumbing the depths of the past, have every square inch of our psyche "understood" according to some school of thought, then what we will know is not freedom, but the cosmic loneliness of one who has become master of one's own destiny. Our deepest longings are not to know ourselves but to be known, but for that we have to leave ourselves in order to find ourselves in the Light of another reality.

Dying to Self vs. Self-Fulfillment

ANOTHER REASON WHY we may be seeing so little personal change or transformation in the church is because we cannot decide whether it is better
to die to self or to nurture the self. It is admittedly not an exciting prospect
contemplating the Gospel's injunctions to die and lose oneself while living
in a culture where the people around us are talking about self-fulfillment,
nurturing the self, and developing ways whereby we can become
autonomous, self-authenticated beings with lives created and controlled
by the Almighty Self. In *A History of Pastoral Care In America: From
Salvation to Self-realization,* the historian E. Brooks Holifield traces the history of how a gospel that once had dying to self and self-denial at its heart
slowly got turned into a gospel of self-love, self-actualization, and self-
realization. At best, the church has become an institution of double
options. Option A—the Gospel—is offered from the pulpit on Sunday, but
if it finds no takers then it reverts to Option B, functioning as a referral
base for those who offer a more palatable way of teaching us how to view
ourselves.

The church has always tended to adapt its message to the prevailing
culture, but rarely when the culture's message has been so blatantly antag-
onistic to its own. The sociologist Daniel Yankelovich, in his book *New
Rules,* writes of how the modern search for self-fulfillment has destroyed
many of the traditional rules of conduct. The new rules, Yankelovich
claims, "Simply turn the old ones on their head, and in place of the old
self-denial ethic we find people who refuse to deny anything to themselves—not out of bottomless appetite, but on the strange moral principle
that 'I have a duty to myself'."[390] Humanistic psychology has turned the
self into a sacred object that needs to be nourished, "unblocked" so that it
can be "real," unrestrained so that it can be spontaneous, and freed from
all that would repress the natural goodness inherent within.
Unfortunately, as Yankelovich observed, "The error of replacing self-denial
with a duty-to-self ethic has proven nearly fatal, for nothing has subverted
self-fulfillment more thoroughly than self-indulgence."[391]

When Jesus said, "I have come that they may have life, and have it to the full" (John 10:10), how can that be made consistent with all that Biblical talk of dying and losing oneself? Does dying and losing oneself abort our development, or is it the secret door to a world where dying is the condition of entry? I have learned that it is harmful to take any one verse or idea from the Bible and remove it from the setting of full gospel revelation. If the Bible calls us to die and to deny ourselves, then it does so in the setting of offering "life more abundantly," "joy unspeakable," and in keeping with the fruits of the Spirit: joy, peace, love, and ultimately, freedom. Gospel dying must therefore be seen not as an attitude of morbidity but rather as a clue to life itself.

In spite of our culture's more palatable ways of dealing with oneself, I found myself more ready to re-examine Jesus' command to die and to deny oneself after reading back through Christian history. I had gone back in history looking for those through whom the Light of God had shone brightly and purely; what I discovered at the same time was that a dark shadow has always threatened to engulf the Light wherever it has appeared. Religion has a dark and shameful side to its history. As Eugene Peterson noted, "Religion is the most dangerous energy source known to humankind. The moment a person (or government or religion or organization) is convinced that God is either ordering or sanctioning a cause or project, anything goes. The history, worldwide, of religion-fueled hate, killing, and oppression is staggering."[392]

The critics of Christianity are especially gleeful when they can point out how much evil has been done in the name of religion. It does seem evident that if religion does not transform us, then it will actually harden and feed whatever is worst in us.

History is full of examples of those who have allowed religion to provide the justifying cover behind which their unpurified passions could go raging, disguised as religious zeal. Our latent hostility, fear, and prejudices have so often been pressed into the service of religion, hypocritically fueling the drive to instate God's supposed kingdom of love. Our obsessive love of power has so often been dressed up in the finery of religion. There have been so many who were ready to tap into humanity's need for God in order to get a strip of stolen power whereby they could go along for the ride, using religion as a means to serve personal ambition, personal pride, or the personal ego. There are just too many stories of divine love being awakened, getting confused, becoming transferred onto the human, and then being reduced to mere human lust. How often has man tried to spread the gospel with his diseased nature, but then managed to spread nothing but his disease?

I believe that if we took a poll as to why people don't go to church, one of the main reasons would be people who are in the church. The gap between the tenets of Christianity, the life of its leader, and the lives of those who attempt to proselytize in its name is just too great to stomach. What is missing from much modern religion is the reality of the cross. Too often we, in the church, want to claim that we are saved before we have died. True Christianity, however, is an invitation to die.

It is religion without an understanding of the art of dying that allows it to become an abusive weapon. Much of the modern world's abhorrence and reaction against religion is justified. William Law justly noted, "When religion is in the hands of the mere natural man, he is always the worse for it; it adds a bad heat to his own dark fire and helps to inflame his four elements of selfishness, envy, pride, and wrath." Romano Guardini was just articulating the obvious when he wrote, "Everything evil in man functions also (there all the more powerfully) in his religion."[393] Pascal, caught in one of the nasty conflicts that religion so readily gives rise to, noted, "Men never do evil so completely and cheerfully as when they do it from religious conviction." Thomas Merton, himself part of the movement that condemned war and who was then silenced by the church because of his protests, observed that the "the reason why so many pious men fail to become saints is that they do evil for the glory of God."[394] In the words of C. S. Lewis, "For the Supernatural, entering a human soul, opens to it new possibilities both of good and evil. From that point the road branches: one way to sanctity, love, humility, the other to spiritual pride, self-righteousness, persecuting zeal. And no way back to the mere humdrum virtues and vices of the unawakened soul. If the Divine call does not make us better, it will make us very much worse. Of all bad men religious bad men are the worst. Of all created beings the wickedest is one who originally stood in the immediate presence of God."[395]

It is not theories of atonement that save us; it is an encounter with the reality of the cross. As John Howard Yoder observed, "The cross is not a detour or a hurdle on the way to the kingdom, nor is it even the way to the kingdom; it is the kingdom come."[396] If we, ourselves, are to be kept from contributing to Christianity's dark history, then we will need to discover and learn to love the reality of the cross; we will need to discover the life that is revealed through dying.

In a world where power, possessions and proud demeanor are the signs of having achieved the pinnacle of success, Jesus came to reveal the nature of a new humanity; "Here at the cross is the man who loves his enemies, the man whose righteousness is greater than that of the Pharisees, who being rich became poor, who gives his robe to those who took his cloak, who prays for those who despitefully use him."[397]

Forget about charismatic or powerful or talented personalities; I believe that, in religion, one should only follow leaders and listen to the gospel from those in whom the cross has been allowed to leave a deep and visible imprint in their lives. Too often it is those who are rich, beautiful, successful, intelligent, or talented who are chosen to be spokespersons for the new Kingdom. That, in itself, is a sign that we have missed seeing its reality. The new humanity can only be revealed where something of the old nature has been put to death; it exists amongst those who know "the fellowship of sharing in his sufferings, becoming like him in his death" (Philippians 3:10). The cross, the central symbol in Christianity, is an ever-present reminder that dying always precedes new resurrection life. In fact, the art of true Christianity could possibly be seen as the art of learning to die—dying rightly and well.

We live our lives on the portal of two kingdoms—one visible, the other invisible. We live our moments perched between death and resurrection. One of the richest facets of the cross is to see it as the tension point we agree to live in between all that has happened to us, all that we have done, all the pressures of our world, and the ever-present call of new life.[398] By reaching out towards a reality existing outside of our world formed by action and reaction, by learning to say, like Jesus on the cross, "Thy will be done" with increasing trust and faith, we are thereby led into the ways of a new Kingdom that teaches us how to live according to new laws.

The cross is thus the reality that stands as a permanent symbol against all of the world's wisdom and offers us the greatest clue into resurrection life. As Rufus Moseley writes, "The Cross is a way of life; the way of love meeting all hate with love, all evil with good, all negatives with positives."[399] Christianity itself "is the life and death and resurrection of Christ going on day after day in the souls of individual men and in the heart of society."[400]

Forgiving those who have hurt us, dismantling our barricades and offering kindness where it makes us vulnerable, learning to see Christ in difficult people and treating them accordingly, building relationships on the basis of love where only resentment and retaliation before existed, overriding our learned distrust and survival mechanisms in order to learn new ways of response, all can leave us feeling exposed and fragile. We attempt the impossible not because it "works" or because we won't be further wounded, but because we have caught a vision of the new.

Inseparable from the story of the cross is the symbol given to us from the other side of the cross and its darkness—that of the curtain of the temple being torn apart. The two symbols—the cross and the torn curtain—form two views of the same reality. Whenever the cross is the reality we live by, then at the other side of our darkness, God tears apart the curtain of separation and comes to reside with us. Resurrection happens. Christ is born wherever something of the old has died. Our capacity for God is determined by how deep the imprint of the cross has been in our lives.

It is one thing to believe in the cross as the place where God tricked the devil (Origen), or the place of transaction where God struck a deal with the devil to release our souls from hell (St. Anselm); it is quite another to believe in the cross as a place where Jesus modeled for us the way into resurrection life (Abelard). Since Jesus asked us to take up our cross daily and follow Him, I believe the last interpretation is significant as imaging our door into life.

However, as important as it is to accept the need to die, it is just as important to recognize exactly what it is that needs to die. The Bible is filled with references as to how God created the world to be good, how God was satisfied with what He had created, and how man was the climax of that creation. Clearly, it is wrong to attempt to destroy what God created and declared to be good.

At one time, reading of the ascetic extremes within the Middle Ages left me feeling slightly queasy; I was afraid that might be what the call of faith was about. It took a long time before I was capable of seeing that the Christian life was obviously not a denial of the world or of the nature that God had created, but rather, a dying to all that had diminished, destroyed, and hidden its original glory. Perhaps a good example of rightful dying can be seen in the life of Henry Suso.

Suso was a fourteenth century Dominican monk who lived in Germany at a time when he came under the influence of the powerful teacher and mystic Meister Eckhart. It was perhaps Eckhart's influence that persuaded Suso that his nature was too "lively" and made him determined to subject his flesh to the spirit. Suso designed for himself an undergarment of hair to which one hundred and fifty sharply filed nails were attached. Since his bed was covered in vermin, he designed rings of leather that locked his hands around his throat so he could not scratch and gain relief. He next had leather gloves made with brass tacks attached by a tinsmith, so that if he tried to relieve himself of the vermin, he would lacerate himself. Wishing to identify with the sufferings of Christ, he designed a wooden cross to which thirty nails were fastened. Attaching it to his back, it became an instrument of torture so he could castigate himself for perceived lapses in behavior. Still not content, he made for himself a scourge to which he had attached pointed brass tacks. Suso denied himself food, water, a bed, and baths until his body was an emaciated, trembling mass of wounds. Suso kept up his practices for sixteen years until, in a vision, God revealed to him that He did not want this of him, and so Suso threw all his instruments of torture into the river. Suso thought himself ready for a life of ease, but that was not to be. In his time of meditation, he was visited by a young man who said, "You seem to think that God has removed your yoke from you and cast off your fetters, and that you should live a life of ease. This is not how it is going to be. God is not taking your bonds off you. He just wants to change them and make them heavier than ever they were."[401] What happened next gives us a revealing example of how different are God's ways of producing righteousness from our ways. In one of the villages where Suso lived, there resided a woman who, as an act of vengeance, spread the rumor that the illegitimate child born to her had been fathered by Suso. Suso quickly learned the difference between internal and external suffering. Whereas his former life had earned him a reputation for great holiness and made him a respected member of the religious community, now that reputation was threatened. All that self-mutilation, he realized, had left his pride intact. Now humiliation opened the door to true humility. Not only had his former life not taught him detachment from self or dethroned the ego, it had actually strengthened the ego in its illusions of self-mastery. Now, in desperation, he learned to throw himself on the mercy of God. As former friends refused to associate with him, he learned to rely on God alone. At the height of his misery, he was approached by a sympathetic woman who believed in his innocence and offered to murder the baby; once the baby was out of sight, she reasoned, it would be out of the minds of the people and Suso could reclaim his former reputation. Suso was horrified. When the woman offered to at least place the child in a public orphanage so that the scandal would disappear, Suso asked instead that the child be brought to him. As Suso held the child, tears of compassion flowed down his face. No longer obsessed with himself, he could feel real empathy for the child who had been brought into the world under such adverse circumstances. Although his support had been largely cut off, he vowed to share as much bread as he had with this child, even though the act would implicate him further.

What Suso's new life demonstrated was how different change led by the Spirit was to change attempted by human effort. God used circumstances to reveal to Suso how pride and ego made real life impossible. Once he found himself dependent on God, then God could lead him on paths that effected his transformation. Where rightful dying had been allowed to be brought into his life, God also compensated for the suffering by bringing radiant peace, grace, and repose. Suso became a man of such depth of wisdom, compassion, and grace that he became the spiritual counselor of many, his life itself became a beacon of light in the land, and his wisdom long outlived his life.

Psychology works on the principle that with enough knowledge and self-understanding, we can gain the confidence and capability to take charge and control of our lives. However, when the personal ego is in charge of life formation, then it always perverts and distorts the very nature that God created to be good. True religion teaches that it is precisely the ego that needs to die. We are no more able to eradicate the evil within ourselves than to amputate one of our limbs with a kitchen knife; we have neither the capability nor the stomach for the task. Our salvation begins at that point where, in however so small a way, we dethrone our ego in order to allow someone else to be God to us. It is in trust, not knowledge, wherein our salvation lies. It is in allowing the ego-life to die that the new Christ-life takes root.

As Suso revealed, religious attempts at holiness are often also just ego-driven exertions; the imperialistic ego that does not dare defy God any longer can turn into itself and do just as much damage in the name of religion. The imperialistic ego that gets thwarted in its drive towards rebellion can, in the name of religion, just don a new religious cloak and continue its work, now working towards self-destruction instead of self-enhancement.

What needs to die is not our God-created human nature, but rather, the personal ego that would design a life according to its own appetites and understanding. When St. Paul said, "I have been crucified with Christ and I no longer live, but Christ lives in me" (Galatians 2:20), he revealed the secret to a life made powerful, effective, and meaningful. It was the crucifixion of the ego, of the "I" that demands control that allowed him to be grafted onto a new life source. We cannot be filled with God if we are filled with our self. The ego will always demand the attention and the worship that is due to only God.

The ego is a rapacious appetite that takes all God-given reality and then devours it in service of the self. It stands before God's creation and feels no awe, but sees only self reflected. The ego, which refuses to bow before a higher, transcendent life, becomes an appetite that never achieves a place of satiety. It rather "seeks to transform the world into a new solar system with itself as the sun."[402] In doing so, it destroys meaning, relationships, and the ability to find oneself placed within a larger unity. The ego that has been allowed to become the center of its own personal universe is perpetually striving, clutching, wounded, unable to find rest or satisfaction, for the natural propensities of the ego are towards self-pity, envy, bitterness, anger, pride, and covetousness. Egoistic self-absorption blinds us to the life of God and the larger society and universe; it keeps us from finding our harmony and participation in a larger whole, turning us into ourselves instead.

The one verse that modern spiritualities love to quote is that of Jesus saying, "The Kingdom of God is within you." Scholars claim that this is actually a mistranslation of the text. A closer translation would be that the Kingdom is "upon" or "amongst" us. By mistranslating it as "within you," it has become the proof text for modern spiritualities that believe that the highest and only truths are those that can be found within ourselves. It justifies the supremacy of the ego. That verse, however, can only be claimed by those who have allowed the kingdom of self to die so thoroughly that another Kingdom of righteousness could find welcome within. One can only live with one overriding locus of attention; if it is the self, then God will have become a peripheral awareness. It is the self that needs to get off of God's throne in our life.

The clue to life itself seems to lie in the example of the one who "emptied himself" or "made himself nothing" (Philippians 2:7). Somehow, that was an attitude and reality that allowed us, in Jesus, to get a glimpse of the fullness of the divine/human potential. Unlike religious societies or moral efforts that work from the outside in, Jesus modeled the access to life that flowed in the opposite direction.

In dethroning the ego, we leave room for something completely new to be born within us, a new life that can be recognized, named, and indwelt by a holy God—a new life that can walk without desecrating a holy way. Resurrection life arises wherever we have allowed something of our own ego-life to die. When Meister Eckhart wrote, "The kingdom of God is only for the perfectly dead," he was describing the state of human nature perfected, not destroyed. In allowing God, not our egos, control of our lives, it is our very humanity that is to be redeemed.

The Bible teaches that God has breathed His own life into us. He has placed eternity in our hearts (Ecclesiastes 3:11). We are God-infused, living souls. That life lives threatened by the Luciferian ego that has raised itself above the throne of God in our hearts.

The assumption has long existed in the church that the therapeutic is an aide to religion, existing to help straighten our broken natures, helping us undo what has gone wrong with us, helping us to re-order our lives. That attitude, however, masks and ignores the fundamental difference that lies between religion and the therapeutic. Religion tells us that our fatal flaw lies too deep to be mended. It is precisely the ego, the "I," that is fallen, so that trying to change by means of our own understanding or by strengthening the ego and its ability to make its own choices only hardens what is wrong with us. It is that conscious "I," my ego, that must be transcended so that I can learn to live out of a center other than my own. Jesus said, "I am the vine; you are the branches" (John 15:5). We are actually grafted onto a new life source so that it is that new life source, not the personal ego, which directs and nourishes our life.

The Bible also uses other metaphors that conjure up the image of death and dying being the prerequisites for life. One of those images is that of circumcision. Circumcision is the biblical image that counters the modern idea that we need to just acknowledge, accept, and integrate all that we find within ourselves. There is always old flesh that needs to be cut off. Self-absorption, pride, envy, lust, greed, and hostility are always present with us, threatening to accompany even the good that we would accomplish. Without circumcising away their presence, even the good we attempt can result in evil.

Old Testament circumcision had always been the means whereby the people of God could be identified. Circumcision was the first symbolic sign of what would eventually lie at the heart of the Christian gospel—the message that creation and destruction, life and death are inextricably linked. The very source of life requires the painful cutting away of flesh. In the Old Testament, circumcision was a physical, outward cutting away of flesh that needed to be ritually carried out once. In the New Testament, it became a spiritual reality, "A man is not a Jew if he is only one outwardly, nor is circumcision merely outward and physical. No, a man is a Jew if he is one inwardly; and circumcision is circumcision of the heart, by the Spirit, not by the written code" (Romans 2:28).

In religious work, it is often the temptation to think that as long as we are doing something great for God, then the invisible sins—pride, lust, greed, jealousy, resentment, and self-absorption—don't matter. In actual fact, they are what matter most. God looks on the heart. The people of God are not defined as those who do great deeds for God, but rather, as those with circumcised hearts.

The difference between a circumcised and uncircumcised heart can be seen by examining a simple act. Let us say, for example, that we decide to invite someone home for lunch after church. Let us say, to make it more interesting, that they are a newcomer to church, but have a "bad" reputation that has preceded them. According to the Bible, it is the heart of our actions that God looks at, but what does lie in our heart? We could be a professional paid by the church and just doing our job and earning money. Or we could have self-consciously realized that in extending the invitation, we would be lauded for our "tolerance" and anticipated the reflected glory. We could have felt self-righteous and superior in the newcomer's presence and liked the way our own insecurity was thereby diminished.

We could have noticed that they had a great body and allowed ourselves to start toying with some fantasies. We could have been running for church office and needed to be seen as involved in church outreach. Or we could be desperately lonely and glad for anyone who will give us notice. We could also have extended the invitation because we recognized in the individual one for who Christ died and we could be attempting to serve Christ in that individual. The outward gesture would be the same in all the above instances, even though only one act arose out of purity of heart. As stated in Proverbs 16:2, "All a man's ways seem innocent to him, but motives are weighed by the Lord." It is the motive or heart of our actions that God looks at. We need to do our works with circumcised hearts. The Old Testament foretold of the need for spiritual circumcision, saying, "For the days are coming when I will punish all who are circumcised only in the flesh" (Jeremiah 9:25). People of circumcised heart are people who not only do good, but who do it for the right motive.

Without circumcision our "vices are generally camouflaged under the cloak of virtue and so do not blush, but rather swell up with pride at being revealed to human eyes.".[403] Pride is the chief of all the vices, but anger, lust, envy, sloth, greed, and gluttony all tend to grow like morning glory or some other pernicious weed, first attaching itself and then insinuating itself around all the good we would do. Without circumcision, even our most well-meaning and religious acts are competing for their life alongside the wild outgrowth of our old fallen nature. The spiritual sins can slip in and become a virulent growth accompanying all of our most religious and holy acts, choking the life from what we consider our best endeavors. Without a constant cutting away of their growth, even the good we wish to do can become an evil.

Another image that exemplifies Biblical dying is that of Abraham and his wells.[404] When the Bible gives us the story of Abraham, it completely ignores the more advanced civilizations and technological feats that were being accomplished at the same time. In Egypt, for example, great pyramids were being erected. The very design of the pyramids was religious, their shape allowing for the sun's rays to move down their surface, and it was by climbing up those rays of light that the king's soul was to climb to join the gods in the sky

Abraham, in contrast, kept busy digging wells. The need for water created a dependency that caused frequent tension among neighbors. The locating, digging, and maintaining of wells was a crucial activity at which Abraham seemed especially adept; the skill and effort required meant removing all dirt and sand that impeded access to the necessary water. That is why well digging is such an apt metaphor for the spiritual life. We cannot produce eternal life or, as did the pharaohs, create our own staircase to heaven. So much, in the name of religion is akin to the building of those impressive pyramids; they were designed to reach heaven, but housed only death. In contrast, the spiritual life, like well digging, consists in removing all that would close off access to God. Antoine de Saint Exupery, the French author, said that perfection was achieved "not when nothing more can be added, but when nothing more can be taken away."[405] True spirituality is about dying, about removing all that keeps God from coming closer and from forming the true center of our life. It is not what we do for God that is important in religious life, but how emptied of ourselves we can become so that we can become channels of God's grace.

Pruning is another image the Bible uses. The therapeutic would have us believe that we need to nurture ourselves and that nothing should be cut off or repressed. That is like watering and fertilizing a rose bush without believing in a need for pruning. The bush will become an unmanageable tangle of prickly vines with very few blossoms.

In the Middle Ages, sin was seen not as the lapses in moral conduct that we are all prone to but as the vices—anger, lust, greed, envy, etc.— that form root systems that blossom into immoral acts. Our society now needs those vices in order to be kept afloat. Capitalism would collapse without greed and envy. How could our political structures survive without pride? Take lechery out of the movie industry and who would support it? Gluttony and anger support our country's GDP; armaments and satisfying palates craving new taste sensations are big business. The West flourishes on the vices. Religion that has not the courage to preach the cross and dying will not be a counter-cultural force, but will function as a fertil-izer nourishing and sanctifying all that is worst in society and in human nature.

Dying, pruning, and circumcision have become unfashionable topics in a society that expends so much energy on self-fulfillment. We spend our energy, instead, following the "science" of psychology, which offers us the proper care, preservation, development, and the nurturing of our selves and our human nature. It is not morbidity that causes us to focus on dying when all around us people are working towards reaching one's human potential. It is, rather, the understanding of how death and life are two views of the same reality; wherever we've died to self, we have also made room for another reality to come to life within.

At the heart of all major religions lies the belief in the need for man's un-selfing and the overcoming of his ego needs. At the very time pluralis-tic awareness has made that evident, the Christian church has been inte-grating into itself therapeutic systems that have man's self and his ego needs the center of its concern.

While pluralistic awareness has informed us that at the heart of all major religions lies belief in the need for self-surrender to a reality greater than ourselves, the Western church has countered that growing awareness by integrating into itself a system that teaches theories of the autonomous self, self-actualization, individuation—all euphemisms for self-godhead. The self is not surrendered, but rather, affirmed, validated, and fortified.

Coventry Patmore wrote, "Emptiness of self is the supreme merit of the soul because it is the first condition of her capacity for God."[406] We, however, have preferred the therapeutic gospel that has the self at the cen-ter of its focus and concern.

Past Versus Becoming

WE HUMANS ARE CREATURES who are cursed by memories. The past will therefore always be a problem for us until we allow God to turn our mistakes into wisdom; our sins into redemption stories; our weaknesses into strengths.

Without an ability to face and acknowledge all that lies in our past we will stumble into the future; without an ability to face and acknowledge the past it will be the hidden power that accompanies and haunts all our attempts to create ourselves anew. However, it also has to be acknowledged that when we try to overcome our past in our own strength and by our own understanding we just become trapped by it. The inner or wounded child that we try to nurture can become the fiend that never allows the adult to break free. The therapeutic can help us uncover, analyze, and give theories of understanding as to what lies in the past, but it cannot help us break free from what we agree to see and know. The past is a fixity; focusing on it does not engender movement. It is, I found, dangerous to submerge oneself in the past without a Transcendent vision of the new that we are being drawn towards and the presence of God with us in the journey.

What makes religious faith so appealing and powerful is that it places divine love, acceptance, and forgiveness at the forefront of its gospel. Forgiveness does not eliminate the past; it is what allows us to face the past. Perhaps it is only the Christian who has experienced an awakened awareness of the love and forgiveness of God that can truthfully face the past without resorting to excuses, rationalizations, without building defense mechanisms, and without developing neurotic responses.

There was a time when I thought it coincidental that an awakened interest in the Transcendent was coupled with, as I said at the time, someone opening the trap door of my life and allowing all that I had repressed, cut off, and left behind, to re-attach itself and start to bleed. Now I know that it wasn't coincidence at all; that is how God works. All is revealed, not out of condemnation, but for the purpose of "bringing every thought captive to Christ". We need to be able to face the past if we are going to be able to change for the future.

First, however, I bought completely the idea that if one gathered the broken threads of one's life, analyzed them, brought them to full consciousness and awareness, then they would form themselves into a ball that could finally be thrown away, or at least be under one's control. I didn't understand why those broken pieces didn't form themselves into a ball at all, but rather into a net; the more I struggled the more I was caught and bound by my past. There came a time when I finally stopped, stepped back to get a good look at how many broken threads and how much garbage there actually was in my life, with new loads arriving each day. I figured that at the rate I was going, picking through it all, I might be finished in time to die – without ever having really lived. I began to wonder if there was anything after this life, other than this life. The more I wondered about that question the more it got turned into an all-consuming passion.

When I turned from myself to seek someone other, the coincidences in my life began to happen; coincidences that became so pronounced, I told myself that there must be someone there who wanted to be known. To whoever that was, I began to address my many questions, and slowly I discovered a quiet place where one becomes aware of being listened to. As I grew in courage, I began to bring the broken and shattered fragments of my life into that quiet place. In the quiet, those broken pieces, like filings before a magnet, were revealed according to a Higher Light, and I knew I was being given the option of turning my life in new directions, of allowing the broken pieces to be formed into new patterns. It was on two different occasions that I, in that quiet place I now called prayer, was suddenly startled by two particular memories, and, surprised, I realized that someone had just shown me two incidents from my past; two long-forgotten incidents that existed in long-forgotten settings. For the first time in my life I realized that I actually made sense.

I'm not sure why I was suddenly made to feel free, as though I could begin to move to a new place. Perhaps it was because in a life where loneliness sat like a permanent ache I realized that I am not and have never

294 THE ALTARS OF AHAZ

been alone. Perhaps it was because in a world where I felt I moved like the Invisible Man, no one ever having seen me, I realized that the Biblical standard for knowledge was the degree to which I am now and always have been known. Perhaps it was the realization that under all that garbage there were two primary sources that, like cancerous flesh, kept metastasizing throughout my being. Being made aware of their presence also made me aware of the choices I had opened to me as to how to respond differently. Whatever the reason, I felt I was finally free to begin to move on. That pile of garbage did not disappear. It is a pity there's quite so much, but it exists as archives; I go back to get pieces I need. I, however, was given a new option as to how to live life other than living under its control. I found myself ready to live life on new terms.

I began to wonder, however, if I had discovered what had run as a theme through the writings of the saints that I had been reading, but that I had not understood: "Know God and you will know yourself"; "Find God and you will find yourself." Or the Biblical paradox, "For whoever wants to save his life will lose it, but whoever loses his life for me will save it"(Luke 9:24). What ran as a theme through the lives of the saints and the Bible was the fact that we cannot know ourselves until we find ourselves in God. For example, "It came also that I was able to see with absolute certainty that it was easier for us to get to know God than to know our own soul...God is nearer to us than our own soul, for he is the ground in which it stands...So if we want to know our own soul and enjoy its fellowship, as it were, it is necessary to seek it in our Lord God in which it is enclosed (Julian of Norwich). Or, in the words of Martin Luther, "God is closer to everything than anything is to itself."

Therein lies one of the great paradoxes of the gospel; the more we take our focus off of ourselves and shift our attention to God, the more we will become aware of ourselves and who we truly are. Faith asks us to lose sight of ourselves, to forego our attempts to save ourselves according to our own means, to leave our self-absorption in order to seek God, and then to our surprise we find ourselves in Him.

In turning our backs to the past to seek God, not only will we not be allowed to leave everything behind, but we will keep tripping over the past until we learn to use it as the raw material that we allow God to transform in the process of our becoming. Not only does faith not allow us to escape the past but in new ways and on new ground we are led on paths whereby that past becomes the raw material that is redeemed and reworked.

I found it interesting that in Dante's "Inferno" Lucifer and the worst sinners were portrayed as frozen in ice. As Charles Williams wrote, "Hell is an image that bears no more becoming." It is a pity that so much religion has consigned people to that frozen hell: by defining religion in static terms and according to theological theories that ignore the deeper realities of our being it has actually prevented us from facing our broken pasts (they have been forgiven, have they not?), our deep inner struggles (we are saved, are we not?) and has prevented Christ from leading us beyond ourselves (Christ is already born in us, is he not?). Too often religious belief does not engender movement. True faith, however, is not only a place of rest but also of constant becoming.

The therapeutic claims that self-knowledge will free us and allow us to be masters of our fate, and that awareness will allow us to manipulate the past into a new future. I, however, have found that knowledge and awareness can be unbearable burdens. The advantage of leaving, losing ourselves to find ourselves in God, is that what God reveals He also frees us from. We are shown the past so that we can be offered new choices, a new path. The past is revealed in the light of forgiving love and acceptance, so that we will no longer need to bury, cut off, or rationalize away that which has deformed us but rather be freed of it.

I now know that the first sign of the nearing of the Light will always be a growing awareness of what that Light reveals; it will reveal how little health there is in us. What we do with our awakened awareness is crucial to the development of faith. The choice the growing awareness presents us with is as to whether we will continue on in our approach to the Transcendent, or whether we will choose to re-focus our attention onto ourselves, our past memories, and the emerging unconscious. The fateful error in the life of faith is to turn from God in order to turn into ourselves.

Will versus Emotions

IF WE ARE GOING TO BE CAPABLE of change, we will have to choose whether we use our will or our emotions to propel the engine of change. We live in a world where emotions are fast becoming the barometer for truth, the measure of personal success, and the guide for making life's choices. Could that be another reason why people become trapped in lives that they seem incapable of changing?

If emotions are our guide and measure of success, then St. Paul can be dismissed as a basket case. In light of modern therapeutic understanding, St. Paul's cry—"What a wretched man that I am! Who will rescue me from this body of death?" (Romans 7:24)—would have to be interpreted as a personal failure to integrate his inner life. If, however, St. Paul can be seen as a guide to the spiritual life, then what the Bible may be preparing us for is the awareness that increasing spiritual consciousness and growth may not initially bring us peace, but rather, greater inner turmoil and conflict.

Our current pre-occupation with our emotional health could not have come about if we had not first destroyed the concept and awareness of soul. The reality of soul is actually born and grows out of inner emotional turmoil and struggle. It is the belief in personal responsibility and the freedom of choice that is most intimately connected with the function of soul. However, if our wills are truly free to chart our course in life, then the greatest obstacle they will face will be runaway emotions and passions.

The imagery of struggle and warfare are intrinsic to the gospel message. Considering their prevalence in the Bible, it is interesting looking back and reflecting on how little the people around me spoke of their personal inner struggles. In fact, looking back, I can't remember being in a place where it was all right to admit to how deeply divided we can inwardly be, and how deep the inner struggles are. Of course, it could be claimed that the therapeutic encounter was set up precisely to deal with those inner battles, but they helped one articulate the struggle in therapeutic terms. They were oriented towards the personal ego and the subjective, not towards helping us see our lives in terms of great cosmic themes. In the church, it seemed as though we were either expected to be living a "saved" or victorious Christian life or, if that wasn't working, then we were referred to a therapist who helped us to see our struggles in secular, humanistic terms. It was our emotional health we were made attentive to, not some overarching drama of good versus evil that could play havoc with our inner states.

Various theorists have speculated on it being the loss of objective truth that has led us to rely so heavily on our feelings to be our guide.[407] At one time we would have explained our actions by saying "I believe." Now we preface our explanations by saying "I feel." Our truths are not external truths, but are emotional truths. When we stopped scripting our lives according to something large such as religion, tradition, culture, or national identity, then subjective emotions became the only barometer left to gauge our actions, or to take the measure of how well we were doing. Without a belief in an objective order, feelings became the only sure guide and measure of our success—success defined not as the furtherance of a cause, but rather, as the ability to further some emotional state such as happiness. Christopher Lasch observed, "Therapy constitutes an antireligion, not always to be sure because it adheres to rational explanation or scientific methods of rational explanation or scientific methods of healing, as its practitioners would have us believe, but because modern society 'has no future' and therefore gives no thought to anything beyond its immediate needs. Even when therapists speak of the need for 'meaning' and 'love', they define love and meaning simply as the fulfillment of the patient's emotional requirements."[408]

It was in the 1970s—in the decade after the 1960s when we had become suspicious of and rebelled against all external forms of authority—that emotions became the new barometer for truth. The "me" decade found salvation in emotional discovery, emotional honesty, emotional intelligence, and emotional communication. Self-help books suddenly dominated the publishing industry and the encounter group became the new cultural phenomenon. By the middle of the decade, it was thought that six million Americans were in encounter groups.[409] New Therapies and groups burgeoned, all intent in helping us overcome our emotional inhibitions. The Esalen Institute, Primal Therapy, Scream Therapy, Est, TA, Rebirthing, and nude encounter groups were some of the perhaps more novel attempts at helping us get in touch with our true feelings, but everybody got into the action to varying degrees. It was the beginning of the Psychological Age; our attention was slowly turned from an external, objective order and the old ways of viewing life in order to become refocused on inner, subjective experience.

Where all that emotional honesty finally brought us was to the realization that we were really sick. Whereas in the seventies someone who asked themselves, "Who am I?" was seen as a person of openness and honesty who was moving towards personal integrity, by the nineties they were regarded as having a "identity disorder" and therefore sick. A person who asked about the meaning of life would have been seen, in the seventies, as a person of depth attempting to see beyond the superficialities of life; by the nineties, even the attempt to face the question was a marker for depression and Valium and Prozac were prescribed to eliminate the questions. All those recovered and found emotions became, not the fertile ground out of which emotional health could flourish, but rather a fetid swampland in which the therapeutic could discover all manner of pathology. By the eighties and nineties, the encounter groups were being replaced by support and recovery groups as we were increasingly discovering how sick we really were. Of course, we needed help coping with all that we had discovered and uncovered within ourselves, and the DSM diagnosis and its labels of pathology became our new mode of self-definition. At this time, it is thought that in the United States there are more than three million recovery groups.[410] An estimated 40% of Americans participate in groups for the support of the particular affliction for which they need help coping.[411]

Slowly our society has turned those who admit to pathology or dysfunction into the new heroes. Stories of heroism, adventure, creativity, and inspiration are being replaced by reality TV. There need be no depth of character, conviction, or vision in our entertainment; as long as people "let it all hang out," they qualify to become our new heroes.

Initially, it was the twelve-step programs that made our problems and the therapeutic idea of the talking cure mainstream. Then, with the spreading influence of the therapeutic, our preoccupation with our problems grew until it finally spawned Donahue, *The Oprah Winfrey Show*, Ricki Lake, Geraldo, and Jerry Springer, all shows that turned our emotional problems into public amusement. It was cyberspace, however, that really turned our fascination with our personal pain into a universal phenomenon. Therapeutic chat rooms and support groups are now available twenty-four hours a day, as are counselors for any affliction we may have just discovered within ourselves. A mental-health Web site that provides a comprehensive list of such groups gets over thirty thousand hits per day.[412]

What started out as a movement that had the honorable intentions of getting ourselves out of our heads and into our feelings eventually took us to where we have become dependent on others for the management of our emotions. Strong emotions are "worked through," buried emotions are "found," emotions are identified, and then all those emotions are either pathologized, turning us into their victims, or else we are "helped" through drugs, counseling, or encounter groups until we become an insipid blend of well-managed emotions.

Our growing dependence on the therapeutic seems to be a final act of defeat and despair. Unable to find anything large and grand to devote our lives to, unable to believe that our lives and efforts matter, we have resigned ourselves to the management of our emotions. We trust what feels good, we believe what can be emotionally validated, and as long as we are in a good space emotionally, then the rest of the world can go to hell; it is not our responsibility. Of this generation, Daniel Yankelovich wrote, "They speak the tongue of 'need' language: they are forever preoccupied with their inner psychological needs. They operate on the premise that emotional cravings are sacred objects and that it is a crime against nature to harbor an unfulfilled emotional need. This psychological attitude affects precisely those crisis points in their lives when their attention might more productively be turned outward—toward the world and its vicissitudes."[413]

When our search for truth no longer meant a search for some external, objective source of meaning, but rather became inwardly focused onto the meaning of ourselves, then nothing higher than our current emotional states could validate our lives and choices.

Ironically, in our preoccupation with our emotions, all passion has been drained from life. The word "emotion" comes from the Latin word *ex movere,* or "to move out."[414] Our emotions are social and connect us to the outside world. Therapy takes those social emotions and introverts them; we are taught to work on them not within a social context, but rather, internally. Now fearful of passion or deep commitment, we have become afraid of devoting ourselves to anything higher than the maintenance of our state of insipid peace. Fearful of passionate beliefs, we ignore the fact that all significant change for the better in our world has been accomplished by those for whom life has become a passion towards an end, for whom life is lived according to strongly held beliefs. As Coventry Patmore noted, "In vulgar minds the idea of passion is inseparable from that of disorder.... Hence the passions, which are the measure of man's capacity for virtues, are regarded by the pious vulgar as being of the nature of vice; and, indeed, in them they are so; for virtues are nothing but ordered passions, and vices nothing but passions in disorder."[415] It was Hegel who noted, "Nothing great in the World was ever accomplished without passion."

What several observers have noted is that all our preoccupation with our inner selves seems to be directly linked with social and political apathy. As Eva Moskowitz observed, "Starvation, illness, and warfare ravage the world while we obsess about anxiety, shyness, and denial."[416] I went to hear a talk given by Steven Lewis, the United Nations envoy to HIV Aids in Africa. When meeting with the various leaders of African countries, he noted that they were using language such as "holocaust," "annihilation," and "extermination" to describe what was happening in their countries. We in the affluent West are ignoring the tragedy as we obsess about happiness, self-fulfillment, about self-esteem, and about how to get our heads into the right framework. One disillusioned psychoanalyst asked,

> Why are the intelligent people—at least among the white middle class—so passive now? Why? Because the sensitive, intelligent people are in therapy! They've been in therapy in the United States for thirty, forty years, and during that time there's been a tremendous political decline in this country ....Twenty or thirty years of therapy have removed the most sensitive and the most intelligent, and some of the most affluent people in our society into child cult worship. It's going on insidiously, all through therapy, all through the country. So of course our politics are in disarray and nobody's voting—we're disempowering ourselves through therapy.[417]

Once the pursuit of self-fulfillment, self-esteem, and self-understanding became seen as necessary and laudable goals, then it only became a matter of time before the narcissistic, self-preoccupied life became seen as an honorable life and we could feel justified in ignoring the needs of others.

I think that one of the most dangerous ideas I picked up from the therapeutic was the notion that I needed to listen to and attend to all my feelings, emotions, desires, and passions, for to ignore them would be to repress them. Repressed emotions were supposedly a dangerous thing and for that I would pay the consequences later.

I hadn't realized what a dangerous attitude all this attention to our emotions and feelings was until I had a conversation one day with someone who was trying to tell me that he couldn't engage in an activity that I regarded as harmless because he feared being overcome by the experience and by certain urges. I was incredulous; I couldn't understand the deep anxiety over what I considered to be an innocuous activity. As we talked, I came to realize that he was actually terrified of his own emotions. I argued that our wills are free to choose our course of action; we are not pawns at the mercy of unconscious urges or runaway passions. It was a hard sell. Although the individual would have never read Freud he was, I realized, part of a therapeutic culture that had unquestioningly accepted Freud's ideas of the libido, not free will, as being determinate in life. He did not seem to think himself capable of fighting and overcoming emotions or passions he found threatening—his freedom lay in avoiding all situations that seemed threatening.

I could not help but think back to my oppressive religious roots where smoking, drinking, movies, dancing, and even bowling alleys were thought to be threats, and how righteousness had become an avoidance of life rather than the freedom to enter it fully because we had been freed of its destructive power.

That conversation had me pondering the question of what actually determines the direction of our lives. By attempting to overthrow the constraints of religion, we don't seem to have gained our freedom, we have just discovered a new form of enslavement; we have become enslaved by the id and its unruly depths.

There was a time when our deepest inner struggles were interpreted as spiritual struggles; we understood them by means of holding them against an external reference point, which we called God. Then Sigmund Freud came along and turned the reality of God into an abstract concept that he called the Superego. Since Freud did not believe in God, he thought to free man from the torment of guilt, alienation, and all the inner struggles that accompanied those outdated ideas. He thought to accomplish that feat by means of strengthening the ego. Yes, there was still the id—all our emotions, feelings, passions, urges (especially sexual ones)—but once the ego was sufficiently strengthened, it would be master of our being. Or at least that was the plan. What actually happened is best told in the words of Anna Freud—the daughter of Sigmund Freud and a prominent psychoanalyst in her own right—who also worked in close association with her father. She wrote, "We've come full circle, I'm afraid…we started out trying to use our wits to help people be less anxious, less driven by a tyrannical Superego, and we've come to the point that people are more anxious and even alarmed and fearful, but not of the Superego, but of—themselves, their 'drives', we say, or their 'situation', their 'existential fate', their 'nature,' others put it."[418]

Anna Freud then described the effect of their work on children, saying, "They are scared that they will be able to do anything, that there are no limits."[419] Freud's attempt to free us from the tyranny of God did not, according to his daughter, free us at all; it just left us in deeper trouble as it managed to subject us to the tyranny of our emotions, passions, and desires.

Perhaps we have been slow to return to religious answers because we have seen so little validation of their truths. It must be admitted that religion at its worst has tried to repress much within our humanity that should have been allowed to grow and flower. For that it has been justifiably condemned. But religion at its best did offer us a way of life that did not deny us our emotions, but that would free us from their enslavement. In Christianity, healthy emotions are not a goal but are rather a byproduct of gospel life.

The therapeutic has made us so afraid of repressing what lies in the id that we have allowed it to dominate our lives. We often forget that repression is not the same thing as suppression or sublimation. Repression is an unconscious mechanism that allows us to bury the deep forces of life that we would rather not face. Suppression is the acknowledgement that all that lies in our deepest regions does not necessarily need to be expressed. It can be a conscious choice made out of a desire to follow a higher calling— a higher calling that offers a greater vision of what it means to be human than a reduction of man to an instinctual animal. Suppression actually creates strength of character and reveals man to be a being that is able to be responsible for his own destiny.

Sublimation, on the other hand, can take a destructive impulse and modify or divert it into a higher good. Vladimir Solovyev revealed a lot of wisdom when he wrote, "The actual goodness of a saint involves the ability to be evil; man attains such heights of holiness because he is able to be so colossally wicked: he has brought this power of evil into subjection to the supreme principle and in consequence this very power has become a foundation of goodness."[420]

If we are going to live changed and transformed lives, then we are going to have to again believe that we are not beings determined by biology, chemistry, the past, the unconscious, or our emotions, but that we are free to choose our own destinies. We will have to again believe in the freedom and supremacy of the will. Descartes observed that it is free will that gives us our God-like quality, saying, "Now free will is in itself the noblest thing we can have because it makes us in a certain manner equal to God and exempts us from being his subjects; and so its rightful use is the greatest of all the goods we possess, and further there is nothing that is more our own or that matters more to us."

Whereas we initially used our free will to usurp our independence from God, desiring to be "in a certain manner equal to God" rather than remain His subjects, our free will rightly used is also how we return to God. Free will, however, seems to be one of the hardest truths to keep a hold of. The philosopher Iris Murdoch speculated on why: "Determinism is always reappearing in new forms since it satisfies a deep human wish: to give up, to get rid of freedom, responsibility, remorse, all sort of personal individual unease, and surrender to fate and the relief of 'it could not be otherwise'."[421]

And yet free will, the ability to choose our own destiny, is what releases us from necessity and distinguishes us from the animal kingdom. In the words of William Temple, "For the supreme mark of a person is that he orders his life by his own deliberate choice."

Outside of relationship to God, however, our free wills actually present us with a dilemma. Two philosophers—Schopenhauer and Nietzsche—offer the two responses that have been taken up by the West. According to Schopenhauer, we can use our free will to escape from the world of cares and striving. Schopenhauer is significant for our world in that he took Buddhist notions and Eastern concepts and introduced them into Western thinking. According to Eastern thinking, by destroying will and desire in oneself, one can live in some mystical sphere where one

306 THE ALTARS OF AHAZ

becomes free from the torments and horrors of history.

At the other extreme lies Nietzsche, who first proclaimed the death of God and then envisioned the kind of individual capable of asserting his will and becoming the replacement for God. However, instead of using one's will to achieve either self-extinction (Schopenhauer) or self-Godhead (Nietzsche) there is another option offered by Christianity. It is the option expressed so well in "In Memoriam A. H.H." by Lord Alfred Tennyson, in which he wrote,

> Our wills are ours, we know not how;
> Our wills are ours, to make them thine.

The Christian option is the voluntary placing of one's will in the hands of a personal God in order to learn a life of obedience. It is at that point that Christianity offers us a host of paradoxes; by giving up our life, we save it; by learning obedience to God, we gain true freedom; by seeming to so lose our life, we actually find it. Our conversion begins at that place where, in however small the gesture, we use our free will not to assert our God-like status, but rather, to place our wills in the hands of God and allow for a Higher Being to be God to us.

One psychoanalyst proposed that our age should be seen as the "Age of the Disordered Will."[422] Left to our own devices, we tend to turn our wills towards that which is either unattainable or else will destroy us. Anxiety is created because of the gap between what we crave and the reality we have to face. Achieving what we think we desire can be precisely what destroys us. Too often, even religion is pressed into serving our disordered wills as we attempt to press God into the service of satisfying our cravings. The Bible says, "What causes fights and quarrels among you? Don't they come from your desires that battle within you? You want something but don't get it. You kill and covet, but you cannot have what you want. You quarrel and fight. You do not have, because you do not ask God. When you ask, you do not receive, because you ask with wrong motives, that you may spend what you get on your pleasures" (James 4:1–3).

When the Bible claims, "God works in you to will and to act according to his good purpose" (Philippians 2:13), it reveals that our salvation begins with a reordering of our distorted wills. In order to change, we need to discover something more appealing than what we presently crave. True salvation affects the will or heart. Without a powerful vision to capture the imagination, our wills just become subservient to the demands of the id.

We humans are strange creatures. We live caught between instinctual forces and desires and the pull of holy longings. Freud and the therapeutic tried to convince us that the repression of those instinctual forces—especially sexuality and hostility—are what created neurosis and psychoses. We have discovered, however, that repression of our holy longings is what creates depression. The psychotherapist Viktor Frankl used the expression "repressed transcendence" to describe our "unrest of the heart."[423] Denying the call of transcendence can create even more inner distress than denying our instincts. Our problem was not, as the therapeutic tried to convince us, that religion and the call of the Holy, or the Superego, was too strong causing repression; our problem was that it was not strong enough. It is when we live with a divided will—wanting to give in to the forces of our instinctual urges but also wanting to give the Holy its due—that we develop mental problems in our attempt to live inside the tension. By capitulating wholeheartedly to the call of the Holy, we discover that those instinctual forces are not repressed, but are rather freed to become the servants of our unified nature. Instincts are not seen as determinative or fixed, but as "changing through positive disintegration, losing their primitive strength and evolving to new levels of expression in the cycle of human life."[424] Sexual energy, harnessed, becomes the driving force serving compassion, love, and charity. Latent hostility becomes the force driving one towards a zeal for justice and mercy. When religion was allowed to provide the rituals and symbols through which our emotions were channeled, then those emotions provided the energy that became utilized in our journey toward transformation and transcendence.

Real faith never requires us to repress or cut off necessary emotions and passions. It leads us through the inferno of their burning until we overcome them and harness their energy. When we speak of the breaking in of a wild horse, we don't mean the destruction of a good animal but the harnessing of its energy so it can be used to good purpose. Even so, the conquering of our emotions and passions is for the purpose of making them servants to our surrendered will. Our emotions, passions, and desires are the driving force feeding and nurturing a higher life; we will be in trouble if we try leaving them behind.

Religion is always influenced by the culture around it and the last centuries have been no exception. To a large extent, the Enlightenment had been allowed to set the agenda and the terms of religion. During the Enlightenment period, religion was allowed to be reduced to right thinking and right living—theology and morality. However, theology and morality did not take into account our full humanity with its desires and emotions. We next brought the therapeutic into the church to fill the vacuum, giving full attention to those emotions and desires. Broken emotions and unfettered instincts, however, have also proven to be insufficient guides for charting the course of our lives. Once we began to free and sacralize our emotions and instincts, they just turned and made us their slaves and victims.

In our world, Rational Man or Enlightenment Man has given way to Psychological Man. It is no more feasible for Psychological Man to accept a reality higher than his desires, emotions, and passions than it was for Rational Man to accept a reality higher than his reason. For Psychological Man, the full expressing of one's emotions and desires has become one's new credo, the new categorical imperative. The era of Rational Man ended with the coming of deconstruction and the individual's growing suspicion over whether we can ever truly know anything. The era of Psychological Man has resulted in a populace who are afraid of facing the full range of human emotions. The pharmaceutical industry is becoming rich discovering drugs that can free us from the very emotions we have spent so much attention and time getting in touch with.

In the Enlightenment, we humans were turned into thinking animals.

Now, thanks to the therapeutic, we have become instinctual animals. Both positions are soul-destroying. What we seem to have been trying hard to avoid is facing the concept of soul. It is the denial of soul that will have us consistently missing the mark when seeking self-understanding.

Soul is a reality that will never be discovered by science or proven by analytic thought. The "empirical self" that has been so thoroughly examined by the therapeutic is not going to prove or reveal the existence of soul. I suppose that is why we have chosen to ignore it. The Bible gives us the picture of God breathing His own breath into us. It also tells us that God has placed eternity in our hearts. That is as close to a definition of soul that the Bible gives us. The concept of soul, like the wind analogy that Jesus uses, can be seen in its effects rather than by direct vision. We can achieve and acquire all we wanted out of life and still feel empty. We can sit in a room full of people and still be haunted by loneliness. We can obtain and achieve all that we thought we wanted and yet still be longing for "something more." We can pursue our desires in a search for happiness, but then discover that we are happiest when we deny ourselves some of those desires.

On the other hand, we can be surprised by moments of illumination and intuitive insight that we can give no explanation for. We can be all alone and yet feel accompanied. We can know moments of awe and wonder in observing nature and feel we have touched the trail of some glorious reality. What is more, it is precisely at those moments that we seem to be more "alive" in the true heart of our being than in all our attempts to pursue pleasure. Ignore the reality of soul and all our attempts to understand and "fix" ourselves will only reduce and destroy our humanity.

Sometimes it helps leaving the Christian tradition so that one can return and see what one has missed due to over-familiarity. It was that noble pagan, Plato, who prepared me to return to the Bible ready to see and acknowledge the reality of soul. Plato helped me purge myself of the modern therapeutic belief that all that raged within me only needed to be "named," "understood', "expressed," "articulated," and "integrated"; some things actually needed to be struggled with and overcome. We are beings at war with ourselves; by reintroducing the concept of soul, Plato helped me to see those places of struggle as places where the soul could grow.

The religion of my past had been over-intellectualized. That is why I, a housewife, found myself trying to read through the collected works of Plato. The concept of soul allowed me to believe in a larger unifying principle that was much greater than, but encompassed both, mind and emotions. It gave me dignity by bestowing on me the ability to choose and contribute to my final destiny. The concept of soul allowed me to reroute my attention and energies beyond myself to the source of life itself.

Plato prepared me to return to the Bible and recognize the supreme importance God places on the freedom of the human will. It is the human will that is most closely tied to the function of the soul. One of my greatest steps into freedom came when I finally accepted that not only did I not need to analyze or listen to all my emotions and feelings, but I could actually see them as my enemy. By placing my will in a Higher Will, my emotions and desires might give me terrible trouble for a while but then, as I discovered, they could actually become tamed to become the servants of my will.

Because Christianity calls us to live according to a Transcendent Reality that asks us to deny ourselves, it has often been caricatured as a life of repressed emotions. That could not be further from the truth. Repressed emotions are one of the surest signs of having missed the mark. When we read the Bible with its offer of "joy unspeakable," "peace that passeth understanding," its invitation to mourn with those who mourn, to enter into the suffering of others, it's hard to see how it can be accused of repressing emotions. It does, however, bring us to the place where we can live free of their tyranny. In the words of St. Dominic, "A person who governs his passions is master of the world. We must either rule them, or be ruled by them. It is better to be the hammer than the anvil." We were created to be free, not mastered by instincts like the animals.

By living out of a will placed under a Higher Will, we can learn to love our neighbor passionately without being threatened by our feelings. We can enter the suffering of the world without being afraid of being overcome by the pain. We can know joy and peace that aren't tied to the changing circumstances of life. By living out of our will and not our feelings, it is precisely our emotions that are finally freed to live in larger-than-life dimensions. First, however, comes the struggle to live according to a will lived in surrender to a Higher Will. Then comes the struggle *against* our emotions until we can discern between those craving easy surface pleasure and those that arise out of the deepest eternal heart of our being.

When we learn to live according to a transcendent vision rather than fixated on our emotional health, we are ready to discover that the fruits of the Spirit—peace, joy, love—are not the products of emotional intelligence, but are what they claim to be—gifts given to meet and counter our turbulent emotions. What the gifts of the Spirit do is free us from reliance on our human emotions, for when emotions are our guide, then they will also be our downfall. The emotions that are gifts of the Spirit are not tied to circumstances or to our inner health (or lack thereof). They are linked, rather, to the Presence of God who steadfastly remains with us, an anchor for the soul once adrift and shipwrecked by turbulent emotions. When our spirituality has begun to mature, then it is our very desires, will, and emotions that God uses as the means through which He leads us. There comes a time, in spiritual maturity, when the gifts of the Spirit—love, joy, peace, freedom, etc.—become the way we discern the true path. We follow our peace, joy, and love to wherever they lead.

Faith offers us a paradox; the more we struggle with God, and, through the struggle, manage to submit our wills to God's will, the freer we will be. The other option is that of claiming freedom on our terms and then being tyrannized by our passions, desires, emotions, and instinctual urges.

The defining question of the therapeutic seems to be, "How do you feel about that?" The defining question of faith is. "What do you choose to do about that?" It can be the questions we ask as much as the answers we receive that end up defining us.

Choose to live out of a Transcendent source and not under the control of our emotions, feelings, and passions, and we may find ourselves in for a rough ride for a while—until we discover that we have thereby entered the territory of grace. God knows we cannot do what He asks, but He takes the intent of our wills as supreme. When we try to blend our will with His, He comes to struggle with us. We may soon find ourselves living in completely new country.

Obedience versus Self-understanding

I WAS RAISED IN A TRADITION that immersed me in knowledge of the Scriptures. It had never occurred to me that knowledge of the Scriptures was not enough, and that I would need to learn how to read them and then learn how to apply them before I could know the life they were meant to reveal. It was when I eventually found myself in a place of deep darkness and began to read through the Bible in a new way—not out of expected religious duty, or for confirmation of previously held beliefs, or in order to add more knowledge to a personal database—but rather out of personal need, looking for clues as to the God the Bible claimed to reveal, that I discovered I was in a unique position that allowed me to see the Bible as though for the first time. In fact, the Bible just kept surprising me, as I would repeatedly stop and tell myself, "I don't think that is what I was taught."

When I got to the gospel story of the wise and foolish builders deciding whether they should build their houses on sand or rock, I was so surprised by what it said that I had to stop and check the other gospel versions to see if one gospel writer had managed to get the story wrong. All the gospels, however, said the same thing. Still surprised at how I could have gotten it so wrong, I then went to ask others raised in the same tradition as me as to what they thought that foundation was. They, like I had been taught, said it was Jesus Christ. That seems like such a laudable answer that perhaps that is why I never before noticed that it is not what the Bible actually says. What the Bible says is that if we try to build our structures of faith on anything other than a firm foundation of obedience, then we are given Gospel assurances that they won't survive.

Now the necessity of obedience to a Word that lies outside of my self and is often beyond my understanding is a hard reality for me, as a modern individual, to accept. I live in a culture where truth is deemed to be personal and relative and is formed by a personal search according to personal understanding. I was formed by Vietnam and Watergate, which taught me that blind and unquestioning obedience to authority could be the source of our greatest error, and that we should be suspicious of all external authority. The idea that all authority should be suspect is therefore deeply inscribed in my psyche. I am also a female living in awareness of how all the power structures of history—both religious and political—have combined to keep women in suppression. For me, therefore, the concept of obedience was closely allied, if not synonymous, with suppression. With that past in mind, it could perhaps be understood why the idea of obedience to a reality that lay above and beyond my grasp of understanding was deeply inimical to the very essence of my being.

I think I was originally attracted to psychology because it seemed to have a better understanding of human nature than the Bible. It allowed me to live by what I could understand rather than unquestioning obedience. After all, humility, gentleness, and meekness were not the attributes needed for getting on in this world. Forgiveness, self-denial, and turning the other cheek were human impossibilities. In a time when women's rights were being championed, submission was not an idea that appealed to me. When the therapeutic was brought into the church, I welcomed it with a sense of relief. It allowed me to consign much of the gospel to the realm of otherworldly idealism while giving me a more tangible and realistic way to see and deal with the "real world" and my "real" nature.

Sometimes God in His goodness allows our "real world" to collapse so that we can experience the "otherworldly" as real. At that time of real despair in my life, I decided to read my Bible to see if there was anything in it that would allow me to hold onto a belief in God any longer. I had the novel idea that if this was going to be a serious quest, then I should try to live out what I was reading to the best of my ability. What I discovered in a new way was how hard to accept, how difficult to understand, and how contrary to my nature those hard gospel edges really are. What I also discovered, however, was that in being deeply offended, deeply perplexed, and in finding the gospel sayings hard to accept, I was in good company.

What I discovered was that whenever Jesus found his popularity rising, He seemed to have a consistent way of dealing with it; He would offend the people. Those following Jesus had become a crowd when Jesus told them they would need to eat His flesh and drink His blood. Now, in old pagan cultures, the blood was thought to contain the life force, and therefore, the drinking of blood was a pagan practice by which the people hoped to magically increase their power. Not only was the drinking of blood a pagan rite, but for the Jewish mind raised on Kosher rules with their special treatment of blood and dietary restrictions, the effect of Jesus' statement should have been predictable: horror and revulsion. The results were understandable, "From this time many of his disciples turned back and no longer followed him" (John 6:66). The disciples who remained did not remain because they found the teachings easy to accept. On the contrary, as it says in the Scriptures, "On hearing it many of his disciples said, 'This is a hard teaching. Who can accept it?'" (John 6:60). Neither did Jesus enlighten them further at the time so that they found acceptance easier. No, it would be a long journey through the Last Supper, the Crucifixion, and the Resurrection before understanding would finally come.

Of all those seeking after Jesus, there were probably few more eager and more sincere than the rich young ruler. Jesus honored his interest with sayings so harsh that the ruler turned away and even the disciples were left saying, "Who then can be saved?" (Mark 10:26). If the rich young ruler would have hung around and, as the disciples did, confront Jesus with the impossibility of His demands, then He may have heard Jesus' complete response; real obedience is impossible without God's help, and we give up everything so that being free from their control and power, we can eventually be free for them and be trusted with them. If the rich young ruler had hung around, he may have ended up richer than he ever was before:

"I tell you the truth," Jesus replied, "no one who has left home or brothers or sisters or mother or father or children or fields for me and the gospel will fail to receive a hundred times as much in this present age (homes, brothers, sisters, mothers, children and fields" (Mark 10:29).

Clearly, the clue to obedience lay in learning how to get past those places of offence. I don't believe that we ever get to the point where the

Bible no longer presents us with harsh sayings that we find hard to accept. Those who find the Bible to be only a book of comfort cannot be reading it in its entirety, or else have so hardened their hearts that they have become numbed to what it actually says. There is something in the Bible to give offense to everyone.

History is full of those who would deal with the offense of the gospel by ignoring or eliminating portions of Scripture. Perhaps none went farther than Marcion, a teacher and religious leader from the second century. Marcion did not like the God of the Old Testament; he therefore tried to eliminate all Jewish influence from religion. That meant that he needed to reject all of the Old Testament and anything in the New Testament that would favor Jewish readers. What he was left with was a portion of Luke's Gospel and ten letters of Paul.

I personally felt a kinship with Marcion, as it was the God of the Old Testament that I found hard accept. There was just too much male language, power, violence, domination, and unreal expectation to make the reading of the Old Testament a pleasant experience. But I kept reading anyway. One day I was reading Revelation when it was as though a time capsule had been detonated; the language of worthiness seemed to fill the entire book. I realized that what the gospel was portraying was someone who held power, glory, and honor purely out of worthiness. That was a novel concept for me. I lived in a world where power was an end that was gained and held by means of oppression, suppression, intrigue, and manipulation. Power that dies, power that serves, power that loves, power that does not exalt itself, power that is held purely on the basis of worthiness, was humanly inconceivable. I decided that it would be worth gaining heaven just to experience the novelty of that power. From that point on, the Old Testament became my favorite part of the Bible. It spoke to me of a God who had an outstretched arm and mighty hand. I discovered that from the encircling comfort of the outstretched arm, the power held in the mighty hand loses its terror. It is a good.

That first lesson in meeting the offense of the gospel has given me courage to keep on reading even when I keep coming upon its hard and impossible edges. I now see those places of offense to be like the knots that form in my thread when I try to sew. In order to be able to pull the thread through, I need to get rid of the knots. Try and force the thread through with the knots intact and the thread will tear. Real obedience never tries to force the knots. The knots take time and special care to undo. Those places in the Bible that seem most impossible and most offensive, I have discovered, are due to the very places in my psyche where something needs to be straightened, or corrected, or needs new understanding. That is why real obedience can never be separated from prayer. We need revelation, moments of special insight, and divine help to undo the knots in our being. As it says in John 6:44, "No one can come to me unless the Father who sent me draws him." True obedience resides in patiently waiting and trusting in God to draw through the knots.

The desire to live free from the necessity of obedience to God and the desire to choose good and evil according to our own understanding is not unique to our relativistic culture; it is an attitude that goes back to our origins and is implicit in the story of our fall. The serpent offered Eve an alternative to obedience—with seductive arguments, he convinced Eve that she could understand and choose what was good for herself in a way that was superior to blind obedience to God. The fruit from the Garden of Eden never loses its allure. An attitude that I have repeatedly encountered is that of the following psychologist who claimed that Eve made the right decision in the plucking of the fruit; it was what allowed for her growth into adulthood. Marsha Mirkin writes,

> Eve uses all her expanding capacities to observe the situation and decide how it will impact her... this fruit, if she is ready to eat it, can give her the opportunity to fulfill her potential and create/birth future generations. Pulled by the lure of growing into adulthood, aware of only the benefits and not the risks of maturity, she chooses to eat the fruit.... With that bite, life as it was known changed forever, and people moved into being more full human beings, more adult human beings, forever grappling with the joys and sorrows inherent in all our choices. Eve had listened

to her need for growth, she had reflected on the rightness of the decision; she had the courage to leave childhood behind and move toward adulthood. But she hadn't yet begun to understand or even predict the loss attached to any major developmental step. Later, God would do that with her.[425]

The voice of that original serpent is not silent, but still speaks through the voice of every counselor who helps us to live by our own understanding, who convinces us that living an authentic existence means living free from external constraints, and who helps us interpret life and truth according to our own inclinations.

Why was the tree of the knowledge of good and evil a necessary part of the Garden of Eden? What placing the forbidden tree in the Garden of Eden did was place freedom of choice before the human animal. The other animals were not given commandments; they had instincts to guide them. Their lives were driven by necessity. However, by being given freedom, the human was given the option of relationship. Obedience gave us the opportunity to link our free wills with the reality of God and live in relationship. When we pray, "Thy will be done on earth as it is in heaven" we link our wills to God's will and to the hope for the restoration of God's purposes here on earth. The forbidden fruit offered the alternative.

Paul Tillich noted, "Holiness cannot be experienced without its power to command what we should be."[426] God can draw near to the degree that we obediently respond to the demands of that love. Our knowledge of God and our obedient response to what we have perceived are intricately linked. We all go through periods of time where we seem to be living in some desert or void with no experiential knowledge of God's Presence with us. Obedience to what God has already revealed as to His purposes can be the way we signal our interest in closer relationship. It is like priming a pump; if one wants water, sometimes one has to first add water. Similarly, Goethe claimed, "Only they who have added to it find the substance." It is irrelevant asking whether aligning our lives with the purposes of God is what allows God to draw near, or whether God's nearness is what allows us to leave our rebellious ways—the two motions work in tandem.

Having given us free will, God allows us to follow our own understanding, even though it always leads to disaster. It was Chesterton who sagely noted, "When Man goes straight he goes crooked. When he follows his nose he manages somehow to put his nose out of joint, or even to cut off his nose to spite his face."[427] Man is the only creature that, if left to its own understanding and devices, will always follow some hidden bias causing him to self-destruct. And yet, if the human race could have chosen a theme song to accompany it through history, then the song would undoubtedly be that of Frank Sinatra crooning "I Did It My Way." All the evils of history come as a result of our chosen and willful independence.

The lure of freedom from God and from all religious constraints entices us from every corner of our modern world. What we don't initially seem to recognize is that when we claim the freedom to choose our own path, it is our freedom that we lose; the freedom thus gained is just a chimera hiding slavery to desires, external influences, or to the impossible needs that the ego demands. Paradoxically, to know freedom, we first have to learn obedience. It was Augustine who could see that sins against God were actually sins against ourselves, for, as he wrote in his *Confessions*, those who sin against God "do wrong to their own souls."[428] Obedience actually allows us to become free from "the chains which we have forged for ourselves."[429] In the *City of God*, Augustine observed, "If man despise the will of God, he can only destroy himself; and so he learns the difference between consecrating himself to the common good and reveling in his own."[430] Obedience gives recognition to the fact that we, as human beings, need help navigating the shoals of life. The God who created us also left us with operating instructions. Only our Creator knows the purposes and ends for which we were created.

I think the best definition of judgment that I have ever come across is that of the splinters we get when we go against the grain of the universe. Eve and all her progeny have known the pain of those splinters. The Bible gets the same idea across but with different imagery, saying, "He will be a sanctuary; but…a stone that causes men to stumble/and a rock that makes them fall" (Isaiah 8:14). We are presented with two options in life. A cornerstone was presented to us to use as a reference point that made the invisible realm visible and against which we could take all the measurements for our life. When we use that cornerstone as the plumb line around which we orient our lives, then that cornerstone becomes both the rock on which we stand and the sanctuary that keeps us safe. The other option is to see the rock as a nuisance or impediment on our road to some destination that we have chosen according to our own understanding. In that case, that same stone becomes the stumbling block against which we fall. The choice is ours; use the rock as a firm place to stand or discover it to be that against which we fall.

I like to picture obedience in terms of the rock that the Israelites encountered on their journey to Canaan. For the Israelites crossing the desert sand, the rock would at first sight have been seen as an obstacle blocking the way to their destination. However, in listening to God and in following His instructions, Moses and the Israelites were surprised to discover that the rock in their path actually became the source of the refreshing water that sustained their lives. For all of us pilgrims, the first glimpse of what real obedience might entail initially looks like that rock; it appears as an obstacle on our road to self-fulfillment.

I remember sitting with a friend who was giving me her exegesis of the story in Genesis about Cain and his unacceptable sacrifice. Cain, according to this friend, grew vegetables and therefore should have been allowed to offer a sacrifice commensurable with his work. An offering of vegetables would have been the self-expression of his life that he was offering to God. Why should he have to go to Abel, his hated brother, to ask for an animal in order to offer to God a sacrifice that did not express his own unique individuality? I thought we were having a theological conversation, but only realized later that this friend was deeply involved in an extramarital affair and the question of whether we should obey rules that seem arbitrary and go against our own inclinations was the question of her whole present being. I suppose the story of the hurt and devastation that followed was an answer to her question.

Edward Farley, the Professor of Theology at Vanderbilt University, noted in his book *Deep Symbols* that in American religion one no longer hears many "thou shalts." Religion, instead, has become invaded by the language of "our lives, what we need in our lives, what makes us sad and unhappy, what we are up against and have to cope with, the resources of that coping, and what gives us wholeness."[431] As Edward Farley noted, if the "therapeutic is the prevailing ethos and discourse of the church, then the idea of the law is sitting on the very back pew, perhaps is not even in the church building but out on the front step."[432] Self-understanding rather than obedience becomes the focus of our attention.

The therapeutic is actually destroying the authority of the metaphysical systems that in the past allowed us to ground our lives in higher reality. Obedience to a personal God has been replaced by the supposed need of the individuals to choose their own values. The authority of revealed religion, of society, of traditions, and of cultural institutions have all been undercut to make way for the relative and subjective values of each individual. Our identity is now seen as derived, not from some attachment to a transcendent vision or to an institution or a tradition that mediates that vision, but has rather become self-referential; we create our own autonomous self and identity. The guide and arbiter of our success has gone from being the clergyman or spiritual guide to being the therapist. The source of our guidance has gone from being sacred texts to the inner emotions and feelings that justify our choices and behavior. The purpose and meaning of life has gone from being created to be in relationship with and to live in obedience to God to being seen as the need to achieve personal well being. There are Christian enclaves that fight the secularizing and relativistic influence of psychology, but their alternate religious schemes are framed within the language and conceptual frameworks of the therapeutic. Biblical morals are attached to the ideals, frameworks, assumptions, language, and techniques of psychology. They are not alternatives to the therapeutic worldview, but rather, a futile attempt to Christianize it.[433]

Freud saw God as the infantile projection of an immature nature. Thinking to rid people of such a regressive device as God, he thought to use psychoanalyses as the means whereby the ego could be strengthened to the point where it no longer had any need for God. With a firm foundation built on self-understanding, self-reliance, and the ability to strengthen the ego and increase its capacity to direct one's own life and choices, Freud tried to ensure that society need never return to the immature religious responses based on obedience, trust, and learned dependence. Although much of what Freud wrote has been discounted and discredited, the foundation that he established still forms the basis for the therapeutic movement. That is why it is so interesting seeing the "Christian Counseling" movement proliferate. Its foundations are built on Freud, not Jesus Christ. The Bible may claim, "For no one can lay any foundation other than the one already laid, which is Jesus Christ" (1 Corinthians 3:11), but then we, in the name of Jesus, offer to help people lay foundations built on self-understanding, self-sufficiency, and self-reliance. The foundational life of trust, obedience to the Father, and learned dependence that Jesus came to reveal are foregone. I have found it sad watching those who would at one time have called themselves Christians finally reach a place where their entire belief system collapses. When religion tries to build over Freud's foundations, then there will come a time when one discovers one has built over a sinkhole—the religious structures thus erected just tend to collapse in and of themselves.

Self-understanding is not the way, but rather, a byproduct of the life of faith. Augustine said, "Understanding is the reward of faith." Faith calls us to right action; only later does that resolve itself into understanding and wisdom. The Bible's claims are now being threatened by the competing claims of psychology that provide us with an alternative religion of man. The new religion is self-referential, being mandated to help us set our boundaries, our limits, and our parameters according to personal safety. In place of brokenness and contrition, it helps us develop appropriate "ego defenses," good "adaptive reflexes," and it helps us "individuate." Instead of the call to be poured out sacrificially, it helps us avoid becoming "over-involved," or keeps us from "over-identifying." In other words, it creates a cocoon wherein the imperialistic self can be kept safe from the claims of the larger society, from the harsh intrusions of reality, and from the burden of sacrificial relationships. It also helps us to justify our self-absorption by creating a new sacred vocabulary out of words such as "self-fulfillment," "self-awareness," and "authenticity." The new religion helps us justify our focus on personal needs rather than obedience. It offers us a personal salvation disconnected from a greater good. It offers us healing without the need for discipline. It offers us self-knowledge outside of relationship. It offers us health and wholeness without obedience and censure.

When we found ourselves with congregations full of emotionally unhappy and disturbed people, we meant well in forging an alliance with the therapeutic, hoping to bring more health to the people in the pews. However, eventually we need to admit that we are not seeing increasing health, we are just seeing the therapeutic increasingly free people from the constraints of the gospel. Listen to the language of the therapeutic long enough and the other gospel that calls us to obedience will have been rendered obsolete.

It was in attempting obedience to what I had begun reading in my Bible that again began to sensitize me to what the gospel was actually saying. How quickly I began to notice the competing claims of the two gospels that we have tried to blend within the church. I personally discovered that God can and does frequently ask us to do what sets off all the alarm bells of the therapeutic. God does not seem interested in nurturing the imperialistic self but in helping us leave the limits of its confining cocoon in order to help us fly, to live life in relationship, and to see life from the wider horizons of eternity. Therapeutic self-understanding with all its boundaries may help us feel safe for a while, but what we may have been made most safe from are those rich intrusions of grace that I began to discover and that surprised and accompanied me as I attempted to follow that hard road of obedience.

However, even after acknowledging the need for obedience to a reality higher than my own self-understanding, it was still a long time before I could begin to understand what true Biblical obedience looks like. It is not only the therapeutic that can be blamed for giving obedience to a higher authority a bad name; religious legalism has to share equal blame. We will all need to be converted from something; if it is not from a life of rebellion and self-absorption, then it will probably have to be from a life of self-righteousness, self-inflicted asceticism, legalistic moralism, scrupulosity, and proud prudery. Legalism can just be another way we avoid relationship with God. Lacking the courage for radical self-surrender, we think we can instead throw up our morality and self-righteous acts like a sop to God's eternal face. Charles Finney has noted, "Few things are a greater curse than a legal state of mind. It is often as bad as open wickedness, if not worse. Often it is such a misrepresentation of religion as makes the little children more afraid of such a religious man than of a fiend. Does he recommend religion? He could not possibly disparage and misrepresent it more than he does. Far better if he were never thought to be a Christian at all; for then his somber, morose and harsh spirit would be ascribed to its true cause, the selfishness of his heart and the utter absence of the gentle spirit of gospel love."[434]

True obedience, I had to eventually understand, lies along a very narrow path that runs between two equally dangerous and lethal precipices: the precipices of licentiousness on the one hand and that of legalism on the other. Both positions kill the life of Spirit.

I was raised in a culture where to be religious meant one did not go to movies, did not dance, smoke, drink, or basically have much fun in life. Religion functioned like a strong bleach; in an attempt to remove all the dirt from life it also removed all the color. For a while, as a child, I lived in a town where both a proposed coffee shop and a bowling alley raised such objections over what they would do for the morality of the young that both projects were dropped. In our culture, not only a strict ethical code, but also even one's very appearance, could give recognition to one's religious status. I incredulously told another Mennonite relative that I had heard of groups that had split up over whether they should wear zippers or buttons. She, living in Mennonite country, said it got worse than that; groups had actually split over whether hat ribbons should be worn at the back or the front.

The New Testament is filled with warnings against those who thought true religion was about prohibitions, rules, and life-denying practices. That is why Paul's warning—"For everything God created is good, and nothing is to be rejected if it is received with thanksgiving" (1 Timothy 4:4)—had to be repeated so frequently. The Gnostic belief that the material world was inherently evil kept insinuating itself into the Christian church and had to be constantly battled. As noted by Coventry Patmore, "Good people, who do not know that all evils are corrupted goods, in their anxiety to avoid evil, are apt to call the greatest goods, of which the worst evils are corruption, evil; and such may have to live maimed lives even in eternity; for all denial here is corresponding privation hereafter."[435]

After a long history of rebellion, the Jewish people went through a period of religious zeal by means of which they tried to recover their heritage. The law was no longer a problem. They, in fact, took to it with such zeal that by the time of Christ, the prohibitions had grown to 365 specific laws and the positive commands had grown to 248. The reaction of Jesus to the Pharisees shows that they had missed the way of true obedience. When we can no longer live in defiance of God, then turning to work on ourselves and working on our own salvation can be the same willfulness, just turned in a new direction. Self-inflicted righteousness and scruples can be as destructive to the life of soul and spirit as open rebellion.

Paul was obviously fighting the tendency towards legalism when he wrote, "Since you died with Christ to the basic principles of this world, why, as though you still belonged to it, do you submit to its rules: "Do not handle! Do not taste! Do not touch!" These are destined to perish with use, because they are based on human commands and teachings" (Colossians 2:21, 22).

Galatians is a book written to a church getting caught up in legalistic scruples. It is a resounding cry to the freedom that is ours by grace, by the power brought by Jesus Christ, and in the reality of the Holy Spirit. We do not need therapists who supplant the gospel out of concern for our human natures; we need spiritual guides who, like Paul in Galatians, cry "freedom" when our obedience is becoming derailed into something unhealthy. We need to be taught to pray truly so that we do not take the guilt from our infantile repressions and unconscious regions and project it out into the voice of God, turning God into a tyrannical and unhealthy Father image. We need to learn to read the Bible and meditate in ways that remove the cultural blinkers that distort our hearing. We need help walking the thin line that keeps us free from torturous self-inflicted righteousness and scruples.

The purpose and end of all religious life is not the keeping of rules, but is rather for the breakthrough of the kingdom of God into the reality of our temporal world. If the devil can't convince us to live in defiance of God's rule, then he can do almost as much damage by isolating us into false spiritual ghettos where we have no influence in the world, and where we no longer function as agents of redemption in the world God created and loves. When we no longer choose to live in rebellion towards God, we can still be duped by the devil into thinking that obedience to God requires the destruction or limiting of our humanity and the denial of what's good in creation. As Coventry Patmore wrote, "When the Tempter can no longer persuade us to our destructions by representing unclean things as clean, he perpetually harasses us, and endeavors to delay our progress by representing clean things as unclean. In the first stage of our advance we are purified by self-denial, in the second by denial, almost equally laborious, of the enemy's false charges."[436] Human understanding can trip us up not only by enticing us into licentiousness, but also by seducing us into creating our own systems of self-inflicted righteousness.

Having known the destructive side of religion, I turned to my Bible hoping for something that would bring life, not death. If I was going to allow my life to be formed by the gospel, then I was going to have to trust that, as Irenaeus wrote, "The glory of God is a human fully alive" and I would need to believe that following would bring "life more abundantly" and not the constriction or distorting of life. I would need to have faith that, as St. Thomas Aquinas wrote, "Grace does not eliminate nature but perfects it" and I would need to trust that following would make me not less but more alive. If sin, as Northrop Frye wrote, is "a matter of trying to block the activity of God, and it always results in some curtailing of human freedom," then I was going to have to learn to see obedience as that which opened me up to the free flowing of God's life within and not that which stunted the maturing of my humanity. I had to realize that if it is true that "to the pure, all things are pure" (Titus 1:15), then true obedience should not cause one to reject the world, but perhaps the obedient would be the only ones capable of living in the world, for they would be the only ones able to live in it in a manner suitable for the purposes for which it was created. I needed to recognize that obedience was for the purpose of allowing our humanity to be free to become all that God had created it to be.

True obedience, I eventually discovered, offered a way to live true to the heart of my eternal being rather than being a legalistic approach to life. If pride, envy, or licentiousness lurked within my heart, then no prohibitions placed on my external appearance or behavior was going to help stamp out those sins. If rebellion lay within my heart, then staying away from movies, dances, or TV was still not enough to fill it with the joy or graces of the Holy Spirit. When obedience tries to work itself from the outside in rather than being from the inside out, then it becomes destructive and life-denying.

True obedience is about getting close enough to the heart of God so that our hearts are touched by what moves the heart of God, so that God's concerns become our concerns, and so that we begin to see the world through God's eyes. Obedience means turning from our path of self-understanding in order to follow in the direction that God is moving. Obedience is about learning enough of the purposes of God so that we can be agents of their ends here on earth.

Therapy, as one psychoanalyst noted, "has made a philosophical mistake, which is that cognition precedes conation—that knowing precedes doing or action."[437] Therapy attempts to place reflection and understanding first and foremost. In actual fact, reflection happens after action. We learn and know through doing. It is obedience that teaches us that Christian spirituality is a "kinesthetic spirituality." Knowledge is imparted kinesthetically, by means of the body. As Rodney Clapp wrote in his book *Tortured Wonders: Christian Spirituality for People, Not Angels,* "We learn with, through, and as our bodies. We keep that learning fresh and sharp by the ongoing, repeated workouts of our bodies. Christian spirituality is exercise, even or especially bodily exercise."[438]

The body has its own acquired knowledge, as I was reminded of when I decided to knit a blanket for my first grandchild. Before my oldest son was born, I asked my mother to teach me to knit a baby blanket. She patiently helped me learn how to knit. Eighteen years later, my son was to leave for university, so I picked up knitting needles again to knit an afghan to wrap himself in while he read and studied. It is hard the first time one realizes one's child has grown and is ready to leave home. Keeping my fingers busy knitting stitch after stitch brought emotional relief; love and grief and resolution were knit right into the blanket. Twelve years later, that same son phoned home to say that I was going to become a grandmother. Once again, I went out to buy knitting wool and needles for a baby blanket; the cycle was about to start over again. However, I soon realized that I had forgotten how to cast on the first stitches. I went off to the library to find a book on knitting. With the book before me, I gazed at the diagrams but just could not make sense of them. All my attempts to follow their directions proved futile. Finally, in sheer frustration, I closed my eyes, stopped my mind from reflecting on the how of knitting and just let my fingers follow what seemed to be still instinctually imprinted in them. My fingers instinctually knew what to do—as long as my mind did not get in their way. When I told my husband about how my fingers knew what my mind had forgotten, he said he knew exactly what I was talking about; when asked his locker combination at the club, he never remembers it, but when he's at the club, his fingers instinctually repeat the combination. The body is capable of acquiring and keeping its own knowledge behind which the mind lags.

A Biblical example of how understanding follows obedience comes in the story of Moses. Moses was instructed to return to Egypt, the land from which he had fled for his life and in which he had become a stranger. He was returning because he believed he was called by God to lead the Israelites out of their slavery. Under the circumstances, he could be excused for wanting knowledge of whom it was that he was trusting his future to. God's response to his hesitancy and need for assurance was, "And this will be the sign to you that it is I who have sent you: When you have brought the people out of Egypt, you will worship God on this mountain" (Exodus 3:12). In other words, the knowledge and the certainty would come after and arise out of the obedience. When Jesus said, "I am the Way the Truth and the Life," He put the way we walk before the truth we know. The knowing and certainty arise out of the following. We humans usually want to follow only what we understand. Faith teaches us to reverse the process. First we follow and then knowledge and understanding come after.

The gap between mind and body is what kinesthetic spirituality attempts to overcome. There is something in the Christian Scriptures to appeal to everyone, even atheists. Something seems to happen, however, between the truths we admire in the Bible and their ability to be realized in one human life. I personally learned that for the Bible to become a Living Book, one had to start responding to its life. I had that discovery confirmed by watching others who had begun to read the Bible. In watching and meeting with people, I have been repeatedly struck by how quickly and effectively the Bible can touch what seems to lie at the heart of one's difficulties. Individuals would give word to the special force with which the Bible suddenly addressed them personally and in a meaningful way by using expressions like, "I suddenly saw," or "I was struck by," or "I was touched," or "The Bible spoke to me." Something happened after those moments of revelation, however. Having left a deep impression in their heads, those insights made absolutely no difference in their lives. They would go off and live as they had been living with no visible change in attitude or lifestyle. I have come to believe that God never reveals more than what we have been obedient to. Soon, in the lives I observed, the Bible would once again become a dead book and its reading a chore. Obedience is the long and arduous journey that brings Scriptural realities

from the realm of idea and turns them into the story of our personal existence: " To act holy is a simple thing. To be holy is the lifelong process of
bringing the dull, dry demands of daily life into conjunction with ideals.
That process requires patience, endurance, the strength to aspire, and the
grace to grow through failure. No set of rules will do it. What is required
here is an attitude of mind and a centeredness of heart."[439]

Real obedience starts with the small, with the invisible, and with the
hidden. Jesus described the Kingdom in terms of that which is so hidden
and so small that it could be easily overlooked or else rendered invisible.
It was yeast, the mustard seed, salt—all overlooked because of seeming
insignificance—that were seen to be the essential ingredients of that eternal Kingdom.

When obedience to God seems too difficult, frightening, offensive, or
unappealing, then one way we can avoid it is by transferring our obedience over to people, institutions, or religious groups. Whereas obedience
to God frees us, when obedience is translated by another source we usually end up with our freedoms curtailed. Obedience to God draws us into
the heart of the gospel, where we discover the life and relationship for
which our deepest being has always yearned. Obedience diverted and
mediated by human institutions and systems can create moral societies,
but not the life and freedom that only God can give.

Another way we avoid wholehearted obedience is by means of
exchange. We all have an insatiable need to feel justified and righteous in
our own eyes, so we choose an area in which to work out and prove our
zeal, which then allows us to avoid submission in some other area of our
lives. Our society seems to be divided between those who are obsessed
with personal ethics and those who are concerned with social ethics. Half
the society would have us aware of social causes and humanitarian efforts
while refusing any outside authority with regards to personal morality. The
other half of society would impose on us religious views on abortion,
homosexuality, euthanasia, stem cell research, and other moral issues
while at the same time fighting for lower taxes, the death penalty, and
imperialistic foreign policies, refusing to see that they are thereby not hon-

oring life but are rather diminishing or destroying the lives of others. The true religion in North America is that of individualism; we live according to our own understanding and then offer up to God either our bodies or our money as a sop to buy our independence in those areas where we really desire God's absence. Instead of obedience to Christ, we offer commitment to our chosen ideals.

Obedience is seen in the Scriptures as the foundation, the gateway, and the door to the kingdom of God. Try to enter that Kingdom and one is sure to discover how deeply inimical to our nature that way can be. Disciples are not people who find the way easy or less offensive; they are people who would rather struggle with God until they receive the grace to go on rather than turn their backs to God and walk according to their own understanding.

Integrating the therapeutic into the church has brought us the illusion, for a while, that the hard edges of the gospel can be smoothed out. It has offered us the false hope that self-understanding can create a parallel path that allows us to be "saved" while following our own understanding, rather than committing ourselves to that hard road of obedience. It has offered us systems that lead us to believe that we need not be broken or measured against a "capstone" that's not of our making. It's a way, I discovered, that brings disillusionment and a dead end.

CHAPTER SIX

THEOLOGICAL PROBLEMS

Knowledge and Faith: Can There Be a Harmony?

Where is the wisdom we have lost in knowledge?
Where is the knowledge we have lost in information?

(T.S. Eliot "The Rock")

CONSIDERING THE EMPHASIS ON FAITH in the church, it is surprising to see how often the Bible enjoins us to "know." "Be still, and know that I am God" (Psalm 46:10); "I did this so that you might know that I am the Lord your God" (Deuteronomy 29:6); "The knowledge of the secrets of the kingdom of heaven has been given to you" (Matthew 12:11); "Then you will know the truth, and the truth will set you free" (John 8:32); "They will all know me, from the least of them to the greatest" (Hebrews 8:11); "To know this love that surpasses knowledge" (Ephesians 3:19); "I know whom I have believed" (2 Timothy 1:12); "I know that my Redeemer liveth" (Job 19:25). The Bible defines "faith" as "being sure of what we hope for and certain of what we do not see" (Hebrews 11:1). That is certainly not an attitude that I would normally have associated with faith.

What were those gospel writers talking about? Was their "knowing" intellectual, experiential, or wishful thinking? In contrast to all those confident assertions of "knowing," had I been asked to define what I meant by "faith," I could not have come up with anything more concrete than H. L. Mencken's definition, which was, "Faith may be defined briefly as an illogical belief in the occurrence of the improbable." "Knowing" is a term I would have applied to the increasing accumulation of information and scientific knowledge that we humans have amassed, while "faith" was a term I would have applied to the spiritual and invisible realm which, by definition, was not capable of being observed or proven in the material realm. I just assumed that the great divide between faith and confident knowing could not be bridged in this life.

There came a time, however, when finding a bridge that would secure my life in that other reality became imperative. Life was coming apart, I was sinking deeper and deeper into an endless pit of depression, and if I was going to be able to go on, I needed to know that my life was grounded in something surer than my disintegrating temporal existence. Faith as an "illogical belief in the occurrence of the improbable" was not sufficient to carry a life, and I no longer had patience for a faith that was a form of wishful thinking. God as an abstract ideal or as a theological construct was also no longer adequate; my life had become haunted by God's absence and I wondered whether there was some further way in which He could be "known." After an entire lifetime of Sunday services, I gathered up my courage to approach the church during the week to question someone there as to why, in the most inopportune time imaginable, God seemingly left me. I needed to know what to do with my loneliness and with God's profound absence.

After an entire life of listening to the gospel on Sunday, I finally heard what it sounded like during the week. I was astounded by how far that weekday gospel flew from Sunday's pulpit message.

I started listening to others, to those for whom the church was created—the broken, the lost, the wounded, the lonely, and the weak. I became aware of how suffering parishioners were being offered a therapeutic gospel for the answers to their unease. They were being offered "aid" according to humanistic systems of knowledge—knowledge that actually undercut and destroyed the very message offered from the pulpit. The need for faith was still preached from the pulpit, but secular, human knowledge was offered for real life. We were told, from the pulpit, to trust God to save our souls, but then referred to those trained in secular forms of understanding for the salvation of our bodies, our relationships, our attitudes, and our human natures. What is more, I noticed how churches offering two contradictory gospels could still claim to be proudly and even stridently evangelical. I also began to realize that many who preached the gospel from pulpits did not really believe in what they preached. They were preaching ideas, not reality.

I was not in a liberal church, but rather, a church that prided itself on its adherence to Scripture. That "knowledge" of Scripture, however, seemed to be slotted into a small portion of our brains where it could live unthreatened by the encroaching "knowledge" offered by secular disciplines such as psychology. Faith did not inform or illuminate all our realities, but had retreated to a small enclave in our brains where it could set up its defensive positions, zealously guarding a diminishing cache of "truths." Those truths, however, were of a different epistemological order than the truths that we lived by. Or to use another image, our religious beliefs had become a beautiful coat of paint applied to a structure that was humanistic in origin. As attitudes about our identity, our anxiety, our sense of self-worth, our relationships, and our sexuality became increasingly formed according to therapeutic understanding, that coat of paint was drying up, shriveling, and as it peeled away, I could see clearly the humanistic structure over which it had been applied. I tried to object, but the responses I got only made me aware of how deeply we had come to believe in and have faith in the "knowledge" offered by psychology.

I found that I could no longer live as a schizophrenic with two conflicting voices inside my head giving competing views as to my identity, life, and reality. Something had to give, but how could I maintain my identity as a rational and intelligent creature and still question therapeutic sensibilities that were being presented as knowledge and science?

It was not only the therapeutic that destroyed my ability to believe. I later realized that my entire belief system had been erected over faulty foundations. As that belief system became threatened, as it developed cracks and strains, as the foundations were eroded, my faith was finally subjected to a few too many blows, blows that finally allowed all that I had ever believed in to come crashing down. As the walls of belief caved in, the dark came rushing in—the darkness with its overwhelming questions about truth; is there any such thing as "truth?"

For me, that period brought back a flood of memories. Once before I had been caught in a period of crisis where intellectual honesty seemed incompatible with faith, and in order to maintain the supremacy of reason, I had felt it necessary to give up on faith. I was raised in a culture where higher learning was frowned upon; it was apparently a threat to faith. I was raised with stories of those who had gone to university and then consequently lost their faith. I had heard condemnations aimed at those who took in too much higher learning and consequently held "strange" ideas. Knowledge and higher learning, in my past, were viewed with suspicion. The implication seemed to be that faith could only survive in an atmosphere of unquestioning innocence. I chose to become an atheist at a young age, deciding I would go insane if I tried to fit my mind into the belief system I had inherited.

At that time, I was brought back to faith by the influence of poetry and literature. Strangely, I recovered my faith in university. Our lives are a series of choices where at any moment we may be presented with a chance to reroute. One of those formative turning points for me came as a college student riding a city bus in Medicine Hat, Alberta, and reading Tennyson's "In Memoriam A.H.H." Tennyson was a true Enlightenment product. He rode the crest of rationalism's wave, which was unlocking the secrets of the universe. He had a keen mind, and as geology, biology, and astronomy probed the secrets of the universe, he was part of a worldview that increasingly thought they were gaining mastery of their universe. Tennyson could have identified with Swinburne's worship-filled cry, "Glory to Man in the highest! For Man is the master of things."[440] Or with Comte's quip about the heavens declaring not the glory of God but rather of Kepler and Newton.[441] Or with the cry of Robert Ingersoll, "Give me, the storm and tempest of thought and action, rather than the dead calm of ignorance and faith! Banish me from Eden when you will; but first let me eat of the fruit of the tree of knowledge!"[442]

But then Tennyson's best friend and mentor drowned. Tennyson got a good view of where they, the arrogant Enlightenment thinkers, were actually standing. He realized that man is not—and never will be—the master of his universe but exists, rather, completely at its mercy. Tennyson's poem reads like a long cry of agony as he looks across a world where reason has been allowed to pave over the entire landscape, leaving little chance for faith to put down roots and grow. Written over seventeen years, it shows the slow progression from despair back to faith and hope.

By the time I left the bus in Medicine Hat, I had decided that man could not have been created with such longings without there being something corresponding meant to satisfy them. I decided I was going to search until I discovered that "something." I still had difficulty accepting much that came in the name of religion, but as long as I kept God as a question that hovered over my existence, then that question, itself, seemed to guide me.

Now, once again, I stood at a crisis point where faith and reason were offering different views, not of the nature of the universe and of physical reality this time, but rather of the reality of my own human nature. Biblical revelation about my nature, existence, and how I should live it out was in direct conflict with psychological understanding. I could see that the therapeutic was increasingly being allowed to provide the frameworks of understanding into which we were invited to place our lives, while religion was left with a room in the attic where faith was invited to provide some soothing furniture—but I wanted truth, not soothing furniture. A gospel could not have much substance or reality if it could be preached from the pulpit with such evangelical rigidity, but was translated into therapeutic form and meanings when it left the pulpit.

Once again I found myself at a crossroad. Subterranean depths that had seemingly waited for cracks to form in my psyche so they could erupt threw up all the unanswered questions of my youth, questions about faith versus reason; wisdom versus knowledge; information versus truth; human words versus the Word. How could we humans with intelligent brains, with the capability of exploring, discovering and knowing, ever find the harmony in those tensions? Rather than running from those questions any further, I embraced them all. I became a pilgrim.

Once again I struggled until I found myself back at a place of faith, but not before the foundations on which I based that faith were completely changed. I eventually realized that the "knowing" of God that we were invited into lay on a different plane than the scattered bits of information we gather up and then claim as "knowledge." Religious knowledge cannot be given a separate folder in our documents file. It is more like the hard drive that we are rarely aware of but that makes the accumulation of other files and knowledge possible. It can be susceptible to viruses that come with malevolent intent, but its purpose is to allow the accumulation of knowledge and to facilitate the ways we categorize and process it.

Jacques Ellul, in his book *The Meaning Of The City*, wrote of how the city is used in the Bible as a symbol for all that man accomplishes in defiance and outside the authority of God. The city symbolized "the triumph of objective knowledge, of man's intellectual conquest, of his piracy of the world."[443] The first recorded city was built by Cain, who also happened to be the first murderer and the first individual to try designing his religious acts according to his own preferences rather than the ordinances of God. The ultimate city, Babel, was also built as an act of defiance, uniting mankind in a godless enterprise to build a tower "that reaches to the heavens"; it was a human endeavor attempting to usurp God's space, creating a challenge and an act of defiance to the kingdom of God.

In the Biblical narrative, it is Eve who was first tempted by fruit from the Tree of Knowledge. The serpent offered it as "desirable for gaining wisdom" (Genesis 2:6) and claimed it would make her "like god." Eve succumbed to the temptation and discovered that the serpent was right. Adam and Eve, indeed, needed to be as god to themselves, because they became separated from their relationship with a real God.

Our human history seems to endlessly repeat the same sequence of events: human knowledge is used as the means of displacing obedience to God, we glory in our freedom and ability to play god to ourselves, and then we face the bitter consequences. First, Eve found that the fruit from the Tree of Knowledge did not allow her to become the self-appointed Goddess of the Garden as she had thought was promised, but rather found herself banished from the Garden forever. Civilization progressed to the point where it could create the city of Babel, a city where human genius could devise a tower built up to the heavens, but then it became a civilization that collapsed as they found themselves not co-hosts of the heavens, but rather, scattered across the earth, consigned to living in mutual incomprehension. Eventually we arrived at the Enlightenment. We felt we had really arrived, our intelligence producing thinkers who were unlocking all the secrets of the universe. What we actually found, however, was that we, like Tennyson, were trapped within the universe we thought we were unlocking. Squeezed into Darwin's closed box, we didn't have room to move, much less control the universe. What has become evident is that the appropriation of knowledge so that we can be as god to ourselves was not only man's original sin, it has also been man's perpetual sin.

The Bible actually offers us two contrasting stories of man accomplishing technological feats of wonder: the tower of Babel and the ark. The tower was built by human invention and desire; it was not made of stone (representing the use of God-given creation), but rather, of brick (that which man had invented), and it was an attempt to pierce the heavens with the workmanship of man. It resulted in the dissolution of society. The ark was also a technological feat of wonder for its age. However it, in contrast to the tower of Babel, was built under the specific directions of God and resulted in the preservation of man. Obviously, it is not our knowledge or accomplishments that are the problem, but the terms of reference under which we operate.

Interestingly, in the Biblical narrative, we are never offered a return to the Garden of Eden. Our lost innocence is irretrievable. Our banishment from the garden is secured by angels with flaming swords. Feigned simplicity and naivety will not bring us back to Eden. Any attempt, as in my past culture, to disassociate faith from reason, to attempt a return to simplicity and to innocence, is doomed to failure. The way back is blocked.

Our temptation, rather, will be to continue to engorge ourselves on the fruit of that original rebellion. We too, like Eve, will at some point stand before the Tree of Knowledge and realize that we, too, need to decide between obedience, or the fruit promising life according to our own reasoning powers and understanding. We, at some point, will realize that we, too, have inherited the craving for that original fruit and are beguiled by the power inherent in following dictums like Kant's "Dare to Know." Knowledge that allows us to be as god to ourselves, which allows us to forego the fearful life of faith and obedience, is a powerful seduction.

However, before we fearfully react to the role that reason and knowledge play, we must notice that they are not condemned in the Bible. Although we are not invited back to Eden and to our lost simplicity, we are not left stranded. We are invited, instead, to make our way towards a new city, the New Jerusalem. Whereas cities in the Bible represent man's living according to his own capabilities and his defiance of God, it is an image that eventually becomes redeemed. In the book of Revelation, it is actually a city—the New Jerusalem—that will eventually gather up the people of God. In the New Jerusalem, all that we've done will be redeemed; all that we have dared to discover and to know will once more be illuminated by the Light of a Higher Reality (Revelation 22:5); all that we have accomplished will be again nourished by that "river of the water of life" (Revelation 22:1). It is interesting that the formation of the New Jerusalem is said to be according to "man's measurement, which the angel was using" (Revelation 21:17), and "the glory and honor of the nations will be brought into it" (Revelation 21:26). The New Jerusalem is a place where our humanity and what we have achieved is not destroyed, but is rather honored and brought back under the life of God.

It is knowledge that gets separated from relationship with God that always seems to get us into trouble. We often tend to forget that the Bible is not a book about facts; it is a story about relationship and meaning. The Bible offers us a context into which we can place the knowledge we gather and which also offers the plumb line against which we can test the veracity of the ideas we develop. As Thomas Traherne wrote, "He knoweth nothing as he ought to know, who thinks he knoweth anything without seeing its place and the manner how it relateth to God, angels and men, and to all the creatures in earth, heaven and hell, time and eternity." It is in allowing knowledge to become separated from that context that has been our constant temptation and downfall.

When I finally got around to reading my Bible, I was relieved to find that the pursuit of knowledge was not condemned, as implied in my background, but encouraged. We are told, "Study to show yourselves approved unto God." We are told to add knowledge to faith (2 Peter 1:5). A God who had said, "Come now, let us reason together" (Isaiah 1:18), was not going to ask me to squelch my mind for the sake of blind obedience, or to give Himself an unfair advantage in the dialogue. And yet there is a reason why it was the Tree of Knowledge from which the fruit of our destruction was plucked. There is a reason why we are not told to seek God with our minds but rather to love Him with our minds, and there is a reason that the word "demon" has its origin in a Greek word meaning "knowledge."[444] There is a reason why the Apostle Paul, who was once the brilliant mind within Pharisaism, said that he now served the Lord "with all humility of mind,"[445] and asked the Colossians, likewise, to take on "humbleness of mind."[446] There is a reason why Martin Luther claimed, "The intellect is the Devil's whore." Jesus praised God for having "hidden these things from the wise and learned, and revealed them to little children" (Luke 10:21), and Paul could ask, "Has not God made foolish the wisdom of this world?" (1 Corinthians 1:20). Knowledge that asserts its autonomy becomes the demon that destroys us. Knowledge that gets abstracted from wisdom, life, and charity is a force bringing great destruction. In Christian history, both "agnostic" and "gnostic" are negative words because "wisdom is not identified either with knowledge or with the denial of knowledge."[447] It is important to realize the role reason can play, and it is even more important to recognize its limitations.

When I struggle over the relationship of knowledge to wisdom I think of Martin Buber's visual picture of knowledge sitting on the lap of Mother Wisdom. Human knowledge is the offspring of Divine Wisdom. The problem, however, is that human knowledge has always been an errant child. Leaping from Wisdom's lap, it offers to take a few steps of its own. Gaining in courage, it soon offers to walk alongside Wisdom, holding its hand. Eventually, knowledge gets puffed up and invites Wisdom to sit on its lap. In that inverted position, Wisdom is never anything more than lifeless form; smothered and abused, it becomes the inanimate plaything of human knowledge.

The Bible places such an emphasis on faith because of the inadequacy of our minds to comprehend eternal realities. Although the Bible does not clearly define faith, it does give us stories that reveal what it looks like when in action. In Hebrews 11, we are given the Hall of Fame of those who have lived by faith. Interestingly, faith is only mentioned twice in the Old Testament, and yet the examples of faith given in Hebrews 11 come from there. The individuals in Hebrews 11 were commended because when God asked them to go, to do, to live by what lay beyond their understanding, they had become so sure of what they hoped for, so certain of what they could not see, they could confidently follow. Their actions—building an ark, sacrificing one's son, leaving home to journey to a promised land, etc.—all look foolish when first observed by the eye of cool reason. Yet they followed God even when He led them on ways that were difficult and inscrutable. It was God they knew, and certainty of this knowledge allowed them to follow what they could not yet understand.

In the examples given in Hebrews 11, the supremacy of reason is obviously foregone in order to live in response to some invisible power. It is as though God, at some point, invites us to take our crowning glory— our ability to reason, to "know," that faculty that allows us to direct the course of our own lives—and invites us to place it back in the lap of higher

342 THE ALTARS OF AHAZ

wisdom. It appears from the stories in Hebrews that in that homecoming—
the return of knowledge to the lap of Wisdom—the intimacy we severed
at Eden can once more be restored.

Last night my son's friend entered my room to say, "I don't believe in
Christianity. What do you have to say to that?" What he was wanting was
an apologetic defense of Christianity that appealed to his reason. I felt too
old and battle-weary to give him what he wanted. I told him, instead,
about C.S. Lewis's metaphor of the climbers who had climbed a mountain
to arrive at a cliff's edge where they could see the shelter that they desired
far down below them. C.S. Lewis then differentiated between nearness of
distance and nearness of approach. We may climb great heights by means
of our intellectual prowess, but reason, by itself, cannot get us to the place
of warmth and comfort that, from reason's peak, is so near and yet so far.
We need to discover another approach. Leaving the peak—where we can
view the shelter with its lights and chimney-smoke offering warmth and
shelter—may feel like defeat after all the strain of the climb, but by
choosing another path—a path that leads circuitously through dark
woods, away from the visual sight-line of the shelter—we discover the
nearness of approach as we begin to hear the music and sounds emanat-
ing from the shelter. We probably needed reason to climb the heights and
to give us a view of the other side of the mountain, but if we don't find a
way to descend, then we will know no more of the reality of the shelter
than what we can view from reason's lofty peak.

I probably should have engaged my son's friend on his terms. After all,
I still remember my youth when it was imperative that I trust nothing but
what lay within reason's terrain. However, I now know that trying to
approach God by means of reason alone is like asking a dog to run a race
by means of using only one leg. God had told the Israelites that He would
be found if they sought Him "with all your heart and with all your soul"
(Deuteronomy 4:29). The mind is included in what is meant by the soul,
but it is not given any special mention. The Greeks later came to exalt
human reason, which is perhaps why the mind was given special attention
in the New Testament, our being told, "Love the Lord your God with all

your heart and with all your soul and with all your strength and with all your mind" (Luke 10:27). The mind, although mentioned, is still only given partial credit for our approach to God. To know God, we need to approach Him with the totality of our being, and the mind is only a part of that being.

We are not actually commanded to know God; we are commanded to love Him. Love arises out of relationship, not out of propositional truths. Our knowledge of God does not arise out of books or seminars, but out of a life lived in relationship to God. As long as our knowledge of God is left in the realm of abstraction and idea, as mine had been, then it will always be made vulnerable to the newest discoveries of "science" threatening to broadside faith. Considering that the Apostle Paul condemns those who are "always learning but never able to acknowledge the truth" (2 Timothy 3:7), I think it is safe to assume the knowing that the Gospel calls us to enter into is of a higher and different order than the information that we normally gather in order "to know."

The overwhelming question for all us pilgrims living east of Eden is how can we use our God-given intelligence in a way that returns us to relationship with God, rather than having it reinforce and make permanent our estrangement. How does our reason find its way back into the lap of God? How can we use knowledge in a way that brings us to the New Jerusalem? Perhaps the best way of understanding that is to see how reason and knowledge have managed to separate themselves from the life of God. In reading through history, I realized that religion itself is not free from the effects of the curse, and the seeds from the Tree of Knowledge have developed two especially pernicious root systems that have persistently sucked the life from organized religion: Pharisaism and Gnosticism.

Pharisaism is the attempt to substitute knowledge about God for true knowing. The Scriptures are full of people who "knew" God. The Hebrew word for "know" is the same word that they used for sexual intercourse.[448] It obviously meant intimacy and relationship. Intimacy, however, comes with a lot of difficulties; it requires a lot of self-giving and a lot of effort. Knowledge used for abstraction, in contrast, can help us avoid those difficulties. Abstraction allows distance, it leaves us with feelings of control, and it eliminates the messiness and commitment of relationship. Abstraction also opens the door to ways we can play games with the truth. Bonhoeffer aptly pointed out that the first recorded religious question was the devil's, asking Eve, "Did God really say?"[449] Rather than seeking the face of God to inquire directly as to how to respond to the serpent, Eve chose to turn to the serpent and engaged in "the first conversation about God, the first religious, theological conversation."[450] Whenever we speak about God without first speaking to God, we make ourselves vulnerable to deception and expose ourselves to the lie.

Pharisaism first arises in the book of Job, arguably the oldest book in the Bible. I used to find Job the most frustrating book of the Bible. Job obviously had a bad attitude and faulty theology, but everything his friends said seemed so scripturally sound—there were biblical references for it all. And yet every time the book ended the same way. Job found himself at the center of God's answering Presence and approval and God ended up expressing His anger with Job's friends. I would shut the book and tell myself, "Now who is ever going to understand a God like that?" I hadn't realized that I had gotten the point. It was Martin Buber who helped me understand Job by alerting me to who they were addressing. The friends spoke about God; Job addressed his angry cries to the silent skies where he persistently asked to speak *to* God, crying, "But I desire to speak to the Almighty and to argue my case with God" (Job 13:3). As Buber wrote, "God can be addressed, not expressed." Job stands as a permanent warning that if our knowledge of God lies in ideas *about* God rather than in knowledge of intimacy and relationship, we may have done little more than arouse the displeasure and anger of a Living God.

I had never questioned why exactly Jesus became so angry with the Pharisees until I read *Sages and Dreamers,* a book by the Jewish writer Elie Wiesel. Wiesel gave living, biographical form to the rabbis and leaders in Jewish history, including some from Jesus' time. By the time I had finished reading the book, I found myself confused. The Pharisees as depicted by Wiesel were obviously admirable characters. In fact, they experienced their religion in much the same way that the people in my inherited tradition believed and practiced their religion.

The Pharisees were a group committed to keeping the essentials of their religion alive: their scriptures, their traditions, and right moral living. Wiesel depicted men spending their lives reading, learning, discussing, and arguing over their scriptures. When 2 Timothy 3:16 says, "All Scripture is God-breathed and is useful for teaching, rebuking, correcting, and training in righteousness," the New Testament canon had not yet been formed. The writer was referring to the same scriptures that both Jesus and the Pharisees had been studying and living by. The very titles given to Jesus—"rabbi" and "teacher"—show that the group Jesus would have been most closely identified with would have been the Pharisees. One would have thought the Sadducees should have been the primary targets of Jesus wrath; they were the corrupt, liberalizing, humanizing element trying to rid religion of the supernatural. Jesus, however, seemed to largely ignore them. It was the Pharisees who seemed to bear the brunt of Jesus anger and to be the target of his most vitriolic language and condemnation. I eventually came to see that the Pharisees were such a threat precisely because they came so close; they came so close they had the capacity to "shut the kingdom of heaven in men's faces" (Matthew 23:13). As revealed by the Pharisees, one could live by the scriptures, by inherited traditions, and keep up right moral living, but still miss what lies at the heart of true religion.

Coming from a revivalist background, I was surprised to read the Bible and realize that the very words which rang out before the altar calls—"You must be born again" or, "Behold I stand at the door and knock"—were not addressed to sinners or unbelievers; they were addressed to the religious of the day. "Behold I stand at the door and knock" was actually addressed to a Christian church, a church with a religious system so complete the only thing they had managed to leave out was a Living God. That Living God was left standing outside, knocking and offering all the intimacy of the communal meal if only He could be invited in. I was surprised to read the Bible and realize that Jesus did not directly threaten sinners with hell or damnation. Jesus mostly seemed to save that language for the Pharisees—perhaps because Pharisees can be the hardest people to save; they have too much confidence in their self-created systems and traditions.

Both Jesus and the Pharisees were distancing themselves from the corrupt temple cult, which was under the control of the Sadducees. But they differed over what would replace it. For the Pharisees, it was their scriptures and their traditions that were to replace the temple. The Pharisees eventually came to say that where two or more were gathered studying the Torah, then the Shekinah would be there. The Scriptures formed the center of religious life. Jesus, in contrast, said that where two or more were gathered in His name, then He would be there. Community and the known Presence of Christ formed the center of the new religion. The difference between Jesus and the Pharisees is the difference between the Scriptures opening one up to the continuing work of God, or trusting in the Scriptures as a closed system. That is why Jesus could turn to the Pharisees and say, "You diligently study the Scriptures because you think that by them you possess eternal life. These are the Scriptures that testify about me, yet you refuse to come to me to have life" (John 5:39). Jesus said it was the reality of His own life that would replace the temple; He came to initiate an experiential knowing that would be available to all.

Jesus did not reduce or belittle the importance of the Scriptures—with Jesus, they became more important than ever before. It is not possible to safely navigate the spiritual realm without firm guidelines, a framework, and sure stepping-stones. The more one becomes aware of the spiritual realm, the more one will need to rely on the Scriptures, as one becomes aware of how far one can fall if one missteps. But with the coming of Jesus, it was the life of Spirit, not the Scriptures, that formed the basis of relationship with God and that became the center of the new religion. It was prayer, not Bible study, which provided the formational basis of the new life. When the Scriptures, rather than the living reality of Christ, are made the center of faith, then religious life becomes reduced to a mode of knowing, an intellectual adherence to a set of interpretations rather than the following of a Living God.

Perhaps the best modern example of Pharisaism comes from the last century and from our own continent. One writer suggested that it was a reaction to the Enlightenment; tired of being seen as anti-intellectual, the church decided to compete with the world on Enlightenment terms. She writes,

> Since the late nineteenth century, American fundamentalists had responded to the challenge of modernity by trying to make their faith wholly rational. They had emphasized the virtues of reason and plain sense; they had embraced a sober literalism that eschewed imagination and fantasy; they had organized the world into watertight compartments in which right was utterly and obviously distinct from wrong, and true believers in an entirely different category from secularists and liberal Christians…it was a faith that offered cast-iron certainty and hierarchy to challenge the doubts, open questions, and shifting roles of the modern world….By trying to make their faith scientific and rational, the fundamentalists had pushed religion into an unnatural mode.[451]

The essential problem of the Fundamentalists was that they had lost awareness of the difference between knowledge and faith and had succumbed to the cultural pressure to reduce faith to the level of reason and knowledge. Slowly, as they summed up the Gospel mystery, encapsulating it in a compendium of human knowledge called "The Fundamentals," they didn't even realize how they were destroying the reality of faith. No longer was faith the realization that we were created with souls that have the capacity to apprehend God; no longer was it the realization of our ability to live in increasing awareness and co-creation with our Creator; no longer was faith the ability to stand before mystery with a sense of overwhelming awe and wonder and live in response; no longer was faith the ability to live in the wide horizons of the Gospel and then interiorize it all in one human life. Faith, instead, became the intellectual adherence to a system of theology, compliance with certain accepted traditions, and a strict code of morality. Once faith had been reduced to that position, then it was inevitable that it would next become "an act of knowledge that has a low degree of evidence,"[452] or an act of will determined to believe the unbelievable. Faith, thus understood, was bound to create conflict as dogmatic systems collided.

The fundamentalists, however, didn't even seem to notice how badly they were losing their balance until they ended up in Dayton, Tennessee at the Scopes Monkey trial, landing flat on their proverbial faces as they tried arguing faith in a court of human reason. The faith they had attempted to reduce to knowledge, reason, and good common sense was in danger of being destroyed by knowledge, reason, and good common sense.

The evolution debate has often been caricaturized as a conflict between reason and faith. That is a false dichotomy. It has since been the scientists, and especially the physicists, who have reopened the closed box that Darwin stuffed us into and have instead posited us in a participatory universe where our presence—even our observations—can affect reality around us. The linking of the Fundamentalist camp with true faith is also misleading; they were not defending faith, but had actually lost sight of what faith is. In seceding to the pressure of the Enlightenment, they had allowed faith to become redefined and forced into an unnatural mode.

When the historian James Turner wrote his history of unbelief, he claimed he started out fully expecting to write a history of the external forces that caused the erosion of faith. To his surprise, he concluded, "Religion caused unbelief. In trying to adapt their religious beliefs to socioeconomic change, to new moral challenges, to novel problems of knowledge, to the tightening standards of science, the defenders of God slowly strangled Him."[453] In tailoring belief to human understanding, they "forgot the tension that, by definition, must exist between an incomprehensible God and the human effort to know Him."[454] Religious knowledge had been reduced to intellectual modes of knowing that were only appropriate for understanding the realities of the physical world. Mystical, nonrational and intuitive ways of knowing had always balanced and renewed religion in the past, but by the nineteenth century religion "had abandoned those nonrational, sometimes noncognitive, roads to belief, left them weed-grown traces of once broad avenues."[455]

The theory of evolution was one of those dividing issues that seemed to catch everyone off-guard and, as in a game of freeze-tag, awakened in everyone an awareness of what position they were actually standing in. Many lost their faith. Too many just redoubled their efforts to patch up their intellectual religious systems that were crumbling—and consequently left a trail of strident insecurity that haunts us still, for "repressed doubt can lead to the worst kind of fanaticism: the zealot, the fascist, the spiritual rapist who assaults the souls of others and bombards the world with the noise of his own insecurity.[456] For some others, however, it led to a re-examination of what faith actually is and it became a place of spiritual rebirth and growth.

What became evident in the whole Fundamentalist debacle was the realization that when reason is allowed to set the perimeters of faith, then faith itself becomes unreasonable. When faith tries to make itself intelligent, then it itself becomes unintelligent. Faith is something we discover in its own right and cannot be forced into a foreign mode without itself becoming destroyed. Fundamentalists are often portrayed as people existing in the backwaters of reason, but that is to miss the point; they were trying to be reasonable. They erred in their attempt to reduce faith to reason. As Pascal wrote in his Pensee 188, "Reason's last step is the recognition that there are an infinite number of things which are beyond it. It is merely feeble if it does not go as far as to realize that." Religion is essentially about the Holy, the numinous, about the "permeation of the rational with the nonrational."[457] In the words of Saint Thomas, "The final attainment of man's knowledge of God consists in knowing that we do not know Him, in so far as we realize that He transcends everything that we understand concerning Him." Faith is not anti-knowledge. Faith does not call us to go against our mind; it just helps us to become aware of and live by what lies beyond our ever knowing.

The Scopes Monkey trial and the humiliation of the Fundamentalists came at a time when man was beginning to shift his major focus of attention. After unlocking the secrets of the world, the universe, of nature, and of history, man next turned his attention onto himself. Man discovered that he could unlock the secrets of himself, and with that he began the long study of his own biology, chemistry, genetics, and his own DNA. He discovered that he could create and alter life; he could decide the terms whereby life enters this world, leaves this world, and he could set the terms of his existence. And then he came to that ultimate act of hubris; man, without finding God, could look within himself and uncover the secrets of his own inner life and his soul.

Edwin Starbuck, the one-time student of William James who did the groundbreaking work that then formed the basis of James' work, began his study in *The Psychology of Religion* with the words,

> Science has conquered one field after another, until now it is entering the most complex, the most inaccessible, and, of all, the most sacred domain—that of religion. The Psychology of Religion has for its work to carry the well-established methods of science into the analysis and organization of the facts of the religious consciousness, and to ascertain the laws which determine its growth and character. It will be a source of delight to many persons, and of regret to others, that the attempt is at last made to study the facts of religion by scientific methods.[458]

A study was thus begun of what were thought to be the inner secrets of religion, which, it was thought, could, by means of reason, be understood and then duplicated according to man's own capabilities. Whereas God had once been seen as the source of our inner life and healing, now man was ready to assert his dominion over those areas. Man, with the aid of science, it was thought, could become the means and source of his own inner healing, his own salvation. It was only a matter of time before man could then take the next step, could take the size and shape of his own spiritual longings, and could begin to design spiritualities and gods made to measure. Where it brought us was to a form of "knowing" that has become part of the second pernicious root system that runs through all of Christian history: that of Gnosticism.

When Jesus told a Pharisee, "You must be born again," and likened rebirth as a spiritual being with learning to discern the movements of the wind, He was describing what we feel most uncomfortable with. It is more in keeping with our nature to build a safe shelter from the wind. From a self-designed safe shelter, we can then stridently acclaim, "I believe in the wind." The wind is that which we can never capture, contain, or control. It can be harnessed for good use; one can certainly move to a place exposed to its force and learn to "follow." Yet we know that if someone claims to have caught the wind, they are deluded. But from the beginning of Christianity, this did not stop man from trying, and Gnosticism was the means he used.

What lies at the heart of both Gnosticism and Pharisaism is the failure to find the relationship between knowledge and faith. Gnosticism makes the same mistake as Pharisaism, but from the side of intellectual pretension. Rather than trying to reduce faith to an intellectual system, it adds an intellectual system to give it more sophistication.

Gnosticism comes from the root word *to know*—it means "one who knows." The attachment of some system of knowledge to Christianity allows man to live with the illusion that some of the power, some control has been allowed back into his own hands. Gnosticism helps man to live not by faith, but by knowledge. It attempts to add some intellectual respectability to what was a very humble religion. After all, we human beings are intelligent creatures. By adding a system of knowledge to faith, the Gnostics hoped to raise faith up to the level of our intellectual pretensions.

The greatest Gnostic century—before our own—was the second century. In Chapter 1, I noted how the early Christian fathers were conflicted over what to do with the brilliant pagan thinkers such as Plato. On many levels, Plato seemed to presciently articulate what lay at the heart of Christianity. It seemed only natural to baptize him and allow him to enlighten Christian thinking. That integration, however, proved fatal. Plato's duality created an enmity between the soul and the body, which undid the work of the Incarnation. The new Gnosticism also confuses, and then subverts, the biblical revelation as to our nature. The therapeutic, with its interest in our inner wholeness and healing, actually seems to be working towards the same ends as the gospel. So once again we have bought into a Gnostic pairing—this time of the gospel with therapeutic knowledge—in order to make the gospel more intelligent, pragmatic, and accessible.

Ever since Jesus was born in a stable, there has been something lowly and humble about the Christian religion. As William Temple wrote, "The last resort of human pride is to attribute a proud dignity to the object of its worship. But even that has to go. In the light of Christ's revelation no place is left for pride at all."[459] Our ability to perceive the secrets of the universe will depend more on humility than on our intellectual capabilities. Gnostics are people who cannot abide the humility required for true knowing. Gnostics instead attach a system of knowledge to Christianity in order to create a doorway that is a little more respectable; it does not require one to stoop quite so low. That attached doorway, however, never leads us into the kingdom of God, but rather, into the Kingdom of Self. As H. Richard Niebuhr noted, early Gnostics "sought to disentangle the gospel from its involvement with barbaric and outmoded Jewish notions about God and history; to raise Christianity from the level of belief to that of intelligent knowledge, and so to increase its attractiveness and its power."[460]

Gnosticism is hydra-headed; it can never be fully eradicated or, what makes it so insidious, never clearly defined. It exists as a parasite living off of religion, sucking out its life until it has reduced the host religion to an empty shell. However, as the work on Gnosticism written by R. M. Grant points out, certain characteristics are common to all its variations.

First and foremost, Gnosticism is self-centered; the "Gnostic is a Gnostic because he knows, by revelation, who his true self is."[461] Whereas true religion is God-centered, Gnosticism is self-centered. In Christian baptism, we symbolically enact our dying to self in order to be raised into God-consciousness. In Gnosticism, however, attention is turned back onto the knowing self. Gnosticism allows the shell of religion to exist while simultaneously tearing out religion's heart, soul, and substance; it replaces slowly learned dependence on the divine with human knowledge, human control, and human self-sufficiency.

Secondly, Gnostic salvation comes by means of self-knowledge. Whereas traditional Christianity says that we can only know ourselves by means of finding ourselves in God, in Gnosticism, "we return to our ontological condition, to the deep, total and permanent reality of our ego."[462] The spiritual journey is thus redirected from being a search for God into an inward journey.

Thirdly, Gnosticism is completely subjective, foregoing objectivity for the sake of self-discovery.[463] It is ultimately about freedom—freedom from the God of the Old Testament, from law, and from all external constraints.[464] It is, above all, a freedom for novelty; it eschews law and tradition for a new personal mythology. Salvation becomes detached from life in order to live in some parallel realm of ideas or some nebulous spiritual plane. The external Word is not born in, revealed, and incarnated in life; subjective experience becomes pre-eminent and passes judgment on the Word. Gnostics ignore the world and history in order to retreat into the mind and introspection.

Grant was writing about the second century, the century in which, until our own, Christianity was most threatened by Gnostic influence. In reading about second century Gnosticism, however, I realized that Gnosticism had never been eradicated, but lay dormant until it could reach a new and full flowering in our present century. It was the study of Gnosticism that caused a lot of self-examination in me and made me realize how many of the beliefs and practices I had picked up in current evangelicalism were not Christian beliefs at all, but the result of Gnosticism again penetrating the church and substituting its parasitic views where the Gospel once held sway.

I have often wondered if the current debate over homosexuality—like Darwinian evolution—isn't one of those dividing issues that catches us as in a game of freeze-tag, revealing where we stand. I am convinced that the current turmoil in the church over homosexuality is not primarily a disagreement over sexuality at all. Rather, it is about the collision of

354 The Altars of Ahaz

two disparate gospels that we have erroneously tried to blend. Inevitably, the attempted integration of two contradictory gospels had to eventually result in a seismic eruption, as two gospels, like two tectonic plates, eventually attempted contrary movements along some previously invisible fault line. I believe the furor over homosexuality should be seen as God's gift, a rattling of the systems we have created, warning us that we have been trusting that which we, ourselves, have created.

If we had stuck to one gospel, would sexuality have become such a problem for us? Let us look at how we understand ourselves. Were we taught to see the deepest imprint in our being as love, the emanation from a personal God, or were we taught to see it in terms of sex, a function of the libido? Did we allow Jesus to define our attitudes of love, or did we allow Freud to make sex the prism through which we viewed our relationships?

The original gospel offers revelation and law to provide a structural form within which we work out our relationship to God and, consequently, the pursuit of meaningful life. The new therapeutic gospel places the knowing ego at center, allowing us to choose what is right for us.

The original gospel offers grace as the means whereby we can transcend ourselves to live a supra-human life; we do not create ourselves but are, by grace, made new. The therapeutic gospel offers knowledge as the means of autonomy, self-realization, self-actualization, and the means whereby we create an authentic self. We create our own destiny.

The Bible claims that the reason we recognize sin is because it has dropped its seed into every one of our hearts. Were we taught how to overcome all that lives in contradiction to the life of God, or were we taught to accept our shadow side, to integrate it all?

The unconscious is a chaotic region that will never form itself into moral structure. However, to what degree have we elevated it to become the determination and the excuse for our being? Were we taught to see the role of the unconscious as determinate, or were we taught that as sons of God we would be made free from slavery "to the elemental spirits of the universe?" (Galatians 4:3)

Were we taught to live according to divine obedience or according to more "scientific" theories of self-understanding?

To what degree does the problem of our sexuality arise out of the universal problem of loneliness? Were we taught to see community as the means whereby we discovered our identity and were formed into Christlikeness, or were all problems in living referred outside of the church? Whatever happened to spiritual friendship, soul mates, or spiritual directors who could help us see God in all the confrontations of our life?

From the Christian point of view, we need the Other to know ourselves. From within the therapeutic point of view, we need others to reflect ourselves. When reality is seen through the subjective lens of self, then it is imperative to be around others who affirm one's own view of the world; from that perspective, someone of the opposite sex can be too much of a shock to one's autonomous, self-realized existence.

It has been my experience that belief in the inherent goodness of homosexuality and the need to bless its practice comes as part of a cluster of beliefs; it comes attached to a psychologized view of man, and where it is linked to a form of spirituality, then it bears the imprint of either Carl Jung or else Eastern influence, where the sacramental view of life has been discarded. I believe the issue of homosexuality is just a red herring; it is the vision of God and of ourselves that is the problem. We, in the church, have allowed our understanding of ourselves to be formed by therapeutic, and not biblical, understanding.

Being a former Anglican living amidst the crisis over the blessing of same-sex unions, I sometimes feel this is another Dayton, Tennessee, where those who are most to be pitied are the ones who can't see that there has been a major earthquake, and those who claim to be living by orthodoxy have been revealed to be standing on anything but solid ground. The homosexual debate has often been linked to the issues of slavery and women's rights. That, I believe, is the wrong association. It is, rather, a parallel to the evolution debate. Both conflicts arose out of an inability to find the harmony between faith and knowledge.

Knowledge of the Pharisaical kind resulted in the crisis of faith triggered by the evolution debate. I believe that knowledge of the Gnostic kind is what has caused the current furor over sexuality. In both cases, it was the use of man's reason and knowledge in a way that destroyed faith that brought the church to a point of crisis where one dividing issue—evolution or homosexuality—could reveal the church to be bankrupt. The first crisis could not be resolved by means of arguments over evolution any more than the current debate can be resolved by arguing over homosexuality. When the church allowed the therapeutic to integrate its systems of knowledge into its institutions, it opened itself up to a Gnosticism that allowed all that the original gospel reveals about our natures to be supplanted and destroyed. The church has since been living with two contradictory gospels offering competing answers as to our identity and our unease.

Did not the current debate over sexuality arise out of that point around 1974 when the American Psychiatric Association and then, following suit, the American Psychological Association, both declared homosexuality to be "normal"? But are those not the very sources we, in evangelical churches, have become completely dependent on to answer for us the once religious questions of: Who are we? What has gone wrong with us? What shall we do about it?

When we were broken by life, were we told that broken soil is needed for germinating the seed of life? Were we taught how to tend and nurture the ever-so-slow-growing life of that eternal seed until it could fully flower and blossom? Or was our care subcontracted out to those in the "science" of psychology who could "fix" us according to their humanly designed forms of health?

When life stripped the foundations from under our feet, leaving us suspended in terror, were we taught how to clear our minds and vision so we could become aware of the Invisible Reality in which we live, move, and have our being? Were we helped to persist until those invisible arms holding us became even more real and more certain than all the physical world around us? Or were we offered the scaffolding of therapeutic knowledge systems so that we could keep our feet fully grounded on visible soil and firmly back in our own hands?

In both the Old and New Testaments, my Bible uses the metaphor of the Word that tastes as sweet as honey in our mouths but then turns sour in the stomach. 1 Peter states that it is suffering that is going to do away with sin in our lives. Were we encouraged to take the bitter with the sweet, to accept inner suffering as the way that gospel medicine brings its life and health into our being? Or were we taught to savor the honeyed taste of Gospel words, sweet in the mouth, and then offered the therapeutic as an antidote so we need never know the bitter taste and inner suffering as those gospel words began to work their way into the heart of our being?

When the raging fires of our personal hells consumed us, were we taught how to enter the silence where someone could bring salvation to all that so badly festered and burned within? Or were we helped to white-wash over all that so badly festered and burned with assurances that we were saved, and then, for all that so badly festered and burned within, offered psycho-babble, more human, relative words?

Were we taught to walk by faith, or has it become the ever-increasing pattern of the evangelical church to stand at all those places where man has traditionally taken his first steps of faith and then just offered, instead, human knowledge systems? How much of the present evangelical church can still be defined as Christian, or to what degree has it just become pure Gnostic cult?

We live in a time when movies and books are exploiting apocalyptic imagery to create a doomsday atmosphere. Coming from a revivalist background where that same imagery was used liberally to scare people into the Kingdom, I am especially leery of adding to the popular speculation. However, since that time, innumerable writers have helped me to see past the literalist interpretations of my childhood and to see how the Bible hides its truths by means of metaphor, story, symbol, and allegory. Our literalist approach to the reading of the Bible, I discovered, was a fairly recent phenomenon. It came out of the scientific revolution. Before that, it was understood that it was not enough to read the Bible; one needed to learn how to read it. The Bible has so many ways of keeping its realities in mystery until we are ready to see them.

When we attempt to turn what is metaphorical, allegorical, or vision-ary into something literal, it loses its ability to instruct. The danger can be seen by looking at the Psalms and noting how God is repeatedly referred to as a rock. Now all primitive cultures were want to worship nature, and sacred stones were a part of that nature worship. A literalist could have justified his nature worship by means of the Psalms. By calling God a rock, however, the Psalmist was not being literal, but was revealing something of the characteristics of God that lie beyond the ability of language to cap-ture or express.

Having left a past where the Bible was plumbed for literalist end time clues, I have now come to approach the apocalyptic, metaphorical, and visionary language of the Bible as instruction for our present time. Apocalyptic language is not only about celestial secrets and seeing into the future; it is also about learning to see through to the essence of things. Apocalyptic imagery is an imaginative, visionary way of portraying other-worldly reality. Just because it is otherworldly, however, does not mean that it is futuristic or that it does not have this-worldly relevance. N. T. Wright explained the difference between "apocalypticism" and apocalyp-tic language when he wrote, "Apocalyptic language exploits the heaven/earth duality in order to draw attention to the heavenly signifi-cance of earthly events; apocalypticism exploits apocalyptic language to express a non-biblical dualism in which the heavenly world is good and the earthly bad."[465] The "apocalyticism" of the religious right is an attitude that is impatient with earthly limitations; it attempts to find clues that would allow us to pierce the veil and peer into God's mysteries. What were meant to be clues then become dogmatic weapons. Apocalyptic literature, in contrast, aims to accomplish the opposite. Once our imaginations are awakened by cosmic imagery, then we turn and see the eternal in all that is supremely normal and everyday. Far from polarizing reality into present time and end-of-the-world scenarios, it teaches us to see the cosmic and eternal that runs through the fabric of the present and earthy and normal. For example, I now cannot read my morning newspaper without realiz-ing that those apocalyptic horsemen are on the move; death, famine, bloodshed and conquest are the order of reality wherever man, not God, is establishing his Kingdom. I have personally been a member of the church at Laodicea, and chose it precisely because it was not too hot and not too cold, but just the right temperature for the comfort of my humanity. God could have told Daniel that Babylonia, Medo-Persia, Greece, and then Rome would be the chronological succession of the coming rulers in the land. God did not. He rather gave Daniel a vision of a lion, a bear, a leopard, and an unknown, terrifying beast. The vision revealed that God not only saw the visible time-bound realities of the successive kingdoms, but also their essence and characteristics. God-revealed history gave a point of view that was greater than the particularistic view of the individual residing within history.

In an attempt to see how apocalyptic language can reveal our present realities, it is perhaps an appropriate time to look at one of the major apocalyptic images—that of the Antichrist. Considering the religious right's absorption with end time scenarios, it is surprising how many biblical clues they choose to ignore.

CLUE #1: From my revivalist, literalist background, the Antichrist was usually looked for as an individual. That, however, is not Scriptural. 1 John 2:18 claims, "Even now many Antichrists have come." Since the Antichrist was already in the church in New Testament times, it certainly cannot be an individual. Although an individual can become a manifestation of its power, it cannot be reduced to an individual. It has to be a hydra-headed, ever-present reality. As such, it becomes the challenge of each succeeding generation to perceive the current form in which it comes.

CLUE #2: The church has always looked for the Antichrist as the manifestation of evil, but that is naïve and unscriptural. Paul claimed, "Satan himself masquerades as an angel of light. It is not surprising, then, if his servants masquerade as servants of righteousness" (2 Corinthians 11:14, 15). Because of that, Paul Tillich reconsidered his own views of the Antichrist, coming to believe that the Antichrist comes as a perceived good; that may be the reason for its great seduction. Tillich wrote of the Antichrist, "In the very place where Christ is supposed to be represented, everything is done which stands against Christ."[466] At a place where we should be expected to receive the fruit of the completed, perfected, fulfilled work of God that Jesus won for us, something is allowed to stand that causes us to fall short.

CLUE #3: The book of Revelation does not mention the Antichrist, but it is thought that the Beast of chapter 13 represents the Antichrist. Plato (427-347 B.C.), in his *Republic Book VI*, had introduced the image of the beast to represent the mindless, conforming ways of mass humanity, which acts out of its collective prejudices and mass reactions rather than engendering personal quests for goodness and truth.

The Beast of Revelation is pictured as having multiple identities, as multi-headed, and as having multiple sources of power, again confirming the impression that it comes not as an individual but in multiple forms that need to be discerned. The Beast, the mob mentality, the collective unconscious; however one articulates the reality of mass humanity, it has a power that causes the writer of Revelation to ask, "'Who is like the beast? Who can make war against him?'" (Revelation 13:4). The mass of common humanity has a force that few can withstand.

Revelation 13:18 says that deciphering the number of the Beast "calls for wisdom. If anyone has insight, let him calculate the number of the beast, for it is man's number. His number is 666." The Antichrist "is man's number"; it is the purely human. It is that which has forfeited transcendence. It is when humanity has allowed itself to become the measure of all reality that it becomes the Beast. Humanity, at the peak of its rebellion, is allowed to become an autonomous being; both individually and collectively humanity becomes the Beast as it attempts to live in separation from God.

It is with those images in mind that we can begin to understand the number ascribed to the Beast. What is hidden in the number 666? To begin with, the numbers are multiples of 3. The number 3 is the divine number. When the Bible wants to emphasize something, it repeats or multiplies a number. If one, for example, would want to emphasize Divinity, then one would take the divine number, expand it to the divine measurement, or three times: 333. If one would want to express the completed, perfected, fulfilled work of Divinity, then one would take the divine number, expand it by the measure of Divinity, and then multiply it by the measure of Divinity to express the work of Divinity completed, perfected, fulfilled: 999. It is the Trinity of Trinities. Joseph Campbell, the man who became the expert on ancient mythologies, wrote, "Nine is the number of the descent of the divine power into the world."[467]

What, however, if the divine number measured out to divine measurement but then stretching towards completion fell just short? Then one would have the number 666, the number of the Antichrist. If one only focused on the good inherent in that number (after all, the Antichrist number contains the divine number—3—repeated and enlarged), then one might not even notice that the full descent of divine power into the world has been blocked. Divinity, or the action of God, has been prevented from entering history.

So what is the application and relevance for us? Look at the role that the therapeutic plays in the church. The problem with bringing the therapeutic into the church is not that it cannot aid us with life's challenges— the problem is that it can. Human effectiveness can block divine power that seeks to enter history. Instead of the human being becoming a tablet on which God inscribes a story revealing Himself, the human instead exists as a self-created, autonomous being that authenticates itself. It becomes "the number of man": a human, not a divine story.

CLUE #4: The Scriptures teach the Antichrist is that which denies the fleshly nature of Jesus (1 John 4:2; 2 John 7). How can human flesh and Divinity so coexist that neither nature is destroyed but rather both are revealed in their perfection? Those who think that to be a merely abstract or theological question have not yet discovered the enigma of their own existence. As beings partially animal but with a spark of the divine implanted in our breasts, we struggle to understand the enigma of our existence—who are we? Jesus offers the clue.

For Jews, the idea of God taking on flesh and coming in a human form was blasphemous. God was too holy to be abased by the human.

Even now we try to get rid of the offense by offering a spiritualized salvation that bypasses our flesh. Jesus can be the answer to the spiritual side of our being, but by spiritualizing the gospel, His relevance to our earthly existence is limited. It is the Incarnation, however, that lies at the heart of the gospel. The Incarnation re-affirms the gospel's recurrent theme, that the means whereby God has chosen to reveal Himself is by human flesh living in human history.

The Incarnation, however, is a hard reality to grasp and keep hold of. Christianity itself has been puzzled and offended by its message. When Maximus the Confessor, a monk who lived in the seventh century, dared to suggest that Jesus had so "emptied himself" that he had a human will, he had his right hand cut off and his tongue pulled out of his mouth so that he could no longer spread such heresy. That, however, did not clarify the confusion.

The history of Christianity is filled with heresies that confused the message of the Incarnation. An early heresy called Cerenthianism decided that the divine entered Jesus at baptism, only to leave Him before His death. The Docetists, another early heresy, claimed that Jesus only seemed to be human; in actual fact God, in Jesus, came disguised as a human. Appollinaiarians decided that Jesus could not have had a human soul. Sabellians claimed that God could only exist in one "mode" at a time, so in Jesus, the difference between God and Son disappeared. In contrast, the Arians claimed Father and Son were of completely different substances. The Ebionites thought Jesus was an ordinary human indwelt by God's power upon baptism. The Photinians said there was no Divinity in Jesus and the Manicheans argued that there was no humanity in Him.

The enigma of Jesus casts its shadow over our own lives. We, too, were created as beings with two natures. Who are we? It was because of the conflict over Jesus' nature that in 451 A.D. the Council of Chalcedon was summoned. Over six hundred bishops met to argue over the two natures of Jesus. They did not come to a consensus of belief, but rather, created a careful compromise statement wherein the two natures of Jesus were kept carefully separate. The bishops from the east were strongly opposed. They believed the document again opened up a crevasse whereby the divine and the human were separated. What they insisted on was that in Jesus, "the divine and human had been joined in Christ in a manner that transfused the human person of Christ with the divine, to such an extent that even the touch of His fingers was sufficient to bring healing to the sick."[468] Peter Brown, in his book *The Rise of Western Christendom,* wrote about how, ten months after the Council of Chalcedon, one of its opponents, the Bishop of Maiouma, was presiding over the communion service when blood rushed from the broken loaf of bread and covered the altar. He turned to see Christ, who said, "Break the bread, bishop... I have done this for my glory, that everyone may know where the truth is and who are they who hold the orthodox faith."[469]

The Antichrist works in that confusion over humanity and Divinity; what the Antichrist does is create and maintain a bifurcation of being. It prevents the divine from being revealed in the human. Gospel truths are instead relegated to some nebulous spiritual realm, while "hard" knowledge (such as that offered by psychology) is allowed to direct our tangible human lives. The truth of the Incarnation is destroyed. Jesus is no longer Lord and exemplar and guide and actual life for our human natures, but he becomes, rather, an assigned answer to some spiritual aspect of our being. His uniqueness no longer comes from having incarnated Divinity in a human body. His relevance to our human lives is instead blurred.

Our bodies, however, are "an essential part of who we are, and no redemption that omits it is full redemption."[470] Redemption and resurrection and salvation are first of all realities that we begin to discover in this world in our human bodies. They are not realities that can be channeled into some spiritual realm while we bring in the therapeutic to care for our "real" lives: our lives of broken relationships, depression, and frightening passions. The therapeutic may feel it is helping us towards the ends to which the gospel would bring us—towards healing and wholeness—but by turning us into ourselves rather than helping us focus on God, it actually blocks the descent of divine power into the world.

CLUE # 5: The name of the Antichrist is itself a clue. It is that which goes against the work of Christ. Jesus came to be mediator between God and man; what he mediated was a new way of relationship. Jesus revealed the Fatherhood of God. We are defined eternally by our relationship to God here in life on earthly soil. Through Jesus, God offered His final, completed, and perfected revelation of Himself as loving Father to our fallen humanity. When spiritual realities are allowed to become separated from our tangible day-to-day existences, then our relationship to and experience of God also changes. God is no longer Father to our humanity.

How can a church claim to be Christian if it has no human stories of God to tell? Why do churches that claim to be bearers of God's final revelation have so little evidence of God's loving Presence? I think one of the major reasons is because we have allowed knowledge to replace faith as the way we fashion our lives.

Psychology is not an evil; it can be a good. It, however, becomes an evil when it is allowed to place itself where it has no right to be. To a large extent, the therapeutic just shadows and mimics the divine life. It offers salvation by means of knowledge rather than the fearful walk of faith. It offers us self-knowledge without the pain and deep sorrow of repentance. It offers us wholeness without costly dying. It offers us integration without the cross. It offers autonomy rather than learned and holy dependence. It allows the fortifying of the ego to replace the way that allows us to find ourselves in God. It offers us self-realization without the fearful act of self-surrender. It places the knowing ego at the center of one's personal universe, instead of calling us to walk the dark path into unknowing and mystery. It offers us the "professionalization" of relationships, helping us avoid costly commitment. If we are not careful, we could end up with lives so autonomous, so self-realized, so fully individuated, that when Jesus came announcing the Kingdom as here, it has arrived; when the Bible defines the sons of God as those who are led by the Spirit of God; when Jesus says, "My sheep listen to my voice," we may not even be aware that we have no experiential knowledge as to what the Gospel is actually talking about. We have fallen short of the final, perfected, and completed revelation of God that Jesus won for us.

Whenever the church stands at those places of our inner chaos and disorganization and uses the opportunity to reintegrate life around the ego and our own ways of understanding rather than helping us reorder life on a higher level, then that church may be functioning as the Antichrist.

Whenever the church stands at our places of brokenness and helps us to adjust to the situation we find ourselves in rather than using the situation to help us adjust our lives to the Reality of God, then that church is functioning as the Antichrist.

Whenever the church stands at those places of our potential awakening or rebirth and functions not as the midwife of potential new life, but instead offers knowledge that allows us to hold on to the supremacy of the ego, then that church is functioning as the Antichrist.

Whenever a minister stands with us in our emotional turmoil and encourages us not to open, expand our lives out towards the wide horizons of Gospel life; does not encourage us to use the opportunity to reform ourselves to the plumb line given in the Gospel, but rather allows subjectivity to reign—"If that's how you feel, then that is the truth"—then that minister is functioning as the Antichrist. Whenever the priest/parishioner relationship becomes "client-centered," driven by the client's inner devices and the client's inner wisdom rather than by an external vision, then that priest has given up his function as mediating the life of God to man and is functioning as the Antichrist.

Hildegard of Bingen (1098-1179), in one of her visions, has the devil whispering to the soul, "Who are you, and whence do you come?"[471] Whenever the church succumbs to the temptation to offer us self-knowledge, to help us ask and then answer questions of our identity outside of reference to God, then it is in danger of functioning as the Antichrist.

The church exists for one purpose only—to mediate the life of God to its suffering parishioners. A church that gets distracted and decides to help people find easier paths, or that decides to get into the business of helping people manage without God, is in danger of becoming the church of the Antichrist.

Thanks to the introduction of the therapeutic into our seminaries and colleges, we seem to be raising a generation of clergy who can help us live successfully and competently without God, but who cannot teach us how to live with God; who can help us listen to our "inner child" and our feelings and desires, but cannot teach us how to listen to God; and who can help us become aware of the unconscious and how it controls our life, but cannot help us become aware of the God who comes alongside and also wants control of that life.

Pharisaism and Gnosticism are not mutually incompatible. In a sense, they are exactly the same thing: they give to reason and knowledge a supremacy that allows faith no room to grow. They both create intellectual boxes so small that mystery is destroyed and the Eternal Spirit is squelched for want of compatible soil. If one were to reduce knowledge of God to the ideas that one holds about God instead of the knowledge that arises out of intimacy and relationship (Pharisaism); if one were to stand at all those places where God is needed as Living Reality, not as an idea, and then in that position help those in need to live by therapeutic self-knowledge rather than by faith (Gnosticism), then one could have developed one of the most foolproof systems ever for keeping people safe from a Living God.

If I now had to describe the relationship between reason and faith, I would explain it by means of an analogy—that of the sailboat at sea. The ability of a sailboat to keep its balance and stay upright while driven by forceful winds will depend to a certain extent on the depth and strength of its keel. The keel on a sailboat is the structural component that runs along the base and can extend downwards in order to increase its stability. Our expression "to keel over" gives evidence to the relationship between the keel and stability. Reason and knowledge, I believe, are the means whereby we create a keel capable of keeping our craft steady and upright. It is not, however, what the experience of sailing is about. When Jesus described the experience of being born again, he likened it to being awakened into the awareness of a wind blowing across our being, a wind that we can be receptive to and follow. The failing of much of modern theology and religion is that they turn religion into an effort to create a deeper and deeper keel without ever having the courage or faith to take that sailboat out to sea. Left in dry-dock, that keel functions as nothing more than dead weight. However, one of the reasons we do not have more sailors is because of the examples of those who thought they could brave the sea and winds without the development of an adequate keel and "keeled over." Faith and reason were meant to work in harmony.

At both crisis periods in my life where faith seemed threatened and then almost destroyed by human knowledge, I actually arrived back in a place where faith not only gained supremacy but was actually strengthened and grew. What my long journey finally revealed to me was that faith is not the opposite of reason; it is actually what keeps reason and our intellectual endeavors from getting derailed; it safely grounds our intellect to keep it in harmony with the larger universe that we will never completely understand. Faith is also the framework that can give form and meaning to all the knowledge we gather; it is what turns information into wisdom. Faith is the light that enlightens all our intellectual groping, for in this world, no matter how brilliant our minds and scholastic achievements, we can never see more than partially and darkly.

The greatest paradigm shift I have ever had to make in my life was when I finally realized that our reasoning, intellectual faculty is not our highest faculty—faith is. We were created with souls or hearts that can know much more that our minds are ever capable of grasping:

> It is the heart which experiences God, and not reason.
> This, then, is faith: God felt by the heart, not by reason (Pascal, Pensee 278).

> The most beautiful thing we can experience is the mysterious. It is the source of all true art and science…. To know that what is impenetrable to us really exists, manifesting itself as the highest wisdom and the most radiant beauty, which our dull faculties can comprehend only in the most primitive forms—this knowledge, this feeling, is at the center of true religiousness.[472] (Einstein)

> For it is with your heart that you believe (Romans 10:10)

CHAPTER SEVEN

THE

BANKRUPTCY

I have spent much of my life struggling with deep depression. My husband once bleakly observed that my moods seemed to vary all the
way from mild depression to severe depression. Darkness was my
closest friend (Psalm 88:18).

There came a time, however, when the darkness took over. With a
mind entertaining thoughts such as how to best exit this world gently,
being allured by the temptation of a planned exit, I happened to come
across a book by an author whose life had also hit a dead end, but who had
discovered that what seemed to be the end of life actually revealed a doorway into another life. The clue to entering that other life, she claimed, lay
in surrendering one's life with all of its details up to a Living God.
Fascinated, I turned to face the dark that was oppressing me and wondered
what I had to lose. It later occurred to me that there were two equally
frightening forms of suicide: to take one's own life, or to relinquish it to a
Higher Power. The former choice would leave me with one last grand gesture of self-assertion; I could choose the terms of my exit. The second
choice would take a leap of faith and trust that seemed equally suicidal considering the image of God that I had been raised with. Nevertheless, I chose
the latter option. To the God who just might exist beyond that overwhelming darkness, and with all the generosity that can only come when one is

not really offering anything but one's last burned ashes, I turned and said, "You can have this life if you want it." To my very great surprise, there seemed to be someone there, someone who addressed me.

What is perhaps not surprising was that my problems were not thereby eradicated, but rather, compounded. An experience of God's Presence can raise more questions than it answers. However, what was brought into my life from that moment on was the new phenomenon of hope. Hope, but also the overwhelming need to understand who and what that hope was based on.

We humans are sign-making beings. We require words, concepts, and a framework to secure the space that we inhabit. We cannot live as pure spiritual beings. To keep our equilibrium, or even our sanity, we need some paradigm of thought or vision of the true that can keep us balanced. However, what I realized was that I did not have the right words to understand life before that God; I did not have the right theology or conceptual paradigm needed in order to understand or survive or learn how to follow.

As I, in my fearful, stumbling way attempted to follow and to keep from closing off the doors of perception, someone increasingly "spoke" into the various parts of my life. I watched in growing horror as all of life as I had known it began to unravel. That "Someone," that inner voice, seemed to warn me that it would be very dark for a while, but then filled my life with promises and expected me to trust. I, however, had never trusted anyone I could see in my life. I certainly couldn't trust someone I couldn't see. I began to entertain dark thoughts about some cosmic monster that plays with us.

I did eventually grope my way to a place of peace and certainty. I did eventually come to see that life as I had known it—life as an unbearable burden—had needed to be taken apart so that it could eventually be returned as special gift. I did eventually come to understand that the Divine Hand that I had initially feared and had considered to be too heavy was actually the hand of Perfect Love; Perfect Love slowly, painfully straightening what had been so badly broken and deformed. At the time, however, I just felt like the fox in Aesop's fable who, climbing a fence and finding himself falling, grabbed hold of a brier-bush to break his fall. Landing hard, but now with paws ripped and bleeding, he turned to that brier-bush and said, "I turned to you for help and you have made me worse off than I was before."[473] Life stopped, as I needed to know who it was that had addressed me.

And how could I have said that someone "spoke" into my life when I heard nothing at all? I was a rationalist who could only trust what my mind could comprehend. How could I even say that someone had "addressed" me when that apprehension lay on a different epistemological plane than all my other perceptions of reality?

Martin Buber, in his classic *I and Thou*, wrote that prayer is the sign that a religion has stayed true to the reality of God, who works through religious forms. Religions, he wrote, "Live so long as it [true prayer] lives in them. Degeneration of the religions means degeneration of prayer in them."[474]

In the same vein, the philosopher William James listed prayer as the heart of living faith; remove the heart from any living organism and one will not be left with anything more than lifeless form. William James quotes, and then assents, to Auguste Sabatier's description of prayer:

> Prayer is religion in act; that is, prayer is real religion. It is prayer that distinguishes the religious phenomena from such similar or neighboring phenomena as purely moral or aesthetic sentiment. Religion is nothing if it be not the vital act by which the entire mind seeks to save itself by clinging to the principle from which it draws its life. This act is prayer, by which term I understand no vain exercise of words, no mere repetition of certain sacred formulae, but the very movement itself of the soul, putting itself in a personal relation of contact with the mysterious power of which it feels the presence.... Wherever this interior prayer is lacking, there is no religion.[475]

One writer that I respect gave her book on prayer the title of *Clinging*.[476] Buffeted by what the world is doing to us, struggling with unruly passions, threatened by doubts, overcome by fear, unable to come up with even the words with which to cry out to God, all we are capable of mustering is an act of clinging to that life principle from which to be separated from we now recognize as the meaning of death.

John V. Taylor, the once Bishop of Winchester, wrote,

> Traditional religious instruction has so stressed the importance of prayer that we are prone to lose sight of the fact that Christian prayer was such a new experience for the church in New Testament times that it could properly be ranked as one of the signs of the new manhood of Jesus . . . . We tend to read back into the Old Testament and into the devotional patterns of other faiths those meanings which Jesus gave to the word 'prayer', and so conceal the fact that what was so characteristic of Jesus is almost unique amid the formal recitations which are the commonplace of religion everywhere else, including most of the churches.[477]

If prayer was so vital to true religion, then how could I, a person so steeped in life-long religious observance, be left feeling so terrified and confused and lost at having discovered its reality? I needed firm ground to stand on. I needed words, stories, traditions, and adequate theology.

As I looked back, I wondered what I had been trusting in. George Bernard Shaw once quipped, "If you cannot have what you believe in, then believe in what you have." I suppose prayer, for me, had become spiritual monologue, soliloquies, or my daily job list sent up to some celestial servant. Prayer seemed to be the celestial blessings we called down on all we had so proudly accomplished for God, and if God just finished up what we had so proudly accomplished for Him then we would split the glory fifty-fifty. Prayer had become magic, an attempt to tap into God's power. Prayer had become a quiet place of peace away from life that we could access. In my world, I could go on and on. But as I went back through the history of Christianity, it seemed that prayer was the key that had been discovered whenever the church had become vibrantly alive. The rediscovery of prayer seemed to precede every period of revival, every period of renewal, every journey into mature faith. And prayer that was allowed to become effective and real always seemed to be defined the same way—prayer as nothing other, nothing less, than man's ability to live in awareness of God; man's ability to live in communion and in communication with one's Creator. Prayer was man's ability, through the reality of the Holy Spirit, to become awakened into awareness, to become attentive, and then to live in response and in co-creation with God. Prayer was the realization that, as A.W. Tozer articulated it, "God is speaking. He is, by His nature, continuously articulate. He fills the world with His speaking voice."[478]

God and prayer. That is how my odyssey began. The need to find some person or place where I could be helped to understand God and prayer formed the goal of the journey. At first, the precipitate of that journey was anger, a most un-Christ-like anger as I began to notice what we in the church had done to the realities I had need of. One example was an encounter I had with a pastor's wife. In the sheer frustration of hearing how a ministerial couple were handling a woman struggling with deep depression I, outraged, asked the minister's wife why they were referring all their people to therapists. What, I asked, about God and prayer? When I was told, "That's what we're trying to get away from," I realized that I had a problem with anger. I am no longer unreasonably angry. I now realize that the ministerial couple, like so many of us, came from a religious background where "God" and "prayer" were toxic ideas inappropriately applied and mishandled in such a way that made the retreat to a safe intellectualism seem a necessary corrective. I realize it is hard serving a God who does not seem to be interested in pragmatism, effectiveness, or in helping one survive a vestry vote of confidence. I am glad I do not have to make my living off of the gospel. However, in rendering the church safe, sane, and hopelessly effective, we have also lost the only realities that justify its existence.

Seeking understanding of the reality of God and prayer became, for me, an obsession. Leaving the church that had become too modern for outdated applications of God and prayer to life, I began to wander from church to church to church, looking for someone who could help me. The more I searched, the more I began to realize the degree to which we have preferred to shift our focus away from gospel realities in order to make room for the world's easier answers.

Where, in our churches, do we now get our answers to the questions that were once fundamental to our humanity and to religion; the questions of : Who are we? What has gone wrong with us? What should we do about it? We know ourselves to be living east of Eden, we live with intimations of something that we have lost, but how do we journey home?

What we have done is gone to the world for answers to our unease and identity. We have brought into the church humanistic systems created by man, for man, and derived out of the study of man. We have forfeited the God-revealed answers to the riddle of our existence in order to embrace secular humanism's answers that seem much easier to accept. We have chosen systems of understanding that with our human eyes seem more immediate, tangible, concrete, and pragmatic. However, we, in our search for easier answers, have also, as in the time of Jeremiah (Jeremiah 2:13), been creating man-made cisterns that hold no Living Water.

Paul Johnson, in his book *A History of Christianity,* wrote of the spread of Gnosticism in the second century—until our own time the greatest Gnostic century. He wrote, "'Gnosticism' is a 'knowledge' religion—that is what the word means—which claims to have an inner explanation of life. Thus it was, and indeed still is a spiritual parasite which used other religions as a 'carrier'. Christianity fitted into this role very well.... The most dangerous Gnostics were those who had, intellectually, thought their way quite inside Christianity, and then produced a variation which wrecked the system."[479]

Having come, thanks to the Enlightenment, to regard reason as supreme and its findings as sacrosanct, we again became susceptible to Gnosticism. As we allowed the therapeutic to offer us explanations as to our inner workings, we became people of two gospels: one gospel for some nebulous spiritual realm that we claim we "believe" in and another for the "real" world that we live in. Much of modern Christianity just exists as pure Gnostic cult.

However, if we are ever again going to know the "spiritual" realities revealed in the gospel, then it is going to be through and in our palpable, physical existences. A "salvation" that bypasses or is not about our human natures is not Christian salvation. The nature that the therapeutic exists to study is the nature that Christianity exists to reveal and redeem.

BIBLIOGRAPHY

Aelred of Rievaulx, *The Mirror of Charity,* Kalamazoo, Michigan, Cistercian Publications, 1990.

Aikman, David, *Hope: The Heart's Great Quest,* Ann Arbor, Michigan, Servant Publications, 1995.

Armstrong, Karen, *A History of God,* New York, Ballantine Books, 1994.

Armstrong, Karen, *Buddha,* London, Phoenix Paperback, 2002.

Armstrong, Karen, *The Battle For God,* New York, Ballantine Books, 2000.

Armstrong, Louise, *And They Call It Help: The Psychiatric Policing of America's Children,* Reading, Massachusetts, Addison-Wesley Publishing Co., 1993.

Augustine, *Confessions,* New York, Penguin Books, 1961.

Augustine, *The City of God,* New York, Random House, 2000.

Barrett, William, *Death of the Soul: From Descartes to the Computer,* New York, Anchor Press, 1987.

Barth, Karl, *The Holy Spirit and the Christian Life,* Louisville, Kentucky, John Knox Press, 1993.

Battle, James, *Self-Esteem: The New Revolution,* Edmonton, James Battle and Associates, 1990.

Becker, Ernest, *Escape From Evil,* New York, The Free Press, 1975.

Becker, Ernest, *The Denial of Death,* New York, The Free Press, 1973.

Bellah, Robert N. et al, *Habits of the Heart,* Berkeley, University of California Press, 1996.

Berdyaev, Nicolas, *Spirit and Reality,* London, The Centenary Press, 1939.

Bernard of Clairvaux: *The Classics of Western Spirituality,* Mahwah, New Jersey, 1987.

Bibby, Reginald W., *Restless Churches,* Kelowna, Wood Lake Books, 2004.

Bill W., *Alcoholics Anonymous Comes of Age,* New York, Alcoholics Anonymous World Services, Inc., 1979.

Bloom, Anthony, *Beginning to Pray,* New York, Paulist Press, 1970.

Boisen, Anton T., *The Exploration of the Inner World: A Study of Mental Disorder and Religious Experience,* New York, Harper & Brothers, 1962.

Bondi, Roberta, *To Pray & To Love,* Minneapolis, Fortress Press, 1991.

Bonhoeffer, Dietrich, *Creation and Fall,* London, SCM Press, 1960.

Bonhoeffer, Dietrich, *Letters and Papers from Prison,* New York, Macmillan Publishing Co., 1971.

Bonhoeffer, Dietrich, *Life Together,* HarperSanFrancisco, division of HarperCollins, 1954.

Bonhoeffer, Dietrich, *The Cost of Discipleship,* New York, Macmillan Publishing Co., 1961.

Borg, Marcus J., and Wright, N.T., *The Meaning of Jesus: Two Visions,* HarperSanFrancisco, 2000.

Borg, Marcus, *Meeting Jesus Again for the First Time,* HarperSanFrancisco, 1995.

Bounds, E.M., *Power Through Prayer,* edited by Penelope Stokes, Minneapolis, World Wide Publications, 1989.

Brand M.D., Dr. Paul and Yancey, Philip, *Pain: The Gift Nobody Wants,* New York, HarperCollins, 1993.

Breggin M.D., Peter R, *Toxic Psychiatry,* New York, St. Martin's Press, 1991.

Brown, Michael L., *How Saved Are We?,* Shippensburg, PA, Destiny Image Publishers, 1999.

Brown, Peter, *The Rise of Western Christendom,* Massachusetts, Blackwell Publishers, Inc., 1997.

Buber, Martin, *I and Thou,* New York, Macmillan Publishing Co., 1958.

Buber, Martin, *Meetings,* La Salle, Illinois, Open Court Publishing, 1973.

Buchanen, Mark, *Your God Is Too Safe,* Sisters, Oregon, Multnomah Publishers, 2001.

Cahill, Thomas, *Sailing the Wine-dark Sea,* New York, Nan A. Talese, Doubleday, 2003.

Campbell, Joseph with Moyers, Bill, *The Power of Myth,* New York, Doubleday, 1988.

Campolo, Tony, *Let Me Tell You a Story,* W Publishing Group, 2000.

Caplan, Paula J., *They Say You're Crazy: How the World's Most Powerful Psychiatrists Decide Who's Normal,* Reading, Massachusetts, Perseus Books, 1995.

Carretto, Carlo, *The God Who Comes,* London, Darton, Longman & Todd, 1974.

Chambers, Oswald, *My Utmost for His Highest,* Grand Rapids, Michigan, Discovery House Publishers, 1992.

Chesterton, G.K., *Saint Francis of Assisi,* New York, Image Books, Doubleday, 1990.

Chesterton, G.K., *The Everlasting Man,* San Francisco, Ignatius Press, 1993.

Chittester, Joan, *The Fire in These Ashes,* Franklin, Wisconsin, Sheed and Ward, 1995.

Chittester, Joan, *The Heart of Flesh,* Grand Rapids, William B. Eerdmans Publishing Co., 1998.

Clapp, Rodney, *Tortured Wonders: Christian Spirituality for People, Not Angels,* Grand Rapids, Michigan, Brazos Press, 2005.

Clement, Olivier, *The Roots of Christian Mysticism,* New York, New City Press, 1995.

Coles, Robert, *The Secular Mind,* Princeton, Princeton University Press, 1999.

Conyers, A.J., *Eclipse of Heaven,* Downers Grove, Illinois, Intervarsity Press, 1992.

Cox, Harvey, *Fire From Heaven,* Reading, Addison-Wesley Publishing Co., 1995.

Crabb, Larry, *The Pressure's Off,* Colorado, WaterBrook Press, 2002.

Darling, Frank C., *The Restoration of Christian Healing,* Boulder, Colorado, Vista Publications, 1992.

Dawn, Marva J., *Reaching Out Without Dumbing Down,* Grand Rapids, Michigan, William B. Eerdmans Publishing Company, 1995.

De Caussade, Jean-Pierre, *The Sacrament of the Present Moment,* HarperSanFrancisco, division of HarperCollins, 1989.

Dryness, William A., *How Does America Hear the Gospel?,* Grand Rapids, Michigan, William B. Eerdmans Publishing Company, 1989.

Dunn, James D.G., *Jesus and the Spirit,* Grand Rapids, Michigan, William B. Eerdmans Publishing Company, 1997.

Edwards, Jonathan, *Religious Affections,* Portland, Multnomah Press, 1984.

Elchaninow, Alexander, *The Diary of a Russian Priest,* New York, St. Vladimir's Seminary Press, 1982.

Eldredge, John, *The Journey of Desire,* Nashville, Thomas Nelson Publishers, 2000.

Eliade, Mircea, *Myths, Dreams, and Mysteries,* New York, Harper Torchbooks, 1960.

Ellul, Jacques, *The Humiliation of the Word,* Grand Rapids, Michigan, Eerdmans Publishing Co., 1985.

Ellul, Jacques, *The Meaning of the City,* Grand Rapids, Michigan, Eerdmans Publishing, 1970.

Erlandson, Charles, editor, *F.B. Meyer: The Best From All His Works,* Nashville, Thomas Nelson Publishers, 1988.

Farber, Leslie H., *The Ways of the Will,* New York, Harper & Row, 1966.

Farley, Edward, *Deep Symbols,* Valley Forge, Pennsylvania, Trinity Press International, 1996.

Farrer, Austin, *Saving Belief,* New York, Morehouse-Barlow Co., 1965.

Ferm, Robert O., *The Psychology of Christian Conversion,* Westwood, New Jersey, Fleming H. Revell Company, MCMLIX.

Fine, Cordelia, *A Mind of Its Own,* New York, W.W. Norton & Company, 2006.

Finney, Charles G., Power, *Passion, & Prayer,* Gainseville, Florida, Bridge-Logos, 2004.

Forsyth, P.T., *Positive Preaching and Modern Mind,* London, Hodder and Stoughton, 1907.

Forsyth, P.T., *This Life And The Next,* London, Independent Press, 1946.

Fowler, James, *Stages of Faith,* HarperSanFrancisco, division of HarperCollins Publishers, 1995.

Frankl, Viktor E., *The Unconscious God,* New York, Simon and Schuster, 1975.

Friedman, Maurice, *Encounter on the Narrow Ridge,* New York, Paragon House, 1991.

Frye, *The Great Code,* Toronto, Academic Press, 1982.

Furedi, Frank, *Therapy Culture,* London, Routledge, 2004.

Gallagher, Winnifred, *Working on God,* New York, Random House, 1999.

Gallup, George H., and Jones, Timothy, *The Saints Among Us,* Harrisburg, PA, BSC LITHO, 1992.

Gilbert, Daniel, *Stumbling on Happiness,* New York, Alfred A. Knopf, 2006.

Grant, R.M., *Gnosticism and Early Christianity,* New York, Columbia University Press, 1966.

Guardini, Romano, *The Lord,* London, Longmans, 1959.

Harrold, Charles Frederick, editor, *A Newman Treasury,* New Rochelle, New York, Arlington House Publishers, 1975.

Herman, E., *Creative Prayer,* Santa Fe, Sun Books Publishing, 1995.

Herman, E., *The Meaning and Value of Mysticism,* New York, Books for Libraries Press, 1971.

Herrick, James A., *The Making of the New Spirituality,* Downers Grove, Illinois, InterVarsity Press, 2003.

Heschel, Abraham Joshua, *God in Search of Man: A Philosophy of Judaism,* New York, The Noonday Press, 1996.

Hildegaard of Bingen: *The Classics of Western Spirituality,* Mahwah, New Jersey, Paulist Press, 1990.

Hillman, James and Ventura, Michael, *We've Had a Hundred Years of Psychotherapy and the World's Getting Worse,* New York, HarperCollins Publishers, 1992.

Hilton, Walter, *The Ladder of Perfection,* London, Penguin Books, 1988.

Hoffman, Edward, editor, *The Wisdom of Carl Jung,* New York, Citadel Press Books, Published by Kensington Publishing Cop., 2003.

Holifield, E. Brooks, *A History of Pastoral Care in America,* Nashville, Abingdon Press, 1984.

Holland, Bernard, editor, Baron Friedrich Von Hugel: *Selected Letters,* London, J.M. Dent & Sons, 1933.

Hugel, Baron Friedrich von, *Essays and Addresses on the Philosophy of Religion,* London, J.M. Dent & Sons, 1924.

Hugel, Baron Friedrich Von, *Eternal Life,* Edinburgh, T. & T. Clark, 1913.

Hugel, Baron Friedrich von, *The Mystical Element of Religion,* New York, Crossroads Publishing, 1999.

Hunter, James Davison, *The Death of Character,* New York, Basic Books, 2000.

Huxley, Aldous, *Brave New World,* Glasgow, Collins Publishing, 1977.

Huxley, Aldous, *The Perennial Philosophy,* New York, HarperCollins Publishers, 2004.

James, William, *The Varieties of Religious Experience,* New York, Collier Macmillan Publishers, 1961.

Johnson, Paul, *A History of Christianity,* New York, Macmillan Publishing Co., 1976.

Jones, Alan, *Exploring Spiritual Direction,* HarperSanFrancisco, division of HarperCollins, 1982.

Jones, Alan, *The Soul's Journey,* HarperSanFrancisco, division of HarperCollins, 1995.

Jones, Rufus M. editor, *The Journal of George Fox,* Richmond, Indiana, Friends United Press, 1983.

Jung, C. G., *Memories, Dreams, Reflections,* London, Collins and Routledge & Kegan Paul, 1964.

Jung, Carl, *Modern Man In Search of a Soul,* in the Bollingen Series XX, Psychology and Religion: West and East, Princeton, Princeton University Press, 1989.

Kavanaugh, Keiren O.C.D. and Rodriguez, Otilio, O.C.D. translators, *The Collected Works of St. Theresa of Avila,* Washington, D.C., ICS Publications, 1987.

Keating, Thomas, *Open Mind Open Heart,* New York, Continuum Publishing Co., 1997.

Kierkegaard, Soren, *The Sickness Unto Death,* London, Penguin Books, 1989.

Kierkegaard, Soren, *Works Of Love,* New York, Harper & Row, 1962.

Kilpatrick, William Kirk, *Psychological Seduction,* New York, Thomas Nelson Publishers, 1983.

King Jr., Martin Luther, *Strength to Love,* Philadelphia, Fortress Press, 1981.

Kreeft, Peter, *Three Philosophies Of Life,* San Francisco, Ignatius Press, 1989.

L'Engle, Madeleine, *The Irrational Season,* HarperSanFrancisco, division of HarperCollins, 1977.

Lasch, Christopher, *The Culture of Narcissism,* New York, Warner Books, Inc.,1979.

Leech, Kenneth, *Spirituality and Pastoral Care,* Cambridge, Massachusetts, 1989.

Leech, Kenneth, *True Prayer,* New York, Harper & Row, 1986.

Lewis, C.S., *Mere Christianity,* London, HarperCollinsPublishers, 1997.

Lewis, C.S., *Reflections On The Psalms,* New York, Harcourt Brace Jovanovich, 1958.

Lewis, C.S., *The Four Loves,* Glasgow, Fontana Books, 1989.

Lewis, C.S., *The Screwtape Letters,* London, Collins, 1972.

Lindbergh, Anne Morrow, *Gift From the Sea,* New York, Random House, 1991.

Lindbergh, Charles A., *The Spirit of St. Louis,* New York, Ballantine Books, Inc, for Charles Scribner's Sons, 1971.

Lloyd-Jones, D. Martin, *Spiritual Depression,* Grand Rapids, Michigan, Wm. B. Eerdmans Publishing Company, 1992.

Macdonald, George, *An Anthology,* London, William Collins Sons & Co Ltd, 1990.

Macdonald, George, *Life Essential,* Wheaton, Illinois, Harold Shaw Publishers, 1974.

Macdonald, George, *The Curate's Awakening,* Minneapolis, Bethany House Publishers, 1993.

Macdonald, George, *Unspoken Sermons (Series Two),* Eureka, CA, Sunrise Book, Publishers, 1989.

Macdonald, Gordon, *Ordering Your Private World,* Nashville, Thomas Nelson Publishers, 2003.

MacIntyre, Alasdair, *After Virtue,* Notre Dame, Indiana, University of Notre Dame Press, 2002.

MacNutt, Francis, *The Nearly Perfect Crime,* Grand Rapids, Michigan, Chosen Books, 2005.

Marius, Richard, *Martin Luther,* Cambridge, Massachusetts, Harvard University Press, 1999.

Marty, Martin E., *A Cry of Absence,* Grand Rapids, Michigan, William B. Eerdmans Publishing Co., 1997.

Masson, Jeffrey Moussaieff, *Against Therapy,* New York, Macmillan Publishing Company, 1988.

McGinley, Phyllis, *Saint-Watching,* New York, The Viking Press, 1969.

McGinn, Bernard, *The Foundations of Mysticism,* Vol. 1, New York, Crossroad Publishing Co., 1994.

McNeil, John T., *A History of the Cure of Souls,* New York, Harper & Brothers, 1951.

Menninger, Karl, *Whatever Became of Sin?,* New York, Hawthorn Books, 1973.

Merton, Thomas, *Conjectures of a Guilty Bystander,* New York, Doubleday, 1989.

Merton, Thomas, *New Seeds of Contemplation,* New York, New Directions Publishing Corporation, 1972.

Merton, Thomas, *The Ascent to Truth,* San Diego, Harcourt Brace & Co., 1981.

Mirkin, Marsha, *The Women Who Danced by the Sea,* New York, Monkfish Book Publishing Co., 2004.

Moore, Thomas, *Care of the Soul,* New York, Harper Perennial 1994.

Moseley, J. Rufus, *Perfect Everything,* Saint Paul, Minnesota, Macalester Park Publishing Co., 1980.

Moskowitz, Eva, *In Therapy We Trust: America's Obsession With Self-Fulfillment,* Baltimore, The John Hopkins University Press, 2001.

Moulton, Philip, editor, *The Journal and Major Essays of John Woolman,* Richmond, Indiana, Friends United Press, 1989.

Mowrer, O. Hobart, *The Crisis in Psychiatry and Religion,* Princeton, New Jersey, D. Van Nostrand Company, Inc., 1961.

Mowrer, O. Hobart, editor, *Morality And Mental Health,* Chicago, Rand McNally & Company, 1967.

Moynihan, Ray and Cassels, Alan, *Selling Sickness,* Vancouver, Greystone Books, 2005.

Murdoch, Iris, *Metaphysics as a Guide to Morals,* Toronto, Penguin Books, 1993.

Neuhaus, Richard John, *As I Lay Dying,* New York, Basic Books, 2002.

Nicolson, Adam, *God's Secretaries,* New York, HarperCollins Publishers, 2003.

Niebuhr, H. Richard, *Christ & Culture,* HarperSanFrancisco, 2001.

Niebuhr, Reinhold, *The Self and the Dramas of History,* New York, Charles Scribner's Sons, 1955.

Noll, Richard, *The Aryan Christ,* New York, Random House, 1997.

Noll, Richard, *The Jung Cult,* Princeton, Princeton University Press, 1994.

Oates, Wayne E., *Christ and Selfhood*, New York, Association Press, 1961.

Otto, Rudolf, *The Idea of the Holy*, London, Oxford University Press, 1958.

Paternak, Boris, *Doctor Zhivago*, New York, Pantheon Books, 1991.

Patmore, Coventry, *The Rod, The Root, and the Flower*, Freeport, New York, Books For Libraries Press, 1968.

Peck, M. Scott, *The Road Less Traveled*, New York, Simon & Schuster, 1978.

Peterson, Eugene H. editor, *Stories for the Christian Year*, Toronto, Maxwell Macmillan Canada, 1992.

Peterson, Eugene, *Christ Plays in Ten Thousand Places*, Grand Rapids, Michigan, BakerBooks, 2003.

Philips, J.B., *Making Men Whole*, London, Collins, Fontana Books, 1955.

Pieper, Josef, *On Hope*, San Francisco, Ignatius Press, 1986.

Rahner, Karl, *Everyday Faith*, New York, Herder and Herder, 1968.

Raschke, Carl, A., *The Interruption of Eternity*, Chicago, Nelson-Hall, 1980.

Rieff, Philip, *The Triumph of the Therapeutic*, Chicago, The University of Chicago Press, 1987.

Riesman, David, *The Lonely Crowd*, New Haven, Connecticut, Yale University Press, 1967.

Robinson, H. Wheeler, *The Christian Experience of the Holy Spirit*, Great Britain, Fontana Books, 1962.

Rogers, Carl R., *On Becoming a Person*, New York, Houghton Mifflin Co., 1961.

Rollheiser, R., *The Holy Longing*, New York, Doubleday, 1999.

Roof, Wade Clark, *Spiritual Marketplace*, Princeton, Princeton University Press, 1999.

Rosenstock-Huessy, Eugen, *I am an Impure Thinker*, Norwich, Vermont, Argo Books, Inc., 1970.

Rupnik, Marko Ivan, *In the Fire of the Burning Bush*, Grand Rapids, Michigan, William B. Eerdmans Publishing Company, 2004.

Ruusbroec, Jan van, *The Spiritual Espousals*, Collegeville, Minnesota, The Liturgical Press, 1995.

Sabom, Michael B. M.D., *Recollections of Death*, London, Corgi Books, 1982.

Sayers, Dorothy, *The Whimsical Christian*, New York, Collier Books, 1987.

Shea, John, *Stories of God*, Chicago, Illinois, The Thomas More Press, 1978.

Shoemaker, Samuel, *With the Holy Spirit and With Fire*, London, Word Books, 1960.

Sine, Christine, M.D., *Sacred Rhythms*, Grand Rapids, Michigan, BakerBooks, 2003.

Soelle, Dorothee, *The Silent Cry*, Minneapolis, Fortress Press, 2001.

Solovyev, Vladimir, *God Man & the Church*, translated by Donald Attwater, Cambridge, Great Britain, James Clark & Co. Ltd., 1974.

St. John of the Cross, *Ascent of Mount Carmel*, Liguori, Missouri, Triumph Books, 1983.

Starbuck, Edwin, *The Psychology of Religion,* New York, Charles Scribner's Sons, 1903.

Steere, Douglas, *The Hardest Journey,* Wallingford, PA, Pendle Hill Publications, 1969.

Stein, Murray, editor, *Encountering Jung On Christianity,* Princeton, Princeton University Press, 1999.

Steiner, George, *Nostalgia for The Absolute,* Montreal, CBC Enterprises, 1983.

Stokes, Penelope J., E.M. Bounds: *Power Through Prayer,* Minneapolis, MN, World Wide Publications, 1989.

Szasz, Thomas S. M.D., *The Myth of Mental Illness,* New York, Harper & Row, 1974.

Taylor, John V., *The Go-Between God,* London, SCM Press, 1975.

Temple, William, *About Christ,* London, SCM Press, 1962.

Thielicke, Helmut, *The Waiting Father,* New York, Harpur & Row, 1959.

Tillich, Paul, *A History of Christian Thought,* New York, Simon and Schuster, 1968.

Tillich, Paul, *Dynamics of Faith,* New York, Harper Torchbooks, 1958.

Tillich, Paul, *The Courage To Be,* New Haven, Yale University Press, 1952.

Tobin, Frank, editor and translator, Henry Suso: *The Exemplar,* New York, Paulist Press, 1989.

Tocqueville, Alexis de, *Democracy In America,* New York, Doubleday, 1969.

Tournier, Paul, *Guilt & Grace,* New York, Harper & Row, 1962.

Tozer, A.W., *The Pursuit of God,* Camp Hill, Pennsylvania, Christian Publications, Inc., 1982.

Traherne, Thomas, *Centuries,* New York, Harper & Brothers, 1960.

Tugwell, Simon, *Prayer: Living With God,* Springfield, Illinois, Templegate Publishers, 1975.

Turner, James, *Without God, Without Creed,* Baltimore, The Johns Hopkins University Press, 1985.

Underhill, Evelyn, *Light of Christ,* London, Longmans, Green & Co., 1949.

Underhill, Evelyn, *Mysticism,* New York, Penguin Books, 1974.

Underhill, Evelyn, *The Ways of the Spirit,* New York, Crossroad, 1993.

Van Dusen, Henry P., *Spirit, Son and Father,* New York, Charles Scribner's Sons, 1958.

Vitz, Paul C., *Psychology As Religion,* Grand Rapids, Michigan, Eerdmans Publishing, 1994.

Walkenstein, Eileen, M.D., *Don't Shrink to Fit,* New York, Grove Press, Inc., 1976.

Walker 111 M.D., Sidney, *A Dose of Sanity,* New York, John Wiley & Sons, Inc., 1996.

Wallis, Jim, *God's Politics,* New York, HarperCollins Publishers, 2005.

Ward, Candace, editor, *Plato: Symposium and Phaedrus,* New York, Dover Publications, Inc., 1993.

Warmington, Eric H., and Rouse, Philip G., editors, *Great Dialogues of Plato,* Markham Ontario, Penguin Books, 1984.

Watter, Ethan and Ofshe, Richard, *Therapy's Delusions,* New York, Scribner, 1999.

Weil, Simone, *Gravity and Grace,* London, Ark Paperbacks, 1987.

Weil, Simone, *Waiting for God,* New York, Harper & Row, 1973.

Wells, David F., *No Place For Truth,* Grand Rapids, Michigan, Eerdmans Publishing Co., 1993.

Whyte, Alexander, *Lord, Teach Us To Pray,* Vancouver, Regent College Publishing, 1998.

Wiesel, Elie, *Sages and Dreamers,* New York, Simon & Schuster, 1991.

Wilken, Robert Louis, *The Spirit of Early Christian Thought,* New Haven, Yale University Press, 2003.

Willard, Dallas, *Renovation of the Heart,* Colorado Springs, Navpress, 2002.

Willard, Dallas, *The Divine Conspiracy,* HarperSanFrancisco, division of HarperCollins, 1998.

Wise, Robert L., *Quest For the Soul,* Nashville, Thomas Nelson Publishers, 1996.

Wood, Garth, *The Myth of Neurosis: Overcoming the Illness Excuse,* New York, Harper & Row, 1986.

Wright, N.T., *Jesus and the Victory of God,* Minneapolis, Fortress Press, 1996.

Wright, N.T., *The Millennium Myth,* Louisville, Kentucky, Westminster John Knox Press, 1999.

Wuthnow, Robert, *Acts of Compassion,* Princeton, Princeton University Press, 1991.

Yancey, Philip, *Rumours of Another World,* Grand Rapids, Zondervan, 2003.

Yankelovich, Daniel, *New Rules: Searching for Self-Fulfillment in a World Turned Upside Down,* New York, Bantam Books, 1982.

Yoder, John Howard, *The Politics of Jesus,* Grand Rapids, Michigan, William B. Eerdmans Publishing Co., 1975.

Zilbergeld, Bernie, *The Shrinking of America,* Boston, Little, Brown and Company, 1983.

ENDNOTES

[1]Kavanaugh, Kieren and Rodriguez, Otilio, translators, *The Collected Works of St. Theresa of Avilla,* (Washington, D.C., ICS Publications, 1976), 276-7.

[2]Marty, Martin E., *A Cry of Absence,* (Grand Rapids, Michigan, William B. Eerdmans Publishing Company, 1997), 183.

[3]James, William, *The Varieties of Religious Experience,* (New York, Collier Macmillan Publishers), 393.

CHAPTER 2: LIFE IN THE BORDERLAND

[4]A concept and title I took from Mark Buchanen's *Your God Is Too Safe,* (Sisters, Oregon, Multnomah Publishers, 2001), Part One.

[5]Wilken, Robert Louis, *The Spirit of Early Christian Thought,* (New Haven, Yale University Press, 2003), 9.

[6]Cahill, Thomas, *Sailing the Wine-dark Sea,* (New York, Nan A. Talese, imprint of Doubleday, 2003), 258.

[7]Bonhoeffer, Dietrich, *Creation and Fall,* (London, SCM Press, 1960), 44-5.

CHAPTER 3: THE HUMILIATION OF THE WORD

[8]Job 14:9.

[9]Stokes, Penelope J., editor, *E.M. Bounds: Power Through Prayer,* (Minneapolis, MN, World Wide Publications, 1989), 15-16.

[10]Van Dusen, Henry P., *Spirit, Son and Father,* (New York, Charles Scribner's Sons, 1958), 73-75.

[11]Ibid, 75.

[12]NIV Study Bible, (Grand Rapids, Michigan, Zondervan, 1984),1626.

CHAPTER 4: THE GREAT COMPROMISE

[13]Ferm, Robert O., *The Psychology of Christian Conversion,* (Westwood, New Jersey, Fleming H. Revell Company, MCMLIX), 201.

[14]Jones, Alan, *The Soul's Journey,* (HarperSanFrancisco, 1995), 42.

[15]Menninger, Karl, *Whatever Became of Sin?* (New York, Hawthorn Books,1973), 217-218.

[16]Hunter, James Davison, *The Death of Character,* (New York, Basic Books, 2000), 7.

[17]Ibid, 7.

[18]Willard Dallas, *The Divine Conspiracy,* (HarperSanFrancisco, 1998), 36.

[19]Vitz, Paul C., *Psychology As Religion*, (Grand Rapids, Michigan, Eerdmans Publishing,1994), 65.

[20]Dyrness, William A., *How Does America Hear the Gospel?* (Grand Rapids, Michigan, William B. Eerdmans Publishing Company, 1989), 102.

[21]Nicolson, Adam, *God's Secretaries,* (New York, HarperCollins*Publishers,* 2003), 153-4.

[22]Ibid, 236.

[23]Ibid, 236.

[24]Farber, Leslie H., *The Ways of the Will,* (New York, Harper & Row, 1966), 150.

²⁵Conyers, A.J., *The Eclipse of Heaven*, (Downers Grove, Illinois, InterVarsity Press, 1992), 193.

CHAPTER 4(A): LIFE: A SECULAR OF SACRED ENDEAVOUR?
²⁶Underhill, Evelyn, *Light of Christ*, (London, Longmans, Green &Co., 1949), 38.
²⁷Weil, Simone, *Gravity and Grace*, (London, Ark Paperbacks, 1987), 132.
²⁸Rahner, Karl, *Everyday Faith*, (New York, Herder and Herder, 1968), 88.
²⁹Chambers, Oswald, *My Utmost for His Highest*, (Grand Rapids, MI, Discovery House Publishers, 1992), Nov. 2.
³⁰Elchaninow, Alexander, *The Diary of A Russian Priest*, (New York, St. Vladimir's Seminary Press, 1982), 204.
³¹Eliade, Mircea, *Myths, Dreams, and Mysteries*, (New York, Harper Torchbooks, 1960),153.
³²Tillich, Paul, *Dynamics of Faith*, (New York, Harper Torchbooks, 1958), 1.
³³Sine, Christine, M.D., *Sacred Rhythms*, (Grand Rapids, Michigan, BakerBooks, 2003), 79.
³⁴Rupnik, Marko Ivan, *In the Fire of the Burning Bush*, (Grand Rapids, Michigan, William B. Eerdmans Publishing Company, 2004), 32.
³⁵Shea, John, *Stories Of God*, (Chicago, Illinois, The Thomas More Press,1978), 63.
³⁶As translated in Augustine, *The City of God*, (New York, Random House, 2000), 733.
³⁷Borg, Marcus J. and Wright, N.T., *The Meaning of Jesus: Two Visions*, (HarperSanFrancisco, 2000), 126.
³⁸Peterson, Eugene, *Christ Plays In Ten Thousand Places*, (Grand Rapids, Michigan, Wm. B. Eerdmans Publishing Co., 2005), 180.
³⁹quoted in Sine, Christine, M.D., *Sacred Rhythms*, (Grand Rapids, Michigan, BakerBooks, 2003), 108.

CHAPTER 4(B): REDUCTIONISM VERSUS MYSTERY
⁴⁰Moskowitz, Evan S., *In Therapy We Trust: America's Obsession with Self-fulfillment*, (Baltimore, John Hopkins University Press,2001), 1.
⁴¹Ibid, 283.
⁴²Bullfinch's *Greek and Roman Mythology*, (New York, Dover Publications, Inc. 2000), 121.
⁴³Walkenstein, M.D., *Eileen, Don't Shrink to Fit!* (New York, Grove Press, Inc., 1976), 10.
⁴⁴Coles, Robert, *Migrants, Sharecroppers, Mountaineers*, (Toronto, Little, Brown and Company, 1971), 26.
⁴⁵quoted in Yancey, Philip, *Soul Survivor*, (Large edition, New York, Random House, 2001), 193.
⁴⁶Nietzsche, Friedrich, *Twilight of the Idols*, (Penguin Books, 1978), 76.
⁴⁷Toqueville, Alexis de, *Democracy in America*, (New York, Doubleday & Co. Inc., 1969), 437.
⁴⁸Herman, E. *The Meaning and Value of Mysticism*, (New York, Books for Library Press, 1971), 66.
⁴⁹Elchaninow, Alexander, *The Diary of a Russian Priest*, (New York, St. Vladimir's Seminary Press, 1982), 87.

[50]Coles, Robert, *The Secular Mind,* (Princeton, Princeton University Press, 1999), 123.

CHAPTER 4(C): WHO ARE WE? TWO ANSWERS
[51]Becker, Ernest, *Escape From Evil,* (New York, Macmillan Publishing Co., 1975), 157.
[52]Lindbergh, Charles A., *The Spirit of St. Louis,* (New York, Ballantine Books, 1971), 330-1. Reprinted with the permission of Scribner, an imprint of Simon & Schuster Adult Publishing Group, from THE SPIRIT OF ST. LOUIS by Charles A. Lindbergh. Copyright 1953 by Charles Scribner's Son; copyright renewed 1981 by Anne Morrow Lindbergh. All rights reserved.
[53]Lindbergh, Charles A., 338-9.
[54]quoted in Breggin, M.D., Peter R., *Toxic Psychiatry,* (New York, St. Martin's Press, 1991), 373.
[55]Oates, Wayne E., *Christ and Selfhood,* (New York, Association Press, 1961), 112.
[56]Traherne, Thomas, *Centuries,* (New York, Harper & Brothers,1960), 205-6.
[57]Bonhoeffer, Dietrich, *Creation and Fall,* (London, SCM Press Ltd., 1960), 82.
[58]quoted in Hunter, James Davison, *The Death of Character,* (New York, Basic Books, 2000), 140.
[59]quoted in Clement, Olivier, *The Roots of Christian Mysticism,*(New York, New City Press, 1995), 77.
[60]Becker, Ernest, *Escape From Evil,* 157.
[61]L'Engle, Madeleine, *The Irrational Season,* (HarperSanFrancisco, 1977), 171.
[62]quoted in Zilbergeld, Bernie, Ph.D., *The Shrinking of America,* (Boston, Little, Brown and Company, 1983), 23.
[63]quoted in Darling, Frank C., *The Restoration of Christian Healing,* (Boulder, Colorado, Vista Publications, 1992), 489.
[64]Ibid, 489.
[65]quoted in Zilbergeld, 23.
[66]Patmore, Coventry, *The Rod, The Root, And The Flower,* (Freeport, New York, Books For Libraries Press, 1968), 53.
[67]Dunn, James D.G., *Jesus and the Spirit,* (Grand Rapids, Michigan, William B. Eerdmans Publishing Company, 1997), 315.
[68]Ibid, 311.
[69]Ibid, 234.

CHAPTER 4(D): KNOWLEDGE SYSTEMS VERSUS NARRATIVE
[70]Eliade, Mircea, *Myths, Dreams, and Mysteries,* (New York, Harper & Row, 1950), 153.
[71]Stephen R. Lawhead, "Christ The King", in *Stories For The Christian Year,* (New York, Macmillan Publishing, 1992), 202-3. Copyright currently held by Baker Books, a division of Baker Publishing Group.
[72]Huxley, Aldous, *The Perennial Philosophy,* (New York, HarperCollins Publishers, 2004), 21.
[73]The insights on narrative relied heavily on Frye, Northrop, *The Great Code,* (Toronto, Academic Press, 1982), see 198.
[74]Wilken, Robert Louis, *The Spirit of Early Christian Thought,* (New Haven, Yale University Press, 2003), 68.

[75] quoted in MacIntyre, Alasdair, *After Virtue*, (Notre Dame, Indiana, University of Notre Dame Press, 2002),211.

[76] Ibid, 216.

[77] Eliade, Mircea, *Myths, Dreams, and Myteries*, 143.

[78] NIV Study Bible, (Grand Rapids, Michigan, Zondervan, 2002), 727.

[79] Bonhoeffer, Dietrich, *Letters and Papers from Prison*,(New York, Macmillan Publishing Co.,1971), 157.

[80] Ibid, 157.

[81] Huxley, Aldous, *The Perennial Philosophy*, (New York, Perennial Classics, 2004), 114.

[82] Farber, Leslie H., *The Ways of the Will*, (New York, Harper Colophon Books, 1966), 133.

[83] I loved this image from Brian McLaren's book, *A New Kind of Christian*

[84] Bellah, Robert N, et al, *Habits Of The Heart*, (Berkely, University of California Press, 1996), 290.

[85] quoted in Dawn, Marva J., *Reaching Out Without Dumbing Down*, (Grand Rapids, Michigan, William B. Eerdmans Publishing Company, 1995), 233.

CHAPTER 4(E): THE UNCONSCIOUS VERSUS TRANSCENDENCE

[86] Tillich, Paul, *A History Of Christian Thought*, (New York, Simon and Schuster, 1968), 419-488.

[87] Tillich, Paul, *A History Of Christian Thought*,(New York, Simon and Schuster, 1968), 448.

[88] Raschke, Carl A., *The Interruption of Eternity*, (Chicago, Nelson-Hall, 1980),135, 139.

[89] quoted in Masson, Jeffrey Moussaieff, *Against Therapy*, (New York, Macmillan Publishing Company, 1988), 106.

CHAPTER 4(F): INTEGRATION VERSUS OVERCOMING

[90] Underhill, Evelyn, *Mysticism*, (New York, Penguin Books, 1974),X1V.

[91] ibid, 444.

[92] Ibid, 445.

[93] Stein, Murray, editor, *"Encountering Jung On Christianity"*, (Princeton, Princeton University Press, 1999), 79.

[94] Murdoch, Iris, *Metaphysics As A Guide To Morals*, (Toronto, Penguin Books, 1993), 468.

[95] Wright, N.T., *Jesus and the Victory of God*, (Minneapolis, Fortress Press, 1996).

[96] Macdonald, George, *Life Essential*, (Wheaton, Illinois, Harold Shaw Publishers, 1974),65.

[97] Chesterton, G. K., *Saint Francis of Assisi*, (New York, Image Books, Doubleday, 1990), 52.

[98] This version of the story comes from Chesterton's *Saint Francis of Assisi*, pages 50-2.

[99] Wise, Michael O., Abegg Jr., Martin G., Cook, Edward M.., editors, *Dead Sea Scrolls*, (HarperSanFrancisco, 2005), 122.

[100] Buchanen, Mark, *Your God Is Too Safe*, (Sisters, Oregon, Multnomah Publishers, 2001), 230.

CHAPTER 4(G): RELATIONSHIPS: KNOWLEDGE VERSUS LOVE

[101] Oates, Wayne E., *Christ and Selfhood*, (New York, Association Press, 1961), 63.

[102] quoted in *FQ Magazine,* (Toronto, Kontent Publishing Inc., Summer Issue 2004), 37.
[103] Eldredge, John, *The Journey of Desire,* (Nashville, Thomas Nelson Publishers, 2000), 182.
[104] Ibid, John, 182.
[105] Tugwell, Simon, *Prayer: Living With God,* (Springfield, Illinois, Templegate Publishers, 1975), 96.
[106] Ibid, 118-120.
[107] Ibid, 310.
[108] Bonhoeffer, Dietrich, *Letters and Papers from Prison,* (New York, Macmillan Publishing Co., 1972), 303.
[109] Plato, *Symposium,* from the *Great Dialogues of Plato,* (Markham, Ont. Penguin Books1984), 86-87.
[110] Klima, Ivan, *Love and Garbage,* (New York, Penguin Books, 1990), 31.
[111] Ibid, 31.
[112] Lasch, Christopher, *The Culture of Narcissism,* (New York, Warner Books, Inc. 1979), 330.
[113] Forsyth, P. T., *Positive Preaching and Modern Mind,* (London, Hodder and Stoughton, 1907), 186.
[114] This idea was from Peter Marshall
[115] Jung, Carl, *Psychotherapists or The Clergy,* 333.
[116] Bill W., *Alcoholics Anonymous Comes of Age,* (New York, Alcoholics Anonymous World Services, In., 1979), 114-5. Step Twelve says that "Having had a spiritual awakening as the result of these steps, we tried to carry this message to alcoholics, and to practice these principles in all our affairs." (page 50).
[117] Bonhoeffer, Dietrich, *Life Together,* (HarperSanFrancisco, Harper & Row Publishers, 1954), 21.
[118] Keating, Thomas, *Open Mind Open Heart,* (New York, Continuum Publishing Co., 1997), 103.
[119] Lindbergh, Anne Morrow, *Gift From the Sea,* (New York, Random House, 1991),81.
[120] Lindgergh, Anne Morrow, *Gift From the Sea,* 106.
[121] Shea, John, *Stories of God: An Unauthorized Biography,* (Chicago, Illinois, The Thomas More Press,1978), cover.
[122] Rupnik, Marko Ivan, *In the Fire of the Burning Bush,* (Grand Rapids, Michigan, William B. Eerdmans Publishing Co., 2004), 26-7.
[123] Lewis, C. S. *The Four Loves,* (Glasgow, Fontana Books, 1989), 7.
[124] Bellah, Robert N., Richard Madsen, William M. Sullivan, Ann Swidler, and Steven M. Tipton, *Habits of the Heart,* (Berkeley, University of California Press, 1996), 84.
[125] Yankelovich, Daniel, *New Rules: Searching for Self-Fulfillment in a World Turned Upside Down,* (New York, Bantam Books, 1982), 59.
[126] Furedi, Frank, *Therapy Culture,* (London, Routledge, 2004), 103.
[127] Ibid, 80.
[128] Lasch, Christopher, 64-5.
[129] Furedi, Frank, *Therapy Culture,* (London, Routledge, 2004), 103.

CHAPTER 4(H): SELF-LOVE VERSUS ACCEPTING LOVE
[130] Wilken, Robert Louis, *The Spirit of Early Christian Thought,* (New Haven, Yale University Press, 2003), 307.

[131] quoted in Furedi, Frank, *Therapy Culture*, (London, Routledge, 2004), 153.

[132] Battle, James, *Self-Esteem: The New Revolution*, (Edmonton, James Battle and Associates, 1990), 3.

[133] quoted in Battle, 6.

[134] quoted in Battle, 24.

[135] quoted in Battle 9-10.

[136] quoted, in Battle, 36.

[137] Furedi, Frank, *Therapy Culture*, 156.

[138] Ibid, 157.

[139] Ibid, 158.

[140] Ibid, 158.

[141] Ibid, 158.

[142] Armstrong, Karen, *A History of God*, (New York, Ballantine Books, 1994), 382.

[143] Ibid, 199.

[144] quoted in Zilbergeld, Bernie, Ph.D., *The Shrinking of America*, (Boston, Little, Brown and Company, 1983), 66-7.

[145] Bonhoeffer, Dietrich, *Creation and Fall*, (London, SCM Press, 1960), 83.

[146] Ibid, 83.

[147] Ibid, 84.

[148] .Tournier, Paul, *Guilt & Grace*, (New York, Harper & Row, 1962), 152.

[149] Tari, Mel, *A Mighty Wind*, (Harrison, Arkansas, New Leaf Press, Inc., 1980), 148.

[150] Bernard of Clairvaux, *The Classics of Western Spirituality*, (Mahwah, New Jersey, 1987), 192-197).

CHAPTER 4(I): WOUNDS: REDEMPTION VERSUS CURE

[151] Stowe, Harriet Beecher, *Uncle Tom's Cabin*, (New York, Penguin Books, 19860, Introduction, page 20.

[152] Stowe, Harriet Beecher, *Uncle Tom's Cabin*, (New York, Penguin Books, 1986), from the Introduction, page 20.

[153] Keller, Helen, *Light In My Darkness*,(West Chester, Pa. Chryssalis Books, 1995), 134.

[154] McKibben, Bill, "The Christian Paradox", from Harper's Magazine, August, 2005.

[155] A great example of how our wounds are used to help others is in the Betel program, wherein former drug addicts successfully minister to drug addicts. The work of this program can be read about in the book "We Dance Because We Cannot Fly" by Guy Chevreau.

[156] Zilbergeld, Bernie, Ph.D., *The Shrinking of America: Myths of Psychological Change*, (Boston, Little, Brown and Company, 1983), 267.

[157] Ibid, 266.

Chapter 4(J): Depression: Illness versus "The Shadow of Thy Hand"

[158] Fine, Cordelia, *a mind of its own*, (New York, W.W. Norton & Company, 2006), 23.

[159] Brand, Dr. Paul, and Yancey, Philip, *Pain: The Gift Nobody Wants*, (New York, HarperCollins, 1993), 219.

[160] Breggin, Peter R., *Toxic Psychiatry*, (New York, St. Martin's Press, 1991), 32.

[161] Breggin, Peter R., *Toxic Psychiatry*, (New York, St. Martin's Press),170.

[162] Gilbert, Daniel, *Stumbling on Happiness*, (New York, Alfred A. Knopf, 2006), 4.

[163] quoted in Sabom, Michael,B. MD, *Recollections of Death*, (London, Corgi Books, 1982), 250.

[164] Collins, Francis, "His Beautiful World", in *Guideposts*, Volume lX1, Issue10, December, 2006, 44.

[165] this view of our return to ancient views of the relationship between the body and emotional states comes from Neuhaus, Richard John, *As I Lay Dying*, (New York, Basic Books, 2002), 47 ff.

[166] Quoted in *Guideposts*, Volume LV1,ISSUE 5, pg 56.

[167] Lewis, C.S. *A Grief Observed*, (New York, Harper Collins, 1961), 6.

[168] *The Medical Post*, August 27,2002, pg.11.

[169] *The Globe and Mail,*Thursday, May 30, 2002, .A18

[170] Herxheimer, Andrew; Mintzes, Barbara, "Antidepressants and adverse effects in young patients: uncovering the evidence" *Canadian Medical Association Journal*, February 17, 2004, Vol. 170, No. 4, 487.

[171] *The Medical Post*, August 27, 2002, .52.

[172] Block, Dr. Joel, and Greenberg, Diane, *Women and Friendship*, ((New York, Franklin Watts, 1985), 225.

[173] *The Globe and Mail*, Wednesday, January 9, 2002, .A7.

[174] Kilpatrick, William Kirk, *Psychological Seduction*, (New York, Thomas Nelson Publishers, 1983),181-195. Kilpatrick has a chapter comparing Christian and psychology's attitudes to suffering.

[175] Rieff, Philip, *The Triumph Of The Therapeutic*, (Chicago, The University Of Chicago Press, 1987), 29.

[176] Ibid, 34.

[177] Becker, Ernest, *Escape From Evil*, (New York, The Free Press, 1975), 151.

[178] Rieff, Philip, *The Triumph of the Therapeutic*, 30.

[179] Ibid, 154.

[180] Ibid, 8.

[181] Ibid, 108.

[182] Jung, Carl, *Modern Man In Search Of A Soul*, in Bollingen Series XX, *Psychology and Religion:West And East*, (Princeton, Princeton University Press, 1989), 334.

[183] Jung, C. G., *Memories, Dreams, Reflections*, (London, Collins and Routledge & Kegan Paul, 1964), 313.

[184] Ibid, 313.

[185] Steiner, George, *Nostalgia For The Absolute*, (Montreal, CBC Enterprises, 1983), 23.

[186] Becker, Ernest, *The Denial Of Death*, (New York, The Free Press,1973), 57.

[187] Ibid, 57

[188] Harrold, Charles Frederick, ed., *A Newman Treasury*, (New Rochelle, New York, Arlington House Publishers, 1975), 197.

[189] Underhill, Evelyn, *Mysticism*, (New York, Penguin Books, 1974), 19.

[190] Tillich, Paul, *The Courage To Be*, (New Haven, Yale University Press), 175.

[191] Wiesel, Elie, *Sages and Dreamers*, (New York, Simon & Schuster,1991), 400.

[192] Pieper, Josef, *On Hope*, (San Francisco, Ignatius Press, 1986), 50.

[193]Lloyd-Jones, D. Martin, *"Spiritual Depression"*, (Grand Rapids, Michigan, Wm. B. Eerdmans Publishing Company, 1992), 265.

[194]Bloom, Anthony, *Beginning To Pray,* (New York, Paulist Press, 1970), 17

[195]Macdonald, George, *An Anthology*, (London, Collins,1990), 102.

[196]St. John of the Cross, *"Ascent Of Mount Carmel"*,(Liguori, Missouri, Triumph Books, 1983), 19-20.

[197]Berdyaev, Nicolas, *Spirit and Reality*, (London, The Centenary Press, 1939), 102.

[198]Campbell, Joseph with Bill Moyers, *The Power of Myth,* (New York, Doubleday, 1988), 39.

[199]Bill W., *Alcoholics Anonymous Comes of Age*, (New York, Alcoholics Anonymous World Services, Inc. 1979), 256.

[200]Chesterton, G.K., *The Everlasting Man,* (San Francisco, Ignatius Press, 1993), 206.

[201]Sayers, Dorothy, *The Whimsical Christian*, (New York, Collier Books, 1987).

[202]Underhill, *Mysticism,* 18.

[203]Huxley, Aldous, *Brave New World*, (Glasgow, Collins Publishing, 1977), 235.

[204]Ibid, *Brave New World*, (Glasgow, Collins Publishing, 1977), 43.

[205]Ibid, 226.

[206]Tillich, Paul, *The Courage To Be*, (New Haven, Yale University Press, 1952), 83.

CHAPTER 4(K): SPIRITUALITY: HOLY SPIRIT VERSUS UNIVERSAL SPIRIT

[207]Macleans, June 20, 1994, 28.

[208]Ibid, 28

[209]Ibid, 28.

[210]The Globe And Mail, Tuesday, October 19, 2004, A22.

[211]Bibby, Reginald W., *Restless Churches*, (Kelowna, Wood Lake Books), 86.

[212]Niebuhr, Reinhold, *The Self And The Dramas of History*, (New York, Charles Scribner's Sons, 1955), 125.

[213]Barth, Karl, *The Holy Spirit And The Christian Life*, (Louisville, Kentucky, John Knox Press, 1993), X1V.

[214]Noll, Richard, *The Aryan Christ*,(New York, Random House, 1997).

Noll, Richard, *The Jung Cult*, (Princeton, Princeton University Press, 1994).

[215]Peck, M.Scott, *The Road Less Traveled*, (New York, Simon & Schuster,1978), 283.

[216]Ibid, 270.

[217]quoted in McGinn, Bernard, *The Foundations of Mysticism*, Vol. I, (New York, The Crossroad Publishing Company, 1994), 128.

[218]quoted in Leech, Kenneth, *True Prayer*, (New York, Harper & Row, 1986), 13.

[219]Clement, Olivier, *The Roots Of Christian Mysticism*, (New York, New City Press,1995), 76.

[220]quoted in Leech, Kenneth, *True Prayer*, (New York, Harper & Row, 1986), 13.

[221]quoted in Rupnik, Marko Ivan, *In the Fire of the Burning Bush*, (Grand Rapids, Michigan, William B. Eerdmans Co., 2004), 11.

[222]Peck, M. Scott, *The Road Less Traveled*, 273.

[223]quoted in Roof, Wade Clark, "Spiritual Marketplace", (Princeton, Princeton University Press, 1999), 89.

[224]Hoffman, Edward, PhD. editor, *The Wisdom of Carl Jung*, (New York, Citadel Press Books, published by Kensington Publishing Co., 2003), 156.

[225]Holifield, E. Brooks. *A History of Pastoral Care in America*, (Nashville, Abingdon Press, 1984), 290.

[556]Ibid, 290.

[227]quoted in Leech, Kenneth, *True Prayer*, (New York, Harper & Row, 1986), 156-7.

[228]One such study is reported in "Spirituality, Religion, and Pediatrics: Intersecting Worlds of Healing", Pediatrics: Journal of the Ambulatory Pediatric Association, Volume 106, Number 4, October 2000, pg. 899.

[229]*The Medical Post*, September 14, 2004, page 30.

[230]quoted in MacLeans, Sept. 25, 1995, 42.

[231]Ibid.

[232]Huxley, Aldous, *The Perennial Philosophy*, (New York, Perennial Classics, 2004) 244.

[233]Rupnik, Marko Ivan, *In the Fire of the Burning Bush*, (Grand Rapids, Michigan, William B. Eerdmans Publishing Company, 2004), 10.

[234]Underhill, Evelyn, *The Ways Of The Spirit* (New York, Crossroad, 1993), 187.

[235]Clement, Olivier, *The Roots of Christian Mysticism*, 168.

[236]quoted in Sabom, Michael B. MD, *Recollections of Death*, (London, England, Corgi Books, 1982), 254.

[237]Heschel, Abraham Joshua, *God in Search of Man: A Philosophy of Judaism* (New York, The Noonday Press, 1996), 317.

[238]Weil, Simone, *Waiting for God*, (New York, Harper & Row, Publishers, 1973), 24.

[239]Bill W., *Alcoholics Anonymous Comes of Age*, (New York, Alcoholics Anonymous World Services, Inc., 1979), 63.

[240]Cox, Harvery, *Fire From Heaven*,(Reading, Addison-Wesley Publishing Co.,1995), 315.

[241]Van Dusen, Henry P., *Spirit, Son and Father*, (New York, Charles Scribner's Sons, 1958), 126.

[242]Maximus the Confessor, quoted in Wilken, Robert Louis, *The Spirit of Early Christian Thought*, (New Haven, Yale University Press, 2003), 131.

[243]Berdyaev, Nicolas, *Spirit and Reality*, (London, The Centenary Press,1939), 134.

[244]Armstrong, Karen, *The Battle For God*, (New York, Ballantine Books, 2000), 23.

[245]Becker, *Escape From Evil*, (New York, The Free Press, 1975), 169.

[246]quoted in George H. Gallup, Jr; Timothy Jones, *The Saints Among Us*, (Harrisburg,PA, BSC LITHO, 1992), 21.

[247]quoted in Wilken, Robert Louis, *The Spirit of Early Christian Thought,* 131.

[248]MacNutt, Francis, *The Nearly Perfect Crime*, (Grand Rapids, Michigan, Chosen Books, 2005),194.

CHAPTER 4(L): SIN VERSUS PATHOLOGY

[249]Reported in Furedi, Frank, *Therapy Culture*, (London, Routledge, 2004), 113.

[250]Reported in *The British Medical Journal: BMJ* 2002;324:859-860.

[251]Ibid

[252]Wood, Garth, *The Myth of Neurosis: Overcoming the Illness Excuse*, (New York, Harper & Row, Publishers, 1986), 97.

[253] Breggin, Peter R., M.D., *Toxic Psychiatry*, (New York, St. Martin's Press, 1991), 18.

[254] Ibid, 58.

[255] Ibid, 26.

[256] Szasz, Thomas S. M.D., *The Myth of Mental Illness*, (New York, Harper & Row, Publishers, 1974), 262.

[257] Ibid, 182.

[258] Ibid, 27-28.

[259] Ibid, 56.

[260] Ibid, 77.

[261] Ibid, 263.

[262] Ibid, 257.

[263] Masson, Jeffrey Moussaieff, Against Therapy, (New York, Atheneum, 1988), 249.

[264] Ibid, 249.

[265] Hunter, James Davison, *The Death of Character*, (New York, Basic Books, 2000), 191.

[266] Ibid, (New York, Basic Books, 2000), 23.

[267] Ibid, 23.

[268] Boisen, Anton T, *The Exploration of the Inner World: A Study of Mental Disorder and Religious Experience"* and R. Frederick West, *Light Beyond Shadows: A Minister and Mental Health* These books are personal testimonies, but the book which is a more comprehensive study of the relationship between mental health and morality is that of O. Hobart Mowrer, *Morality and Mental Health.*

[269] Boisen, Anton T., *The Exploration of The Inner World: A Study of Mental Disorder and Religious Experience,* (New York, Harper & Brothers, 1962), 238.

[270] quoted in Breggin, Peter R., M.D., *Toxic Psychiatry*, (New York, St. Martin's Press, 1991), 30.

[271] Boisen, Anton T., *The Exploration of the Inner World*, 181.

[272] Ibid, 181.

[273] Caplan, Paula, *They Say You're Crazy: How the World's Most Powerful Psychiatrists Decide Who's Normal*, (Reading, Massachusetts, Perseus Books, 1995), 39.

[274] Walkenstein, M.D., Eileen, *Don't Shrink To Fit*, (New York, Grove Press, Inc., 1975), 97-98.

[275] Ibid, 79.

[276] Ibid, 7.

[277] Ibid, 141.

[278] Ibid, 86.

[279] Ibid, 31

[280] Armstrong, Louise, *And They Call It Help: The Psychiatric Policing of America's Children*, (Reading, Massachusetts, Addison-Wesley Publishing Company, 1993), 132.

[291] Breggin, Peter R. M.D., *Toxic Psychiatry*, (New York, St. Martin's Press, 1991), 182.

[22] Caplan, Paula, *They Say You're Crazy*, 90.

[283] Moskowitz, Eva, *In Therapy We Trust: America's Obsession With Self-Fulfillment*, (Baltimore, The Johns Hopkins University Press, 2001), 255.

[284] Caplan, Paula, *They Say You're Crazy*, 231.

[285] quoted in Caplan, 234.

[286]Ibid, 234.

[287]Quoted in Moynihan, Ray, and Cassels, Alan, *Selling Sickness*, (Vancouver, Greystone Books, 2005), 179.

[288]Moynihan and Cassels, *Selling Sickness*, 189.

[289]Ibid, 182.

[290]Ibid, 78.

[291]Ibid, 103.

[292]Armstrong, Louise, *And They Call It Help: The Psychiatric Policing of America's Children*, 153.

[293]quoted in Caplan, Paula, *They Say You're Crazy*, 262.

[294]quoted in Caplan, 280.

[295]Armstrong, Louise, *And They Call It Help: The Psychiatric Policing Of America's Children*, (Reading, Massachusetts, Addison-Wesley Publishing Company, 1993), 132.

[296]Ibid, 154.

[297]Moskowitz, Eva S., *In Therapy We Trust*, (Baltimore, The Johns Hopkins University Press, 2001) 4.

[298]Ibid, 4.

[299]Lasch, Christopher, *The Culture of Narcissism*, (New York, Warner Books, Inc,1979), 356.

[300]Lottie Marcus quoted in Caplan, Paula, *They Say You're Crazy*, 72-3.

[301]Breggin, Peter R., M.D., *Toxic Psychiatry*, (New York, St. Martin's Press, 1991), 325.

[302]Turner, James, *Without God, Without Creed*, (Baltimore, The Johns Hopkins University Press, 0985), 68.

[303]MacIntyre, Alisdair, *After Virtue*, (Notre Dame, Indiana, University of Notre Dame Press, 2002), 38.

[304]Ibid, 38.

[305]Barrett, William, *The Death of the Soul: From Descartes to the Computer*,(New York, Anchor Press, 1987), 91.

[306]MacIntyre, Alisdaire, 38.

[307]This is a poor summary of brilliant ideas in *After Virtue*, a book that should be read.

[308]Turner, James, *Without God, Without Creed*, (Baltimore, The Johns Hopkins University Press, 1985), 84.

[309]Robinson, H. Wheeler, *The Christian Experience of the Holy Spirit*, (Great Britain, Fontana Books, 1962), 182.

CHAPTER 4(M): SCIENCE VERSUS FAITH

[310]Wood, Garth, *The Myth of Neurosis*, (New York, Harper & Row, Publishers, 1986), 275-6.

[311]quoted in Masson, Jeffrey Moussaieff, *Against Therapy*, (New York, Atheneum, 1988), 182-3.

[312]quoted in Masson,, 184.

[313]Ubell, Earl, "Has Psycho-Probing Helped Anyone?" reprinted in Mowrer, O. Hobart, *Morality and Mental Health*, (Chicago, Rand McNally, 1967), 21.

[314]Ubell, Earl *Has Psycho-Probing Helped Anyone?* Reprinted in Mowrer, O. Hobart, *Morality and Mental Health*, (Chicago, Rand McNally, 1967), 21.

315 Ibid, 21.
316 quoted in Masson, Jeffrey Moussaieff, *Against Therapy*, (New York, Atheneum, 1988), 183.
317 quoted in Zilbergeld, Bernie, Ph.D., *The Shrinking or America,* (Boston, Little, Brown and Company, 1983) 169.
318 Ibid,. Bernie, 133.
319 Ubell, Earl, "Has Psycho-Probing Helped Anyone, 21.
320 Kilpatrick, William Kirk, *Psychological Seduction*, (Nashville, Thomas Nelson Publishers, 1983), 29.
321 Zilbergeld, Bernie, Ph.D., *The Shrinking of America,* (Boston, Little, Brown and Company, 1983), 185-6.
322 quoted in Wood, Garth, *The Myth of Neurosis*, 286.
323 reported in Walker 111, Sydney, M.D., *A Dose of Sanity*, (New York, John Wiley & Sons, Inc., 1996), 127.
324 Kilpatrick, William Kirk, *Psychological Seduction*, 29.
325 reported in Walker 111, Sidney M.D., *A Dose of Sanity*, 140-1.
326 Ibid, 141.
327 Zilbergeld, Bernie, *The Shrinking of America*, 19.
328 quoted in Walker 111. Sidney M.D., A Dose of Sanity, 145.
329 The Globe and Mail, Monday, February 10, 2003, Social Studies.
330 Zilbergeld, Bernie, *The Shrinking of America*, 164.
331 The Vancouver Sun, Wednesday, March 31, 2004, pg. A2.
332 Included in the chapter on Loving Oneself versus Accepting Love
333 Furedi, Frank, *Therapy Culture,* 157.
334 Ibid, 158.
335 Ibid, 158.
336 Ibid, 158.
337 Hunter, James Davison, *The Death of Character*, (New York, Basic Books, 2000), 268.
338 Ibid, 152. Anyone wanting to pursue the studies further can get a list of some of the studies in the end-notes of the book: pages 268-273.
339 Ibid, 152.
340 The Lancet, Volume 360, Number 9335, 07 September.
341 Reported in *The Globe* and *Mail,* Friday, September 6, 2002.
342 Moynihan, Ray and Cassels, Alan, *Selling Sickness*, (Vancouver, Greystone Books, 2005), 2005), 134.
343 Ibid, 5.
344 Furedi, Frank, *Therapy Culture*, 160-161.
345 Lehrman, N.S. "*The Potency of Psychotherapy*", in Mowrer, O.Hobart, *Morality and Mental Health,* (Chicago, Rand McNally, 1967), 80.
346 Ibid, 80.
347 quoted in Zilbergeld, Bernie, *The Shrinking of America*, 170.
348 Wood, Garth, *The Myth of Neurosis*, 284.
349 Watters, Ethan and Ofshe, Richard, *Therapy's Delusions*, (New York, Scribner, 1999), 247-8.

[350]Linda L. Barnes, et al, *"Spirituality, Religion, and Pediatrics: Intersecting Worlds of Healing"*, American Academy of Pediatrics, October 2000 Volume 106, Number 4, Part 2 of 2, 899.

[351]MacLeans, September 25, 1995, 42.

[352]reported in Herrick, James A., *The Making of the New Spirituality*, (Downers Grove, Illinois, Intervarsity Press, 2003), 29.

CHAPTER 4(N): GOD VERSUS GODS

[353]quoted in Herrick, James A., *The Making of the New Spirituality*, (Downers Grove, Illinois, InterVarsity Press, 2003), 241.

[354]Aikman, David, *Hope: The Heart's Great Quest*, (Ann Arbor, Michigan, Servant Publications, 1995), 20-21.

[355]Armstrong, Karen, *A History Of God*, (New York, Ballantine Books, 1993), 41.

[356]Hoffman, Edward, PhD., *The Wisdom of Carl Jung*, (New York, Citadel Press Books, published by Kensington Publishing Co., 2003), 176.

CHAPTER 4(O): WELL ADJUSTED VERSUS TRANSFORMED

[357]Wallis, Jim, *God's Politics*, (New York, HarperCollins Publishers, Inc., 2005), 61-2.

[358]Jones, Rufus, editor, *The Journal of George Fox,* (Richmond, Indiana, Friends United Press, 1983), 106.

[359]quoted in Leech, Kenneth, *Spirituality and Pastoral Care*, (Cambridge, Massachusetts, 1989), 12.

[360]Leech, Kenneth, *Spirituality and Pastoral Care*, (Cambridge, Massachusetts, 1989), 69-70.

[361]Frankl, Viktor E., *The Unconscious God*, (New York, Simon and Schuster, 1975), 74-5.

[362]Lewis, C.S., *Mere Christianity*, (London, HarperCollins*Publishers,* 1997), 178.

[363]Starbuck, Edwin, *The Psychology of Religion*, (New York, Charles Scribner's Sons, 1903), 364.

[364]Merton, Thomas, *New Seeds of Contemplation,* (New York, New Directions Publishing Corporation, 1972), 190.

[365]Erlandson, Charles, editor, *F.B Meyer: The Best from All His Works,* (Nashville, Thomas Nelson Publishers, 1988), 271.

[366]King Jr., Martin Luther, *Strength to Love*, 1981),

[367]Jung, Carl, *Memories, Dreams, Reflections,* (London, Collons and Routledge & Kegan Paul), 1964), 327.

[368]Riesman, David, *The Lonely Crowd*, (New Haven, Connecticut, Yale University Press, 1967), 21.

[369]Ibid, 307.

CHAPTER 5(A): EXTERNAL VERSUS INTERNAL VISION

[370]Rogers, Carl R., *On Becoming A Person*, (New York, Houghton Mifflin Co., 1961), 63.

[371]Ibid, 61.

[372]Ibid, 62.

[373] quoted in Masson, Jeffrey Moussaieff, *Against Therapy*, (New York, Macmillan Publishing Co., 1988), 190-1.

[374] McNeil, John T., *A History of The Cure of Souls*, (New York, Harper & Brothers , 1951), 171.

[375] Ibid, 95.

[376] Ibid,, 98.

[377] Masson, 201.

[378] Hunter, James Davison, *The Death of Character*, (New York, Basic Books, 2000), 151..

[379] Zelbergeld, Bernie, PhD., *The Shrinking of America*, (Boston, Little, Brown and Company, 1983), 21.

[380] Ibid, 21-2.

[381] Masson, 193.

[382] Walkenstein, M.D., Eileen, *Don't Shrink to Fit*, (New York, Grove Press, Inc,. 1976), 5.

[383] Watters, Ethan, and .Ofshe, Richard, *Therapy's Delusions*, (New York, Scribner, 1999), 14.

[384] Quoted in Watters and Ofshe, *Therapy's Delusions*, 144.

[385] Ibid, 123.

[386] Watters and Ofshe, 93.

[387] Ibid, 149.

[388] Ibid,, 149.

[389] Ibid, 192.

CHAPTER 5(B): DYING TO SELF VERSUS NURTURING THE SELF

[390] Yankelovich, Daniel, *New Rules*, (New York, Bantam Books, 1982), xvi.

[391] Ibid, 243.

[392] quoted in Wallis, Jim, *God's Politics*, (New York, HarperCollins Publishers, Inc, 2005), 137.

[393] Guardini, Romano, *The Lord*,(London, Longmans,1959), 506.

[394] Merton, Thomas, *The Ascent To Truth*, (San Diego, Harcourt Brace & Co, 1981), 177.

[395] Lewis, C.S., *Reflections On The Psalms*, (New York, Harcourt Brace Jovanovich, 1958), 31-32.

[396] Yoder, John Howard, *The Politics of Jesus*, (Grand Rapids, Michigan, William B. Eerdmans Publishing Company, 1975), 61.

[397] Yoder, 61.

[398] I believe it was Kenneth Leach who helped me to understand this facet of the cross.

[399] Moseley, Rufus, *Perfect Everything*.

[400] Thomas Merton in Augustine, *The City of God*, (New York, Random House, 2000), XVl.

[401] Tobin, Frank, editor and translator, *Henry Suso: The Exemplar*, (Paulist Press, New York, 1989), 100.

[402] Conyers, A.J. *The Eclipse of Heaven*, (Downers Grove, Illinois, Intervarsity Press, 1992), 85.

[403]Aelred of Rievaulx, *The Mirror of Charity*, (Kalamazoo, Michigan, Cistercian Publications, 1990), 129.

[404]The image comes from a talk by Eugene Peterson.

[405]quoted in Martin Marty and Micah Marty, *When True Simplicity Is Gained*, (Grand Rapids, Michigan, William B. Eerdmans Publishing Co., 1998), 8.

[406]Patmore, Coventry, *The Rod, The Root and The Flower*,(Books For Libraries Press, 1968), 148.

CHAPTER 5(C): WILL VERSUS EMOTIONS

[407]Wuthnow, Robert, *Acts of Compassion*, (Princeton, Princeton University Press, 1991), 88.

[408]Lasch, Christopher, *The Culture of Narcissism*, (New York, Warner Books, Inc., 1979), 42

[409]Moskowitz, Eva S., *In Therapy We Trust: America's Obsession with Self-Fulfillment*, (Baltimore, The Johns Hopkins University Press, 2001), 219.

[410]Ibid, 247.

[411]Ibid, 248.

[412]Ibid, 270.

[413]Yankelovich, Daniel, *New Rules: Searching for Self-fulfillment In a World Turned Upside Down*, (New York, Bantam Books, 1982),56.

[414]Hillman, James, and Ventura, Michael, *We've Had a Hundred Years of Psychotherapy – And the World's Getting Worse,* (HarperSanFrancisco, A Division of HarperCollinsPublishers, 1992), 11.

[415]Patmore, Coventry, *The Rod, The Root and the Flower,* Freeport, New York, Books For Libraries Press, Inc., 1968), 146.

[416]Moskowitz, Eva S., 284.

[417]Hillman, James, and Ventura, Michael, *We've Had a Hundred Years of Psychotherapy – And the World's Getting Worse,* (HarperSanFrancisco, A Division of HarperCollinsPublishers, 1992), 5-6.

[418]Coles, Robert, *The Secular Mind,* (Princeton, Princeton University Press, 1999), 120.

[419]Ibid,119.

[420]Solovyev, Vladimir, *God Man & the Church*, translated by Donald Attwater, (Cambridge, Great Britain, James Clarke & Co., Ltd., 1974), 111.

[421]Murdoch, Iris, *Metaphysics As A Guide To Morals*,(London, Penguin Books, 1992) 190.

[422]Farber, 48.

[423]Frankl, Viktor E., *The Unconscious God*, (New York, Simon and Schuster, 1975.), 68.

[424]Dabrowski, Kazimierz, *The Theory of Positive Disintegration*, in Mowrer, O. Hobart, *Morality and Mental Health,* (Chicago, Rand McNally 7 Co., 1967),161.

CHAPTER 5(D): OBEDIENCE VERSUS SELF-UNDERSTANDING

[425]Mirkin, Marsha, Ph.D., *The Women Who Danced By The Sea*, (New York, Monkfish Book Publishing Company, 2004), 8-10.

[426]Tillich, Paul, *Dynamics of Faith*, (New York, Harper Torchbooks, 1958), 56.

[427]Chesterton, G.K., *Saint Francis of Assisi*, (New York, Image Books, Doubleday, 1990), 28.

[428]Saint Augustine, *Confessions*, (New York, Penguin Books, 1961), 66.

[429]Ibid, *Confessions*, 66.

[430]Saint Augustine, *The City of God*, (Toronto, Random House of Canada Limited, 1999), 431-2.

[431]Farley, Edward, *Deep Symbols*, (Valley Forge, Pennsylvania, Trinity Press International, 1996), 89.

[432]Ibid, 89.

[433]Hunter, James Davison, *The Death of Character*, (New York, Basic Books, 2000), 146-7. This is a transferring and utilization of the ideas worked out by Hunter in his attempt to study the deterioration of morals due to the psychologizing of moral instruction in the schools.

[434]Finney, Charles G., Power, Passion, & Prayer, (Gainseville, Florida, Bridge-Logos, 2004), 51-2.

[435]Patmore, Coventry, *The Rod, The Root And The Flower*, (New York, Books For Libraries Press, Inc., 1968), 183.

[436]Patmore, Coventry, *The Rod, The Root And The Flower*, (Freeport, New York, Books for Libraries,

Press, Inc., 1968), 156.

[437]Hillman, James, and Ventura, Michael, *We've Had a Hundred Years of Psychotherapy – Ant the World's Getting Worse*, (HarperSanFrancisco,1992), 12.

[438]Clapp, Rodney, *Tortured Wonders: Christian Spirituality for People, Not Angels,* (Grand Rapids, Michigan, Brazos Press, 2005), 222.

[439]Chittester, Joan, *The Heart Of Flesh*, (Grand Rapids, William B. Eerdmans Publishing Co.,1998), 75.

KNOWLEDGE AND FAITH: CAN THERE BE A HARMONY?

[440]quoted in von Hugel, Baron Friedrich, *Essays & Addresses on the Philosophy of Religion*, (London, J.M. Dent & Sons Limited,1926),145.

[441]Ibid, 145.

[442]Turner, James, *Without God, Without Creed*, (Baltimore, The Johns Hopkins University Press, 1985), 234.

[443]Ellul, Jacques, *The Meaning Of The City*, (Grand Rapids, Michigan, Eerdmans Publishing,1970), 207.

[444]Augustine, *The City of God*, (New York, Random House, 2000), 298.

[445]Acts 20:19, King James Version, The Word Publishing Company.

[446]Colossians 3:12, King James Version, The Word Publishing Company.

[447]Frye, Northrup, *The Great Code*, (Toronto, Academic Press, 1982), 67.

[448]Borg, Marcus, *Meeting Jesus Again For The First Time*, (HarperSanFrancisco, 1995) 38.

[449]Bonhoeffer, Dietrich, *Creation And Fall*, (London, SCM Press, 1960), 66.

[450]Ibid, 70.

[451]Armstrong, Karen, *The Battle For God*, (New York, Ballantine Books, 2000), 356.

[452]Tillich, Paul, *Dynamics of Faith,* (New York, Harper Torchbooks, 1958), 31.

[453]Turner, James, *Without God, Without Creed,* (Baltimore, The John Hopkins University Press, 1985), xiii.

[454]Ibid, 267.

[455]Ibid, 198.

[456]Leech, Kenneth, *True Prayer,* (HarperSanFrancisco, 1980), 136.

[457]Otto, Rudolf, *The Idea Of The Holy,* (London, Oxford University Press, 1958), 109.

[458]Starbuck, Edwin Diller, *The Psychology of Religion,* (New York, The Walter Scott Publishing Co., Ltd, 1903),1.

[459]Temple, William, *About Christ,* (London, SCM Press, 1962), 137.

[460]Niebuhr, H. Richard, *Christ & Culture,* (HarperSanFrancisco, 2001), 86.

[461]Grant, R.M., *Gnosticism and Early Christianity,* (New York, Columbia University Press,1966), 8.

[462]quoted in Grant, 12.

[463]Ibid, 9.

[464]Ibid, 12.

[465]Wright, N.T., *The Millennium Myth,* (Louisville, Kentucky, Westminster John Knox Press, 1999), 36.

[466]Tillich, Paul, *A History of Christian Thought,* (New York, Simon and Shuster, 1968) 208.

[467]Campbell, Joseph, *The Power of Myth,* (New York, Doubleday, 1988), 27.

[468]Brown, Peter, *The Rise of Western Christendom,* (Massachusetts, Blackwell Publishers, Inc., 1997), 75.

[469]Ibid, 112.

[470]Willard, Dallas, *Renovation of the Heart,* (Colorado Springs, Navpress, 2002), 163.

[471]Hildegard of Bingen; *The Classics of Western Spirituality,* (Mahway, New Jersey, Paulist Press, 1990), 531.

[472]quoted in Cahill, Thomas, *Sailing the Wine-dark Sea,* (New York, Nan A. Talese, Doubleday, 2003), 150.

CHAPTER 7: THE BANKRUPTCY

[473]*Fables of Aesop,* (Middlesex, England, Penguin, 1974), 4.

[474]Buber, Martin, *I and Thou,* (New York, Macmillan Publishing Co, 1958), 118.

[475]James, William, *The Varieties of Religious Experience,* (New York, Macmillan Publishing Co., 1961), 361.

[476]Griffin, Emilie, *Clinging: The Experience of Prayer*

[477]Taylor, John V., *The Go-Between God,* (London, SCM Press, 1975), 225,

[478]Tozer, A.W., *The Pursuit of God,* (Camp Hill, Pennsylvania, Christian Publications, Inc., 1982), 73.

[479]Johnson, Paul, *A History of Christianity,* (New York, Macmillan Publishing Co., 1976), 45.